China's Emerging
Middle Class

China's Emerging Middle Class

BEYOND ECONOMIC TRANSFORMATION

CHENG LI

editor

BROOKINGS INSTITUTION PRESS
Washington, D.C.

Library of Congress Cataloging-in-Publication data

China's emerging middle class : beyond economic transformation / Cheng Li,
editor.
    p.   cm.
  Includes bibliographical references and index.
  ISBN 978-0-8157-0405-8 (pbk. : alk. paper)
    1. Middle class—China. 2. China—Economic conditions—2000–
3. China—Social conditions—2000– I. Li, Cheng. II. Title.
  HT690.C55C398 2010
  305.5'50951—dc22   2010037417

9 8 7 6 5 4 3 2 1

Printed on acid-free paper

Typeset in Sabon

Composition by Cynthia Stock
Silver Spring, Maryland

Printed by R. R. Donnelley
Harrisonburg, Virginia

In memory of

BROOKE SHEARER

(1950–2009)

Personal friend, inspiring member of

the extended Brookings family,

and American goodwill ambassador

to an ever-changing world

Contents

Foreword

KENNETH G. LIEBERTHAL
John L. Thornton China Center

China's development of a middle class is of potentially enormous consequence for its domestic future, for the global economy, and even for the world's capacity to limit climate change. Yet the growing body of work to date that studies this phenomenon and its implications has been characterized, overall, by imprecise descriptions, little agreement on data, and a great deal of speculation (based in no small part on analogies from the West's historical experience). Against this backdrop, this volume provides the best basis to date for further work on this important subject.

Despite its phenomenal record of sustained GDP growth, the People's Republic of China's domestic social and political evolution remains uncertain. For China has, in tandem with its exceptional decades-long surge in GDP growth, transitioned from a remarkably egalitarian society to one of extraordinary inequalities in wealth. Given the state's pervasive role in the economy and the importance of connections to the state for accumulating wealth, serious political repercussions may stem from this combination of economic growth and inequality. China's simultaneous embrace of the information revolution has arguably further upped the ante, for Chinese citizens now know, to an unprecedented degree, what others are experiencing, liking, and disliking.

The emergence of a middle class, as well as the popularization of its attitudes and consumption habits, may provide the bridge to a stable and prosperous future for the PRC. Clearly, a large number of Chinese citizens have, since the early 1990s, acquired sufficient personal wealth to turn them into the types of discretionary consumers—of housing, appliances, vehicles, clothing, home-use products, information, and services—that are the hallmarks of a middle class. But overall China still ranks below 100 in a list of countries sorted by per capita GDP. It is likely crucial for stability, therefore, that opportunities to join the middle class continue to expand at a pace sufficient to enable those who are still poor to feel they or their children have a realistic chance of becoming middle-class citizens.

In brief, the middle class in China is still in many ways inchoate. It is less than two decades old and consists of some who got there through private entrepreneurship, others who joined via educational achievement and jobs in foreign-invested enterprises, still others in the state system itself (both officials and middle management in state-owned enterprises), and increasingly also members of the intellectual and cultural backbone of China's educational, entertainment, and *belles arts* circles. These are very different groups, with appropriately diverse sentiments.

It appears that many of the integuments of the middle class elsewhere—extensive civil organizations, a particular social ethos, and fundamental conservatism with respect to the value of the system itself—are still not dominant features of the Chinese middle class. Indeed, the way the emerging Chinese middle class shapes itself along these several tangents will likely be very consequential for the evolution of the overall system.

Systemic reforms since the Maoist era have permitted the development of China's middle class, but this increasingly important social stratum may become a destabilizing element if the system does not continue to evolve with sufficient speed. There is already widespread anger that rapid escalation in housing prices is creating obstacles to new entry into the middle class and is barring people's return to it when health expenses or some other exigency adversely affects their fortunes. In addition, many feel that the very wealthy are exempted from paying for the state's obligations, while the middle class faces increasing burdens because it both has resources and is not powerful or unified enough to defend its interests.

China's middle-class lifestyle is also still not fully formed. Until recently middle-class aspirations were quite clear: American living standards—including high-quality housing, one or more family cars, good clothing, travel opportunities, and relatively conspicuous consumption overall—provided the gold standard of what it means to be middle class and modern. Because of the global financial crisis and, increasingly, the reality of climate change, these views may change if given sufficient guidance by China's government and propaganda apparatus. The simple truth is that the world cannot sustain a large Chinese middle class that continues to strive for American levels of consumption (especially of fossil fuels). The sensibilities and social ethos of China's middle class will thus potentially have profound global repercussions.

Indeed, sociopolitical stability in China and the country's greenhouse gas emissions will have enormous impacts on Asia and globally. To an extent not widely acknowledged in the Western media, China's emerging middle class will shape the broad parameters of China's future on these issues. This volume cannot delineate precisely how China's middle class will develop: too many variables are in play, and too little empirical information is available. With so many things changing so rapidly and on such a large scale in China, it is not possible to model accurately their dynamic interactions and likely consequences. But this volume succeeds in examining the issues from every important angle—the conceptualization of the middle class, data describing its characteristics and evolution, questions about the implications for systemic change in China, and comparisons with developments elsewhere—and provides the best available data on each of these approaches to the overall issue. Chapter authors, moreover, represent each generation, from current graduate students to senior scholars in the field. As such, this volume significantly advances our ability to understand and research two of the biggest questions of our time: How is China's middle class evolving? And how will it interact with the state to shape the future of China?

The right way to read this volume, therefore, is as a set of contemplations, each supported by both evidence and expertise, on the nature, aspirations, and potential consequences of the emerging Chinese middle class. Cheng Li, as editor, has not imposed a single analytical scheme on the contributors but rather has sought to ensure consistent quality while allowing the diversity of views and approaches of serious scholars to show through and inform the reader. This is in the best tradition of edited volumes in that it addresses a subject that warrants both the richness of the data relied upon and the uncertainties inherent in the topic. As a whole, this volume provides a significant foundation for the ongoing examination of the current and future middle class in China.

Acknowledgments

For a subject of such intuitive importance, it is no small wonder that this is the first edited volume of scholarly work on the Chinese middle class to be published in English. The project, whose research phase culminated in an international conference of scholars, held at the Brookings Institution in September 2009, grew out of a creeping awareness that English-speaking scholarly circles had begun to lag behind PRC scholars—especially a small coterie of pioneering PRC sociologists—when it came to studying the Chinese middle class. And yet at the same time the English-language literature still had much to offer in terms of the breadth of analytical perspectives represented and the sophistication of certain scholars' approaches to the topic. This innovative and eclectic volume is the fruit of this international meeting of the minds.

Many thanks are in order. First and foremost, thank you to John L. Thornton, chairman of the board of the Brookings Institution, for his impassioned and farsighted leadership, both of the center that shares his name and of the institution as a whole. This volume is merely the latest of many projects that would be unimaginable without his enduring personal commitment to in-depth, holistic analysis of change in China at both the grassroots and the elite levels.

I am also grateful to Strobe Talbott, president of the Brookings Institution, who has lent his unwavering support to the John L. Thornton

China Center since its inception by presiding over its rise to prominence in the Washington policy scene. Martin Indyk, vice president of Brookings and director of the Foreign Policy program, is also owed a debt of gratitude, both for overseeing the progression of this volume and for giving a stirring set of opening remarks at last September's conference. The volume also benefited substantially from the incisive observations and very constructive comments of Michael O'Hanlon, senior fellow and director of research for Foreign Policy, who reviewed an early typescript of the book.

A special note of appreciation goes to Kenneth Lieberthal, director of the China Center, whose knee-deep involvement in all of the center's activities over the last year has already placed it on firm footing for many years to come. It was kind of him to take time out of his schedule to write the insightful and comprehensive foreword that graces this volume's first few pages. Jeffrey Bader, former director of the China Center and current senior director for Asian Affairs on the National Security Council, lent his support to this project at its earlier stages. Ted Piccone, senior fellow and deputy director for Foreign Policy at Brookings, helped steer the China Center through a period of transition and remains a major source of support for all of its activities.

The conference "China's Middle Class: Beyond Economic Transformation," held at Brookings on September 23–24, 2009, was itself an elaborate endeavor to which many contributed. Thanks go to our panel moderators, Richard Bush, Erica Downs, Kenneth Lieberthal, Margaret Pearson, and Dennis Wilder, as well as to our two distinguished keynote speakers, the Harvard University professor and historian William C. Kirby, who offered illuminating remarks on the role of educational development in the formation of the Chinese middle class, and James Fallows, one of our most thoughtful public voices and a longtime national correspondent for *The Atlantic*. Thank you, as well, to all of this volume's contributors for presenting earlier versions of their chapters as conference papers.

Several leading Chinese sociologists were especially helpful in the earliest stages of the research process, helping to frame the debates and set the volume's agenda. They include Li Peilin, director of sociology at the Chinese Academy of Social Sciences (CASS), Zhang Wanli, also a professor of sociology at CASS, and Li Lulu, professor of sociology at Renmin University.

Thanks are also owed to Evan Greenberg and ACE Charitable Foundation, without whose generous financial support this project would not have been possible. Evan Greenberg has taken a personal interest in the John L. Thornton China Center's activities from very early on, and several of the center's signature accomplishments have stemmed from his support.

I am profoundly indebted to Jordan Lee, my research assistant, essay collaborator, and the most brilliant graduate student any professor or researcher could possibly hope to have, for his thorough research in the relevant literature and meticulous scrutiny of the manuscript. From start to finish, he played a critical role in brainstorming for the volume, in conceptualizing its organization and major themes, and in editing it line by line.

The China Center's tireless staff deserves a special mention. Thank you to Kevin Foley, the center's assistant director, and Iris An, center coordinator, for keeping everything on track. Their predecessors, Elizabeth Brooks, Dewardric McNeal, and Pavneet Singh, were crucial in acquiring the green light for the project and in preparing for the conference. Several other friends and research assistants reviewed individual chapters and offered helpful suggestions on how to clarify the presentation of these chapters. Thank you to Sally Carman and Yinsheng Li (both have worked closely with me since my previous position at Hamilton College) and to Robert O'Brien and Matthew Platkin, both at Brookings, for their generous help. Eve Cary, Henry Fung, Scott Harold, Teresa Hsu, and Paul Wozniak also aided in the process of completing this volume in myriad small ways.

Deep appreciation is owed to everyone at the Brookings Press—Robert Faherty, director, Chris Kelaher, marketing director, Janet Walker, managing editor, Diane Hammond, copy editor, Larry Converse, production manager, and Susan Woollen, art coordinator—all of whom performed, unfazed throughout the process, with the high level of intelligence, creativity, and professionalism for which the Press is known.

Finally, I would like to dedicate this book to the late Brooke Shearer, a close friend and constant inspiration, whose thoughtful reflections on the Chinese middle class helped first animate this project in the fall of 2006, when we traveled together in China with a large delegation of Brookings trustees and friends. In the course of our lengthy discussions about the subject—and about China generally—as well as about her own area of expertise, India's modern development, I would recurrently note to myself how much more peaceful and tolerant the world would be if only her characteristic style of American goodwill were generalized to more U.S. policymakers and the public at large. One can only hope, in this time of rapid global change, when the stakes are so high for the world, that perspectives as thoughtful as hers will begin to acquire greater resonance.

PART I

The Global Significance of China's Emerging Middle Class

CHAPTER ONE

Introduction: The Rise of the Middle Class in the Middle Kingdom

CHENG LI

Among the many forces shaping China's course of development, argu-ably none will prove more significant in the long run than the rapid emergence and explosive growth of the Chinese middle class. China's ongoing economic transition from a relatively poor, developing nation to a middle-class country has been one of the most fascinating human dramas of our time. Never in history have so many people made so much economic progress in one or two generations. Just twenty years ago a distinct socioeconomic middle class was virtually nonexistent in the People's Republic of China (PRC), but today a large number of Chinese citizens, especially in coastal cities, own private property and personal automobiles, have growing financial assets, and are able to take vacations abroad and send their children overseas for school. This trans-formation is likely to have wide-ranging implications for every aspect of Chinese life, especially the country's long-term economic prospects, energy consumption, and environmental well-being.

The importance of China's emerging middle class, of course, extends far beyond the realm of economics. This volume focuses on the socio-political ramifications of the birth and growth of the Chinese middle class over the past two decades. The central question is: What impacts,

I would like to thank Sally Carman, Jordan Lee, Robert O'Brien, and Matthew Platkin for their very helpful comments on an earlier version of this chapter.

current and future, might China's emerging middle class have on the country's social structure and political system? Following this broad line of inquiry, the volume sets itself four tasks:

—To examine the status of research on social stratification and social mobility in China

—To identify the major issues and trends related to the Chinese middle class

—To compare the Chinese middle class with its counterparts in other countries

—And to assess the values, worldviews, and potential political roles of the Chinese middle class as well as its likely impact on China's rise on the world stage.

This introductory chapter provides an overview of the political significance and historical background of the emerging Chinese middle class and summarizes the existing literature and ongoing debates on the topic.

The Sociopolitical Significance of a Chinese Middle Class

Early studies of newly affluent groups in China, including the nascent middle class, tend to emphasize the status quo–oriented, risk-averse nature of these prime beneficiaries of economic reform. However, more recent studies (including many by PRC scholars) suggest that this may simply be a transitory phase in the development of the middle class. There already appears to be widespread resentment among the middle class toward official corruption and the state's monopoly over major industries. Another potential source of sociopolitical ferment lies in the increasing number of college graduates, many of whom belong to middle-class families, who are unable to find work. An economic downturn, led by the collapse of the real estate market or the stock market—two institutions that have contributed enormously to the rapid expansion of the Chinese middle class—will only heighten the middle class's sense of grievance. Furthermore, the middle class is central to China's new development strategy, which seeks to reorient China's economy from one overly dependent on exports to one driven by domestic demand. The increasing economic role of the middle class may in turn enhance the group's political influence.

China's emerging middle class is, of course, a complex mosaic of groups and individuals. Subsets of the middle class differ enormously from each other. In terms of the class's occupational and sociological composition, its members fall into three major clusters:

—An economic cluster (including private sector entrepreneurs, urban small businesspeople, rural industrialists and rich farmers, foreign and domestic joint-venture employees, and stock and real estate speculators)

—A political cluster (government officials, office clerks, state sector managers, and lawyers)

—A cultural and educational cluster (academics and educators, media personalities, public intellectuals, and think tank scholars).

There is a tendency, sometimes, to assume that the relationship between China's middle class and its authoritarian state is one of simple, one-dimensional co-optation, but this is to oversimplify. Undoubtedly some members of the class are the clients of political patrons, but many more are self-made people. Indeed, such an economically aspirant population is a double-edged sword for the Chinese authorities. They are well aware of the fact that the middle class has pushed for democratization in other developing countries (South Korea, Indonesia, and Brazil, among others).

It is also noteworthy that the emergence of the middle class in China parallels the reemergence of the Middle Kingdom on the global stage. To a certain extent, the Chinese middle class has already begun to change the way China engages with the international community, both by playing an active role in this increasingly interdependent world and by keeping abreast of transnational cultural currents. As the PRC's international influence continues to grow, two contending views on how China might understand its role in the world have taken shape. They reflect fundamentally different visions of China's future, and neither can be divorced from the trajectory of its emerging middle class.

In the first, a nightmare scenario, a superpower China, buoyed by decades of double-digit economic growth and military modernization, has birthed a middle class of unprecedented size and scope, whose strongly mercantilist views govern almost all affairs of state. The aggregate demand of hundreds of millions of middle-class consumers, coupled with increasingly severe global resource scarcity and growing international consternation at China's swelling carbon footprint, has led nativist demagogues to peddle a toxic strain of nationalism to the broader populace. In this scenario, an ascendant and arrogant China, still smarting from the "century of humiliation" it endured at the hands of Western imperialists over a century earlier, disregards international norms, disrupts global institutions, and even flirts with bellicose expansionism.

In the second view, China's burgeoning middle class increasingly embraces cosmopolitan values, having forged close economic and cultural links with Western countries, and especially the United States. In this scenario, China's middle-class lifestyle closely mirrors that of the West, and an increasing percentage of China's political and cultural elites have received some Western education. The Chinese middle class has acquired a sophisticated understanding of the outside world, recognizes the virtue of cooperation, and demands that China act as a responsible stakeholder on the world stage. The expectation underwriting this scenario is that if China continues to "evolve peacefully" in the direction of openness and integration, it may experience an eventual democratic breakthrough.[1] If this were to occur, then the time-honored theory of a "democratic peace" would finally be put to the test in a world of great powers integrating ever more closely.[2]

The significance of China's emerging middle class, therefore, lies not only in the economic domain or in its potential to effect domestic politics but also in its ability to shape China's international behavior. A better informed and more comprehensive understanding of the Chinese middle class, from its basic composition to its values and worldviews—from its idiosyncratic characteristics to its evolving political roles in China—will help to broaden the policy options available to the United States and other countries in dealing with this emerging global power. In a broader sense, this study will contribute to the ongoing debate over the Chinese middle class, that is, whether or not it will become a catalyst for political democratization within China and lead to a constructive Chinese presence in a rapidly changing global environment.

China's Middle Class: Fast Ascendance amid Slow Acceptance

Despite the great importance of the subject, scholarly communities outside China have been remarkably slow to accept the notion that the Chinese middle class has become a distinct sociopolitical force. China watchers around the world are nearly unanimous in recognizing the country's rapid economic growth over the past three decades: China's GDP has grown at a pace of roughly 10 percent a year, the average Chinese person's income has quadrupled, about 300 million people have been lifted out of poverty, and a significant portion of the population has become affluent.[3] Yet the use of the term *Chinese middle class* remains controversial. With a few notable exceptions, Western scholars are hesitant to acknowledge the existence of a Chinese middle class, let alone explore its political implications.[4]

There are various reasons for this dearth of Western scholarship on the Chinese middle class. The most notable include the difficulty that foreign researchers have in obtaining extensive empirical data on the issue, cultural differences in conceptualizing the idea of a middle class in the Chinese context, and reluctance on the part of Western analysts to accept the fact that Communist China could produce a middle class similar to those found in the West.[5] This skepticism is not wholly without justification: the nascent Chinese middle class is admittedly a very new phenomenon.

A Foreign Concept and a Nascent Phenomenon

The term *middle class* was rarely used during the first four decades of the PRC. Even in the pre-Communist era, it was largely a foreign concept. According to the late John King Fairbank, capitalism did not grow in earnest in China during the late nineteenth and early twentieth centuries because China's merchant class failed to coalesce into an independent entrepreneurial power outside the "control of the gentry and their representatives in the bureaucracy."[6] Without firsthand experience, the concept of a middle class remained foreign to the Chinese.

This state of affairs changed very little after the establishment of the PRC in 1949. The few groups considered part of the middle class in pre-1949 China—namely, the private entrepreneurs and petty-bourgeois intellectuals who had emerged in preceding decades—either quickly disappeared or were severely curtailed, both politically and economically, after the Communist revolution.[7] Indeed, by the mid-1950s the 4 million private firms and small businesses that had existed in China before 1949 had been systematically dismantled.[8] Maoist ideology dictated that the country had only three social strata (workers, peasants, and intellectuals), and the Marxist notion of intellectuals as an "intermediate stratum" bore little resemblance to the Western concept of the middle class.[9]

Only after Deng Xiaoping instituted reform and opening did the term *middle class* begin to appear in Chinese academic writings. The earliest references to the concept were made in the late 1980s, when scholars began to examine the sudden emergence of rural industrialists—owners of township and village enterprises in the countryside—and the arrival of private entrepreneurs in the cities. At that time, the consensus among Chinese scholars was that the concept of the middle class should not be employed to describe these groups, in large part because many of these rural industrialists and urban entrepreneurs came from underprivileged or uneducated social strata.[10]

Only since the turn of the millennium has research on the middle class found its way into the PRC's intellectual mainstream. It should be noted that in the early phase of research on this concept Chinese scholars often used the terms *middle stratum* (*zhongjianceng*), *middle-income stratum* (*zhongjian shouru jieceng*), and *middle-income group* (*zhongdeng shouru qunti*), rather than *middle class* (*zhongchan jieji*) to refer to this new socioeconomic force. The increasing use of these new terms among PRC scholars over the past decade reflects the profound changes that have occurred in domestic social stratification and social mobility. In addition to the aforementioned rapid development of rural industries and urban private enterprises, numerous other important developments have led to the meteoric rise of the middle class in China. These include the boom in foreign joint ventures, the adoption of a stock market in Shenzhen and Shanghai, urban housing reforms and large-scale urbanization, an enormous expansion of higher education, constitutional changes regarding property rights, and the increasingly cosmopolitan lifestyles created by economic globalization and international cultural exchanges.[11]

Two factors, however, have been particularly instrumental in increasing both public awareness of and scholarly interest in China's middle class. The first is the Chinese business community's drive to promote the image of Chinese consumers as potentially the "world's largest middle-class market"; the second is the Chinese government's decision to "enlarge the size of the middle-income group."

The Business Community's Drive for the "World's Largest Middle-Class Market"

The business community in China, including both domestic and foreign companies, has an interest in promoting the notion of a Chinese middle class. The idea of an extant middle class in China has often been the primary driver of foreign investment and other business activities in the country. It has been widely noted that China's savings rate is one of the highest in the world. In 2008, for instance, Chinese households saved approximately 40 percent their disposable income. That same year, American households saved only 3 percent of their disposable income.[12] While private consumption comprised an average of 59 percent of GDP globally and 72 percent of U.S. GDP in 2006,

China's private consumption made up only 38 percent of its aggregate GDP.[13] The possibility of stimulating domestic consumption in China, the world's most populous country, has understandably captured the imagination of the business community.

The business community recognized very early on that popularizing the idea of a middle class in China would redound to the benefit of their sales figures. As Li Chunling, a sociologist at the Chinese Academy of Social Sciences (CASS) and a contributor to this volume, has observed, it was the business community in China, including manufacturers, company managers, service providers, and their associates in the media, that initially turned the idea of a Chinese middle class from an abstract academic subject to a hot topic throughout society.[14] While most Western social scientists, including academic economists, have been generally dismissive of the idea of a Chinese middle class in the last decade, business leaders and analysts have conducted a substantial number of research projects on the topic. For firms operating in China—including multinational, foreign-owned, and Chinese state-owned, private and joint ventures—this research has helped them to understand the middle class's overall size, consumption patterns, generational composition, and geographical distribution. To the extent that they publicize the middle-class lifestyle, they are also helpful in shaping and promoting the group's continued expansion.

Over the past decade the Chinese media have obsessed over commercial indicators of middle-class growth. One such indicator is the rapid increase in credit card use. In 2003, 3 million credit cards were issued; by the end of 2008 a total of 150 million credit cards were in circulation, 50 million of which were issued in that year alone.[15] Another indicator is the stunning increase in the number of private autos in the country, from some 240,000 in 1990 to about 26 million in 2009.[16] In 2009 China's auto production output and sales volume reached 13.8 million and 13.6 million, respectively, making the PRC the world's leading automobile producer and consumer for the first time.[17]

A variety of companies, especially large multinational banks and consulting firms, have commissioned studies to assess the current size and projected growth of the Chinese middle class. In 2004 the French investment bank BNP Paribas Peregrine predicted that China's middle class would increase from 50 million households that year (13.5 percent of the Chinese population) to 100 million households by 2010.[18] Two years later, Merrill Lynch projected that China's middle class would consist of a total of 350 million people by 2016, constituting 32 percent of the adult population.[19] That same year, the McKinsey Global Institute made an even bolder prediction: China would have a total of 100 million middle-class households by 2009, which would account for 45 percent of the country's urban population. According to McKinsey's projections, the middle class would reach 520 million individuals (or even 612 million if "lower aspirants" are included) by 2025, accounting for 76 percent of the urban population. According to these estimates China will have the world's largest middle class within fifteen years.[20] Another study, jointly conducted by the Hong Kong Shanghai Banking Corporation (HSBC) and MasterCard in 2007, reached a conclusion more in line with BNP Paribas Peregrine, forecasting a total of 100 million middle-class households by 2016.[21]

Most of these studies were conducted by groups of economists consisting of local Chinese researchers, foreign-educated PRC nationals, and expatriates based in China. Their methodologies are often quite opaque, and some might not meet the standards of rigorous academic research. Indeed, some of their more rosy forecasts might obscure the real nature of social stratification and social tensions in present-day China. Regardless, these business-driven empirical research projects have served as an important impetus for further study of the Chinese middle class, especially by raising public awareness of the far-reaching changes taking place in both the Chinese and global economic landscape.

The Ideological and Policy Shift of the Chinese Leadership

For the first two decades following Deng Xiaoping's implementation of economic reforms in 1978, the Chinese Communist Party's (CCP) leadership avoided class analysis, a deliberate departure from the Mao era, during which class struggle dominated all aspects of life in China. The year 2000 marked the beginning of a major ideological and policy shift on the part of the Chinese authorities. Jiang Zemin, then secretary general of the CCP, formulated his "theory of the three represents" (*san ge daibiao*).[22] In contrast to the Marxist notion that the Communist Party should be the "vanguard of the working class," Jiang argued that the CCP should broaden its base of power to include entrepreneurs, intellectuals, and technocrats, all of whom regularly occupy the ranks of the middle-income stratum, the official euphemism for the middle class.

Two years later, at the Sixteenth National Congress of the CCP in 2002, the Chinese leadership called for "enlarging the size of the middle-income group." With this pronouncement, the need to "foster a middle-income stratum in Chinese society" became a clear policy objective of the Chinese government.[23] This policy shift reflected a new line of thinking within the Chinese leadership, which held that the middle class should be considered an asset and political ally rather than a threat to the party's primacy. According to this logic, the real threat to the CCP lies not in the middle class, which is as invested in social and political stability as the authorities, but rather in the prospect of a vicious struggle between rich and poor, a more likely scenario without a rapidly expanding intermediate socioeconomic group bridging the two extremes.

From the CCP's perspective, a growing middle class can provide hope to the country's still massive underclass. In 2007 Zheng Xinli, then deputy director of the CCP Central Committee's Policy Research Office, told the Chinese media that roughly 55 percent of China's population "will be members of the middle class by 2020, with 78 percent of city dwellers and 30 percent of those in rural areas reaching that status."[24] Similarly, Long Yongtu, the former chief negotiator of China's accession to the World Trade Organization, boasted to the foreign media that by 2011 "some 400 to 500 million Chinese would become members of the middle class."[25]

More recently, Chinese authorities have often contrasted the perceived growth of the Chinese middle class in the wake of the global financial crisis with the shrinking of the middle class in the West (and the United States, in particular). This contrast has become a source of national pride for the Chinese public.[26] Several officials and their think tank advisers have turned to the media to publicize the idea that China is entering the "golden age" of its middle-class development.[27] A large number of Chinese scholars, however, have remained circumspect. Mao Yushi, a distinguished economist who works at an independent think tank, recently argued that only a subset of the middle class, namely those officials and managers who work in state-owned firms, grew rapidly over the preceding two years, and that this expansion was actually achieved at the expense of other subsets of the middle class.[28] According to certain PRC sociologists, the Chinese middle class has actually been shrinking in recent years, partly due to the loss of jobs and financial assets as a result of the global financial crisis and partly because of the rapid rise of housing prices in urban China.[29] Recent disputes regarding the status of China's emerging middle class are part of a long series of scholarly debates on this complex subject.

Empirical Questions and Scholarly Debates

These seemingly paradoxical trends in PRC social stratification and social mobility have generated a high degree of uncertainty regarding the country's future socioeconomic trajectory. They have also created a sense of political urgency among the Chinese leadership to address these challenges swiftly. Contradictory assessments of the middle class's growth and evolution have inspired many important empirical questions within the scholarly community. Three key clusters of interrelated questions have emerged:

—First, what criteria define membership in the middle class? What is the conceptual difference between a middle class and a middle-income stratum? What are the educational and occupational backgrounds of the Chinese middle class? What is the size of the middle class in present-day China, and how fast is it growing? How far is China from becoming a middle-class country?

—Second, how unique is the development story of China's middle class? In what respects does the Chinese middle class differ from its counterparts in other countries? Is the middle class a useful conceptual framework or effective analytical angle from which to study present-day China? Does this framework broaden or narrow our perspective on Chinese politics and society? To what degree does this large and internally diverse group have common political interests and a shared class consciousness?

—Third, what role, politically, does the Chinese middle class play? Will this role change as the middle class continues to expand? What factors shape the relationship between the middle class and the lower class, on the one hand, and the relationship between the middle class and the upper class, on the other? How are new notions of consumer rights, taxpayer rights, and property rights affecting state-society relations in China? How can the study of the Chinese middle class enrich the theoretical discourse on the middle class in general?

There are, of course, a variety of answers to these questions. In a sense, the spectrum of possible answers to these three sets of questions corresponds to the three most important scholarly debates on the middle class in general, and the Chinese middle class in particular. The first concerns its definition, the second its characteristics (especially the ways in which the Chinese middle class differs from its counterparts around the world), and the third its potential political roles. In order to ensure a critical, comprehensive, and coherent intellectual inquiry into this relatively new and understandably controversial subject, it is necessary to first briefly survey these debates.

Definitional Criteria

Like many other sociological concepts, the term *middle class* is widely used but lacks a universally accepted definition. There is little scholarly consensus on which criteria should be applied when ascertaining who belongs to the middle class. This lack of a clear, consistent, and consensus-based definition is not limited to research on China's newly emerging middle class. It also afflicts middle class studies in general, including those that focus on the United States or other developed Western nations.

In the United States, income, especially household income, tends to be the most essential criterion in determining middle-class status. American sociologists and economists often use a five- or six-class model to analyze the U.S.'s socioeconomic strata, and some also divide the middle class into upper middle class and lower middle class. In his seminal study of America's class structure, the sociologist Dennis Gilbert adopts a six-class model, which includes the capitalist class (1 percent of the population), upper middle class (15 percent), lower middle class (30 percent), working class (29 percent), working poor (13 percent), and underclass (12 percent).[30] In their widely used sociology textbook, William Thompson and Joseph Hickey combine Gilbert's bottom two classes into one "lower class" (representing 20 percent of the population), along with an upper class (1 percent), upper middle class (15 percent), lower middle class (32 percent), and working class (32 percent).[31] While these two major studies feature similar estimates of the percentage of the U.S. population composed of the middle class—45 percent and 47 percent, respectively—other studies reach far more divergent estimates, ranging from 25 percent to 66 percent of households.[32]

According to Gary Burtless, an economist at the Brookings Institution, the U.S. middle class encompasses the portion of the labor force earning between one-half of the country's median income to twice the median income. Based on U.S. census data from the late 1990s, Burtless believes that middle-class annual incomes in the United States range from roughly $25,000 to $100,000.[33] As a description of middle-class incomes, however, this range has always been controversial. As the Harvard political scientist Iain Johnston notes, "there is no consensus over where the income cut points are to divide the population."[34] The considerable differences in household size, family wealth, geographic locations, housing costs, and other factors related to a family's standard of living all illustrate the problems inherent in the income-based criterion. A population's distribution of household income is also subject to change, requiring that one periodically recalibrate the income range that describes the middle class.

Although American sociologists and economists generally consider income to be the central component in defining the middle class, other factors such as an individual's educational attainment, occupational status, consumption patterns and lifestyle, values, and self-identification as a member of the class are also important. This multifaceted approach to defining middle-class membership can be traced back to C. Wright Mills's classic study *White Collar: The American Middle Classes*.[35] Max Weber's analysis of the interaction of economic wealth, social status, and professional prestige in modern societies has also had a significant influence on Western sociological definitions of the middle class.[36] The Weberian approach to social stratification, which takes into account various professional groups as well as business managers, is particularly influential in European studies of the middle class. European scholars tend to adopt a composite index that combines educational credentials, occupation, and income.[37]

The conceptual complexity and diverse definitional criteria found in Western studies of the middle class suggest that similar definitional difficulties pertaining to the Chinese middle class are to be expected. Yet sorting through these definitional issues is necessary to comprehensively assess China's middle class. A 2005 study of some 263,000 households in urban China, conducted by the State Statistics Bureau of the Chinese government, used income as the primary criterion for determining membership in the middle-income stratum.[38] Using the range of 60,000 to 500,000 yuan annual income for a three-member household, this study estimated that the middle class constituted 5 percent of urban Chinese families in 2005 and would increase to 14 percent in 2010 and 45 percent in 2020.[39] This definition, however, has not been widely accepted in China, even among analysts affiliated with the government. Several factors undermine the utility of this definition, including rapid changes in income, household wealth, and the ownership of property (which often grows faster than income), enormous regional variations in socioeconomic conditions, and the definition's failure to consider purchasing power parity in international comparisons.

Some sociologists who study social stratification in China strongly reject definitions of middle class or middle-income stratum that are based solely on earnings. As Jianying Wang and Deborah Davis incisively point out in their contribution to this volume, "By that metric [income], however, the middle class would never expand beyond the middle 20 percent." Some PRC scholars, such as Chen Yiping and Li Qiang, also explicitly state that there is no difference between the Chinese terms *middle-income stratum* and *middle class* and therefore favor using the latter.[40] Not surprisingly, a large number of PRC scholars have increasingly treated *middle-income stratum* and *middle class* as interchangeable concepts in their academic writings and public comments.[41]

Like their peers elsewhere, many PRC scholars adopt a combination of criteria, or a composite index, to define middle-class membership. Li Peilin, the director of the Institute of Sociology at CASS, has formulated a comprehensive index for the classification of middle-class membership. The index is based on one of three criteria: income, education, and occupation. He then assigns the individual to one of the following three categories: the core, the semicore, and the marginal groups of the middle class. If a person meets all three criteria, he or she is considered to be a member of the core of the middle class; a person who meets two criteria belongs to the semicore; and a person who meets only one criterion is considered part of the marginal middle class. In 2006 Li and his colleagues completed a survey of 7,063 households in China's twenty-eight provinces and cities, finding that 3.2 percent, 8.9 percent, and 13.7 percent of the population could be categorized as the core, semicore, and marginal groups of the middle class, respectively.[42]

Li Chunling, another distinguished scholar at CASS's Institute of Sociology, adopts a well-considered, multifaceted approach to dealing with these classificatory challenges (see table 1-1). First, she uses four sets of definitional criteria—occupation, income, consumption, and self-identification—to determine how many people meet each of these four criteria. Then she calculates the percentages of the four groups—total population (2.8 percent), metropolitan residents (8.7 percent), the labor force (4.1 percent), and the age group thirty-one through forty years (10.5 percent)—that meet all four criteria. Her findings provide both general and specific assessments of the size of the middle class in China.

TABLE 1-1. Size of the Chinese Middle Class by Several Classifications

Percent

Classification criteria	Share of population
Occupation	15.9
Income	24.6
Consumption	35.0
Self-identification (subjective identity)	46.8
Comprehensive criteria (combining all of the above four)	
Total population	2.8
Metropolitan population	8.7
Labor force (age group 16–60)	4.1
Age group 31–40	10.5

Source: Li Chunling, *Duanlie yu suipian—Dangdai Zhongguo shehuijieceng fenhua shizheng fenxi* [Cleavage and fragment: an empirical analysis of social stratification in contemporary China] (Beijing: Shehuikexue wenxian chubanshe, 2005), pp. 485–99.

If one looks only at the urban pool of Li Peilin's study, as many as 25.4 percent of those living in urban areas consider themselves to be core or semicore members of the middle class. Similarly, for each of the four individual categories listed in Li Chunling's study, significant portions of respondents meet at least one criterion for membership in the middle class, and 46.8 percent of respondents consider themselves middle class. Despite this fact, both Li Peilin's and Li Chunling's studies have been criticized by many of their Chinese colleagues for being too conservative in estimating the size of the Chinese middle class. In his 2010 book, which was based on a large-scale nationwide survey, the former director of the CASS Institute of Sociology Lu Xueyi notes that, as of 2009, the middle class constituted 23 percent of China's total, up from 15 percent in 2001.[43] Lu's study also finds that in major coastal cities such as Beijing and Shanghai, the middle class constituted 40 percent of the population in 2009.

In interviews with the Chinese media following his book's publication, Lu predicted that the Chinese middle class will grow at an annual rate of 1 percent over the next decade or so, meaning that approximately 7.7 million people out of a Chinese labor force of 770 million will join the ranks of the middle class each year.[44] Lu also held that in about twenty years the Chinese middle class will constitute 40 percent of the

PRC population—on par with Western countries—making China a true middle-class nation.[45] Lu's prognostication that China will become a middle-class country within two decades is highly debatable. What is not debatable, however, is the fact that China is in the midst of dramatic changes in social stratification and social mobility and that a burgeoning middle class is a central feature of these changes (indeed, Homi Kharas and Geoffrey Gertz suggest, in the following chapter, that it may already be the world's second-largest middle class).

Given the widely divergent approaches to defining the Chinese middle class surveyed above, and the lack of any clear consensus, it is difficult to settle firmly on one uncontroversial standard. Perhaps the most acceptable and ecumenical approach is Li Chunling's four-part typology, which both makes a great deal of analytical sense and produces results that have an intuitive believability. Because this is still an inchoate phenomenon it is highly likely that the most acceptable definition of the Chinese middle class will continue to evolve alongside the vagaries of its development, but for the time being definitions in the style of Li Chunling's composite approach seem most plausible.

Distinctive Characteristics

The Chinese middle class exhibits some extraordinary, perhaps even unique, characteristics. One of the most noticeable is that its rapid growth has taken place alongside an astonishing increase in economic disparities. As the University of Washington professor Ann Anagnost notes, the "expansion of a middle class and its complex relation to increasing social inequality represents a delicate balance between market dynamism and social instability."[46] The World Bank reports that the Gini coefficient (a measure of income disparity) in China increased from 0.28 in the early 1980s to 0.447 in 2001 and is now 0.47 (a statistic the Chinese government has not disputed).[47] It was recently reported by the Chinese official media that the income gap between the top 10 percent and the lowest 10 percent of Chinese earners had increased from a multiple of 7.3 in 1988 to a multiple of 23.0 in 2007.[48]

It has also been widely noted that the rise of the Chinese middle class is primarily an urban phenomenon. Indeed, the middle class is disproportionately concentrated in major cities of coastal regions, such as Beijing, Shanghai, Shenzhen, the lower Yangzi River Delta, and the Pearl River Delta. The economic gap between urban and rural areas has increasingly widened over the course of the past three decades. Economic disparities are now so great that some scholars wonder whether the middle class is even a useful conceptual framework with which to study present-day China. For example, Xu Zhiyuan, a well-known public intellectual in Beijing who writes for influential online magazines such as the *Financial Times*, bluntly refers to the notion of a Chinese middle class as a pseudo-concept (*wei gainian*). In a recent book he argues, "in China during the past ten years, no other popular term has been more misleading than *middle class*."[49] In his view, an analytical approach that places too much weight on the so-called middle class actually narrows one's perspective and risks obfuscating more important issues and tensions in Chinese politics and society.

Lu Xueyi and like-minded sociologists do not deny the seriousness of economic disparities and social tensions in Chinese society but still believe that the concept of middle class is useful. In Lu's view these problems actually reinforce his central argument that China's social structure has lagged behind the country's economic growth for the last fifteen years.[50] Nevertheless, a significant number of scholars have reservations about how unitary the concept of a Chinese middle class is or can be. According to Li Lulu, a professor of sociology at People's University in Beijing, the heterogeneity of the Chinese middle class can be explained by the fact that there are three vastly different means or channels by which individuals can obtain middle-class status. Li and his associate created the terms "power-based executive-type access" (*xingzhengxing jinru*), "market-driven access" (*shichangxing jinru*), and "social network-linked access" (*shehuiwangluoxing jinru*) to characterize these three channels.[51] In other words, various groups—such as the Communist Party and government officials, entrepreneurs, professionals, and cultural elites—constitute a significant portion of China's emerging middle class.

It has also been noted that the Chinese term for middle class emphasizes a sense of ownership (*chan*) or property rights (*chanquan*), a connotation the English term lacks. Some scholars speculate that this shared notion of ownership or property rights may serve as a powerful glue to unify these otherwise starkly different Chinese socioeconomic groups.[52] While members of the Chinese middle class may differ from each other in occupation, socialization, or political position, they seem to share certain views and values. One such value is the "inviolability of the private property of citizens," which was only recently amended into the PRC constitution.[53] In the words of Zhang Yiwu, a professor of

Chinese literature at Peking University, this new notion may prove to be an "important beginning of group consciousness and the sense of rights' protection for the Chinese middle class."[54]

Political Roles

Arguably the most important debate regarding the Chinese middle class is over the potential implications its development will have for the PRC's political system. A long-standing Western maxim postulates that there exists a dynamic correlation, or even a causal relationship, between the expansion of the middle class and political democratization. Pioneering works by Barrington Moore Jr., Seymour Martin Lipset, and Samuel P. Huntington, among many others, all emphasize, from various analytical angles, the vital role of the middle class in a democracy.

For Moore the existence of a forceful middle class—or, in his words, the "bourgeois impulse"—creates a new and a more autonomous social structure in which new elites do not have to depend on coercive state power to flourish, as had been the case under an aristocracy.[55] Lipset believes that a professionally educated, politically moderate, and economically self-assured middle class is an important precondition for an eventual transition to democracy.[56] In his view, mass communication media, facilitated by industrialization and urbanization, provides a broader venue for cultural elites to disseminate middle-class views and values, thus creating a moderate mainstream in the public opinion of a given country. At the same time, political socialization and the professional interests of the middle class also contribute to the growth of civil society and the legal system, key components of democracy.

Huntington, however, criticizes the theory that a market economy or successive capitalist developments, alone, organically lead to political democracy.[57] In his view, a country's transition to democracy often depends on historical and situational factors, both domestic and international.[58] Huntington believes that a middle class tends to be revolutionary in its early development but grows increasingly conservative over time. The newly emergent middle class in a given society tends to be idealistic, ambitious, rebellious, and nationalistic in its formative years. Its members gradually become more conservative, however, as they begin to register their demands through institutionalized means rather than street protests and become engaged in the political system so as to protect and enhance their interests. Both Lipset and Huntington recognize the importance of the middle class in democratic stability, which they attribute to moderate and institutionalized class conflict rather than more radical and potentially violent conflicts.

The Western literature on the relationship between economic development and political democracy, and the political role often played by the middle class, provides a theoretical and analytical framework within which to study China's economic reform and sociopolitical development. A majority of Chinese studies, however, point in a different direction: the Chinese middle class has largely been a political ally of the authoritarian regime rather than a catalyst for democratic change. In their new book on Chinese entrepreneurs, an important subgroup of the middle class, Jie Chen and Bruce Dickson argue that, partly due to their close political and financial ties with the state and partly due to their shared concern for social stability, these new economic elites do not support a system characterized by multiparty competition and political liberty, including citizens' right to demonstrate.[59]

In the same vein, An Chen, a PRC-born, U.S.-educated political science professor at the National University of Singapore, offers a comprehensive four-part answer to the question, "Why doesn't the Chinese middle class like democracy?"[60] First, a significant number of middle-class members are part of the political establishment; as Chen describes, "many have established cozy collaboration with the local top officials."[61] Second, members of the Chinese middle class tend to have what Chen calls "an elitist complex which poses a psychological obstacle to their acceptance of political equality based on the one-citizen-one-vote principle."[62] Third, growing economic disparities and social tensions have often led the new middle class to form alliances with the rich and powerful in the "common cause [of] resisting democratization and averting the collapse of the regime."[63] And fourth, middle-class members tend to "associate democracy with political chaos, economic breakdown, the mafia, and other social evils."[64]

Other empirical studies find that certain widely perceived correlations between the middle class and political democratization in Western countries are simply absent in China. The Chinese middle class lacks the political incentives to promote civil society and is reluctant to fight for freedom of the media. Some middle-class opinion leaders actually act as spokespeople for the Chinese state. According to this view, the middle class has yet to develop an identity, a sense of rights consciousness, and a distinct value system, which characterize their counterparts in other countries.[65] Almost all of these studies, however, acknowledge the inconclusive nature of their arguments and assumptions about the conservatism and pro-regime role of the Chinese middle class. The experiences of many countries in East Asia and South America suggest that the middle class can shift its political stance from anti-democratic to pro-democratic quite swiftly.

Another important development in the recent literature on the topic is that some scholars have challenged the conventional, dichotomous treatment of political stability and democracy. The middle class's current preference for sociopolitical stability does not necessarily mean that it will oppose democracy in the future. In China, if democracy will lead to social instability, political chaos, or even the dissolution of the country, there is no incentive for the Chinese people, including its emerging middle class, to pursue it. In a fundamental way, sociopolitical stability and democracy should be seen as complementary, rather than contradictory, phenomena. A democratic system enhances sociopolitical stability in a given country because it is based on the rule of law and civil liberties, and it provides for the peaceful and institutionalized transfer of power through elections.

The political scientist Zheng Yongnian, for example, recently observed that in Western multiparty democracies, although the party in power may frequently change, there is a remarkably high degree of continuity in terms of political institutions and public policies. Regardless of whether the incumbent party is left wing or right wing, it is incumbent upon the government to avoid undermining the interests of the middle class, which "plays a pivotal role for the country's sociopolitical stability."[66] Social stability is an essential component of political democracy and the peaceful transfer of power from one party to another. The attainment of this stability is due, in large part, to the instrumental and pro-democratic role of the middle class.

The Chinese middle class's current inclination for social stability and gradual political change, therefore, should not be characterized as pro-CCP, anti-democratic, or even conservative. As the Michigan professor Mary E. Gallagher argues, "There may be benefits to delayed political change in China. Integration into the global economy, the increased use of legal institutions to mediate conflict, and the influence of a small but growing middle class may together slowly build up a more stable societal foundation for democratization."[67] Following the same line of reasoning, some PRC scholars have recently expended great effort developing ideas that "conceptually and procedurally make democracy safe for China."[68]

The rapid expansion of the Chinese middle class and its changing relationship to the government has become a focal point of scholarly work on Chinese politics and society. Both the unfolding story of China's drive to become a middle-class nation and the widely differing scholarly assessments of its implications will undoubtedly enrich the literature on this important global subject.

Arguments, Methodologies, and Organization of the Volume

This edited volume is the product of an international conference held on September 22 and 23, 2009, by the John L. Thornton China Center of the Foreign Policy Studies Program at the Brookings Institution. Approximately 300 people attended the conference. Nineteen scholars in the fields of sociology, political science, economics, education, history, and law—including eleven U.S.-based scholars, five from the PRC, one from Taiwan, one from South Korea, and one from Australia—presented fourteen papers. Offered here are all fourteen of these papers, revised to reflect insights gleaned from exchanges during and after the conference.

All of the following chapters are based on firsthand original research and each focuses on one or two specific issues surrounding the Chinese middle class. Several chapters approach the problem from the Chinese perspective or comment extensively on Chinese scholarly debates on the subject. Others painstakingly address the essential definitional and categorical issues, and some provide much-needed cross-country comparisons. One persistent fact is that contributors to the volume have vastly differing views regarding the political role of the emerging Chinese middle class. This volume's rich empirical evidence, diverse perspectives, multidisciplinary nature, and clash of ideas and conclusions make it especially lively and valuable.

Chapter 2 by Homi Kharas and Geoffrey Gertz is unique in two respects: first, it is the only chapter that focuses exclusively on economic issues in the wake of the global financial crisis; second, it provides a macro-level view of the global expansion of the middle class. The authors argue that as the current financial crisis undermines America's customary role as the consumer of last resort, the "center of gravity of global output shifts toward Asia." Based on an absolute definition of the middle class (those with expenditures surpassing $10 a day), the chapter projects that among the world's top five middle-class markets in 2030, four will be in Asia: India, China, Indonesia, and Japan. According to this chapter's predictions, China will surpass the United States by 2020 to become the world's largest middle-class market.

Chapters 3–5 examine the middle class in China primarily from the Chinese perspective, examining the way PRC scholars, government leaders, and the general public have viewed, acted on, and reacted to the major changes taking place in terms of social stratification and political ideology in China.

Chapter 3, by Cheng Li, provides an extensive review of recent Chinese literature on the study of the middle class. With a detailed discussion of several prominent PRC scholars and their most influential work, the chapter highlights the shifting focus in recent Chinese scholarship on the middle class from its effect on social stratification to its possible political implications.

Chapter 4, by Zhou Xiaohong and Qin Chen, examines what they believe to be the two most important contributing factors, one external and the other internal, for the rise of the Chinese middle class. The external factor, economic globalization, represents a synchronic transnational flow of Western capitalism, which has helped nurture middle-class consumerism and lifestyles in urban China. The internal factor, domestic social transformation and upward mobility, reflects diachronic changes in the economic, political, ideological, and structural domains of China in the post-Mao era. These external and internal factors make the Chinese middle class similar to its counterparts elsewhere in terms of consumption patterns and other economic activities but different in terms of political attitudes and behaviors.

Chapter 5, by Lu Hanlong, focuses on the Chinese authorities' pragmatic notion of *xiaokang* or *xiaokang shehui* (a moderately prosperous society). Lu's analysis can be enormously helpful for outside observers not only because the idea of *xiaokang* represents the cultural and ideological foundation for China's transition to a market economy in the reform era but also because it has been used to justify the state's major policy drive to expand the middle class.

The definition of *middle class* employed is inevitably controversial. An extensive discussion of definitional and categorical criteria is therefore essential. Chapter 6, by Li Chunling, and chapter 7, by Jianying Wang and Deborah Davis, both deal with issues relating to the definition, categorization, and internal groupings of the Chinese middle class. Drawing upon a wealth of quantitative data from censuses, national income surveys, and household income surveys of Chinese cities from 1982 to

2006 (some of which the author herself participated in as a principal researcher), Li Chunling offers a clear and comprehensive picture of China's rapid upward social mobility over the past two decades. The chapter finds that among all members of the middle class, 65 percent are from farmer or worker families and 57 percent held blue-collar jobs before obtaining middle-class status. Its heterogeneous family backgrounds and diverse occupations have not only contributed to the "inconsistency between social status and economic status" of the middle class but have also undermined the formation of a collective class identity and a unified class consciousness.

The chapter by Wang and Davis raises one of the most fundamental questions in the study of the Chinese middle class: Should it be treated as singular or plural? Based on their quantitative analysis of major occupational groups, Wang and Davis document several middle classes, rather than finding a single middle class. The chapter shows that an upper middle class of professionals and managers has emerged that is distinct from a more generic middle class and from officials, who are also part of the middle class. The authors argue that any theorizing about the political impact of the Chinese middle class must take into consideration these internal divisions.

The most astonishing aspect of the emerging Chinese middle class is the scale and speed of its expansion. Chapters 8–10 provide comprehensive information and analysis of the crucial factors that have contributed to the rapid growth of the Chinese middle class.

Chapter 8, by the economist Joyce Yanyun Man, reveals that since 1998 the privatization of the housing sector has benefited a large number of people, enabling many families to purchase homes from their work units or the housing market or to obtain houses from developers and local governments through urban relocation. According to recently released data from the large-sample Urban Household Survey, China's homeownership rate reached 82.3 percent in 2007, exceeding the level of homeownership found in many developed countries, including the United States (roughly 67 percent). Though the author argues that the size and wealth of the Chinese middle class are rapidly rising to catch up with middle-class countries, she also recognizes that the problem of affordable housing may constitute a severe sociopolitical challenge.

Chapter 9, by the sociologist Luigi Tomba, also focuses on housing privatization. His analysis challenges the conventional mainstream narrative concerning the "housing effect," which often emphasizes a unified middle-class-based action toward certain goals of political and structural change. Instead, he finds that local variations, the divided nature of the homeowner class, and the various forms of new hierarchy being created all suggest that middle-class homeowners may not soon arrive at a sense of unified collective agency for political change.

Chapter 10, by Jing Lin and Xiaoyan Sun, examines how the expansion of college enrollment has transformed elite higher education into mass higher education over the course of the past decade. This development has, in turn, contributed to the rapid expansion of the middle class and will continue to do so in the future. Lin and Sun's chapter shows that the total enrollment of college students in China increased from 3.2 million in 1997 to 26 million in 2009. A significant portion of the chapter examines the phenomenon of the post-eighties generation, which is not only the main beneficiary of the affluent economy and expansion of higher education in the country but also the first generation of Chinese college students to "face an extremely competitive job market." The chapter discusses the distinct characteristics of this upcoming generation, the future backbone of China's new middle class.

Seeing as middle-class development is a global, and not distinctly Chinese, phenomenon, cross-country comparisons, especially among East and Southeast Asian countries, are invaluable. This is the case not only because these societies also experienced a rapid rise of the middle class in recent decades but also because many have made remarkable democratic transitions, at least partially resulting from the growing influence and political participation of middle-class actors. Chapter 11, by the Taiwanese political scientist Hsin-Huang Michael Hsiao, and chapter 12, by the South Korean sociologist Han Sang-Jin, provide this type of comparative perspective.

Hsiao's chapter argues that one should not perceive the middle classes of the Asia-Pacific region to be uniformly "politically conservative, liberal, or radical." Rather, he describes their subsets as "diverse" and their political standing as "situational," taking into account their various historical contexts; he sees their relations with authoritarian states during democratic transitions as "dialectical." Hsiao finds that in East and Southeast Asian countries, "none of the authoritarian regimes volunteered or self-initiated top-down democratization." Instead, specific subsets of the middle class (that is, the liberal intellectuals and professionals that reached out to civil society organizations) often played a crucial role in the democratic transitions of these countries.

In his chapter, Han compares the role of identity in middle-class development in South Korea and China and argues that, as an independent variable, identity is as significant as education or occupation in influencing middle-class politics. In examining several large data sets in South Korea and China, Han finds that the middle class's development of a "grassroots identity," or pursuit of citizens' participatory initiatives, gives rise to the significant difference in political practice. Han is optimistic about the prospect of democratization in China because the change-oriented and grassroots segment of the middle class, which played a defining role in the democratic transition of South Korea, is beginning to emerge in the PRC.

The final three chapters all directly address the volume's central question: How will the rise of the Chinese middle class impact China's political development? Chapter 13, by Bruce J. Dickson, focuses on private entrepreneurs and calls into question the theoretical proposition that "privatization would create pressures" for democratization, as well as the notion of "social forces as inherently antagonistic toward the state." Instead, "economic development has created material interests [on the part of the middle class] that in turn create a preference for stability and, therefore, support for the current regime." Despite this finding, Dickson also cautiously points out some possible factors—for example, a decline in the pro-business policies of the CCP and middle-class resentment toward official corruption—that may change the relationship between the middle class and the regime in the future.

Chapter 14, by Ethan Michelson and Sida Liu, offers a detailed and sophisticated Internet study of Chinese lawyers, another distinct and increasingly important subset of China's new middle class (the study shows that 70 percent of Chinese lawyers define themselves as middle class). The chapter not only exhibits the key demographic and socioeconomic characteristics of Chinese lawyers but also reveals their political views and values regarding some sensitive issues. Michelson and Liu argue that the fact that Chinese lawyers are economically unstable, politically restricted, and institutionally vulnerable in terms of their occupation-specific work conditions may determine their political stance and behaviors in the years to come.

Chapter 15, by Jie Chen, uses his survey data in offering a comprehensive comparison between middle-class and nonmiddle-class members in China in terms of their political views, values, and behaviors. Chen illustrates that while most members of China's emerging middle class favor individual rights, they continue to shun political liberties, including the freedom to demonstrate or to form organizations, and are not interested in promoting democratic changes such as the implementation of competitive elections. Like other chapters in the section, Chen's chapter also recognizes that dynamic forces and their interactions in the country may eventually change the political equation.

This volume's contributors not only provide a wide range of arguments, insights, and scenarios based on empirical evidence of China's emerging middle class but also put forth some provocative ideas for both intellectual and policy debates. Despite many contrasting views and assessments about the size, composition, characteristics, and even definition of the Chinese middle class, some baseline consensuses have emerged out of this intellectual joint venture. Contributors agree that a new socioeconomic force has profoundly changed China's social stratification and economic landscape. No one seems to doubt that the Chinese middle class is more or less a heterogeneous subset of Chinese society or that it has remained, at least up until now, a political ally of the Chinese authoritarian regime.

Equally important, there are recent indications, as noted in several chapters in the volume, that the Chinese middle class may soon become a crucial force for political change. Sophisticated analysis of this new and rapidly expanding socioeconomic group will allow one to more accurately plot China's likely political trajectory in the years to come. In the broadest sense, promoting a better understanding of the Chinese middle class may help to alleviate some of the misgivings and apprehensions engendered by the Middle Kingdom's reemergence on the world stage.

Notes

1. The American notion of the peaceful evolution of communist regimes through international integration, first articulated by John Foster Dulles in the 1950s, has long been a cornerstone of the U.S. strategy to change the nature of China's political system. For more discussion of this strategy, see Frederick Marks, *Power and Peace: The Diplomacy of John Foster Dulles* (Santa Barbara, Calif.: Praeger, 1995).

2. The democratic peace theory asserts that democracies rarely go to war with one another. For a detailed discussion of the theory, see Michael W. Doyle, "Kant, Liberal Legacies, and Foreign Affairs," *Philosophy and Public Affairs* 12, no. 3 (1983): 205–35; and 12, no. 4 (1983): 323–53.

3. Fareed Zakaria, "Does the Future Belong to China?" *Newsweek*, May 9, 2005, p. 32.

4. Notable exceptions include Alastair Iain Johnston, "Chinese Middle Class Attitudes towards International Affairs: Nascent Liberalization?" *China Quarterly* 179 (September

2004): 603–28; David S. G. Goodman, ed., *The New Rich in China: Future Rulers, Present Lives* (New York: Routledge, 2008); and Deborah Davis and Feng Wang, eds., *Creating Wealth and Poverty in Post Socialist China* (Stanford University Press, 2008). Even some of these scholars, such as David Goodman, have some reservations when they employ the term *middle class*.

5. For example, in David Goodman's view, the argument that members of the Chinese "new rich" are "just like us" can be "very seductive" but obscures the fact that they represent a miniscule elite that has benefited disproportionately from economic reforms. See Rowan Callick, "Myth of China's New Middle Class," *Australian*, January 14, 2008, p. 2.

6. John King Fairbank, *The United States and China*, 4th ed. (Harvard University Press, 1983), p. 51.

7. For the early development of the Chinese bourgeoisie, or the middle class, see Marie-Claire Bergère, *The Golden Age of the Chinese Bourgeoisie, 1911–1937,* translated by Janet Lloyd (Cambridge University Press, 1989).

8. *China News Analysis*, no. 1501, January 1, 1994, p. 2.

9. Ming Yongchang, "Zhongchan jieji zhengzai shixian 'Zhongguomeng'" [The middle class is realizing its "Chinese dream"], in *Lianhe zaobao* [United morning news], October 1, 2008, p. 2.

10. Zhang Wanli, "Zhongguo shehui jieji jieceng yanjiu ershi nian" [Research on classes and social status during the last twenty years in China], in *Shehuixue yanjiu* [Sociological research], no. 1 (2000): 24–39; and also Cheng Li, "'Credentialism' versus 'Entrepreneurism': The Interplay and Tensions between Technocrats and Entrepreneurs in the Reform Era," in *Chinese Business Networks: State, Economy and Culture,* edited by Chan Kwok Bun (New York: Prentice Hall, 1999), pp. 86–111.

11. China's stock market, for example, was ranked the world's largest emerging capital market and the third-largest capital market in 2007. In the same year, the total number of stock accounts exceeded 100 million, and more than half were owned by individual investors. China's property market had an annual growth rate in sales of 20 percent in the past decade. Song Guokai, "Zhongguo zhongchan jieceng jing shinianlai jiakuai jueqi de zhuyao yuanyin" [The main factors in the rapid rise of the Chinese middle-income stratum in the past decade], *Chinese Sociology*, January 29, 2010.

12. *China Daily*, August 31, 2009.

13. Ann Hodgson, "China's Middle Class Reaches 80 Million," *Euromonitor Archive*, July 25, 2007. The data on American consumption as a percentage of GDP refer to the year 2007.

14. Li Chunling, "Zhongguo zhongchan jieji yanjiu de dongli yu quxiang" [The motives and trends of studying China's middle class], in *Hexie shehui yu shehui jianshe* [Harmonious society and social development], edited by Fang Xiangxin (Beijing: Shehui-kexue wenxian chubanshe, 2008).

15. Chen Ziling, "Xinyongka xiyoulu" [Balance sheet on credit cards], in *Shanghai jinrong bao* [Shanghai financial news], October 24, 2008, p. 1; and Shushmul Maheshwari, "China Credit Card Market Outlook to 2013," RNCOS E-Services Pvt. Ltd., March 18, 2009 (www.investorideas.com/news/r031809a.asp. [July 21, 2010]).

16. See http://cn.chinagate.cn/chinese/jj/67931.htm (May 16, 2010).

17. The annual growth rate of output and sales is 48 percent and 46 percent, respectively. Quoted from Zhang Xue, "Domestic Auto Sector Undergoes Structural Adjustments," *Economic Daily*, February 9, 2010. See also *Shijie ribao* [World journal], January 12, 2010, p. 1.

18. *China Daily*, June 2, 2004.

19. Merrill Lynch, *China Consumer Brands Participation Certificate* (Singapore, April 2008).

20. According to the study, the qualification for membership in the middle class is 25,000–100,000 yuan, or $13,500–$53,900 per household, adjusted for purchasing power parity. The group can be further divided into the upper aspirants (with an income of 40,000–100,000 yuan) and the lower aspirants (with an income of 25,000–40,000 yuan). McKinsey Global Institute, "From 'Made in China' to 'Sold in China': The Rise of the Chinese Urban Consumer," November 2006 (www.mckinsey.com/mgi/publications/china_consumer/index.asp).

21. See www.singtaonet.com/chinafin/200712/t20071210_688541.html.

22. *Nanfang ribao* [Southern daily], February 26, 2000, p. 1. For more discussion of the background of Jiang's ideological innovation, the "three represents," see Cheng Li, "China in 2000: A Year of Strategic Rethinking," *Asian Survey* 41, no. 1 (2001): 71–90.

23. Chen Xinnian, *Zhongdeng shouruzhe lun* [Middle-income stratum] (Beijing: Zhongguo jihua chubanshe, 2005), p. 1.

24. Wu Jiao, "50% of people will be middle class by 2020," *China Daily*, December 27, 2007.

25. "China's Middle Class: To Get Rich Is Glorious," *Economist*, January 17, 2002.

26. See, for example, Alexander Brenner, "Zhongguo zhongchan jieji zai ganchao Meiguo zhongchan jieji?" [Is the Chinese middle class catching up to the American middle class?], translated by Hu Yu, in *Qingnian cankao* [Youth reference], September 22, 2008.

27. Lu Xueyi, "Xianzai shi Zhongguo zhongchan jieceng fazhan de huangjin shiqi" [It's the "golden age" of Chinese middle-class development], *Zhongguo qingnian bao* [China youth daily], February 11, 2010.

28. Mao Yushi, "Zhuangda zhongchan jieji: Miaozhun jiuye, gongping chengxiang" [Enlarging the middle class: focusing on employment and the reduction of the urban-rural gap], *Luye* [Green leaf], no. 12 (2009).

29. Li Qiang, "Dao dingzixing shehui yu gongtong fuyu jianxing jianyuan" [A reverse T-type society and further away from common prosperity], *Luye*, no. 12 (2009).

30. Dennis Gilbert, *The American Class Structure in An Age of Growing Inequality* (Belmont, Calif.: Wadsworth, 2002).

31. William Thompson and Joseph Hickey, *Society in Focus: An Introduction to Sociology,* 5th ed. (Boston: Pearson, Allyn, and Bacon, 2005).

32. See http://en.wikipedia.org/wiki/American_middle_class (May 15, 2010).

33. Gary Burtless, "Growing American Inequality: Sources and Remedies," *Brookings Review* (Winter 1999).

34. Johnston, "Chinese Middle Class Attitudes Towards International Affairs," p. 607.

35. C. Wright Mills, *White Collar: The American Middle Classes* (Oxford University Press, 1951).

36. Max Weber, *Economy and Society: An Outline of Interpretive Sociology* (University of California Press, 1978).

37. For cross-country comparisons of the definitions of the middle class, see Olivier Zunz, ed., *Social Contracts under Stress: The Middle Classes of America, Europe, and Japan at the Turn of the Century* (New York: Russell Sage, 2004).

38. Study Group of the General Urban Survey Team of the PRC State Statistics Bureau, "Liuwan dao wushiwan yuan: Zhongguo chengshi zhongdeng shouru qunti yanjiu" [60,000–500,000 yuan: a study of middle-income strata in urban China], *Shuju* [Data], no. 6 (2005).

39. *Huaxia shibao* [China time], January 19, 2005.

40. Chen Yiping, *Fenhua yu zuhe: Zhongguo zhongchanjieceng yanjiu* [Separation and coherence: a study of China's middle class] (Guangzhou: Guangdong renmin chubanshe, 2005), pp. 95–96.

41. A good indicator that supports this observation is the PRC-based scholarly website China Election and Governance. The website has a special section on China's middle class, which includes over 170 articles on the subject since 2002. Most of the authors use the term *middle class* rather than *middle-income stratum*. See www.chinaelections.org/News List.asp?CLassID=93&Pages=1.

42. See Li Peilin and Zhang Yi, "Zhongguo zhongchan jieji de guimo, rentong, he shehui taidu" [Scale, recognition, and attitudes of China's middle class], in *Daguoce tongxiang Zhongguo zhilu de Zhongguo minzhu: Zengliang shi minzhu* [Strategy of a great power: incremental democracy and a Chinese-style democracy], edited by Tang Jin (Beijing: Renmin chubanshe, 2009), pp. 188–90.

43. Lu Xueyi, *Dangdai Zhongguo shehui jiegou* [Social structure of contemporary China] (Beijing: Shehui kexuewenxian chubanshe, 2010), pp. 402–06.

44. Lu Xueyi, "Xianzai shi zhongguo . . . ," *Zhongguo qingnian bao*, February 11, 2010.

45. *Zhongguo xinwen zhoukan* [China newsweek], January 22, 2010.

46. For more discussion of these two simultaneous but seemingly paradoxical developments, see Ann Anagnost, "From 'Class' to 'Social Strata': Grasping the Social Totality in Reform-Era China," *Third World Quarterly* 29, no. 3 (2008): 497–519.

47. World Bank, *World Development Indicators* (various years). Also see Anagnost, "From 'Class' to 'Social Strata,'" p. 498.

48. Xinhua Agency, "Zhongguo pinfu chaju zhengzai bijin shehui rongren hongxian" [China's income gap is approaching the red line of society's tolerance], *Jingji cankao* [Economic reference news], May 10, 2010.

49. Xu Zhiyuan, *Xinglai, 110 nian de Zhongguo biange* [Awakening: China's 110-year reform] (Hubei: Hubei renmin chubanshe, 2009), pp. 194–95.

50. Lu, *Dangdai Zhongguo shehui jiegou*, p. 31.

51. Li Lulu and Li Sheng, "Shutu yilei—Dandai Zhongguo chengzhen chongchan jieji de leixing fengxi" [Different approaches and different types: a typological analysis of the middle class in Chinese cities and towns], *Shehuixue yanjiu* [Sociology studies] 22, no. 6 (2007): 15–37.

52. Wei Cheng, *Suowei zhongchan: yingguo jinrong shibao zhongwenwang dui Zhongguo zhongchan jieji de diaocha* [China's emerging middle class: a survey by *Financial Times*'s Chinese website] (Guangzhou: Nanfang ribao chubanshe, 2007).

53. Wang Jianping, "Zhongchan jieceng—Shehui hexie de jiji liliang" [Middle stratum: a positive force for harmonious society], *Zhongguo gaige luntan* [China reform forum], November 2006.

54. Zhang Yiwu, "Yeshuo zhongchan jieceng" [Comments on the middle stratum], *Huanqiu* [Globe], April 12, 2010.

55. Barrington Moore Jr., *The Social Origins of Dictatorship and Democracy: Lord and Peasant in the Making of the Modern World* (Boston: Beacon Press, 1966), pp. 418, 430.

56. Seymour Martin Lipset, "Some Social Requisites of Democracy: Economic Development and Political Legitimacy," *American Political Science Review* 53, no. 1 (1959): 69–105; and Seymour Martin Lipset, *Political Man: The Social Bases of Politics* (Garden City, N.J.: Anchor Books, 1963).

57. Samuel P. Huntington, *Political Order of Changing Societies* (Yale University Press, 1969).

58. Samuel P. Huntington, *The Third Wave: Democratization in the Late Twentieth Century* (University of Oklahoma Press, 1993).

59. Jie Chen and Bruce J. Dickson, *Allies of the State: China's Private Entrepreneurs and Democratic Change* (Harvard University Press, 2010).

60. An Chen, "Capitalist Development, Entrepreneurial Class, and Democratization in China," *Political Science Quarterly* 117 no. 3 (2002): 401–22.

61. Ibid., p. 411.

62. Ibid., p. 417.

63. Ibid., p. 412.

64. Ibid., pp. 413–14.

65. Margaret M. Pearson, *China's New Business Elite: The Political Consequences of Economic Reform* (University of California Press, 1997); Andrew G. Walder, "Sociological Dimensions of China's Economic Transition: Organization, Stratification, and Social Mobility," Shorenstein Asia/Pacific Research Center, April 2003; Yanjie Bian, "Chinese Social Stratification and Social Mobility," *Annual Review of Sociology* 28, no. 1 (2002): 91–116; and Elizabeth J. Perry, "A New Rights Consciousness?" *Journal of Democracy* 20, no. 3 (2009): 17–20.

66. Zheng Yongnian, "Zhongguo zhongchan jieji he Zhongguo shehui de mingyun" [The middle class and the fate of Chinese society], *Lianhe zaobao*, March 2, 2010.

67. Mary E. Gallagher, "'Reform and Openness': Why China's Economic Reforms Have Delayed Democracy," *World Politics* 54, no. 3 (2002): 371.

68. Cheng Li, "Introduction: Making Democracy Safe for China," in *Democracy Is a Good Thing: Essays on Politics, Society, and Culture in Contemporary China,* edited by Yu Keping (Brookings, 2009), pp. xvii–xxxi.

CHAPTER TWO

The New Global Middle Class: A Crossover from West to East

HOMI KHARAS and GEOFFREY GERTZ

The global economy has grown to rely heavily on American consumption. Thanks to a long-term downward trend in the personal savings rate from 10 percent in the early 1980s to approximately zero by 2007, the growth of U.S. consumption has been faster than the growth of U.S. GDP, making it a driver of both the U.S. and the global economies.[1] At $10 trillion, U.S. private consumption accounts for just under one-fifth of the world economy. In fact, as a source of demand, it is twice the size of the world's next-largest entire economy, Japan.

The structural force behind large U.S. consumption has been a significant middle class. The middle class is an ambiguous social classification, broadly reflecting the ability to lead a comfortable life. The middle class usually enjoys stable housing, health care, educational opportunities (including college) for its children, reasonable retirement and job security, and discretionary income that can be spent on vacation and leisure pursuits. Juliet Schor argues that a "new consumerism" defines the middle class: a constant "upscaling of lifestyle norms; the pervasiveness of conspicuous, status goods and of competition for acquiring them; and the growing disconnect between consumer desires and incomes."[2] In a more academic vein, Kevin Murphy, Andrei Shleifer, and Robert Vishny emphasize the willingness of the middle-class consumer to pay a little extra for quality as a force that feeds investment in production and marketing and drives growth.[3]

The unlocking of the spending power of the U.S. middle class was achieved in part by financial innovations that allowed for rapid growth in consumer credit, mortgages for an ever-larger segment of the population, and home equity withdrawals. Because household wealth grew faster than income, these innovations permitted households to tap into their wealth for current consumption and led to a decline in the household savings rate. But the current downturn has brought this process to a halt. U.S. households are saving again in an effort to rebuild lost wealth. The consensus forecast is that this will be a lasting effect of the global financial crisis.[4]

How can the world economy fill this void in global demand brought on by the retrenchment of the American consumer? All eyes are now turning to Asia, and specifically to the emerging middle class in China and other populous countries, to become the next global consumers. Within Asia there is significant talk of rebalancing toward domestic demand (more specifically domestic consumption) as a way of sustaining growth in the face of potentially sluggish exports. But the policy prescriptions to achieve such a rebalancing are not easy. They involve the creation of a social safety net, medical insurance schemes, and better public education options. In short, Asian consumption is tied in the minds of many analysts to long-term institutional changes.[5] Given the difficulties of implementing such changes, it is hard to be very confident that this rebalancing will happen in the medium term.

This chapter argues that this is too pessimistic a view of Asian consumerism. Instead, we argue that several Asian countries, in particular China and India, have reached a tipping point, at which large numbers of people will enter the middle class and drive consumption. Policies to support such a transformation in China should be focused on increasing the share of household income in GDP—policies that can have almost immediate impacts—rather than lowering the household savings rate.

If this transpires, the world will see a new global middle class—an Asian middle class. There will be a crossover from the West to the East in the products, fashions, tastes, and designs that cater to the mass middle class. According to our estimates, by 2015, for the first time in 300 years, the number of Asian middle-class consumers will equal the number in Europe and North America. By 2021, according to present trends, there could be more than 2 billion Asians in middle-class households. In China alone there could be more than 670 million middle-class consumers, compared with only perhaps 150 million today.

To paraphrase the Nobel laureate Robert Lucas, "The consequences for human welfare involved in questions like these [about economic growth] are simply staggering: once one starts to think about them it is hard to think about anything else."[6]

Defining the Middle Class: An Absolute Approach

While recognizing that the middle class is as much a social designation as an economic classification, most economists choose to measure it in terms of income or consumption levels. The middle class can be defined in relative or absolute terms. William Easterly and separately Nancy Birdsall, Carol Graham, and Stefano Pettinato adopt a relativist approach, defining the middle class as those between the 20th and 80th percentiles of consumption distribution and between 0.75 and 1.25 times the median per capita income, respectively.[7] Surjit Bhalla adopts an absolute approach, defining the middle class as those with annual incomes over $3,900 in purchasing power parity (PPP) terms.[8] Abhijit Banerjee and Esther Duflo use two alternative absolute measures—those with daily per capita expenditures of $2 to $4 and those with daily per capita expenditures of $6 to $10—as estimates of a lower and upper middle class in developing countries.[9]

The choice between these two approaches depends on the purpose at hand. As we are considering comparisons of the size of the middle class across countries, it makes sense to adopt the absolute approach. Obviously, such comparisons require a common definition of the middle class for all countries. It would make no sense to compare Indians earning $2 a day with Americans earning $80 a day and claim that both are comparable in terms of purchasing power because both are middle class.

Taking an absolute approach, we define the global middle class as those households with daily expenditures of $10 to $100 a person in purchasing power parity terms. The lower bound is chosen with reference to the average poverty line in Portugal and Italy, the two advanced European countries with the strictest definition of poverty. The poverty line for a family of four in these countries is $14,533, or $9.95 a day per capita (in constant 2005 international dollars, adjusted for PPP). The upper bound is chosen as twice the median income of Luxembourg, the richest advanced country. Defined in this way, the global middle class excludes those who are considered poor in the poorest advanced countries and those who are considered rich in the richest advanced country.

Based on this definition, we estimate that the size of the middle class for 145 countries accounts for 98 percent of the world's population. These countries have both household surveys, from which household income distribution can be measured, and national income accounts, from which total household consumption expenditures can be measured. From the World Bank's household surveys, we obtain the distribution of household income by decile.[10] This is then inputted into the World Bank's PovCal software to estimate the distributional parameters of a quadratic Lorenz curve.[11] The mean of the distribution is taken from the national income accounts, which provide total household consumption expenditure in constant 2005 PPP dollars.[12] Given the mean and distribution parameters, PovCal generates a head count of those living below any given expenditure threshold. The number in the middle class is defined as the difference between the number of people with expenditures below the $100 a day threshold and the number with expenditures below the $10 a day threshold.

Constructing a Scenario of the Global Economy to 2030

To assess the evolution of the global middle class over time, we need a sense of how countries will develop. To do this, we apply a simple Cobb-Douglas production function to each of the 145 countries in our database.[13] In this production function, growth depends on capital and labor accumulation, coupled with total factor productivity growth. We use demographic projections from the United Nations to estimate the evolution of the labor force for each country.[14] Capital accumulation is arrived at by assuming that future investment for each country will continue at a rate equal to the average investment/GDP ratio of the past ten years.[15] What remains is to estimate total factor productivity (TFP) growth.

One great constant of the last 125 years has been the steady growth of TFP in the United States. U.S. growth per worker has averaged 1.8 percent a year, of which 1.3 percent is attributable to TFP growth. There have been short episodes, including the Great Depression, when U.S. growth was pushed off this trend, but over the long term there has been strong mean reversion: U.S. income levels have reverted to a level that reflects a constant long-run trend growth rate.[16] We make the simplifying assumption that this process of advance in U.S. productivity will continue for the next two decades, notwithstanding the current financial crisis.

Other countries have shown their ability to grow faster than the United States, based on more rapid TFP growth. Using the so-called advantages of backwardness—the ability to import and adopt more advanced production technologies from more developed economies—they have met and in some instances, such as Japan, even overtaken U.S. income levels. The poorer, and therefore less technologically advanced, a country is relative to the world's leading economies, the greater the potential gains are from this process; as technology levels begin to approach those of advanced economies, these potential gains diminish, and growth rates tend to slow. We assume that this process of technological convergence will continue at historic rates, and we model technological catch-up as a function of the gap between each country's income level and that of the United States, taken as a proxy for the global technology leader.[17]

Applying this mechanically to all countries in the world produces a scenario that is not credible. The poorest countries in Africa, for example, would grow the fastest, as their income levels are so low compared to that of the United States. Latin American countries would also start to grow at rates that have not been seen for thirty years on that continent. It is clear that the advantages of backwardness do not apply to all countries.

We therefore use a filter that restricts technology catch-up to advanced economies and to those developing countries that have demonstrated the ability to harness global technology to their advantage. Specifically, the latter are defined as those countries that have achieved a per capita growth rate of 3.5 percent a year over the past twenty-five years, a period long enough to avoid the inclusion of many countries that grow cyclically but have not been able to sustain growth. For transition economies, where we cannot go back twenty-five years because many of the countries did not exist then, or existed with totally different economic structures, we use a criterion of 3.5 percent per capita growth since 1995. This filter restricts catch-up technology to a set of twenty-eight developing and transition economies, including, importantly, China.

The scenario of global economic trends produced by our model has two main features: global growth accelerates, and the center of gravity of global output shifts toward Asia. Global growth accelerates from the rate that has prevailed since 1990, primarily because high-growth developing and transition economies come to account for a larger share of the world economy. In 1990 the high-income but low-growth economies of the OECD accounted for 80 percent of global output, and thus their growth represented most of the growth in the global economy. By 2009 their share had slipped to 65 percent, and it will continue to fall in the coming decades. In their place will be the rapidly growing developing economies. As a consequence, global growth between now and 2030 could rise to 4.8 percent a year, compared with a 4 percent growth rate over the decade 1998–2008.[18]

The rising emerging economies are predominantly in Asia, including notably China and India, as well as Indonesia, Vietnam, and other economies of the Association of Southeast Asian Nations (ASEAN). Thanks to their rapid growth, Asia's share of global output could rise from 28 percent today to 43 percent by 2030. China's share in global output alone rose from 1.6 percent in 1990 to an estimated 8.9 percent in 2009 (at market exchange rates) and could grow further to 19 percent by 2030.

The Global Middle Class Expands to the East

Using assumptions on growth, the existing size of the middle class, and the distribution of income, we can estimate the current size and the future trajectory of the middle class for each country in our sample.[19] Today 1.8 billion people in the world are middle class, accounting for 28 percent of the global population. About half of these people live in developed economies, with another fifth found in Brazil, Russia, India, and China—the so-called emerging BRIC economies. Less than 2 percent of the world's population is rich by our definition; a significant majority, 70 percent, is poor.

In our scenario the world will evolve over the next twenty years from being mostly poor to being mostly middle class (figure 2-1). The year 2022 marks the first year more people in the world are expected to be middle class rather than poor. By 2030, 5 billion people—nearly two-thirds of the global population—could be middle class.

This potential increase in the global middle class is associated with a significant geographical redistribution, as almost all of the new members of the global middle class reside in Asia (table 2-1). Today there are only 500 million middle-class consumers in Asia, one-quarter of whom reside in Japan. Within twenty years there could be a six-fold increase, to some 3.2 billion people. Asia's share in the global middle class would rise from just over one-quarter today to two-thirds by 2030. Meanwhile, North America and Europe could see their combined share drop from

FIGURE 2-1. Global Population of Poor, Middle Class, and Rich Consumers, 2000–30

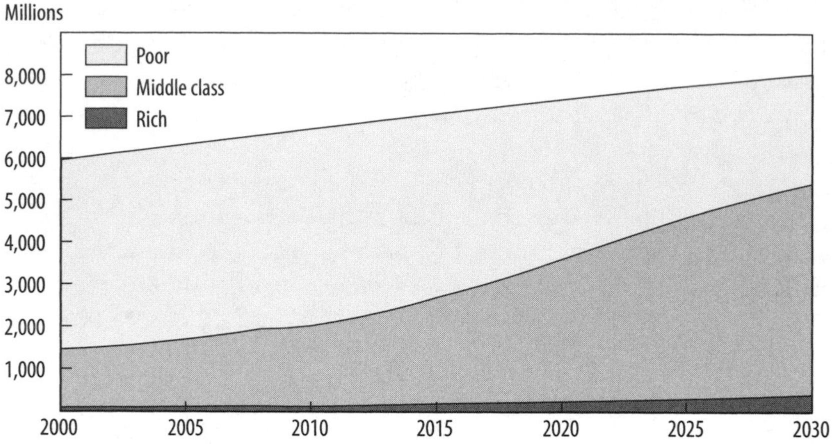

Millions

Source: Authors' calculations.

54 percent to just 17 percent. This reflects, in part, slow population growth in these regions, but it also reflects the fact that many people could graduate out of the middle class and become rich by 2030.[20]

Of course, the number of people in the middle class does not properly capture the spending power of this group. Given the broad definition of *middle class*, some countries have more affluent middle classes than others. Today's middle class in Europe and North America may be 54 percent of the global total in terms of number of people, but they account for 64 percent of total spending by the world's middle class. Looking specifically at the consumption of the middle class, Asia's growth is even more rapid. In 2009 Asia accounted for only 23 percent of the expenditures of the global middle class. By 2030 it may account for 59 percent (table 2-2).

The shifts in potential middle-class spending are starker when decomposed into individual countries. Today six of the ten countries with the largest middle-class consumption are high-income economies (table 2-3). By 2030 only four of the traditional advanced economies—the United States, Japan, Germany, and France—might make the top ten. In our scenario, China, which accounts for only 4 percent of global middle-class spending today (enough to be the seventh-largest middle-class country in the world) could catapult up the global rankings to become the largest single middle-class market by 2020, surpassing the United States. But

T A B L E 2 - 1 . Size of Middle Class by Region, 2009, 2020, 2030

Millions of people and global share (percent)

Region	2009		2020		2030	
North America	338	(18)	333	(10)	322	(7)
Europe	664	(36)	703	(22)	680	(14)
Central and South America	181	(10)	251	(8)	313	(6)
Asia Pacific	525	(28)	1,740	(54)	3,228	(66)
Sub-Saharan Africa	32	(2)	57	(2)	107	(2)
Middle East and North Africa	105	(6)	165	(5)	234	(5)
World	1,845	(100)	3,249	(100)	4,884	(100)

Source: Authors' calculations.

T A B L E 2 - 2 . Middle-Class Consumption by Region, 2009, 2020, 2030

Billions of 2005 PPP dollars and global share (percent)

Region	2009		2020		2030	
North America	5,602	(26)	5,863	(17)	5,837	(10)
Europe	8,138	(38)	10,301	(29)	11,337	(20)
Central and South America	1,534	(7)	2,315	(7)	3,117	(6)
Asia Pacific	4,952	(23)	14,798	(42)	32,596	(59)
Sub-Saharan Africa	256	(1)	448	(1)	827	(1)
Middle East and North Africa	796	(4)	1,321	(4)	1,966	(4)
World	21,278	(100)	35,045	(100)	55,680	(100)

Source: Authors' calculations.

China itself might be overtaken in the following decade by India, thanks to that country's more rapid population growth and more even income distribution, which allows growth to be distributed across all segments of society.

Other studies of the global middle class have found broadly similar results. Though direct comparisons are difficult due to the varying definitions of middle class, a number of authors highlight the potential for a significant increase in the ranks of the global middle class in the decades ahead. Using a more restrictive definition of middle class, the World Bank's *Global Economic Prospects 2007* estimates that the global middle class will expand from 7.6 percent of the world's population in 2000

TABLE 2-3. Middle-Class Consumption, Top Ten Countries, 2009, 2020, 2030
Billions of 2005 PPP dollars and global share (percent)

Country	2009		Country	2020		Country	2030	
United States	4,377	(21)	China	4,468	(13)	India	12,777	(23)
Japan	1,800	(8)	United States	4,270	(12)	China	9,985	(18)
Germany	1,219	(6)	India	3,733	(11)	United States	3,969	(7)
France	927	(4)	Japan	2,203	(6)	Indonesia	2,474	(4)
United Kingdom	889	(4)	Germany	1,361	(4)	Japan	2,286	(4)
Russia	870	(4)	Russia	1,189	(3)	Russia	1,448	(3)
China	859	(4)	France	1,077	(3)	Germany	1,335	(2)
Italy	740	(3)	Indonesia	1,020	(3)	Mexico	1,239	(2)
Mexico	715	(3)	Mexico	992	(3)	Brazil	1,225	(2)
Brazil	623	(3)	United Kingdom	976	(3)	France	1,119	(2)

Source: Authors' calculations.

to between 16.1 and 19.4 percent of the world's population by 2030.[21] A report by Goldman Sachs finds that the global middle class will expand from 29 percent of the world's population in 2008 to approximately 50 percent in 2030.[22]

While the broad trends are agreed upon, our figures may be more optimistic than those of some other analysts, particularly with respect to our high expectations for China and India.[23] While we believe the scenario outlined in this chapter is feasible, it is important to note that this exercise is intended as a scenario, not a prediction. For emerging Asian economies to achieve the high growth and dramatic expansion of their middle classes outlined above will require significant structural transformation and continual policy adjustment. This will undoubtedly be a great challenge, and there is no guarantee of success, yet there are precedents: our scenario for China and India is no more ambitious than what Korea and the other Asian Tigers achieved in the 1970s and 1980s or Japan before them.

China and India do stand apart from these previous high-growth economies in one important respect, however: the sheer size of their populations. This raises another question, one directly tied to the rise of the global middle class: Will the earth be able to support the increase in living standards for the 3 billion people expected to join the middle class over the next twenty years?

There are already some signs that resources are straining in the face of this new demand. Rising incomes in emerging economies was cited as one of the drivers behind the rapid increase in food and fuel prices in 2007 and 2008.[24] With China now the world's largest emitter of greenhouse gases, its burgeoning middle class will be central to any global effort to arrest climate change. The challenge of incorporating new middle-class consumers into global markets in a stable and sustainable manner will require both new technologies and adaptations in human behavior.[25] Yet it would be a mistake to assume that a growing global middle class will exclusively exacerbate resource pressures: the demand for a clean environment, for example, is a view typically associated with middle-class values. As many previously poor people adopt middle-class lifestyles in the decades ahead, they may find themselves not only consuming more but also more forcefully advocating for less pollution and lower emissions.

China's Middle Class Today and in the Future

China's middle class today is large in absolute terms; at 157 million people, only the United States has a larger middle class. This is why so many retailers and businesses are eager to penetrate the Chinese market. In recent years retail sales have been increasing by 15 percent every year, achieving a period of 20+ percent growth in mid-2008, before the financial crisis hit. In certain industries reflective of middle-class consumption, China is already overtaking the United States as the world's most important market. As recently as 2000, for example, the United States accounted for 37 percent of global car sales, while China accounted for barely 1 percent.[26] Today China has emerged as the world's largest auto market, with 13.6 million vehicles sold in 2009, well above the 10.4 million sold in the United States.[27] In 2004 General Motors sold 10 cars in the United States for every 1 car sold in China; the ratio is now quickly approaching 1 to 1, and soon China will be a bigger market than the United States for America's largest automaker.[28]

Similarly, China has recently emerged as the world's biggest cell phone market, home to an estimated 700 million subscribers.[29] In 2008 Nokia, the largest cell phone maker in the world, had net sales of $8.2 billion in China, more than three times its U.S. revenues.[30]

Survey evidence also suggests that China's new middle class is eager to become the world's leading consumers. A 2007 survey of 6,000 Chinese

FIGURE 2-2. Cumulative Share of Population by Consumption Level, China, 2009, 2020, 2030

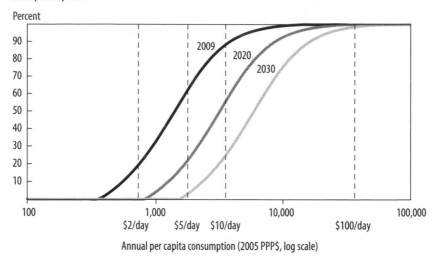

Source: Authors' calculations.

shoppers found that Chinese consumers spend 9.8 hours a week shopping, compared to 3.6 hours for the typical American.[31] Additionally, more than 40 percent of Chinese survey respondents said shopping was one of their favorite leisure activities. It is such attitudes that lead global retailers to bet on the future of China's domestic market: in the fourteen years since opening its first store in China, Wal-Mart has gone on to open an additional 267.[32]

Looking into the future, China's middle class is set to expand exponentially because of two factors: China's rapid growth rate and the fact that a significant share of the population is now close to the lower-bound threshold of our definition of the middle class. The last twenty years of high economic growth have brought many Chinese out of dire, absolute poverty up to the threshold of the middle class. Today 26 percent of the population lives on $5 to $10 a day, and a further 41 percent lives on $2 to $5 a day. These are the people who are primed to become China's new middle class as growth continues in the decades ahead.

Figure 2-2 illustrates these two forces at work. Each curve shows the cumulative percent of the population with consumption below the threshold figure on the x-axis. About 20 percent of China's population consumes less than $2 a day, while 89 percent of the people have

FIGURE 2-3. Poor, Middle Class, and Rich Share of Population, China, 2009, 2020, 2030

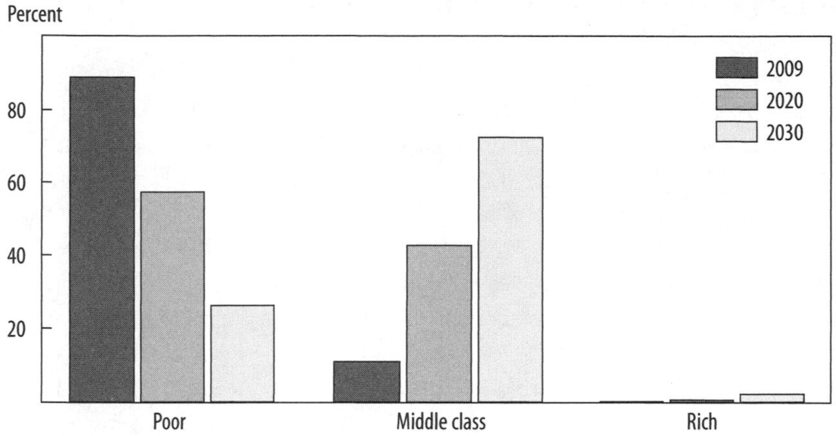

Percent

Source: Authors' calculations.

expenditure levels below $10 a day. But as incomes rise, the number of people with consumption levels above the middle-class threshold will rise. Assuming average income growth of 7 percent (a figure derived from the model with catch-up technology) between now and 2030, the percent of China's population with expenditures surpassing $10 a day will increase to 74 percent (figure 2-3). Within one generation the majority of Chinese could go from being poor to being middle class.

The biggest uncertainty in this scenario is whether China can indeed continue to generate growth at recent levels. Its economy, after all, is famously unbalanced. Household final consumption accounts for only 37 percent of total output, well below the global average (61 percent) and that of economies such as Vietnam (66 percent), Indonesia (63 percent), India (54 percent), and Thailand (51 percent).[33] China is now a middle-income country, and like other middle-income countries it finds itself needing a new growth strategy. The labor-intensive, export-led growth that has served China so well in its development from low-income to middle-income status is showing signs of strain. Global protectionism, China's large trade surplus, and rising real wages are all pressuring Chinese exports of items like garments, toys, and shoes.

Traditionally, middle-income countries have been able to add domestic demand to exports as an endogenous source of growth, once the local market becomes large enough. In most countries, domestic consumption typically starts to grow quickly when per capita income reaches around $6,000 in PPP terms.[34] China is just reaching this threshold level, with an estimated 2009 per capita income of $5,991.

The normal pattern of growth switching to domestic demand, however, may not be followed in China. As the great expansion achieved over the past two decades was led by exports and investment, consumption growth has lagged behind GDP growth by an average of 2.5 percentage points a year since 2000. With such low consumption, China's middle class is disproportionately small for China's level of development. The great uncertainty for China is whether its current growth is sufficiently robust to carry on until the middle-class consumption engine can start to fire or whether growth will stall before the middle class matures.

To see how important this is, contrast the historic cases of Brazil and South Korea. Between 1965 and 1980 Brazil grew at an average of 5.6 percent per capita per year, becoming a middle-income country with a per capita income of $7,600 PPP. Yet due to its high income inequality, Brazil's middle class made up only 29 percent of the country's population in 1980. This made it impossible for the country to rely on middle-class consumption to drive the transformation into an innovation-based economy. Since 1980 the country has remained primarily a commodity exporter and has struggled to sustain growth. Per capita incomes today are only slightly higher than they were thirty years ago (with an annual growth of just 0.7 percent), and the middle class has expanded only marginally, currently accounting for just 38 percent of the total population.

South Korea followed a path similar to Brazil's through the 1960s and 1970s, only a few years behind, growing by 6.5 percent per capita annually between 1965 and 1986. By 1986 it too was a middle-income country, achieving a similar per capita income of $7,700 PPP. Unlike Brazil, however, Korea's evenly distributed growth had produced a sizable middle class by this time, accounting for 53 percent of the population. The country capitalized on demand from this large middle class to grow its services industries and create the building blocks for a knowledge economy; it continued its strong per capita growth at a 5.5 percent rate for another twenty years, in the process becoming one of the most advanced economies in the world. Today 94 percent of Korea's population is middle class.

Japan also benefited from a sizable middle class when growing from a middle-income country to a rich country. In 1965 Japan's per capita income was $8,200, and its middle class was 48 percent of the population. Japan was able to achieve per capita income growth of 4.8 percent per year for the next twenty years.

Today China looks more like Brazil in 1974 (when Brazil also had a per capita income of around $6,000) than like South Korea in 1983 (when per capita income was $6,300). What can China do to increase the size of its middle class? At first glance, addressing income inequality may appear to be a solution. China's Gini coefficient (adjusted for rural-urban cost-of-living differences) had risen to 44.3 by 2005.[35] But in the short term lowering inequality may not have the desired effect. The new middle class is coming from the group consuming $5 to $10 a day, at the top of China's income distribution. Efforts to address inequality may mean that this group would see its incomes grow more slowly than average, as the gap between the rich and poor narrows, which would slow the rise of China's middle class.

This is not to say that China's leaders should embrace income inequality: indeed, there is a significant danger that China may fall into an inequality trap. Because access to health care and education is increasingly linked to income, with local governments unable to provide quality public services, areas and groups with low income levels tend to be less healthy and less educated, factors that result in further income inequalities over a lifetime of reduced earnings. In fact, differences in schooling and educational attainment are already the most significant determinants of income inequality in China.[36]

So addressing basic issues of equality of educational access and opportunity is a central long-term strategy. But in the medium term, the best strategy for increasing the size of China's middle class may lie not in attacking inequality but rather in increasing the share of consumption in GDP. Even without any new policy changes, history suggests that the share of consumption in China's GDP will likely rise in the coming years. Countries in the midst of rapid industrialization often experience falling consumption and rising investment, a process that slowly unwinds as economies mature. In Korea, for example, the boom between 1960 and 1990—when industry's share of output grew from 16 percent to 42 percent—saw consumption drop from above 80 percent of GDP down to 52 percent, as investment rose from 11 percent of GDP to 38 percent. Over the past two decades this trend began to reverse, as consumption rose to 55 percent of GDP.[37] In the early twentieth century the United States experienced a similar fall and then rise in consumption's share of GDP.

Still, given how low consumption is in China today, policies to encourage more rapid consumption growth could play an important role in rebalancing the economy. There are two ways of doing this. First, increase the share of consumption in household income—that is, reduce the savings rate. This would appear to be a long and hard task, requiring significant and credible institutional reform in areas such as health care and social security. Unlike in other countries, even the poor in China save a considerable fraction of their income: the median household savings rate for the near poor—households earning between the poverty line and twice that level—is 17 percent.[38] A high household savings rate appears to be a structural phenomenon in China.[39]

The second way of increasing consumption is to increase the share of household income in GDP. Here there is more scope for direct and indirect policy action. In terms of direct measures, China is now enjoying a considerable accumulation of profits from state enterprises that belong, at least in theory, to the people. State enterprise pretax profits totaled 6.6 percent of GDP in 2007 and have been increasing rapidly for many years.[40] These profits do not get funneled to the Treasury, where they could substitute for income taxes and fees.[41] Instead, they are retained in the enterprises and are directly reinvested. According to the U.S. Bureau of Labor Statistics, the average take-home pay of a Chinese worker is only 65 percent of total compensation, with the difference being made up in social insurance costs, government-mandated labor taxes, and a variety of insurance provisions (health, occupational safety, unemployment, and the like).[42] If the profits from state enterprises were used to reduce these kinds of taxes, China's middle class, most of whom are salaried workers, would instantly grow. Indirectly, if the same savings were channeled into public services that are currently paid for by households, such as health and education, similar effects would result.

Increasing household income, and hence consumption, in China could dramatically accelerate the rise of China's middle class. Figure 2-4 compares the baseline scenario to a scenario in which household consumption as a share of GDP is raised by 10 percentage points, returning China to the consumption levels of the early 2000s. Under this alternative scenario the share of the population that is middle class would increase almost instantaneously by 6 percentage points, rising to a 10 percentage point gain by 2015. That is the equivalent of accelerating the surge in the middle class by three to four years.

FIGURE 2-4. Middle-Class Share of Population, Two Scenarios, China, 2000–30

Percent

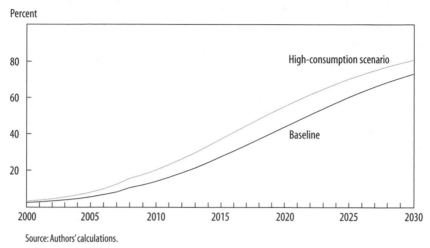

Source: Authors' calculations.

Beyond collecting state enterprise profits for Treasury operations, there are additional means by which China could boost the share of household income. Some analysts argue that China's private sector firms have limited access to finance and so tend to limit employment.[43] As a result, the wage share in GDP has fallen from two-thirds in 1980 to just over one-half of GDP today. This fall in the wage share is all the more remarkable as the growth of human capital in China has been very rapid over the period and as a large part of China's extraordinary growth has been due to the reallocation of labor from low-productivity rural occupations to higher-productivity occupations in manufacturing and services.

The World Bank's *Doing Business* survey finds that China ranks sixty-first in the world in terms of ease of access to credit.[44] Investment climate surveys suggest that less than half of small and medium enterprises have a bank loan.[45] Econometric results indicate that there is low employment growth in firms facing difficulties in accessing credit. According to Jahangir Aziz and Li Cui, China's bank restructuring program tightened rules so as to minimize nonperforming loans, leading firms to cut back further on employment.[46] The corollary is that as banking reforms take root, and as privatization and private enterprise growth moves ahead, employment growth could accelerate. This would raise the share of labor in national income and the share of household disposable income.

Conclusion

In this chapter, we argue that the world is in the throes of a major expansion of the middle class. This is surely good news for the global economy in general and for Asian economies in particular, as most of the expansion in the global middle class will be in Asia.

China is a large part of this story. Its middle class is set to expand exponentially if China can maintain its current rate of economic growth. However, China faces a chicken-and-egg problem. Its middle class is still small by historic standards for a country with its income level, so the engine of domestic consumer demand is not yet fully functioning. If growth happens, the middle class will expand and sustain growth, but domestic demand is not yet in a position to drive growth. If exports and investment are choked off by an unfavorable international environment in the next few years, there is a danger that China's economy could stall before the middle class matures. That would have adverse effects on both China and the global economy.

There are two ways China can accelerate its transformation toward a domestic consumption-led growth pattern. The first, which has been paid considerable attention, is to develop policies to reduce China's high household savings rate. We argue that these policies usually involve long-term institutional change, such as in social security or health delivery reforms. They may not be speedy enough to increase consumption demand.

The alternative strategy is to raise the share of household income in GDP directly. This can be achieved by macroeconomic policy. Two suggestions are to use the large profits of China's state-owned enterprises to reduce labor taxes and fees on employment and to accelerate banking reforms to ease access to credit by small and medium enterprises. Both of these measures would increase the share of labor in the economy and, by extension, the share of household income in GDP.

These measures could accelerate the development of China's middle class by four years or more. That could be sufficient to allow domestic demand to take the place of exports and investment. If China's middle class does develop adequately, it could fuel a self-sustaining boom for decades. China would be at the forefront of one of the great transformations of the world economy—a crossing from West to East of the global middle class.

Notes

1. U.S. Bureau of Economic Analysis (www.bea.gov).

2. Juliet Schor, "The New Politics of Consumption: Why Americans Want So Much More than They Need," *Boston Review* (Summer 1999): 2.

3. Kevin Murphy, Andrei Shleifer, and Robert Vishny, "Income Distribution, Market Size, and Industrialization," *Quarterly Journal of Economics* (August 1989).

4. See, for example, William Galston, "The 'New Normal' for the U.S. Economy: What Will It Be?" Brookings Web commentary (September 2009).

5. See, for example, Martin Feldstein, "Resolving the Global Imbalance: The Dollar and the US Saving Rate," *Journal of Economic Perspectives* 22, no. 3 (2008); and Nicholas Lardy, "China: Toward a Consumption-Driven Growth Path," Policy Brief 06-6 (Washington: Peterson Institute for International Economics, 2006).

6. Robert Lucas, "On the Mechanics of Economic Development," *Journal of Monetary Economics* 22, no. 1 (1988): 5.

7. William Easterly, "The Middle Class Consensus and Economic Development," Policy Research Working Paper 2346 (World Bank, 2000); Nancy Birdsall, Carol Graham, and Stefano Pettinato, "Stuck in the Tunnel: Is Globalization Muddling the Middle Class?" Working Paper 4, Center on Social and Economic Dynamics (Brookings, 2000).

8. Surjit Bhalla, *The Middle Class Kingdoms of India and China* (Washington: Peterson Institute for International Economics, forthcoming).

9. Abhijit Banerjee and Esther Duflo, "What Is Middle Class about the Middle Classes around the World?" Discussion Paper 6613 (London: Centre for Economic Policy Research, 2007).

10. World Bank household survey data for developing countries are found in the PovcalNet database (http://go.worldbank.org/NT2A1XUWP0); data on advanced countries are found in "Inequality around the World: Globalization and Income Distribution Dataset" (http://go.worldbank.org/0C52T3CLM0). There are fourteen countries that are not represented in either database; for each of these we use the average available inequality data of the country's neighbors.

11. The PovCal software can be downloaded from http://go.worldbank.org/YMRH2NT5V0. For a full discussion of the calculations involved, see Gaurav Datt, "Computational Tools for Poverty Measurement and Analysis," Discussion Paper 50 (Washington: International Food Policy Research Institute, 1998).

12. National income accounts data are from the World Bank's *World Development Indicators* online database (2009). *WDI* is the source for all historic GDP and growth statistics included in the chapter, unless stated otherwise.

13. For a full treatment of the methodology, see Homi Kharas, Laurence Chandy, and Geoffrey Gertz, eds., *The Four-Speed World* (Brookings, forthcoming).

14. United Nations, "World Population Prospects" (http://esa.un.org/unpp/).

15. World Bank, *World Development Indicators.*

16. For long-term data for the United States, see Angus Maddison, "Statistics on World Population, GDP, and per Capita GDP, 1-2006 AD" (2009) (www.ggdc.net/maddison/).

17. This follows the methodology used in Dominic Wilson and Roopa Purushothaman, "Dreaming with the BRICs: The Path to 2050," Global Economics Paper 99 (New York: Goldman Sachs, 2003).

18. These growth rates are for global output measured in U.S. dollars after accounting for expected exchange rate movements.

19. For our baseline scenario we adopt two simplifying assumptions: that consumption

grows at the same rate as GDP (share of consumption in GDP will remain constant over time) and that the Lorenz curve remains constant over time (growth is distributionally neutral).

20. The number of rich people in North America and Europe combined increases from 105 million in 2009 to 298 million in 2030.

21. World Bank, *Global Economic Prospects 2007: Managing the Next Wave of Globalization* (2007).

22. Dominic Wilson and Raluca Dragusanu, "The Expanding Middle: The Exploding World Middle Class and Falling Global Inequality," Global Economics Paper 170 (New York: Goldman Sachs, 2008).

23. Interestingly, however, over recent years many analysts have been forced to routinely revise upward their medium- and long-term estimates of Chinese and Indian growth. For a discussion of the Indian case, see Hiroko Oura, "Wild or Tamed: India's Potential Growth," Working Paper WP/07/224 (International Monetary Fund, 2007).

24. See, for example, Joachim von Braun, "Rising Food Prices: What Should Be Done?" Policy brief (Washington: International Food Policy Research Institute, 2008).

25. It is important to note, however, that it is not clear, as is sometimes argued, that higher resource prices will necessarily slow Chinese (or Indian) growth. There is no evidence suggesting that energy prices have a significant impact on long-run growth. Though an international agreement that limits greenhouse gas emissions by raising the price of carbon would undoubtedly lead to significant sectoral shifts in China, as in other economies, there is no a priori reason to believe this would bring an end to China's high growth.

26. Carlos Gomes, "Global Auto Report: July 31, 2009" (Toronto: Scotiabank Group Global Economic Research, 2009).

27. Patricia Jiayi Ho, "Corporate News: China Tops U.S. in Vehicle Sales, Aided by Government Incentives," *Wall Street Journal*, January 12, 2010, p. B2.

28. Gomes, "Global Auto Report."

29. Justine Lau and Joseph Menn, "Apple to Launch iPhone in China," *Financial Times*, August 29, 2009, p. 9.

30. Nokia, *Annual Report 2008* (www.nokia.com).

31. Wai-Chan Chan and Anne Tse, "The Consumer Trap: Retailers Need to Adapt to Entice Fickle Chinese Shoppers into Their Stores" (McKinsey & Company, 2007).

32. Wal-Mart, "China Fact Sheet" (www.walmartstores.com).

33. World Bank, *World Development Indicators*.

34. Nomura International, "China: A Secular Shift," *Asian Bank Reflections* 3 (August 2009).

35. World Bank, *From Poor Areas to Poor People: China's Evolving Poverty Reduction Agenda* (2009).

36. Ibid.

37. World Bank, *World Development Indicators*.

38. World Bank, *From Poor Areas to Poor People*.

39. This conclusion is consistent with Charles Horioka and Junmin Wan, "The Determinants of Household Saving in China: A Dynamic Panel Analysis of Provincial Data," Working Paper 2007-28 (Federal Reserve Bank of San Francisco, 2007).

40. Chunlin Zhang and others, *Promoting Enterprise-Led Innovation in China* (World Bank, 2009).

41. China did abolish all taxes and fees on agricultural incomes as a result of strengthened public finances, but this has helped strengthen poverty reduction programs rather than the middle class.

42. Judith Banister, "Manufacturing Earnings and Compensation in China," *Monthly Labor Review* (U.S. Bureau of Labor Statistics, August 2005).

43. Jahangir Aziz and Li Cui, "Explaining China's Low Consumption: The Neglected Role of Household Income," Working Paper WP/07/181 (International Monetary Fund, 2007).

44. World Bank, *Doing Business 2010* (2009).

45. World Bank, *Governance, Investment Climate, and Harmonious Society: Competitiveness Enhancements for 120 Cities in China* (2006).

46. Aziz and Cui, "Explaining China's Low Consumption."

PART II

The Chinese Perspective: Social Stratification and Political Ideology

Chinese Scholarship on the Middle Class: From Social Stratification to Political Potential

CHENG LI

The emerging Chinese middle class poses a challenge for the China studies community largely because of its sociological heterogeneity and political ambiguity. This new socioeconomic entity consists of many subgroups that differ profoundly from one another in terms of their family origins, occupational identities, levels of educational attainment, and political backgrounds. Such sociological heterogeneity has also contributed to the ambiguity of the Chinese middle class's political role vis-à-vis the authoritarian Communist regime. It is difficult to extrapolate from this emerging class's current state to predict its future political role and potential contribution to democratic change in the People's Republic of China (PRC). As one foreign observer keenly noted, as far as the middle class's political concerns go, "the balance of gains and losses keeps changing."[1]

Despite, or perhaps because of, the conceptual and methodological difficulties inherent in studying China's middle class, PRC scholars and public intellectuals have for some time been engaged in serious academic research on, and have contributed to the public debate over, this socioeconomic force's recent ascendance. Over the course of the last decade, these scholars have published comprehensive and data-rich studies on

I am indebted to Yinsheng Li for his research assistance. I would also like to thank Jordan Lee and Robert O'Brien for suggesting ways in which to clarify the chapter.

China's emerging middle class, which stands in stark contrast to the lack of in-depth scholarly work on the subject in Western academic circles, a deficit noted in the introductory chapter. By 2010 over 100 Chinese scholarly books on the country's middle class had been published in the PRC, most of which can be found in this volume's bibliography.[2] These works represent a variety of methodological angles, including theoretical and conceptual discussions, questionnaire surveys, behavioral analysis, cross-country comparisons, reports on the national income distribution, and regional case studies.

It should be noted that PRC scholars' attention to the concept of a middle class was prefaced at the turn of the century with research into rapidly changing trends in China's social stratification and social mobility. To a great extent scholarly disputes over definitional problems and the heterogeneity of the Chinese middle class stem from earlier theoretical questions related to social stratification in China. Over the past decade, however, the research interests of Chinese scholars have expanded from questions related to the basic existence of, or the definition of, the middle class to topics such as the size of the middle class, its subgroupings, and its members' worldviews, lifestyles, behaviors, and potential political aspirations. As Li Chunling, a sociologist at the Chinese Academy of Social Sciences (CASS) and a contributor to this volume, observes, PRC scholars have moved beyond the question of "whether or not China has a middle class," which still occupies the minds of many Western scholars.[3] Rather, their consensus is that "the emergence of the middle class in China is now beyond any doubt."[4]

This chapter's review of the Chinese literature on the subject also suggests an interesting development—a shift from an early focus on issues related to social stratification during most of the last decade to a more recent, more controversial, and more open-ended inquiry into the political implications of the Chinese middle class's ascendance. An increasing number of PRC scholars have begun to challenge the conventional Chinese (and Western) view that the middle class in China has served, and will continue to serve, as a stalwart political ally of the ruling Chinese Communist Party (CCP). Instead, they believe that the Chinese middle class is beginning to play an important political role that is both conservative, in that it supports the CCP leadership's focus on social stability, and progressive, as is evident in its support for governmental accountability, better legal protections for citizens, restraints on the monopolization of large state-owned enterprises, and greater public participation in the formation of socioeconomic policies.

This chapter examines the last decade of Chinese scholarship on and public discussion of the country's emerging middle class, with an emphasis on two important issue areas: China's social stratification, in light of the development of a middle class, and the political implications of this dynamic new socioeconomic force. By surveying Chinese scholars' quests to understand the subject, this chapter brings to light the growing tensions in the Chinese body politic and the middle class's increasingly serious commitment to fostering changes in China's governance and state-society relations. It is imperative that overseas analysts and observers develop both an accurate knowledge of social stratification in present-day China and a deep understanding of how PRC scholars assess their country's emerging middle class and its implications for China's ongoing transformation and future political trajectory.

Academic Fever on China's Social Stratification: Sociologists' Impetus

For the first five decades of the PRC, social stratification was a politically sensitive subject. After the Communist victory in 1949, the leadership immediately proclaimed that the newly established PRC had only three social strata: workers, peasants, and a small "intermediate stratum" consisting primarily of intellectuals that would, according to Marxist theory, gradually shrink. The ultimate goal of the Communist regime was to establish a "classless society." In the mid-1960s, however, Mao believed that a small number of privileged elites in the CCP, led by the top leaders Liu Shaoqi and Deng Xiaoping, had become a new revisionist ruling class. Mao therefore called for the launch of the Great Proletarian Cultural Revolution to carry forward the "class struggle" against the exploitative classes, new and old, and to restore the "governing role of the working class."

After his return to power in 1978, Deng Xiaoping profoundly changed the course of China's economic and sociopolitical development by abandoning these notions of class struggle and class analysis. The ideological and policy changes that Deng ushered in ended the decade-long large-scale political repression of the Cultural Revolution and paved the way for market reforms. While these market reforms have contributed to the

FIGURE 3-1. Journal Articles with "Middle Class" in Title, China, 1979–2007

Number

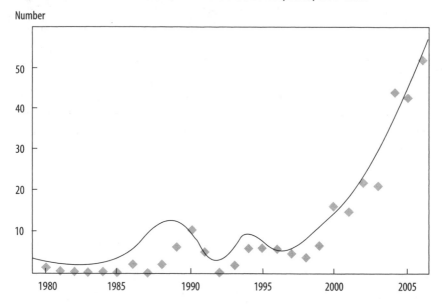

Source: Li Chunling, "Zhongguo zhongchan jieji yanjiu de lilun quxiang ji guanzhudian de bianhua" [Theoretical orientation and the change of focus in the study of the middle class in China], in *Bijiao shiyexia de zhongchan jieji xingcheng: guocheng, yingxiang yiji shehui jingji houguo* [Formation of the middle class in comparative perspective: process, influence, and socioeconomic consequences], edited by Li Chunling (Beijing: Social Sciences Academic Press, 2009), p. 48.

country's remarkable economic development over the past thirty years, they have also aggravated economic disparities and created new socio-political tensions. Given such rapidly changing circumstances, it became essential for China's scholarly and policy communities to reassess social stratification in the PRC.

Figure 3-1, derived from content analysis conducted in 2009 by Li Chunling, shows that from 1980 to 2007, there was a surge in the number of Chinese journal articles that included the term *middle class* in their title. Li generated these numbers using a database of major PRC academic journals and periodicals. The initial small wave of scholarly interest in the late 1980s, as shown in the figure, reflects discussion of the emergence of rural industrialists in township and village enterprises; the second wave, in the mid-1990s, represents an uptick of interest in the middle classes of foreign countries; and the third, most recent, and largest wave is indicative of the surge in multifaceted research on various aspects of the emerging middle class (including its size, composition, rate of expansion, and characteristics such as income, consumption patterns, cultural norms, and political attitudes).[5] These studies and their attendant controversies have increased in frequency year-on-year.

The surge in the number of PRC scholarly studies of China's changing social structure and emerging middle class is not simply a reflection of the importance of these trends. One may reasonably argue that it is also a testimony to the active role and growing influence of Chinese social scientists in the country's intellectual and policy discourse. In other words, PRC sociologists have made their academic pursuits indispensable as a source of information for both the Chinese government and the public.

Chinese Sociologists' Coming of Age

To better review and evaluate the Chinese scholarship on the middle class it is useful to have some basic knowledge of the personal and professional backgrounds of some of the field's most distinguished scholars. Table 3-1 presents an overview of eleven Chinese social scientists who have written extensively on the middle class over the course of the past decade. This list is not comprehensive; rather, it highlights some of the most influential scholars working on the subject and briefly summarizes their different intellectual approaches. All eleven individuals are accomplished senior professors who currently teach or conduct research at China's top universities and research institutions. In addition to the representative works cited here, each has a long list of academic publications to his or her credit. Most also serve as deans, department chairs, directors of research institutions, or in other administrative positions. Three scholars—Li Chunling, Lu Hanlong, and Zhou Xiaohong—are contributors to this volume.

Of the eleven scholars featured here, ten are sociologists by training. Zhu Guanglei is the only exception. Although he received his Ph.D. in economics, he has spent most of his career as a professor of political science. As of 2010, Zhu is the only PRC political scientist to have published a monograph focusing on China's social stratification, including the emerging Chinese middle class, although some have contributed articles on the subject to PRC political science and public administration journals. This may reflect the fact that political controls remain in place over certain academic disciplines. Meanwhile, many of the PRC's academic economists have conducted outstanding studies on more specialized topics relating to the middle class, including the national income distribution, economic disparities, private enterprises, and housing

T A B L E   3 - 1 .   Prominent Chinese Scholars Who Study the Middle Class[a]

Name	Born	Academic field	Education	Overseas studies	Professional affiliation	Professional title	Representative work
Li Chunling	1963	Sociology	Ph.D. CASS	VS (U of Michigan, Sciences Po in Paris, Oxford U, Stockholm U)	Institute of Sociology, Chinese Academy of Social Sciences	Research fellow/ professor	*Formation of the Middle Class in Comparative Perspective* (2009), *Cleavage and Fragment* (2005)
Li Lulu	1954	Sociology	Ph.D. Renmin U	VS (U of Frankfurt, Ruhr U, U of Chicago, U zu Koeln, U of Copenhagen, U DuE)	School of Sociology and Demography, Renmin U	Associate dean/ professor	*Private Entrepreneurs in Transitional Society* (1998), *China's Danwei: Power, Resources and Exchanges* (2000)
Li Peilin	1955	Sociology	Ph.D. (see right)	Ph.D. (U Paris 1 Panthéon—Sorbonne), M.A. (U of Lyon)	Institute of Sociology, Chinese Academy of Social Sciences	Director/professor	*Transformation of China's Social Structure* (1995), *Series of Blue Book of China's Society* (2007–09)
Li Qiang	1950	Sociology	M.A. Renmin U	VS (U of Michigan, Harvard U, Yale U, U of Chicago, Duke U, UCLA)	School of Arts and Humanities, Tsinghua U	Dean/professor	*Social Stratification and Mobility in Contemporary China* (1998), *China's Social Strata in Transitional Period* (2004)
Li Youmei	1955	Sociology	Ph.D. (see right)	Ph.D. (Sciences Po in Paris)	Shanghai U	Vice president/ professor	*Social Structural Changes in Shanghai during the Past 15 Years* (2008)

Name	Birth year	Discipline	Education	Overseas study	Institution	Position	Publications
Liu Xin	1964	Sociology	Ph.D. (see right)	Ph.D. (Chinese U of Hong Kong)	Department of Sociology, Fudan U	Chairman/professor	*Market Transition and Social Stratification* (2005)
Lu Hanlong	1946	Sociology	B.A. Tongji U	VS (Yale U, Cornell U, Duke U, SUNY Albany, Sussex U, Minnesota U)	Institute of Sociology, Shanghai Academy of Social Sciences	Dean/professor	*Social Constructions and Social Governance* (2006), *Shanghai Citizens in Transition* (2008)
Lu Xueyi	1933	Sociology	B.A. Peking U	VS (Waseda U)	School of Social Sciences and Humanities, Beijing Industrial U	Dean/professor	*Research Report on Social Strata in Contemporary China* (2002), *Social Mobility in Contemporary China* (2004)
Sun Liping	1955	Sociology	B.A. Peking U, M.A. Nankai U	VS (Hong Kong Baptist U)	Department of Sociology, Tsinghua U	Professor	*Cleavage: Chinese Society since 1990s* (2003), *Transition and Cleavage* (2004)
Zhou Xiaohong	1957	Sociology	Ph.D. Nanjing U (History)	VS (Harvard U, Nagoya U)	Department of Sociology, Nanjing U	Dean/professor	*Survey of the Chinese Middle Class* (2005), *Series of China's Middle-Strata Studies* (2007–08)
Zhu Guanglei	1959	Political science	Ph.D. Nankai U (Economics)	VS (Ohio State U, York U in UK)	Zhou Enlai School of Government, Nankai U	Dean/professor	*Analysis of Social Strata in Contemporary China* (2007)

Source: Author's database.

a. CASS is Chinese Academy of Social Sciences; MA is Master of Arts; VS is Visiting Scholar; U is University.

reforms. It seems, however, that they prefer to leave general studies of the middle class to researchers at commercial firms, such as those cited in the introductory chapter of this volume.

In a way, the increase in academic interest in social stratification and the middle class has been accompanied by the rebuilding of sociology as an esteemed discipline in China. Sociology, as a "Western import," first found its way to China in the 1920s.[6] Almost all those who helped establish the academic field in China, for example, Pan Guangdan, Fei Xiaotong (Fei Hsiao-Tung), and Lei Jieqiong, studied in the West during their formative years. Pan attended Columbia University; Fei received his Ph.D. from the University of London; and Lei studied at Stanford University and the University of Southern California. After the founding of the PRC, the regime labeled sociology "a bourgeois pseudoscience" and banned it for over three decades. Pan, Fei, and Lei were all persecuted in the course of Mao's various political campaigns. In the Deng era, Fei's dramatic return to the political spotlight as a senior leader (first as vice chairman of the Chinese People's Political Consultative Conference and then as vice chairman of the National People's Congress) was highly symbolic, helping to enhance the professional prestige of Chinese sociologists.

Although the leading PRC scholars studying the Chinese middle class are homogenous in terms of their academic discipline, they represent several different generations. The most senior member, Lu Xueyi, was born in 1933 and was instrumental in rebuilding Chinese sociology after the Cultural Revolution. On the other end of the spectrum are Li Chunling and Liu Xin, the youngest members of the group, who were born in the 1960s. Despite only being in their midforties, their outstanding original fieldwork has already made a mark on the study of China's reform-era socioeconomic transformation. Both frequently participate in international conferences on contemporary China and often publish their work in English and other foreign languages.

For the vast majority of these scholars, their formative years coincided with the Cultural Revolution (1966–76). This qualifies them as members of the "lost generation," a group so named because the decade's political turmoil interrupted their formal schooling. Many were also "sent-down youths," young men and women who were rusticated to rural areas where they were forced to spend many years, sometimes even a decade, working as farmers. Li Qiang, Li Peilin, Li Lulu, Sun Liping, and Zhou Xiaohong all made remarkable comebacks by entering college when the higher education system was reopened in 1977. Though the lives of these sent-down youths were unduly arduous, their experiences in the countryside afforded them invaluable firsthand knowledge of issues that would later become the focus of their careers, including social stratification, social mobility, economic disparities, and distributive justice.

Like the first generation of Chinese sociologists mentioned above, all of the scholars in table 3-1 spent time abroad, participating in international educational exchange programs as visiting scholars or degree candidates, mainly in Western countries and Japan. Three on the list received their doctoral degrees from universities overseas. Upon returning to China they joined the legions of foreign-educated Chinese returnees who are known as "sea turtles" (haigui).[7] Beginning with Deng Xiaoping's landmark decision to send a large number of students and scholars to study abroad in 1978, a total of 1,620,000 Chinese nationals have pursued their studies in foreign countries over the past three decades, with a large number (approximately 37 percent) going to the United States.[8] Over the past decade, China has witnessed a tidal wave of foreign-educated Chinese nationals returning home. By the end of 2009 about half a million foreign-educated Chinese students and scholars had made their way back to the PRC.[9] One of the areas most strongly influenced by returnees is, not surprisingly, higher education, especially leading research institutions such as the Institute of Sociology at CASS. Since returning, these Western-educated scholars have redesigned the curricula and research methods of virtually all of the PRC's academic disciplines.[10] The strong presence of returnees in the group of scholars studying China's middle class demonstrates the power of academic globalization in today's world.

Compared with other groups analyzing China's emerging middle class, these PRC scholars boast many advantages. The time they spent studying at academic institutions abroad generally served to familiarize them with Western social science's cutting-edge theories, paradigms, and methodologies, especially highly technical quantitative surveys. Furthermore, their extraordinary experiences early in life (as sent-down youths) and their intimate knowledge of China's ongoing transformation provide them with an invaluable grassroots perspective. Finally, the fact that many of them hold academic leadership positions, such as department chair or dean, may increase their opportunities to conduct empirical research.

The current dominance of sociologists in the study of China's middle class has its downside. Chinese scholarship on the subject would certainly

FIGURE 3-2. Breakdown of the Chinese Population According to Social Stratum, 2002

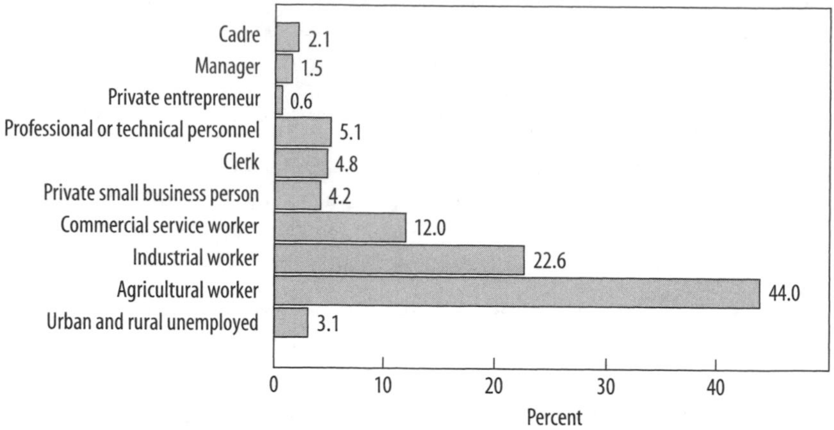

Source: Lu Xueyi, *Dandai zhongguo shehuijieceng yanjiu baogao—Zhongguo shehuijieceng congshu* [Research report on social strata in contemporary China] (Beijing: Shehui kexuewenxian chubanshe, 2002), p. 44.

benefit from more interdisciplinary research, including perspectives from the fields of education, law, social psychology, literature, popular culture, communications, urban development, and the environment.[11] Even so, the sociologists studying the middle class are hardly a monolithic group in terms of the issues they study and policy recommendations they offer. Important intellectual and political disputes often occur among them. These differences of opinion are an important dimension of what makes the Chinese scholars' work on the subject particularly interesting and insightful.

Occupation-Based Strata and Socioeconomic Strata

The most influential study of the social strata of reform-era China (1978 to the present) is the *Research Report on Social Strata in Contemporary China*, published in 2002 by Lu Xueyi, then director of the Institute of Sociology at CASS. Based on three years (1999–2002) of nationwide fieldwork and questionnaire surveys, Lu and his colleagues proposed a ten-stratum framework with which to conceptualize the new configuration of social stratification in reform-era China (figure 3-2).

By categorizing working-age members of society into ten strata according to their occupations, Lu initiated a new approach that owed more to theories of social stratification than conventional Marxist class

FIGURE 3-3. Overlap of Socioeconomic Strata and Occupation-Based Strata in China

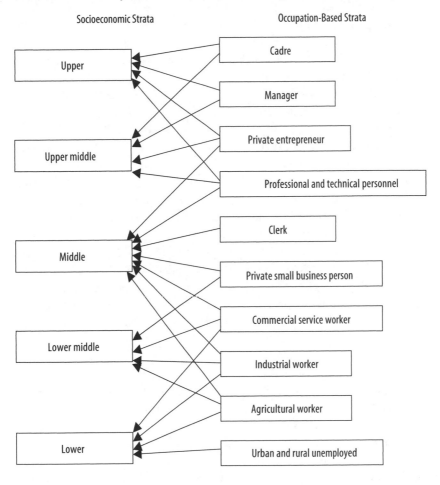

Socioeconomic Strata | Occupation-Based Strata

Source: Lu Xueyi, *Dandai zhongguo shehuijieceng yanjiu baogao—Zhongguo shehuijieceng congshu* [Research Report on Social Strata in Contemporary China], (Beijing: Shehui kexuewenxian chubanshe, 2002), p. 9.

analysis. Occupation is the primary criterion in this approach, but Lu and his colleagues also take into consideration administrative (*zuzhi*), economic, and cultural resources that the members of each stratum may possess or have access to.[12] In addition to occupation-based strata, Lu also employed a five-tiered ranking based on socioeconomic status: the upper, upper middle, middle, lower middle, and lower strata (figure 3-3). In his framework each member of an occupation-based stratum can belong to one of several socioeconomic strata, and vice versa. For example, a private entrepreneur can be a member of the upper, upper middle, or middle strata. Similarly, a member of the upper middle stratum can have one of the four occupational identities (cadre, manager, private entrepreneur, or professional/technical personnel).

Analysis of social stratification in the Chinese context is, of course, not the proprietary creation of Lu Xueyi. Distinguished sociologists outside the PRC, such as Yanjie Bian, Deborah Davis, Nan Lin, Victor Nee, Alvin So, William Parish, Ivan Szelényi, Andrew Walder, Martin Whyte, and Xueguang Zhou, have made important contributions to the subject.[13] Lu's 2002 study of social stratification, however, was truly a landmark study in the PRC for two reasons. First, recognizing and categorizing a vast number of the working class (both industrial and agricultural workers) as belonging to the lower or lower middle strata were political and ideological breakthroughs. Workers, previously considered the "masters of the PRC," are now at nearly the bottom of the Chinese society in terms of their socioeconomic status, occupational standing, and access to resources. Although one might expect this to precipitate an urgent call to build a harmonious society on the part of the government—an agenda item for the populist Hu-Wen administration—it instead revealed, in a striking way, the pyramid-shaped, rather than olive-shaped, structure of socioeconomic and political life in present-day China.[14]

Second, Lu and his colleagues' study provided a more readily applicable and comprehensive paradigm with which to conceptualize the rapid expansion of the middle stratum groups in China and to explicate membership in the middle class. Although Lu used the term *middle stratum* (*zhongjian jieceng*) rather than *middle class*, his new analytical framework nonetheless highlighted the importance of these rapidly emerging groups in society. For example, comparing data from 1978, 1988, and 1991, Lu found that the number of cadres, managers, private entrepreneurs, technical clerks, and private small-business-owners—key constituents of the middle or upper socioeconomic strata—all increased significantly.[15]

In addition to Lu's study, four other important and widely publicized empirical studies were conducted by PRC scholars on social stratification, social mobility, new socioeconomic groups, and intergroup relationships (table 3-2). All of these surveys were conducted within the past decade and provide detailed information about their study pools and

T A B L E 3 - 2 . Major PRC Studies of the Chinese Middle Class

Project	Time period	Study pool and location	Pool number	Research focus	Research method	Middle class as % of population	Research institution	Principal researcher
Social strata in contemporary China	1999–2002	Urban and rural households in 10 provinces	12,000	Social strata	Sampling questionnaire and interview	15	CASS	Lu Xueyi
Survey of changes in China's social structure	2001	Urban and rural residents in 73 counties and cities	6,193	Occupation, income, consumption, self-description	Sampling	4.1 national, 12 major cities	CASS	Li Chunling
Social mobility in contemporary China	2001–04	Urban and rural households in 12 provinces	6,000	Social mobility, generational and occupational change	Sampling and questionnaire	16 in labor force	CASS	Lu Xueyi
Survey of the Chinese middle class	2003–05	Urban households in 5 major cities	3,038	Identity, education, consumption, lifestyle, political participation	Telephone sampling	11.8 in major cities	Nanjing University	Zhou Xiaohong
Survey of China's social condition	2006	Urban and rural households in 130 counties and cities in 28 provinces	7,061	Identity, income, occupation, education	Sampling and questionnaire interview	12.1, including 3.2 core, 8.9 semicore	CASS	Li Peilin

Source: Lu Xueyi, *Dangdai zhongguo shehuijieceng yanjiu baogao—Zhongguo shehuijieceng congshu* [Research report on social strata in contemporary China] (Beijing: Shehui kexuewenxian chubanshe, 2002); Lu Xueyi, *Dangdai Zhongguo shehui liudong* [Social mobility in contemporary China] (Beijing: Shehuikexue wenxian chubanshe, 2005); Li Chunling, "*Zhongguo zhongchan jieji yanjiu de lilun quxiang ji guanzhudian de bianhua*" [Theoretical orientation and the change of focus in the study of the middle class in China], in Li Chunling, ed., *Bijiao shiyexia de zhongchan jieji xingcheng: guocheng, yingxiang yiji shehui jingji houguo* [Formation of the middle class in comparative perspective: process, influence, and socioeconomic consequences] (Beijing: Social Sciences Academic Press, 2009), pp. 46–58; Li Chunling, *Duanlie yu suipian—Dangdai Zhongguo shehuijieceng fenhua shizheng fenxi* [Cleavage and fragment: an empirical analysis of social stratification in contemporary China] (Beijing: Shehuikexue wenxian chubanshe, 2005); and Li Peilin and others, *Zhongguo shehuihexie wending baogao* [Social harmony and stability in China today] (Beijing: Social Sciences Academic Press, 2008).

sampling methods. The Institute of Sociology at CASS, formerly headed by Lu Xueyi and now led by Li Peilin, has assumed a leadership role in empirical research on China's middle class, as evidenced by the fact that affiliated scholars conducted four of the five major national surveys shown. One thing that is immediately apparent is that the estimated size of China's middle class varies from one study to another. This is partly due to the fact that some of these studies focused only on urban areas, but the reason is primarily that they used slightly different definitions of middle class.

In contrast to the reports produced by foreign commercial research groups, which often consider income and assets to be the most important criteria for defining the middle class, PRC scholars usually pay greater attention to other factors, such as occupation, education, and self-identification.[16] In their studies of the Chinese middle class, Li Peilin and Li Chunling both opted for a composite definition along these lines, which the introductory chapter of this volume describes in greater detail. The reported percentage of the Chinese population considered to be part of the middle class ranged from 3.2 percent (the core group of the middle class) in Li Peilin's 2006 study to 16 percent in Lu Xueyi's 2004 report. Other studies conducted in China yield even more divergent assessments.

The Chinese Debate over Sociological Heterogeneity

Studies of Chinese social stratification completed by Lu Xueyi, Li Peilin, Li Chunling, and their associates have often received acerbic criticism from other PRC scholars and public intellectuals. The middle class's lack of sociological homogeneity, in the critics' view, makes many of their generalizations about the Chinese middle class problematic. The critics' reservations generally fall into one of three categories: the Chinese middle class's relatively small size, its distinctly heterogeneous composition, and its lack of a unifying core value.

The first cluster of criticism centers on the group's size. Critics point to the Western norm of the middle class constituting a large proportion of the population in a given country, often a majority of the workforce. As many Chinese critics have observed, the middle class in the United States is a synonym for the "common people," or what the Chinese call the "ordinary people" (laobaixing). They earn an "ordinary income" like the majority of the population and occupy the middle space between a small number of rich and a small number of poor.[17] In China, on the other hand, middle class is sometimes considered a synonym for "moneybags" (*dakuan*); that is, people who spend generously on luxury goods. Li Yining, a prominent professor of economics at Peking University, made headlines with his now famous criterion for middle-class membership: ownership of two houses or condos. This biting remark describes a level of material comfort clearly out of reach of most Chinese.[18]

Some critics believe that the conceptual framework of a middle class is not appropriate for studying present-day China. They often cite Lu Xueyi's studies, which hold that agricultural workers and industrial workers constitute a very large portion of the workforce (44 percent and 22.6 percent, respectively; see figure 3-2). According to the critics, today's China still consists primarily of peasants, migrant workers, and the urban poor, rather than a middle class. These skeptics also assert that even according to the most optimistic assessments, the Chinese middle class still constitutes less than 20 percent of the population, far less than the Western norm of more than half of the population.

According to Niu Wenyuan, a scholar in China's Academy of Sciences, a middle-class country should meet five basic criteria:

—An urban population of 70 percent or above

—A country's labor force made up of more white-collar than blue-collar workers

—An Engel's coefficient (the proportion of total income spent on food) below one-third

—A Gini coefficient (a measure of inequality) in the fairly low range (roughly 0.25–0.3)

—Citizens' education averaging twelve years or more[19]

In Niu's view, China has a long way to go before it meets most of these criteria.

The second cluster of criticism focuses on the belief that the emerging socioeconomic groups in present-day China differ profoundly from each other in terms of their family backgrounds, occupational identities, educational credentials, and political associations. For them, the composition of this broad socioeconomic category is far too heterogeneous to be meaningful. This heterogeneity has been reinforced by the fact that two somehow contrasting subsets—the old middle class (rural industrialists and urban private entrepreneurs) and the new middle class (government officials, managers, professionals, and white-collar workers)—have both experienced rapid, simultaneous growth over the past two decades and are expanding in unison.[20] Critics argue that private entrepreneurs, on the one hand, and white-collar workers in the government or major state-owned enterprises, on the other, have very different values, which lead to different public policy preferences. The former, they believe, tend to prefer less state interference in the market, while the latter are interested in maintaining or even increasing government control.[21]

Several Chinese surveys show that a significant proportion of the private entrepreneurs in both rural and urban China, especially during the first two decades of reform, came from peasant backgrounds. Many of these individuals received only an elementary school education or were illiterate. In fact, a comprehensive survey of 1,440 private entrepreneurs conducted in 1992 by Lu Xueyi and his team at CASS found that 54 percent of entrepreneurs in rural areas were former peasants and 69 percent listed their father's occupation as peasant.[22] Two other studies of private entrepreneurs in Shanghai conducted in the 1990s show that a majority of entrepreneurs (83 percent in one study and 44 percent in the other) received at most a middle-school education.[23] The heterogeneity of these middle-class subgroups' occupational and educational backgrounds leads some critics to doubt whether they can be considered a unified, coherent socioeconomic force.

The third cluster of criticism frequently quotes works by Western theorists, such as Talcott Parsons, on social structure and the middle class, which posit that shared core values must play a central role in the formation of a socioeconomic stratum. Such a value system is normally determined by a society's most influential stratum and becomes the glue that holds together the middle-income group.[24] According to the Chinese critics He Qinglian and Xu Zhiyuan, however, the alleged Chinese middle class lacks such shared values.[25] In line with other critics, they believe that without this shared normative stance, the concept of middle class becomes a reference to income and economic assets and, consequently, loses much of its analytic power. As Yuan Jian puts it, "the middle-income stratum, in fact, exists in any given society in the modern world. Such an identity is meaningless if its members do not have a mainstream consciousness and values that are identical with the middle-class members in other parts of the world."[26]

Proponents of a Chinese middle class reject most of these criticisms. They acknowledge that the middle class in China is still relatively small and indeed very small percentagewise compared to its counterparts in many Western countries. But they hasten to add that no country can have a middle class in the majority in just a few years or even a few decades. Some scholars distinguish between the middle class existing in a given country and that country being a middle-class country as defined by Niu Wenyuan. China appears not to have met the criteria outlined by Niu and therefore cannot be considered a middle-class country, but it is difficult to deny that its middle class has already reached an impressive absolute number and is rapidly expanding. According to an official government report in 2009, the middle class constitutes 16 percent of the workforce in the PRC, or roughly 120 million people.[27]

In his 2010 volume *Social Structure of Contemporary China*, whose findings were based largely on the PRC State Statistics Bureau's 2005 census of 1 percent of the Chinese population and a CASS national survey in 2006, Lu Xueyi reaffirms the trend of middle-class expansion by showing the increasing percentage occupying the upper-middle strata.[28] Private entrepreneurs, for example, increased from 0 percent in 1978 to 0.02 percent in 1988, 0.6 percent in 1999, 1 percent in 2002, and 1.3 percent in 2006.[29] He also concludes that the Chinese middle class constituted 23 percent of the total population in 2009, up from 15 percent in 2001.[30] Lu believes that the annual growth rate of the Chinese middle class appears to be about 1 percent, and he forecasts that its share of the Chinese population will reach 40 percent in twenty years.

Proponents of this mode of analysis argue that the middle class is an inherently flexible concept and that its definition, while imprecise, is equally imprecise for all countries. They observe that members of the middle class in Western countries are just as diverse in terms of their family backgrounds, occupational identities, and educational attainments as their counterparts in China. They also point out that the middle class in Western countries is often subdivided into many groups.[31] Moreover, recalling the Western experience, some argue that the rapid growth of mass higher education in China has contributed significantly to upward social mobility and the expansion of the middle class. In 1977 China admitted only 270,000 college students; three decades later, in 2006, 5.5 million were admitted, a twentyfold increase.[32] This rapid development in higher education mirrors the remarkable growth of American and French universities about a century earlier.[33] In China, however, it took only one generation for most members of the middle class to share the same baseline level of education.

Proponents also reject the notion that the Chinese middle class lacks shared core values. In their view, its constituent members are unified in their appreciation for the middle-class lifestyle, the further development of a market economy at home and economic globalization abroad, the protection of private property rights, a public policy emphasis on primary education, social stability, and pride over China's rise on the international stage.[34] Perhaps most important, the heated public debate over the middle class in China suggests that this new social segment is aggressively searching for its own distinct identity and for ways to express its new values. The public contention over the concept suggests that the middle class's self-consciousness, group identity, and shared values are all on the rise.[35] Underscoring the popularity of the middle-class ideal, Zhou Xiaohong's study of urban residents in five major Chinese cities reports that as many as 85.5 percent of respondents self-identify as members of the middle class.[36]

Rethinking the Political Role of the Chinese Middle Class

Like their overseas counterparts, PRC scholars studying China's middle class have also paid close attention to the political implications of China's ongoing socioeconomic transformation. For most of the last decade, the dominant view within the PRC's scholarly circles has been that China's emerging middle class has contributed to sociopolitical stability. This new socioeconomic force has therefore often been considered a political ally of the Communist regime. More recently, however, an increasing number of the Chinese scholars, including those who have close ties to the political establishment, have begun to challenge this conventional view. They argue that one should rethink the possible political role of the middle class in this rapidly changing country. Just as yesterday's political target could be today's political ally, so too could today's political ally become tomorrow's political rabble-rouser.

Conventional Views of the Middle Class's Political Role

Two ancient philosophers, Aristotle in the West and Mencius in the East, are frequently quoted in Chinese scholarly writings on the correlation between a strong middle class and sociopolitical stability in a given society. Aristotle stated over 2,000 years ago that the middle stratum is a balancing force and a factor for stability. Absent such a stratum, dynastic crises and social upheavals would be far more likely.[37] Mencius voiced roughly the same principle: "Those who have property are also inclined to preserve social stability."[38] Along these lines, Chen Yiping, a scholar at the Guangdong Academy of Social Sciences, argues that the middle class has three functional roles: a leadership role in shaping the market economy, a pioneering role in creating society's social norms, and a buffering role in reconciling political tensions and conflicts.[39]

Tang Jun, a research fellow at the Institute of Sociology at CASS, characterizes the pyramid-shaped social structure as "static stability" and the olive-shaped structure as "dynamic stability."[40] The former appears to be stable but could suddenly collapse if faced with a formidable crisis; the latter, while constantly subject to minor bumps and tensions, is not likely to collapse overnight.[41] According to Tang's optimistic prognosis, China's rapidly expanding middle class will help to establish an olive-shaped structure, with the two small ends representing the rich and poor and the middle class constituting the majority of the population.

In considerations of social stability, Tang and like-minded scholars seem to attribute more significance to a country's socioeconomic structure than to its political system. Some critics, such as He Qinglian, think that the prospect of a democratic China may even become more remote as the middle class rises.[42] The logic behind this pessimistic view holds that members of the new middle class are primarily interested in economic wealth, not political power. As a result, they strike a political deal with the CCP establishment on this hidden rule (*qian guize*) that guides their relationship.[43] Zhou Xiaohong's characterization of the Chinese middle class as the "consumer avant-garde and political rear guard" (*xiaofei qianwei, zhengzhi houwei*) speaks to this question.[44]

New Thinking on Middle-Class Politics

Lately, however, a different assessment has emerged in the PRC scholarly community and has seeped into mainstream public discussions of the middle class. In a large-scale national survey of political attitudes and behaviors across social strata in China, Li Peilin and his team at CASS found that the middle class is more critical of the current social and political situation and less confident in government performance than other strata.[45] The study also suggests that middle-class consciousness, or middle-class values, sometimes differs from mainstream consciousness (*zhuliu yishi*), or the official core values. The work of Li and his team illustrates that, as a group, the middle class often expresses above-average doubt concerning official ideology and China's present-day power structure. In conclusion, they boldly declare it "incorrect to believe that the middle stratum is a force for stability."[46] In their view, the middle class would be unlikely to play a buffering role in reconciling

TABLE 3-3. Central Government Performance, Three Commercial Areas, by Residence, 2008

Percent

Degree of satisfaction	Consumer goods			Stock market			Housing market	
	City	Town	Rural	City	Town	Rural	City	Town
Not satisfied	57.5	47.9	46.9	54.8	43.6	28.0	68.7	55.6
No strong view	17.8	23.9	22.3	26.8	22.3	22.7	15.9	18.9
Satisfied	23.7	27.4	30.0	12.9	15.4	12.2	14.8	18.3
No response	0.9	0.8	0.9	5.5	18.7	37.1	0.7	7.2

Source: Yuan Yue and Zhang Hui, "2008 nian Zhongguo jumin shenghuo zhilian diaocha baogao" [2008 Survey of living standards of Chinese citizens], in *2009 nian Zhongguo shehui xingshi fenxi yu yuce* [Society of China: analysis and forecast for 2009], edited by Ru Xin and others (Beijing: Social Sciences Academic Press, 2008), p. 62.

major sociopolitical conflicts, were they to occur, and might very well oppose the authorities or simply "take a laissez faire attitude" (*tingzhi renzhi*).[47] Li and others believe that this finding should send an important message to the Chinese authorities, as the emerging middle class will have great bearing on China's political trajectory, class structure, and distribution of power in the years to come.

Zhang Yi, a junior colleague of Li Peilin's at CASS, finds (in another study) that the new middle class in China tends to be more cynical about policy promises made by the authorities, more demanding about government policy implementation, and more sensitive as regards corruption among officials.[48] In his analysis, if a large number of middle-class members feel that their voices are suppressed, that their access to information is blocked, or that their space for social action is confined, a political uprising will likely take place. Zhang implies that what happened in South Korea and Brazil, in terms of their middle classes' demand for direct elections, could also occur in China.

A 2008 public opinion survey conducted by the leading Chinese public opinion pollster Yuan Yue and his colleagues echoes some of these findings. Table 3-3 shows the public's evaluation of central government performance on three important commercial issues (consumer goods, the stock market, and the housing market) by area of residence. The study shows that, for each of these three commercial issues, residents in the cities (where the middle class is concentrated) are far more dissatisfied with the central government's performance than are residents of small towns or rural areas. It is particularly notable that this dissatisfaction is directed at the central government rather than at local governments, as has been the case in recent decades.[49]

Middle-class grievances directed at government policy have become increasingly evident in recent years. The growing unemployment rate among recent college graduates (who usually come from middle-class families and are presumed to be members of China's future middle class) should send an alarm to the Chinese government. In a forum on China's response to the global financial crisis held by the Academy of Chinese Reform and Development in Beijing, Chinese scholars argued that the government should pay much greater attention to the needs and concerns of the middle class. Otherwise, in their view, China's "sensitive" middle class will become an "angry" middle class.[50]

The growing number of protests carried out primarily by members of the middle class may reflect the increasing likelihood of this scenario. Examples include the protest against a plan to build an 11 billion yuan chemical factory in Xiamen in 2007, the urban resident movement that blocked the construction of new subway lines in Shanghai in 2008, and the middle-class neighborhood gathering (organized via the micro-blogging service Twitter) that prevented the building of a waste incineration power plant in Guangzhou in 2009. In all of these cases, self-identified middle-class protesters succeeded in pressuring authorities to alter course. Hu Xingdou, a professor of economics at the Beijing Institute of Technology, called the Shanghai resident protest and similar events "a sign of a rising middle class and the awakening of a real sense of citizenship."[51] A well-known NGO in Beijing, the Friends of Nature, published an environmental protection green paper in 2010, reporting on similar protests organized by middle-class residents in various Chinese cities. The principal author of this report, Yang Dongping, a professor of education at the Beijing University of Science and Technology, wrote that China has entered an era in which social protests regarding environmental degradation will take place frequently.[52]

In his study of community governance in Shanghai and other urban centers, Liu Xin finds that members of the middle class have a higher rate of participation in elections and rights-protection activities than other groups. Members of the middle class are also more interested in pursuing legal action when disputes occur and are less tolerant of governance malfeasance than other groups.[53] This is in accordance with the conventional view that because members of the middle class are the main taxpayers in a given society, they have an interest in knowing how their tax revenue is being used. To a certain extent, today's nascent middle class in China represents the first generation of Chinese citizens who are aware of consumer rights. Liu believes that middle-class political participation will be an important factor in the evolution of community governance in the years to come. A report by CASS shows that as of September 2007, China had 360,000 registered civil organizations, including 195,000 social organizations, 164,000 NGOs, and 1,245 foundations.[54] Many scholars believe that the growing number of NGOs and social organizations in the country will also foster greater middle-class consciousness.

In attempting to understand the complex political questions surrounding the middle class in China, some PRC scholars develop sophisticated theoretical frameworks suitable to the Chinese case. Li Lulu argues that the social function, or the political role, of the fast-growing Chinese middle class is neither stagnant nor one-dimensional.[55] He explains that the middle class's fluctuating position in China's social stratification ranks might reveal its seemingly contradictory political preferences and hint at the circumstances under which they will likely change. According to Li, the interaction of three factors—the economic climate, the political system, and the social order (institutionalization)—determines the social function of the middle class, which can be conservative, radical, or dependent.

Li Lulu contrasts this logic with that of a democratic system, in which the middle class tends to become conservative because it benefits from the prevailing social order and power structure. Li calls into question Samuel Huntington's well-known proposition that a middle class tends to be revolutionary in its early development but grows increasingly conservative over time.[56] In authoritarian regimes, Li explains, a nascent middle class tends to depend on the political system in its early development. However, as the economy continues to develop and the middle class becomes more autonomous, the likelihood of the middle class clashing with the government increases. Eventually, it ceases to depend on the regime and might even challenge the authorities. Li also adds three variables to this process: ideology or values, the international environment, and the degree of homogeneity within the middle class. To a great extent, China's emerging middle class is the product of economic and cultural globalization. Li points out that a globally oriented, capitalist, consumer culture—and the transnational political values that often accompany it—will increasingly cause the Chinese middle class to dovetail with, rather than resist, international trends.

Li Lulu's open-ended (and rather optimistic) assessment of the political implications of the Chinese middle class's rise is by no means anomalous within the PRC scholarly community. Many PRC publications on the Chinese middle class highlight the mercurial character of its politics, some portraying the middle class as "vacillating opportunists" (*shoushu liangduan*). In the words of one Chinese writer, the "middle class will neither risk their vital interests to promote democratic changes nor refuse the benefits of democracy that a democratic system can bring to them."[57] In a similar vein, Qin Hui, a distinguished historian at Tsinghua University, argues that no class in the world is born progressive or conservative.[58] Instead, its political orientation evolves according to historical circumstances. In Qin's view, whereas the middle class was a precondition for democracy in Europe, democracy may actually foster the middle class in China.

Hu Lianhe and Hu Angang, a political scientist and an economist, respectively, at the Center for China Studies at the Chinese Academy of Sciences, co-authored a comprehensive article on the middle class and sociopolitical changes. They argue that in China, as in any other country, the political function of the middle class is multiple and malleable. It can be a "stabilizing device" (*wendingqi*), a "subversive device" (*dianfuqi*), or an "alienation device" (*yihuaqi*).[59] The crucial question, in their view, is for what reason or under what circumstances the middle class will shift from one role to another. The authors provide a to-do list for the Chinese authorities to ensure that the middle class remains an ally rather than a challenger. According to the authors, the Chinese authorities need to prevent economic fluctuations, protect property rights, avoid any sense of status loss (individually or collectively) on the part of the middle class, allow more institutionalized political participation, and shield middle-class members from "excessive political attention."

It is interesting to note that all these scholarly writings—whether they offer tips for the Chinese authorities, assess trends from the perspective of a potentially aggrieved middle class, or present more objective analysis—suggest the changing nature of the interaction between the authoritarian regime and the middle class. Arguably the most important factor that might change the relationship is the new notion of a black-collar stratum (*heiling jieceng*). The term refers to the increasing number of urbanites who dress in black, drive black cars, have hidden incomes, live secret lives with concubines, have ties to the criminal underground (*heishehui*, or black society), and, most important, operate their businesses and wield their economic power in an opaque manner. The black-collar phenomenon reflects widespread resentment at the increasingly close associations that exist between officials and the CEOs of large state-owned enterprises, China's powerful bureaucratic capitalists.

It is unclear who first coined the term *black-collar stratum*. Most online postings in China attribute the label to U.S.-educated economist Lang Xianping (Larry Lang), but Lang has publicly denied that he wrote the widely circulated article that popularized the term.[60] Even so, Lang does believe that the black-collar stratum is composed of the true beneficiaries of reform. According to some PRC scholars, three elite groups— namely government leaders, executives of large state-owned firms, and some influential economists—have formed a "wicked coalition" beholden to China's most powerful interest groups (*jide liyi jituan*).[61] These powerful interest groups monopolize China's most important and lucrative business sectors.

Some critics point to the property-development industry as one of contemporary China's most powerful special-interest groups. According to the renowned Tsinghua sociologist Sun Liping, the real estate interest group has accumulated tremendous economic and social capital over the last decade.[62] It has consistently sought to influence government policy and shape public opinion by claiming that it serves the commercial interests of the emerging middle class. Far from uniting with the middle class, however, Sun believes the real estate lobby is profiting from, and increasing the severity of, a "cleavage" (*duanlie*) in Chinese society. The skyrocketing housing prices in large cities in both coastal and inland regions have enriched members of the black-collar stratum but have severely hurt the interests of newlywed, middle-class, urban families who are increasingly unable to pay their mortgages. This explains why the television series *Dwelling Narrowness* (*woju*), which depicts the "middle-class struggle" in coastal metropolitan cities, became one of the country's most popular in 2009.[63]

According to some PRC observers, many members of the middle class, especially small-scale private entrepreneurs, have become increasingly resentful of the Chinese government's policies favoring monopoly-wielding state-owned enterprises. "The state sector's progress at the expense of the private sector" (*guojin mintui*), a new expression widely used in the past few years in China, reflects this public sentiment. The Xinhua news agency, the official Chinese media outlet, reports that in 2010 China's private sector accounted for 60 percent of the country's GDP growth, 70 percent of business firms, and 90 percent of employment for migrant workers. The report also stresses that private firms have made these contributions to the economy despite facing a largely disadvantageous business environment.[64] It seems that the real political ally of the Chinese government is not the white-collar middle class but the black-collar stratum. In fact, these new trends and phenomena are increasingly alienating the middle class.

Conclusion

Over the past century or so, many countries, including the United States, Great Britain, and Japan, experienced a rise of the middle class that profoundly transformed their economies, cultures, and politics. Since the beginning of the reform era, China has also been undergoing drastic changes in social stratification and social mobility, a key feature of which is the emergence of a middle class. It is essential to understand this expanding segment of the Chinese population, as it will likely herald even further-reaching changes in the years ahead.

Over the past decade, a lively intellectual discourse centered on the existence and characteristics of the Chinese middle class has taken shape within China's scholarly community. This ongoing dialogue is replete with open exchanges of striking statistics, bold criticisms, and suggestive analysis. The intellectual fever it represents was spurred, in part, by both admiration for the middle-class way of life in developed countries and consideration of Western social science's maxims and methodologies. As a result, Chinese scholars have enriched, both conceptually and empirically, the world's academic literature on the middle class. In doing so, they have not limited the scope of their intellectual inquiries to the definition, size, and characteristics of this emerging socioeconomic force but have also focused great attention on how the middle class relates to the ruling class and other socioeconomic players in China.

For foreign observers, it is essential to have an accurate picture of China's social stratification and social mobility, and in order to do this, one must understand how Chinese scholars and public intellectuals are wrestling with the profound and ongoing changes to their country.[65] The Chinese scholarly community's careful, straightforward, and often-times bold discourse on the political implications of China's emerging middle class is itself a testimony to these important political dynamics in the making.

Notes

1. An Chen, "Capitalist Development, Entrepreneurial Class, and Democratization in China," *Political Science Quarterly* 117, no. 3 (2002): 422.

2. For example, *Zhongguo zhongjian jieceng yanjiu congshu* [Series on the Chinese middle-income stratum), edited by Zhou Xiaohong, deals with various aspects of this new social group. Shen Hui, *Dangdai Zhongguo zhongjian jieceng rentong yanjiu* [China's middle-income stratum: a study of identity] (Beijing: Zhongguo dabaike quanshu chubanshe, 2008); Wang Jianping, *Zhongguo chengshi zhongjian jieceng xiaofei xingwei* [China's middle-income stratum: consumption behavior] (Beijing: Zhongguo dabaike quanshu chubanshe, 2007); Xu Rong, *Zhongguo zhongjian jieceng wenhua pinwei yu diwei konghuang* [China's middle-income stratum: cultural tastes and social anxiety] (Beijing: Zhongguo dabaike quanshu chubanshe, 2007); and Chen Shuhong, *Zhongguo zhongjian jieceng jiaoyu yu chengjiu dongji* [China's middle-income stratum: education and motivation] (Beijing: Zhongguo dabaike quanshu chubanshe, 2007).

3. Li Chunling, "Zhongguo zhongchan jieji yanjiu de lilun quxiang ji guanzhudian de bianhua" [Theoretical orientation and the change of focus in the study of the middle class in China], in *Bijiao shiyexia de zhongchan jieji xingcheng: guocheng, yingxiang yiji shehui jingji houguo* [Formation of the middle class in comparative perspective: process, influence, and socioeconomic consequences], edited by Li Chunling (Beijing: Social Sciences Academic Press, 2009), p. 53.

4. Ibid.

5. Li, "Zhongguo zhongchan jieji yanjiu de lilun quxiang ji guanzhudian de bianhua," p. 47.

6. Yanjie Bian and Lei Zhang, "Sociology in China," *Contexts* 7, no. 3 (2008): 20–25.

7. In Chinese, the words for *returnee* and *sea turtle* have the same pronunciation.

8. See www.chinanews.com.cn/lxsh/news/2010/03-12/2166360.shtml [March 29, 2010]. The total number of Chinese students and scholars who have studied in the United States referred to the data in 2005. This is based on a speech delivered by China's ambassador to the United States, Zhou Wenzhong, in Seattle on June 1, 2005. See www.chinese newsnet.com (June 6, 2005).

9. See www.chinanews.com.cn/lxsh/news/2010/03-12/2166360.shtml.

10. For further discussion of this topic, see Cheng Li, ed., *Bridging Minds across the Pacific: U.S.-China Educational Exchanges 1978–2003* (Lanham, Md.: Lexington Books, 2005).

11. Exceptions include a study of the middle-class subculture in Shanghai by a scholar in the field of literature and cultural studies. Bao Yaming, *Youdangzhe de quanli xiaofei shehui yu dushi wenhua yanjiu* [The right of a flaneur: consumer society and urban cultural studies] (Renmin University Press, 2004).

12. Lu Xueyi, *Dangdai zhongguo shehuijieceng yanjiu baogao—Zhongguo shehuijieceng congshu* [Research report on social strata in contemporary China] (Beijing: Shehuikexue wenxian chubanshe, 2002), p. 9.

13. For an excellent review of the English literature, see Bian Yanjie, "Chinese Social Stratification and Social Mobility," *Annual Review of Sociology* 28 (2002): 91–116.

14. This pyramid-type structure is most vividly presented in Lu Xueyi's 2004 study. See Lu Xueyi, *Dangdai Zhongguo shehui liudong* [Social mobility in contemporary China] (Beijing: Shehuikexue wenxian chubanshe, 2004), p. 14.

15. Lu, *Dangdai zhongguo shehuijieceng yanjiu baogao,* p. 44.

16. Jiang Shan, *Zhongchan luxiantu* [A roadmap to the middle class] (Wuhan: Changjiang chubanshe, 2004), p. 7.

17. For Zhou Xiaohong's comments see Wei Cheng, *Suowei zhongchan: yingguo jinrong shibao zhongwenwang dui Zhongguo zhongchan jieji de diaocha* [China's emerging

middle class: a survey by the *Financial Times*'s Chinese website] (Guangzhou: Nanfang ribao chubanshe, 2007), p. 3.

18. See www.tianya.cn/publicforum/Content/develop/1/280595.shtml (June 3, 2009).

19. *Financial Times* Chinese online (www.ftchinese.com/specialreport.php?id=005000082).

20. This is in sharp contrast to many Western developed countries, in which it took almost a century for the new middle class to equal the size of the old middle class. See Zhou Xiaohong, *Zhongguo zhongchan jieji diaocha* [A survey of the Chinese middle class] (Beijing: Shehuikexue wenxian chubanshe, 2005). Based on a study conducted by Li Peilin and his associates at CASS in 2008, China's old middle class and new middle class represent exactly the same percentage of China's workforce. Li Peilin and others, *Zhongguo shehuihexie wending baogao* [Social harmony and stability in China today] (Beijing: Social Sciences Academic Press, 2008), p. 198.

21. *Nandu Zhoukan* [Southern capitol weekly], July 14, 2006.

22. Lu Xueyi and others, "Woguo siyou qiye de jingying zhuangkuang yu siyou qiye-zhu de qunti tezheng" [Operational conditions of private enterprises in China and the group characteristics of private entrepreneurs], *Zhongguo shehui kexue* [Social sciences in China], no. 4 (1994): 70.

23. Chen Baorong, "Jiushi niandai Shanghai geti siying jingji fazhan yanjiu" [Study of the development of the private economy in Shanghai during the 1990s] (working paper, Shanghai Academy of Social Sciences, 1994); and Zhu Guanglei, *Dangdai zhongguo shehui gejieceng fenxi* [Analysis of social strata in China] (Tianjin: Renmin chubanshe, 1998), p. 376.

24. For the original argument, see Talcott Parsons, *The Social System* (New York: Free Press, 1951).

25. He Qinglian, "Zhongchan jieji gaibian Zhongguo zhengjushuo shi huanxiang" [The myth of how the middle class will change Chinese politics] in *Dajiyuan* [Epoch], August 2, 2004, p. 1; and for Xu Zhiyuan's comments, see Wei Cheng, *Suowei zhongchan*, p. 208.

26. Yuan Jian, *Zhongguo: Qiji de huanghun* [China: the dusk of the miracle], online book, 2008, p. 116.

27. *Zhongguo jingji shibao* [Chinese economic news], March 3, 2009.

28. Compared with the 1999 data, the percentages of these ten strata in 2006 changed as follows: the category of cadre increased from 2.1 percent to 2.3 percent, managers increased from 1.5 percent to 2.6 percent, private entrepreneurs increased from 0.6 percent to 1.3 percent, professional and technical personnel increased from 5.1 percent to 6.2 percent, clerks increased from 4.8 percent to 7 percent, private small business people increased from 4.2 percent to 9.5 percent, commercial service workers decreased from 12 percent to 10.1 percent, industrial workers decreased from 22.6 percent to 14.7 percent, agricultural workers decreased from 44 percent to 40.3 percent, and urban and rural unemployed increased from 3.1 percent to 5.9 percent. See Lu Xueyi, *Dangdai Zhongguo shehui jiegou* [Social structure of contemporary China] (Beijing: Shehuikexue wenxian chubanshe, 2010), p. 394.

29. Lu, *Dangdai zhongguo shehuijieceng yanjiu baogao*, p. 44; Lu, *Dangdai Zhongguo shehui liudong*, p. 13; and Lu, *Dangdai Zhongguo shehui jiegou*, p. 394.

30. Lu, *Dangdai Zhongguo shehui jiegou*, pp. 402–06.

31. Chen Yiping, *Fenhua yu zuhe: Zhongguo zhongchanjieceng yanjiu* [Separation and coherence: A study of China's middle class] (Guangzhou: Guangdong renmin chubanshe, 2005), pp. 52–53.

32. Ibid., p. 76.

33. Zhou Xiaohong, *Quanqiu zhongchanjieji baogao* [Report on middle classes in the world] (Beijing: Social Sciences Academic Press, 2005), pp. 64, 118–19.

34. For more discussion of the core values in present-day China, especially among members of the emerging middle class, see Pan Wei and Ma Ya, *Jujiao dangdai Zhongguo*

jiazhiguan [Focusing on contemporary Chinese values] (Beijing: Shenghuo dushu xinzhi sanlian shudian, 2008); and Xu Rong, *Zhongguo zhongjian jieceng wenhua pinwei yu diwei konghuang.*

35. Chen Xinnian, *Zhongdeng shouruzhe lun* [Middle-income stratum] (Beijing: Zhongguo jihua chubanshe, 2005).

36. Zhou, *Zhongguo zhongchan jieji diaocha*, pp. 47–48; and Wei, *Suowei zhongchan,* p. 3.

37. Zhou, *Quanqiu zhongchanjieji baogao*, p. 227; also see http://cn.reuters.com/article/columnistNews/idCNCChina-2322520080915 (September 15, 2008).

38. "*You hengchan zhe you hengxin,*" quoted in Jiang, *Zhongchan luxiantu*, p. 32.

39. Chen, *Fenhua yu zuhe*, p. 23.

40. For Tang Jun's view, see *Zhongguo xinwen zhoukan* [China newsweek], January 22, 2010. For a similar argument, see Yu Keping, *Democracy Is a Good Thing: Essays on Politics, Society, and Culture in Contemporary China* (Brookings, 2009).

41. Wei, *Suowei zhongchan*, pp. 109–10.

42. He Qinglian, "The New Myth in China: China's Rising Middle-Class Will Accelerate Democratization," *Finance and Culture Weekly*, November 8, 2006.

43. Wu Si, *Qian guize* [Hidden rules] (Fudan University Press, 2009).

44. For Zhou Xiaohong's argument, see chapter 4 of this volume.

45. Li and others, *Zhongguo shehuihexie wending baogao*, p. 198.

46. Ibid., p. 260.

47. Ibid.

48. Zhang Yi, "Dangdai Zhongguo zhongchan jieceng de zhengzhi taidu" [Political attitudes of the middle stratum in contemporary China], *Zhongguo shehui kexue* [Chinese social sciences] 2 (Summer 2008).

49. Yuan Yue and Zhang Hui, "2008 nian Zhonguo jumin shenghuo zhilian diaocha baogao" [2008 survey of living standards of Chinese citizens], in *2009 nian Zhongguo shehui xingshi fenxi yu yuce* [Society of China: analysis and forecast for 2009], edited by Ru Xin and others (Beijing: Social Sciences Academic Press, 2008), p. 62.

50. Hu Xiao, "Yi gaige yifu jingji weiji" [Accelerate reforms to respond to the economic crisis] in *Zhongguo Jingji Shibao* [China economic times], March 3, 2009, p. 1.

51. Howard W. French, "Shanghai Rail-Line Plan Fuels Middle-Class Protest," *New York Times*, January 27, 2008, p. 6.

52. Yang Dongping, ed., *Zhongguo huanjing fazhan baogao 2010* [Report on China's environmental development 2010] (Beijing: Shehuikexue wenxian chubanshe, 2010).

53. Liu Xin, "Zhongguo chengshi de zhongchan jieceng yu shequ zhili" [Middle classes and community governance in urban China], paper prepared for the conference Middle Class Studies in the Chinese Societies, Changchun, July 22, 2008.

54. Ru Xin and others, *Erlinglingba nian Zhongguo shehui xingshi fenxi yu yuce* [Society of China: analysis and forecast, 2008] (Beijing: Social Sciences Academic Press, 2008), p. 6.

55. Li Lulu, "Zhongjian jieceng de shehui gongneng: xin de wenti quxiang he duo-wei fenxi kuangjia" [The social function of the middle class: the new question-oriented approach and multidimensional analysis framework], *Journal of Renmin University* 4 (April 2008). Also see Li Lulu and Wang Yu, "Dangdai Zhongguo zhongjian jieceng de shehui cunzai: Jieceng renzhi yu zhengzhi yishi" [The social existence of the middle stratum in contemporary China: strata recognition and political consciousness], in *Shehui Kexue Zhanxian* [Social sciences frontline] 10 (2008): 202–15.

56. Samuel Huntington, *Political Order in Changing Societies* (Yale University Press, 1968).

57. Feng Ting, "Biegei zhongchan jieceng tietaiduojin" [Don't gild the middle stratum], *Renmin luntan* (People's forum), no. 10 (April 2010).

58. Qin Hui, "Zhongchan jieji bingfei minzhu biyao tiaojian" [The middle class is not a necessary condition for democracy], *Luye* [Green leaf], no. 12 (2009).

59. Hu Lianhe and Hu Angang, "Zhongchan jieceng: Wendingqi haishi xiangfan huo qita" (Middle stratum: a stabilizer, a disrupter, or something else], *Zhengzhixue yanjiu* [Political science studies], no. 2 (May 2008).

60. See "The Black-Collar Class" (www.chinatranslated.com/?p=407). "Commentary and Analysis on China's Economic and Political Situation," June 12, 2009.

61. *Zhongguo xinwen zhoukan* [China newsweek], January 13, 2006; *Liaowang* [Outlook], December 5, 2005; also see www.chinesenewsnet.com [December 12, 2005].

62. Sun Liping, "Zhongguo jinru liyi boyi de shidai" [China is entering the era of conflicts of interest] (http://chinesenewsnet.com [February 6, 2006]); also see Sun Liping, *Duanlie: 20 shiji 90 niandai yilai de Zhongguo shehui* [Cleavage: Chinese society since the 1990s] (Beijing: Shehuikexue wenxian chubanshe, 2003). Other powerful interest groups include the monopolistic industries, such as telecommunications, oil, electricity, and automotive, which have a huge stake in government policies.

63. *Xinxi Shibao* [Information daily], January 31, 2010.

64. See http://politics.people.com.cn/GB/1026/11602056.html [May 14, 2010].

65. Jean Louis Rocca, "Zhengzhi jiaocha, shehui bianzheng yu xueshu ganyu: Zhongchan jieji zai Zhongguo de xingcheng" [Political interaction, empirical characterization, and academic intervention: formation of the middle class in China], in Li, ed., *Bijiao shiyexia de zhongchan jieji xingcheng*, pp. 59–83.

CHAPTER FOUR

Globalization, Social Transformation, and the Construction of China's Middle Class

ZHOU XIAOHONG and QIN CHEN

Since the 1990s the growth of China's middle class has become an issue of global importance. Its significance in world academia can be attributed not only to the fact that China boasts a population as large as 1.3 billion and a three-decade economic boom that has great bearing on global economic and political affairs but also to the unique ways in which the Chinese middle class has emerged and grown.

As is widely known, the Mao era witnessed political attempts to bridge class gaps, heavy-industry-oriented economic strategies, and intervention in civil life through a particular ideology, all of which contributed to the fact that industrialization before 1978 did not result in a distinct Chinese middle class. Instead, it was China's large-scale social transformation after 1978 that led to today's rapidly growing middle class. In contrast with the West, the Chinese middle class has been influenced by globalization in a way strongly marked by consumerism; further, consumption has become a means for China's amorphously defined middle class to assert its social identity.

Meanwhile, a comparison between China and the former socialist states of Eastern Europe indicates that, on the one hand, the Chinese

This research was cofinanced by a research fellowship from Nanjing University Humanities and Social Sciences Research Council for the project "A Theoretical Study of the Middle Class in the Western Societies" (2006) and a research fellowship from Chinese Social Sciences Research Council for the project "A Comparative Study of Social Construction Theories" (project number 05&ZD037).

middle class's consumption capacity has been boosted by successful economic reforms; on the other hand, its room for action remains confined by the existing political structure. China's radically developing economy and its comparatively retarded political reform have shaped the Chinese middle class into the vanguard of consumption and the rearguard of politics (*xiaofei qianwei, zhengzhi houwei*).

Though seemingly paradoxical, this vanguard/rearguard feature of China's middle class is the natural outcome of a wave of consumerism brought about by globalization and the uniqueness of China's social transformation, especially the continuity of its political system. Globalization and social transformation are interwoven because they both denote a social transition that took place after the 1980s. Globalization signifies a synchronic social transition in which transnational and cross-regional flows of capital, technology, commodities, service, and labor, oftentimes from the United States and other Western capitalist countries, spread throughout the world's modes of production, lifestyles, and cultural representations.

Social transformation, as a diachronic transition, was initiated when the market transition began and thereafter ushered in great changes throughout Chinese society. Social transformation may be regarded as the fruit of globalization; or rather, it is the social transformation of China and the former socialist countries of Eastern Europe and the Soviet Union that has paved the way for globalization in its real sense. Indeed, social transformation has, more than anything else, contributed to changes to the class relations and social structure of socialist countries like China; these domestic changes are also inevitably influenced by global trends in industrial structure, occupational structure, the labor market, and the consumer goods market. In this sense, the birth and growth of the Chinese middle class, as the result of changes to the country's class relations and social structure, cannot be comprehensively and accurately interpreted without the backdrop of globalization and the attendant social transformation.

Due to the comprehensive nature of the issue under discussion, this research does not draw upon original quantitative data. Our analysis of the birth, the growth, and the present features of China's middle class is informed by recent Chinese experiences: its socioeconomic transition over the past six decades, especially the last three, and the contemporary status of China's political scene. We also cite scholarly propositions from a number of empirical studies, including a survey of the middle class the authors conducted in five major Chinese cities in 2005. It is via these empirical resources that we hope to outline the birth and growth of the Chinese middle class and to establish its societal role.

Economic Globalization and the Transnational Expansion of the Middle Class

The modern sense of the middle class has existed since the Industrial Revolution and the French Revolution.[1] Even so, it was never a topic of global importance until the 1970s and 1980s. Besides, the early middle class was confined to the United States and the traditionally capitalist countries of Europe, and even there the middle class was not a mainstream social entity.

Take France in the eighteenth century, for instance. The early form of the French middle class emerged out of the Third Estate, which played an active role in the 1789 French Revolution. Compared with the so-called First Estate (the clergy) and the Second Estate (the aristocracy), the Third Estate, constituting 97 percent of the French population, was an immense group of people. However, only 10–15 percent of it was made up of the middle class in a precise sense, or what the French called the *petit bourgeois,* which included small farmers, small entrepreneurs, and small shop owners as well as a few government employees and professionals, such as writers, doctors, and scholars.[2] It is this social structure that inspired Karl Marx, the first author to use the concept of the middle class in its modern sense, to divide Western society into two rival groups, namely the proletariats and the capitalists, even as he acknowledged the existence of a middle class.[3]

The growth of the middle class has been promoted by two major factors. The first is the transformation of Western capitalist societies from industrial to postindustrial; the second is the spread of Western-style industrialization throughout the world, which is another way of describing globalization. The first transition not only enlarged the scale of the middle class in developed Western countries but also changed its components: small farmers, small entrepreneurs, and small business owners—the "old middle class," in the words of the American sociologist C. Wright Mills—gradually gave way to the new middle class, that is, those engaged in mental work for big businesses or government organizations.[4]

The new middle class first attracted attention in Germany at the beginning of the twentieth century, where industrialization was progressing rapidly. The Social Democrat Eduard Bernstein, citing Gustav von Schmoller, adopted the term *new middle class* to designate salaried employees such as civil servants, technical employees, managers, office workers, and salespeople. Bernstein also modified Marx's theory of class polarization and argued that, in modern capitalist societies, the petty bourgeoisie, or the middle class, was not a diminishing class but one that "increased both relatively and absolutely."[5] This somewhat bold assumption then became a major theme in writings on the middle class by Mills and other authors. Later, in the postindustrial wave as outlined by Daniel Bell, the assumption turned into a reality.[6]

Compared with the first transition, the second is obviously of more importance to the birth and growth of the middle class in Western developed countries. Although the four Asian Tigers (South Korea, Taiwan, Hong Kong, and Singapore), mainland China, India, the former Soviet Union, and socialist countries in Eastern Europe differ from one another in the specifics of their economic booms as well as in their degree of development, the changes they witnessed over the last few decades of the twentieth century were more or less the product of economic globalization. Indeed, the reconfiguration of class formation and birth of the middle class within these countries and regions are intricately linked to the worldwide spread of Western capitalism. Globalization shaped the development of the middle class in the following ways:

—Changing the world's industrial structure and corresponding occupational structure

—Creating a global labor market, which in turn reshaped income distribution

—Ushering in a global consumer goods market and related consumption patterns and lifestyles.[7]

It would be pointless to discuss, in general, whether the influences of globalization are positive or negative, for any such influence is a double-edged sword for every nation and the growth of its middle class. For example, due to globalization, first the four Asian Tigers, and later the People's Republic of China (PRC) and India, witnessed the radical development of low-tech manufacturing industries. In this process, the losses and negative consequences associated with overconsumption of energy, ecological disturbances, and social disorganization have paralleled gains such as the increased and more widespread employment and income.

The double-edged sword proposition can also find evidence in the United States and European capitalist countries. Globalization has enabled them to radically exploit the resources, environment, and labor force of developing countries, hence accelerating their own accumulation of wealth.[8] Moreover, they are not only dumping surplus products onto developing countries but are also exporting their values and ideologies, what Joseph Nye calls "soft power."[9] But developed countries are also paying a price for what they have gained. In spite of the quick and easy money made by financial elites such as Warren Buffett and technological elites like Bill Gates, the middle class in many developed countries, faced with competition from a migrant labor market, is suffering an unprecedented deterioration in living conditions. Although the average annual work time of a middle-class family over the last two decades of the twentieth century increased by over 10 percent (from 3,020 hours a year in 1979 to 3,335 in 1997), its average annual income barely increased by 1 percent.[10] In addition, conditions continue to deteriorate for the middle class in developed countries because of the global financial crisis.

China's Domestic Transformation and the Construction of Its Middle Class

Chinese stories typically follow their own logic. Large-scale industrialization was not initiated in China until after 1949. To be exact, it was initiated when the first Five-Year Plan (1953–57) of national economic development was implemented. From 1949 to 1978, the year marked by the beginning of *gaige kaifang* (reform and opening up), China achieved great strides in industrialization in the face of many trials and tribulations, with annual growth rates averaging 6.1 percent. After many ups and downs, by the time Mao Zedong passed away a fairly comprehensive industrial system had been established in the PRC. Nevertheless, the industrialization experienced during these three decades did not have the capacity to reshape China's class structure, let alone give birth to a middle class.

Unlike its counterparts in the West, China's industrialization process from 1949 to 1978 failed to mold a middle class because China followed a unique political and economic path. From a political perspective, Maoist China's social stratification and class structure had always been affected by two seemingly contradictory policies.

First, after overthrowing rule by former landlords and the bourgeoisie, a fictitious exploitative class was created to oppose peasants and workers. This invented class was identified for as long as three decades in the PRC to support Mao's assumption of the "long-term existence of classes and class struggle" and also to give the Chinese people the idea that they were "boss of the state" (*dangjia zuozhu*). Under the precepts of this class struggle ideology, not only landlords and the bureaucrat-comprador bourgeoisie but also all classes other than workers and peasants were regarded as rivals. The old middle class, labeled either as national bourgeoisie or petty bourgeoisie, had always been the object of socialist rehabilitation. Intellectuals and professionals were also grouped into the petty bourgeoisie. Throughout the first three decades of the PRC, this group was the main target of varied thought rehabilitations, also known as *xizao*.[11] In this way, further class differentiation was checked not only politically but also culturally and psychologically.

Second, among the so-called "people" (*renmin*), egalitarian distribution policies were implemented, which led to a radical destratification of society after 1966. According to research on these egalitarian policies by William L. Parish in the 1960s, even among socialist countries China was the most egalitarian one. High-income people earned only 2.2 to 2.3 times the wages of lower-income earners, and China boasted a Gini coefficient as low as 0.20.[12] Such an egalitarian and destratified social structure was built on varied economic and political policies, including an egalitarian salary system, measures to bridge salary gaps, the abolishment of a military ranking system (which had been in effect for no more than a decade during the Mao era), state allotment of everyday consumer goods, and a housing distribution system.[13] During the Cultural Revolution, piecework wage systems and bonus systems were condemned and later invalidated. After 1966 a series of extreme policies further dragged the moderately egalitarian social structure of earlier years to the radically egalitarian structure of the Cultural Revolution decade. In this situation of destratification, personal efforts, such as raising one's educational level (which in the West is the principal means of becoming a member of the middle class), typically degraded one's occupational status instead of improving it.

Looking from the economic perspective, there were other reasons why China failed to produce a middle class that could have been proportionate to its industrialization process. In particular, affected by the economic patterns of the Soviet Union, China's industrialization had been built upon heavy industry (including military-related industries). Therefore, the development of light industries and service industries, which have great bearing on daily consumption, lagged far behind the

Chinese people's needs. According to statistics, three sectors of the economy (extraction of raw materials, manufacturing, and services) made up 29, 29, and 42 percent, respectively, of China's 1950 GDP; in 1980, however, they were 12.6, 57.8, and 20.6 percent. In that same year other developing countries experienced average proportions of 24, 34, and 42 percent.[14] These statistics are evidence that in Maoist China, while industrialization was advancing fast, development of the tertiary sector of economy was greatly held back. Moreover, in the domain of agriculture, after the 1958 establishment of the People's Commune, the principle of "grain production as the key" and a state monopoly of grain trading caused serious shortages of agricultural consumer goods (the great variety of coupons and certificates was the only silver lining of this shortage).

As far as foreign affairs were concerned, due to China's successive military confrontations with the United States, India, and the Soviet Union, defense expenses had been consuming a considerable portion of total national revenue. All these factors deprived the populace of a substantial income increase during the Mao era.[15] Combined with the political restraints on social stratification, they made the birth and growth of a Chinese middle class nothing but a fairy tale.

However, the following three decades told a different story. After 1978, the year when the Third Plenary Session of the Eleventh Central Committee of the Chinese Communist Party was held, the massive reform and opening-up movement (*gaige kaifang*) began to unfold. Sprouting in the countryside from the household contract responsibility system (*lianchan chengbao zerenzhi*), the movement extended into many cities' economic domains. From then on China began to draw global attention for its economic achievements. Over three decades it boasted an increase of GDP from 364.5 billion yuan in 1978 to 24,953 billion yuan in 2007, making for an annual growth of 9.88 percent. China became the third economic power in the world, ranking behind only the United States and Japan. While the economic boom has created a solid material foundation to better the Chinese people's living conditions, the post-1978 social transformation has been directly and tightly linked with the birth and growth of the Chinese middle class. Initiated by conversion from a mandatory planned economy (or redistribution economy) to a modern market economy, this original economic transformation soon became a driving force of comprehensive social transformation, including changes in class relations and social structure.

Although this social transformation was caused by the market transition in a fundamental sense, the loosening of class relations and social structure, which was frozen for almost thirty years during the Mao era, was triggered by specific policies. In 1979 the Central Committee of the Chinese Communist Party announced it would cease to label landlords (*dizhu*), rich peasants (*funong*), and their children as rivals of the people and to replace the class-struggle-centered principle with the economic-development-centered principle. This policy change, together with other transitions in social life such as occupational differentiation, changed the criteria of social stratification from symbolic class standards to occupational standards, a precondition of the emergence of the middle class.

Once the dam of political stratification collapsed, the power of the market, which became ever stronger after 1978, began to shape a different social structure. When class background ceased to matter as much, new criteria were introduced based on the amount of wealth people earned with their social, economic, and cultural capital.

China's social transformation can be divided into two phases. The fifteen years from 1978 to 1992 constitute the first phase. During this period, thanks to the liberation of private enterprises and the policy "allow some people to get rich earlier than others" (*yunxu yibufen ren xian fu qilai*), two groups became the first members of the Chinese middle class. One group consisted of the early adventurers in the market economy. Having risen from the grass roots, they amassed capital mainly through their keen economic awareness and industriousness. In this sense, they resembled those people, depicted by the influential sociologist Ivan Szelényi, who were engaged in the "second economy" during the early stages of the Hungarian reforms.[16] The other group that became prosperous in this early phase were offspring of cadres (*ganbu*, a Chinese word for government official). Benefiting from their parents' power and from the dual pricing policy (*shuangguizhi*), they translated their parents' political and social capital into their own economic capital. Actually, it was partly their misconduct that triggered the Tiananmen Square turmoil in 1989.

The second phase spans 1993 to the present. With the full-scale switch from a redistribution economy to a market economy and the advance of housing reform (*fanggai*) and other policies, cadres and professionals—who previously enjoyed the privileges of a redistribution economy—now resorted to using their political capital or their cultural capital, which was also of vital importance to the country's overall social transformation. Soon they became the main components of the Chinese middle class, and those poorly educated Chinese who had been the first to rush into the market were now marginalized, which echoes what Szelényi wrote about Eastern Europe.[17]

At the beginning of the reform, people used to remark that "missile makers earn less than egg sellers" and "scalpel holders [surgeons] earn less than razor holders [barbers]," but now such complaints were nowhere to be heard. In the labor market of China today, one's educational level has become a determinant of employment and, hence, an essential factor in influencing social stratification and the growth of the middle class.[18]

Path of the Construction of China's Middle Class

During the three decades beginning in 1949, the political and economic policies of the Chinese Communist Party (CCP) played a vital role in eradicating class inequality. However, implementation of these policies had been dependent upon the planned, or redistributive, economy. While this lack of private ownership of the means of production had put an end to the unequal stratification system, which had existed before the Chinese Revolution, the elimination of the market economy made class differentiation impossible. The redistribution system based on a planned economy had deprived the Chinese people of the opportunity of amassing wealth and capital through free market exchange and had thus prevented Chinese society from differentiation on the basis of economic inequality. As proposed by Szelényi, inequality in socialist societies is typically represented by the distribution of public products, to which power and political loyalty are of critical importance.[19]

Before the *gaige kaifang* in 1978, China was dominated by what Polanyi calls the redistribution economy, in which horizontal relations between producers and consumers were cut.[20] Resource transference and income distribution were realized through a vertical, multistratum bureaucratic system, running from the center to local governments. In the post-1978 era, however, the redistribution system gave way to a market pricing system, which requires that users of production factors reward their providers according to the factors' market prices or their contributions to the ultimate product. It was through this rewarding mode that the policy of "allowing some people to get rich earlier than others" became a reality. Victor Nee insightfully argues that "since the transformation from a redistribution system to a market system incorporates changes in resource transference and distribution modes, chances are that this transformation will reshape the ranking of social stratification."[21]

Accompanied by the GDP boom of the three decades following 1978, three market-inclined distribution modes drove changes in social stratification and the emergence of the middle class. First, the practice of paying rewards based on market pricing inevitably widened the income gap among groups and among individuals of the same group, as evidenced by the rise of the Gini coefficient from 0.21 in the 1960s, to 0.33 in the 1980s, and finally to the present figure of 0.458. The widening of the income gap made it possible for people with comparatively higher incomes to be members of the middle class.

Second, the transformation from a redistribution system to a market system changed the resource-grasping capacity of two fundamental powers, the state and the market. The interest structure was rebuilt, which in turn reshaped the structure of the Chinese middle class. In interpreting such structural change, Victor Nee emphasizes the power of markets and reform. He argues that market transition, while lowering the economic reward of political privileges, raises the economic reward of human capital.[22] Other scholars attach greater importance to the variation and maintenance of power. They either propose that political privileges can be transformed to economic advantages, or they argue that the reward of redistribution power is increased, not decreased, in the process of reform.[23] Each of these perspectives is valid in its own sense: the former stresses the marketization caused by economic reform, while the latter highlights the fact that China's market economy was cultivated in the presence of previous political powers.

Third, along with the advance of marketization, tax reform and housing reform somewhat restrained the widening income gap and facilitated the growth of the middle class.

We now turn to an exposition of the consumption patterns of the middle class, patterns that embody a change of lifestyle and therefore constitute the micro, or psychological, mechanics of their constructing a self-identity and winning social recognition. Considering that, over the past few decades, the Chinese people have been marked by a desire for market transition, a link or interaction between the macro background and the micro mechanics concerning the birth of the middle class may well be described.

Various socioeconomic determinants caused the Chinese middle class to make consumption their principal means of constructing a self-identity and seeking social recognition.[24] From the economic perspective, consumption has become a major means of self-identification by the Chinese middle class because the economic status of this class was not only established by the GDP boom but was also propelled forward by the above-mentioned market-oriented transition. These two factors steadily lifted the income of urban residents. The annual income of the average Chinese worker in 1978 was no more than 615 yuan, but this figure has grown sizably: 1,148 yuan in 1985, 2,140 yuan in 1990, 5,500 yuan in 1995, 9,371 yuan in 2000, and 18,364 in 2005, thus doubling almost every five years.[25]

Meanwhile, consumption was encouraged by the government, with different motives during different eras. Before 1997 a series of policies, including a salary raise, industrial restructuring, and lowering the rate of accumulation, were carried out in order to eradicate the disastrous after-effects of the Maoist Revolution, to improve people's living conditions, and to "overcome the legitimacy crisis."[26] After 1997 consumption was promoted because the Asian financial crisis, combined with insufficient domestic need, had been a bottleneck in the further development of the Chinese economy. Attempting to solve this problem, the CCP and central government proposed that "new consumption highlights such as housing should be created; residence construction should be made a key industry; and consumption of telecommunication, tourism, culture, entertainment, health care and other tertiary industries should be encouraged."[27]

Urged by a variety of government policies, the Chinese middle class updated its consumption items, from consumer durables like televisions, washing machines, and refrigerators to private houses, apartments, and cars, which are considered better manifestations of their status. In one decade, since the beginning of the new millennium, housing prices in China doubled; coastal areas witnessed an increase in population of several times its earlier size, and numerous people became rich through investing in housing. Meanwhile, upon China's joining the WTO in 2001, private cars became common in China. Over the following six years the production and sale of domestically manufactured cars experienced an annual increase of more than 10 percent, from 820,000 cars in 2001 to 5,320,000 in 2007.[28] What's more, to the Chinese middle class, private housing and a car not only represent consumer goods with which they can build their self-identity and win social recognition but also practice fields for molding new notions of consumption.[29]

Encouraged by the CCP and the government, the Chinese middle class accelerated its consumption, which has significant social implications. Under globalization, which became ever more sweeping after the 1990s, consumerist values and lifestyles are evolving among the Chinese people, especially the newly rich, power-and-wealth elite as well as the ever-growing middle class. This trend is contributing greatly to the identity formation of the middle class. As is widely known, the ideological propaganda of the Mao era used to portray consumption as a vile representation of the capitalist lifestyle; to a certain degree it was regarded as equivalent to moral degeneration. After the beginning of *gaige kaifang*, however, and especially after the 1990s, the mainstream discourse transformed the notion of consumption, because the government is aware of the role it can play in advancing the national economy.

Meanwhile, the state's need for economic growth and the market's need for more consumption have ushered in a great variety of consumption-stimulating advertising. Moreover, the appeal of Chinese advertising is beginning to shift from functional value to symbolic value.[30] All of these changes in the public interpretational frames for consumption help to legitimize the improvement of living conditions for the newly rich, including the middle class, and their distinction from the grass roots. Good evidence of this trend are the housing advertisements that have blanketed China over the past decade: houses and apartments are made enticing to consumers not because they are comfortable but because they are guaranteed to manifest and promote the owners' social status.[31] Chinese housing advertisements are replete with slogans like "birds of a feather flock together" (advertisement for Dianyaju Residential District, Nanjing, 2000), "buy a new house and become a real boss" (advertisement for Yongde Xinhua Residential District, Shanghai, 1994), and "the unanimous choice of professors, entrepreneurs, and bankers" (advertisement for Landsea International Residential District, Nanjing, 2005). Boldly linking a housing purchase with one's social stratum and status, these advertisements are very successful, another indication of how important consumption is to the identity of China's middle class.

Vanguard of Consumption and Rearguard of Politics: The Duality of China's Middle Class

The high degree of correspondence between consumption and the Chinese middle class evokes a widely known proposition put forth by the

American sociologist C. Wright Mills. Over half a century ago, in his research on the American middle class, Mills depicted them as "the rearguard of politics."[32] The Chinese middle class presents itself as both the rearguard of politics and the vanguard of consumption. Not only their values, but also their attitudes and behavioral patterns, are directly shaped by this status. Through a comparative study of the development of the middle class in different countries, it can be shown that this dual character of the Chinese middle class has been cultivated by two key trends: globalization and social transformation.

Mills's characterization of the American new middle class, which emerged after World War II, as the political rearguard prompted many challenges and debates. Indeed, the middle class was not born with such an image. Earlier history of the European middle classes witnessed their radical antifeudalism. Having fought as the vanguard of politics, the European middle classes won private ownership of property and the freedom to participate in a market economy and to have a role in deciding public issues. Besides, their efforts resulted in the European tradition of civil society, including the institutions of an elected congress and a free press.

In more recent years, this tradition has played an important role in the social transformation of Hungary and other central European countries.[33] Even in the emerging capitalist countries in other parts of the world, the middle classes often inherited the traits of the political vanguard from their European predecessors. Take the Korean middle class: historically, it was reluctant to take political stands.[34] During the social protest movements from the 1960s to the 1980s, however, they never merely stood by as onlookers. Instead, they took a very active part in democratic reform, which by itself was "a fruit of political democratization."[35]

Just as the French Revolution bestowed the European middle class with the radical traits of the era, the parallel between the rise of the Chinese middle class and the expansion of globalization bestowed upon this group of people characteristics typical of globalization, most prominent among them being consumerism. As a matter of fact, this character is also shared by the Indian middle class, which began to rise at roughly the same time as its Chinese counterpart.[36]

One frequently hears it said that the Chinese middle class can develop its consumption habits only because of the political environment of China. However, this is only half the story. The other side of the coin is that although China and India differ considerably in their political institutions, there are many commonalities in the way the two countries' middle classes consume, largely because the two countries are both deeply involved in the trend of globalization. On the one hand, globalization is expanding capitalist production worldwide and enabling prosperous manufacturing industries and service trades to thrive in developing countries such as China and India. On the other hand, globalization is also cultivating an international consumer market and corresponding values, life attitudes, and behavioral patterns based on consumerism.

In the age of globalization, despite the fact that the middle classes in countries like China and India vary in their origin, political status, occupation, religious belief, and even race, they resemble each other in surprisingly close ways when it comes to constructing their self-identities via consumption. They both emphasize the importance of consumption and lifestyles to one's class categorization and social status. Therefore, in a fundamental sense, both in China and in India, inaction by the middle class in political and social matters has been caused by the fact that cultivating public concerns is compatible neither with consumerism, which is being promoted by globalization, nor with the notion of personal success, which is increasingly defined by one's level of consumption.

Undeniably, besides the factor of globalization, it is also because of China's unique social transformation after 1978 that the Chinese middle class has become the vanguard in consumption and the rearguard in politics. In comparison with Russia and the countries of the former Soviet Union, all of which experienced market transitions, China has followed a completely different path.

In the case of Russia, radical privatization was initiated after the disintegration of the Soviet Union at the end of the 1980s. In less than one decade, the ruling class, consisting of bureaucrats and economic oligarchs, finished their primitive accumulation of capital, which might have taken decades or even an entire century in Western countries.[37] The speed of this accumulation of private wealth far exceeded the speed of the establishment of the market system. This process brought about what Gil Eyal, Ivan Szelényi, and Eleanor Townsley call "capitalists without capitalism." Meanwhile, the Russian middle class that formed at the beginning of privatization was degraded into a poverty-stricken stratum.

In the case of Hungary and other central European countries, thanks to the civil society tradition, the postcommunist era saw a market system established faster than private wealth could accumulate, resulting in "capitalism without capitalists."[38] Moreover, during this process many middle-class intellectuals, namely the well-educated group with abundant cultural capital ("especially those who have been trained in engineering and economics"), were made beneficiaries of the social transformation.[39]

The transformation of Chinese society has its own unique characteristics. On the one hand, reform in China has not undermined the fundamental political position or ruling status of the CCP. On the other hand, it has provided adequate space for the development of a private economy. What's more, the state has pushed the market transition forward at full speed since 1995. Through the interaction of state and market, Chinese reform birthed a typical twofold process: while the socialist state and its agents are actively advancing the market economy, mature market actors and adequate capital owners are equipping the former with an ever stronger capability to adjust the market and grab resources. (In the present financial crisis, the Chinese government invested as much as 4,000 billion yuan, which plainly manifests the increase in its economic capacity.)[40]

Consequently, in both the state and the market—in other words, both inside and outside the institution—a large middle class has developed. In this sense, the Chinese middle class is a political rearguard for two reasons. The first is that the state has not loosened its political grip, and the present political structure leaves the middle class little room for action; the second is that the state, through its advancement of the market economy, guarantees economic benefits to the middle class inside and outside the institution, which undermines its demands for political change.[41]

Political Prospects of China's Middle Class

One of the most frequently discussed issues concerning the Chinese middle class is its probable future development and potential political participation.[42] The discussion was dominated in the past decade by the opinion that such a class can function as a social stabilizer or, as it is put by some scholars, the vanguard of consumption and the rearguard of politics.[43] This opinion has recently come under attack, however.[44] Considering the dishonorable role played by the German middle class in the rise of fascist Germany, it is undeniable that the middle class is a social stabilizer only under certain conditions.[45] However, at least until now, the Chinese middle class has not shown any signs of political radicalism. On the contrary, it interacts with the state in a desirably active way.

In conclusion, China's unique social transformation, influenced as it has been by the continuity of the country's political institutions, is characterized by two distinct traits. First, it has not shaken the status of the CCP as a ruling party or undermined the original political institutions (although it has brought some changes to them). Such a transformation has enabled the intrainstitutional elite and their descendants to reproduce their privileged status. Second, as for the extrainstitutional elite, the market orientation of this transformation has bestowed upon them opportunities for prosperity via economic and educational efforts. As a matter of fact, the dual system of the economy has also driven stratum reproduction along the same dual track, which has guaranteed China's political stability throughout the three decades of social transformation.

Therefore there is little prospect of large-scale conflicts between the state and the middle class as a result of China's social transformation. Problems do exist, however, among the state, the interest groups, and the grass roots. Admittedly, three decades of economic reforms have brought China great economic achievements, but it remains doubtful whether these achievements can be shared broadly by the populace. Due to the unfairness of existing distributional policies, the absence of a social security system, and the inadequacy of government regulation and adjustments, recent years have witnessed many mass events, most of which were triggered by the demands of the lower class (migrant workers, landless peasants, laid-off workers, and the demolished-home owners).

Examples of such events include a clash with rubber farmers in Menglian (a county in Yunnan Province), a taxi strike in Chongqing (a city in Southwest China), and a riot by owners of demolished homes in Longnan (a city in Gansu Province). The Wengan turmoil of 2008 and the Tonghua Steel Company atrocity of 2009 are among the most shocking.[46] Although these clashes broke out between the lower class and those representing capital or local governments, the hostility and resentment of the populace are typically unleashed on middle-class people, such as civil servants, law implementers, managers, and professionals (doctors, judges, and teachers).

Conflicts keep rising between the populace and local governments, as well as between the populace and capitalist groups. The middle class is besieged by all of these conflicts, so whether it can remain unaffected is an open question. Therefore, for the Chinese middle class it may well be concluded that both its future development and the exercise of its political potential will be influenced by the seriousness of social conflicts, like those mentioned above, and the measures taken by the state to solve them. In this sense, chances are that the Chinese middle class has now been brought to a political crossroads.

Notes

1. According to the American historian John Smail, the middle class and its culture originated in the eighteenth century, shortly after the beginning of the Industrial Revolution. John Smail, *The Origins of Middle-Class Culture: Halifax, Yorkshire, 1660–1780* (Cornell University Press, 1994), p. 12.

2. Pamela M. Pilbeam, *The Middle Classes in Europe 1789–1914: France, Germany, Italy, and Russia* (London: Macmillan, 1990), pp. 3–4; and Yuqin Wu, ed., *Shijie Shi: Jindai Shi Bian* [The history of the modern world] (Beijing: Higher Education Press, 1992).

3. Karl Marx and Friedrich Engels, *Makesi Engesi Xuanji* [Selected works of Marx and Engels], vol. 1 (Beijing: People's Publishing House, 1972), p. 250.

4. C. Wright Mills, *White Collar: The American Middle Classes* (Oxford University Press, 1951), pp. 63–65.

5. Eduard Bernstein, *Evolutionary Socialism: A Criticism and Affirmation* (New York: Schocken Books, 1961), p. 48.

6. Daniel Bell, *The Coming of Post-Industrial Society* (New York: Basic Books, 1999), p. 17.

7. Xiaohong Zhou, "Globalization and Making of the Middle Classes: Theories and Realities," *Tianjin Shehui Kexue* [Tianjin social sciences], no. 4 (2007).

8. The annual per capita income gap between developed countries and developing countries increased from $5,700 in 1960 to $15,000 in 1993. UNDP, *Human Development Report* (Oxford University Press, 1996), pp. 2–3.

9. Joseph Nye, *Bound to Lead: The Changing Nature of American Power* (New York: Basic Books, 1990).

10. Will Hutton and Anthony Giddens, eds., *On the Edge: Living with Global Capitalism* (Beijing: Sanlian shudian, 2003), p. 140.

11. *Xizao* literally means "body washing" in the Chinese language. However, in Yang's book, it is a figurative expression of "brainwashing." The English translation of the book is titled *Baptism*. Jiang Yang, *Xizao* [Baptism] (Beijing: People's Literature Press, 2004).

12. William L. Parish, "Destratification in China," in *Class and Social Stratification in Post-Revolution China*, edited by J. Watson (Cambridge University Press, 1984).

13. An egalitarian salary system: Even this virtually egalitarian wage system was condemned and challenged during the Cultural Revolution. For instance, in 1975, one year before Mao's death, he attacked so-called "eight-level wages" implemented among workers, calling it "a bourgeois concept of the right." Measures to bridge salary gaps: Together with others, Mao himself also contributed to bridging salary gaps. For instance, when the "salary system" (*xinjinzhi*) was put into effect in 1956, Mao degraded his own salary from level I to level II, remarking sentimentally, "level I should be granted to the people; me, level II."

14. Cited in Tianyong Zhou, "Why Did We Choose to Reform and Open up Three Decades Ago," *Xuexi Shibao* [Study times], August 2008, p. 26.

15. According to statistics in the *Chinese Agriculture Yearbook* (1980) and the *Chinese Statistic Yearbook* (1981), the average annual salary of employees of state-run organiza-

tions was 446 yuan in 1952 and 529 yuan in 1980, with a gross increase of 18.6 percent throughout the twenty-eight years. In the countryside, under the collectivistic system, in 1953 (after collectivization was completed) the average income per capita was 38.8 yuan, and in 1975 (one year before Mao's death) the amount was 54.4 yuan, with a gross increase of 40.2 percent throughout the twenty-two years. Cited in Roderick MacFarquhar and John K. Fairbank, eds., *Jianqiao Zhonghua Renmin Gongheguo Shi: Zhongguo Geming Neibu De Geming* [Cambridge history of China: revolution within the Chinese revolution] (Beijing: Zhongguo shehui kexue chubanshe, 1992), p. 517.

16. Ivan Szelényi, "Social Inequalities in State Socialist Redistributive Economies," *International Journal of Comparative Sociology* 19 (1978): 63–68.

17. Ivan Szelényi and Eric Kostello, "The Market Transition Debate: Toward a Synthesis?" *American Journal of Sociology* 101 (1996): 1082–96.

18. Margaret Maurer-Fazio, "Earnings and Education in China's Transition to a Market Economy," *China Economic Review* 1 (1999); and Jingming Liu, "Expansion of Higher Education in China and Inequality in Entrance Opportunities: 1978–2003," *Shehui* [Society], no. 3 (2006).

19. Szelényi, "Social Inequalities in State Socialist Redistributive Economies."

20. Karl Polanyi, *The Great Transformation: The Political and Economic Origins of Our Time* (Boston: Beacon, 1944).

21. Victor Nee, "A Theory of Market Transition: From Redistribution to Market in State Socialism," *American Sociological Review*, 54 (1989): 663–81.

22. Ibid.

23. The former proposal is from Akos Rona-Tas, "The First Shall Be Last? Entrepreneurship and Communist Cadre in the Transition from Socialism," *American Journal of Sociology* 100 (1994): 40–69. The latter argument is from Yanjie Bain and John Logan, "Market Transition and the Persistence of Power: The Changing Stratification System in Urban China," *American Sociological Review* 61 (1996): 738–58.

24. Li Chunling, *Duanlie yu suipian—Dangdai Zhongguo shehuijieceng fenhua shizheng fenxi* [Cleavage and fragment: an empirical analysis of social stratification in contemporary China] (Beijing: Shehuikexue wenxian chubanshe [Social sciences academic press], 2005); and Zhou Xiaohong, ed., *Zhongguo zhongchan jieji diaocha* [Survey of the Chinese middle class] (Beijing: Shehuikexue wenxian chubanshe, 2005).

25. National Bureau of Statistics of China, *Zhongguo Tongji Nianjian* [China statistical yearbook] (Beijing: China Statistical Press, 1978; 1985; 1990; 1995; 2000; 2005).

26. Ning Wang, *Cong Kuxingzhe Dao Xiaofeizhe Shehui* [From the ascetic society to the consumer society] (Beijing: Shehuikexue wenxian chubanshe, 2009), p. 235.

27. Rongji Zhu, "Zhengfu Gongzuo Baogao" [Report on the work of the government], paper prepared for the third session of the Ninth National People's Congress, March 5, 2000 (Zhonggong Zhongyang Wenxian Yanjiushi) [Party literature research center of the CCP central committee], in *Shiwuda Yilai Zhongyao Wenxian Xuanbian* [A selection of important documents since the fifteenth national congress of the CCP], vol. 2 (Beijing: People's Publishing House, 2001), p. 1174.

28. Anding Li, "Three Decades of Reform and Opening Up: Millions of Private Cars Driven in Chinese Households," *Jingji Cankao Bao* [Economic information daily], October 3, 2008.

29. Take HP (hire purchase) as an example. The Chinese used to show disapproval of such payment mode, calling it "eating corn in the blade" (*yinchimaoliang*). In 2002 the proportion of the housing loan balance to the total of Chinese financial institutions was below 2 percent. However, in only one year the housing loan balance soared to 10 percent of the total loan balance of Chinese financial institutions.

30. Sheng Chen, "The Channel of Desires: A Content Analysis of Advertisements Published on Yangcheng Wanbao [Evening news] in Past Two Decades," master's thesis, Zhongshan University, 2003.

31. David Fraser, "Inventing Oasis, Luxury Housing Advertisements, and Reconfiguring Domestic Space in Shanghai," in Deborah Davis, ed., *The Consumer Revolution in Urban China* (University of California Press, 2000).

32. Mills, *White Collar*, p. 423.

33. Gil Eyal, Ivan Szelényi, and Eleanor Townsley, *Wuxu Zibenjia Dazao Ziben Zhuyi* [Making capitalism without capitalists] (Beijing: Shehuikexue wenxian chubanshe, 2008).

34. Hagen Koo, "The Social and Political Character of the Korean Middle Class," in *Discovery of the Middle Classes in East Asia*, edited by Hsin-Huang Michael Hsiao (Taipei: Institute of Ethnology, Academia Sinica, 1993).

35. Sangjin Han, "Political Trends of the South Korean Middle Classes," in *Bijiao Shiye Xia De Zhongchan Jieji Xingcheng* [Formation of the middle class in comparative perspective: process, influence, and socioeconomic consequences], edited by Li Chunling (Beijing: Shehuikexue wenxian chubanshe, 2009), p. 427.

36. Pavan K.Varma, *The Great Indian Middle Class* (New Delhi: Viking, 1998), p. 26; N. Rajaram, "The Middle Classes of India and China: Problems and Concerns," and Pradip Kumar Bose, "Rise of the Middle Classes in India and China," both in Li, ed., *Bijiao Shiye Xia De Zhongchan Jieji Xingchen*.

37. Lian Lian, "The Russian Middle Class under Transition," in Zhou Xiaohong, ed., *Quanqiu zhongchan jieji baogao* [Report on the world's middle classes] (Beijing: Social Sciences Academic Press, 2005), p. 310.

38. Eyal, Szelényi, and Townsley, *Wuxu Zibenjia Dazao Ziben Zhuyi*, p. 6.

39. Ibid., p. 42.

40. As far as the market is concerned, echoing the capitalists without capitalism of Russia and the capitalism without capitalists of Central Europe, China may be figured as a country with both capitalists and capitalism.

41. In today's China, the organizational actions of the middle class seldom target the fundamental problems in politics and social life but rather issues of group interest concerning specific actors. A common example of such issues is housing quality, while a special example of them is the Xiamen Paraxylene (PX) project, which could have been a potential source of pollution. See Yingfang Chen, "Ability of Action and System Restrict: Middle Class in the Urban Movement," *Shehuixue Yanjiu* [Sociological studies], no. 4 (2006).

42. Li Chunling, "Change in Theoretical Orientation and Concerns of Studies on the Chinese Middle Classes," in Li, ed., *Bijiao Shiye Xia De Zhongchan Jieji Xingcheng*.

43. David Goldman, "The New Middle Class," in *The Paradox of China's Post-Mao Reform*, edited by Merle Goldman and Roderick MacFarquhar (Harvard University Press, 1999); and Xiaohong Zhou, "The Middle Class: Why and How Can They Grow?" *Jiangsu Shehui Kexue* [Jiangsu social sciences], no. 6 (2002).

44. Yi Zhang, "Are Middle Classes a Stabilizer of the Society?" in Li, ed., *Bijiao Shiye Xia De Zhongchan Jieji Xingcheng*.

45. On the dishonorable role played by the German middle class in the rise of fascist Germany, see Xiaohong Zhou, ed., *Quanqiu Zhongchan Jieji Baogao*, pp. 9–10.

46. On June 28, 2008, in Wengan, a county in Guizhou Province, a middle-school girl student, named Li Shufen, was drowned. Eventually more than 20,000 people became involved in a protest, setting on fire several local public buildings, including those that housed the county government, the public security bureau, the civil administration bureau, and the financial bureau. The drowning of Li was only a superficial cause of the turmoil. The real cause was much more complex and fundamental: with the local underworld dominant in the contention for mineral resources, the populace had been deprived not only of

their economic interests but also of their sense of security. See Zifu Liu, *Xin Qunti Shijian Guan* [New point of collective behaviors and events] (Beijing: Xinhua Chubanshe, 2009).

On July 24, 2009, in Tonghua, a city in Jilin Province, a demonstration involving about 10,000 steelworkers broke out because of conflicts emerging in the process of enterprise restructuring. Believing their own interests at stake and losing confidence in government representatives, the workers of the Tonghua Steel Company initiated a mass protest, during which they battered to death a man named Chen Guojun, the newly designated general manager, who was from a privately run enterprise.

CHAPTER FIVE

The Chinese Middle Class and *Xiaokang* Society

LU HANLONG

China's economic reform and social transformation have drawn academic attention to the issue of the middle class. This attention can be attributed to several factors. First, the proportion of a given population that is middle class is often used as a barometer of that population's social equality. A healthy, sizable middle class is often regarded as the societal foundation for economic development and social stability. However, the concept of middle class should not be defined solely with respect to economic criteria, such as midlevel income, but should also include the group of citizens who creatively contribute to the formation of new lifestyles and a commercial culture. Moreover, the so-called middle class is often thought to be associated with social forces concerned about public affairs, political freedom, and human rights. The middle class is therefore a rather complex and subjective topic.

Chinese scholarly literature on the middle class frequently employs the terms *zhongjian jieceng* (middle stratum) and *zhongjian jieji*, both of which can be translated as *middle class*. Some Chinese scholars suggest that it would be more appropriate to call the middle class the middle-income group (*zhongdeng shouru qunti*).[1] Because the conventional understanding of middle class is mostly derived from the West, it is important to understand the formation of middle class in the West and

The author wishes to thank Yong Lu, research director of the Committee of 100, for her comments and assistance with translation.

the social structure associated with it. On the other hand, we must also consider the meaning of middle class based on Chinese characteristics and traditions.

Western Experiences in the Formation of the Middle Class

The Western experience of the formation of the middle class is largely a story of social productivity development. The middle-class social stratum of Western societies resulted from the self-regulation of production. The term is usually used to describe a social group between the upper class, or capitalist class, and the lower class, or working class.[2] Therefore, the reference point for placing the middle class (that is, between the upper and lower classes) is important. For Western academics, including Karl Marx, the lion's share of the middle class is composed of professionals, small business owners, and the self-employed. The group drifted in an area between capitalists and factory workers.

Gradually, however, corporate managers, administrative officers, and more and more white collars joined the middle class. This phenomenon has been verified repeatedly by sociological surveys. From the Marxist point of view, the middle class has its own class awareness. However, since the 1950s an increasing number of blue-collar workers in Western countries (traditionally regarded as the working class) self-identify as middle class. Research conducted in Hong Kong and Taiwan in the late 1990s also shows that 24.4 percent and 37.8 percent of workers, respectively, regard themselves as middle class.[3] It is therefore relatively unimportant to draw a definite line describing the middle class. Instead, it is important to understand the implications of what might be called the phenomenon of social middlization (*zhongchanhua*).

Social middlization indicates two fundamental changes in the economic development of modern societies. The first is that manpower, or human resources, has become a productivity factor beyond capital. The other is the importance of consumers to production. Consumers have become a driving force for economic activities, even surpassing direct producers in importance. Human rights have played a more important role than property rights, and consumers have become more important than producers. This is the simplest summary for describing the most significant social changes to take place in the twentieth century and is also the fundamental reason for the phenomenon of social middlization.[4]

In the course of the market economy transition of the twentieth century, the notion of capital was generalized.[5] Corresponding to the phenomenon of human power challenging capital in the economic domain, human rights are challenging property rights at the social level. One of the most important consequences of the social transformation of the twentieth century is the emergence of institutional arrangements for limiting capital returns and redistributing social wealth, which prioritize general human rights over private property rights. One such arrangement is to increase the public welfare and social security through federal taxation. Many countries have adopted progressive tax systems, including an income tax, property tax, and inheritance tax, in order to foster greater social responsibility among high-income earners and raise the costs of the transfer or centralization of property. At the same time, the so-called third sector, including NGOs and nonprofit organizations (NPOs), has rapidly developed and come to play an important role between the government and market in protecting and encouraging human rights. Social reallocation in the form of public consumption makes sure to satisfy public needs and realize human-oriented social development goals while also stimulating wealth through the market mechanism. The value created by human labor is reflected as modern consumption at the social level.

Paying attention to labor rights is also an important outcome of the twentieth-century human rights movement. As a result, the situation for the working class has greatly improved, and mass consumption has spread everywhere. With promotion from working-class parties, trade unions, and international labor organizations in many countries, direct producers' rights are extensively protected, labor's socioeconomic values are widely respected, and laborers are no longer being "deprived" by capital. They voice their interests through various channels, including party competition, democratic elections, group negotiations, and civil rights movements, and they are protected by the law to varying degrees. From the New Deal in the United States in the 1930s to the current welfare state systems in many developed nations since the 1960s, protecting basic human rights and sharing the benefits of social development are key elements. The values of labor are recognized by society through the self-regulation of the capitalist-producer relationship. The transition from capitalism to socialism is another important trend in some parts of the world. The working class sense of security, which comes from members' economic benefits and social security, makes them feel that they are members of the middle class. The diffusion of the middle class is exactly due to the ideology of protecting human rights. Once polarized societies are becoming flatter, and the size of the middle class is enlarging.

In fact, the diffusion of the middle class in the West has changed traditional views of class and social hierarchy. Social types within the broad spectrum of the middle class now seem to be more important and widespread than the more confrontational social classes of Marxist theory.[6] As a result, the middle class—those with midlevel incomes earned through their hard work and property rights—have become the foundation for social stability and the primary driver of consumption. Once most members in a given society identify themselves with this group, differences between their levels of wealth and incomes become less important. In addition to wealth and income, there are other factors that affect social inequality, including educational level, professional experience, occupational status, and human capital. The key to change inequality is not only to take from the rich and give to the poor (the Robin Hood approach) but also to develop policies that can provide equal opportunities. Therefore, in the West the middle class is the main body of a consumer society and the main supporter of social security and welfare policies. However, the boundaries of the middle class have blurred. Middle class has become a kind of ideology, which has the same meaning as *xiaokang* (a middlization society, also known as a moderately prosperous, or reasonably well-off, society) in China.[7]

These changes to Western society reveal that the middle class is a natural outcome of economic development but carries with it cultural and social meanings. From the perspective of economic growth, every society will form a *zhongjian jieji* that accords to occupational divisions and economic status. However, the key aspect of the concept of the middle class is its role in eliminating social inequality. This explanation tries to identify a balanced social relationship based on the economic deterministic theory of bipolar class conflicts (Marxism). It originated in America, which has long been considered a middle-class country. Therefore, the middle-class theory can be regarded as an American theory.[8] All other countries may share the same experience in their formation of a *zhongchan jieji* in terms of occupational divisions and economic status. However, every country develops a different process of middlization in its attempt to eliminate social inequality.

China's Economic Reform, Social Transformation, and Ideological Evolution

The renowned American scholar Phillip C. C. Huang has rightly pointed out that Chinese society can be explained neither by the American model, which assumes a majority middle class, nor by the Marxist model, which assumes a majority proletariat.[9]

In the first three decades since the establishment of the People's Republic of China (1949–78), under Maoism, efforts to construct a communist society caused China to go through a process of destratification, which went against history.[10] Landowners, rich peasants, and capitalists were destroyed, and private property and wealth were confiscated. Rural areas were forced to implement the People's Commune. Farming was conducted based on collectivism, and wealth was distributed collectively. Urban areas implemented the *danwei* (work unit) system, characterized by "high employment rates, low incomes, and high benefits." The entire country was categorized into two classes: the working class and the peasant class. Both commune members and urban workers (including intellectuals) became "average human beings," with little to differentiate them.[11]

Social differences within China were then very small compared to capitalist countries and most developing countries. Even among communist countries, China's social inequality was the least severe. In retrospect, however, the redistributive and egalitarian system came at a huge price for Chinese society in several ways:

—The separation of urban and rural economies and societies exacerbated the urban-rural gap, thereby impeding the development of modern industry and the process of urbanization.

—Central planning and the "big rice pot" system nearly eliminated the incentive for enterprises to make profits, making the economy highly inefficient and dysfunctional.

—Destratification was achieved through a series of mass political movements under the name of class struggles, which were disastrous for the nation.[12]

In the 1980s Deng Xiaoping launched a reform program in the spirit of pragmatism. The first step taken was to open up to the outside world and relax government control. China began to transform from the communist goal of establishing a utopian *datong* (commonwealth) society to the pragmatic approach of building "a moderate prosperous society."[13]

The policymaking process in China began to be more rational and scientific, a move away from Maoist idealism and totalitarianism. In the early 1990s China redoubled its efforts to move in the direction of establishing a market economy, further integrated into the global economic system, and made progress in establishing a legal system and modern government.[14] By the end of 2001 China joined the World Trade Organization (WTO). This was an important indication that China's market reform had achieved success and was irreversible. China has gradually abolished the "wartime system," entered into the "normal system," and integrated into the global socioeconomic system.[15] This also has had the effect of increasing the world's labor force by one-fourth and its consumers by one-fifth. In addition, China's social structure has begun to resemble modern social development and to be affected by the world economy, politics, and other civilizations. In sum, China's middle class is taking shape in the context of the global economy.[16]

Marketization and China's opening up have greatly energized the Chinese economy. The country's people also enjoy a degree of freedom never before experienced. China's GDP growth rate has maintained at 10 percent for a decade, and in 2008 China was the world's third-largest economy. The national average GDP per capita is $3,000. China contributes a full 20 percent to the world economy, second only to the United States. According to the criteria used by the World Bank, China has moved from a low-income country to a lower-middle-income country.[17] This economic development has greatly reduced poverty in China: according to some statistics, from 300 million poor before the reforms to 30 million today.[18] The economic structure has also experienced great changes. Although the government relaxed some of its policies during the 1980s, privately owned companies were still less than 100,000 in 1990 but surged to 6.59 million in 2008. The private economy now accounts for about 71 percent of the economy and creates 70 percent of national economic values. It also accounts for 40 percent of the third service sector.[19]

Chinese living standards have also dramatically improved. China has created an economic miracle. At the same time, however, social equality has worsened. The Gini index for urban and rural incomes has greatly increased, reaching .496 in 2006, which is an alarming level for market economic societies (table 5-1).[20] China's Gini index ranked ninety-three in the world and last among Asian countries.[21]

This kind of inequality is partly due to the market mechanism, but it is also due to the residual impact of the state's directed redistribution

TABLE 5-1. Income Distribution Measured by Gini Index, China, 1980–2006

Year	Gini index, total	Gini index, rural	Gini index, urban
1980	0.320	0.241	0.150
1990	0.348	0.307	0.247
2000	0.417	0.362	0.336
2001	0.459	0.365	0.358
2002	0.433	0.370	0.362
2003	0.439	0.376	0.373
2004	0.469	0.369	0.349
2005	0.470	0.375	0.350
2006	0.496	0.378	0.356

Source: National Bureau of Statistic of China. Also see http://baike.baidu.com/view/186.htm; www.stats.gov.cn/tjshugia/zggqgl/t20070411_402398097.htm; http://tieba.baidu.com/f?kz=287968635.

power.[22] Moreover, the consequences for inequality would be disastrous if the newly empowered groups were to use market logic to seek profits for themselves. With the interaction of these two unequal mechanisms, it is worrisome that the social gap is enlarging.

Against this backdrop, the government is focusing on fostering a Chinese middle class and creating a middle-income population. If we examine the development of China's middle class from a midlevel income perspective, we remember that at the beginning of reform Deng Xiaoping emphasized that China's modernization goal was to establish an overall well-off society (*zongti xiaokang shehui*). In the early 1980s he imagined that Chinese people's living standards should reach the well-off level by the end of twentieth century.[23] By the end of 2000 China's statistical indexes had all reached the midlevel. However, these indexes are national averages, which mask dramatic internal variations, especially the gaps between urban and rural areas, among regions, and between officials and civilians. Moreover, there are increasing differences among age groups and between the genders. However, according to Deng Xiaoping, *xiaokang* society means that the national income distribution should benefit everyone; in other words, in such a society there are no extremely rich people nor extremely poor people, but there is all around modest prosperity.[24]

China's strategic goal for the twenty-first century, then, should be to establish an all-around well-off society (*quanmian xiaokang shehui*) in order to realize modernization with Chinese characteristics. I would argue that it is not simply a change of words to substitute *all around (quanmian)* for *overall (zongti)*. This shift emphasizes that China must deal seriously with its internal structural differences. Shifting the focus from improving living standards to building a well-off society also indicates that China's modernization should extend from economic development to social development.

The Chinese government has proposed that building an all-around well-off society includes the following objectives:

—Doubling the GDP between 2000 and 2020

—Enhancing national power and international competitiveness

—Improving democracy, reforming the law, and governing by law

—Improving citizens' moral, educational, and health levels

—Building capacity and leveraging resources to promote harmonious development of both the people and nature.

In other words, the country should strengthen its economic, political, social, cultural, and ecological development.

Xiaokang is a complex cultural concept. In ancient China, *xiaokang* was associated with *datong*.[25] *Datong* in its classic traditional sense is an ideal society, where everything belongs to the public and everyone shares social resources and wealth. It is a harmonious society in which the world is fair. *Xiaokang,* on the other hand, is a realistic and competitive society, in which all members and their families own their private resources and live a life based on law and governed by elites.

Two cultural factors are particularly important in the study of China's social structure and middle class. First, the cultural appeal of *datong* is one of the fundamental reasons the Chinese people accepted communism and the socialist system. Deng Xiaoping proposed *xiaokang* in the 1980s because he recognized that Mao Zedong's *datong* ideal had been proven unrealistic. In the ideological lexicon of the Chinese Communist Party (CCP), Deng Xiaoping described China as being "at the initial stage of socialism development." Here, the relationship between *datong* and *xiaokang* is like the relationship between communism and the initial stage of socialism.

Second, *xiaokang* expresses a respect on the part of the state toward private rights. It recognizes that individuals and families have the right to pursue their interests. It is then easy to convince most Chinese people to pursue *xiaokang*. Its cultural resonance has helped the Chinese to better understand the initial stage of socialism. Over the past decades this pursuit has led the vast majority of Chinese individuals and their families to accept market principles, to contribute to the overall economic miracle, and to improve their lives. This record has led Chinese leaders to continue to use the concept of *xiaokang* into the twenty-first century and, moreover, to adopt the goal of pursuing a *xiaokang* society. That *xiaokang* has become a development model during China's modernization is a breakthrough for CCP ideology and marks a new period of Chinese history.[26] It also suggests that China's leaders have begun to realize that economic reform should be expanded to the social and political arenas.

Xiaokang is a social phenomenon characterized by midlevel incomes. Therefore, China's goal of building a *xiaokang* society will help to reduce social differences and encourage a massive middle class. To deal with increasing inequality, the CCP has proposed several ideas, from the Three Represents formulation proposed by Jiang Zeming in 2000 to scientific development and a harmonious society, concepts initiated by Hu Jintao in 2003–04. All these ideologies laid the foundation for China to develop a modern middle class, or what this chapter calls *xiaokang* classes (*xiaokang jieceng*). China's socialism is currently transforming from state socialism to what might be called an elite-led mass socialism, in which wealth shifts. And although the elite gets the largest share of the pie, the great majority of the populace also benefits.

In reality, all social systems create differences, and it is hard to determine what degree of inequality should be considered unacceptable. One basic requirement of a just society is to offer equal opportunities for social mobility. When opportunities are relatively equal, society can tolerate greater differences. The most unfair and unequal society is one in which hardworking people have few or no opportunities to change their lives for the better.[27] China's economic reforms have realized *xiaokang* by relaxing regulations and stimulating individual economic incentives, and most Chinese citizens have improved their lives. This approach to reform is incremental; that is, it benefits all levels through the wealth created by the market, while protecting and maintaining the direct beneficiaries of the old regime. This is the secret of the success of China's reforms.

Table 5-2 shows the results of two surveys, one conducted in Shanghai, China, and the other in Saint Petersburg, Russia. The survey results reflect how the two publics benefited from their reform programs. As the table shows, more members of the Chinese public benefited than members of the Russian public. The most benefited groups in China are

TABLE 5-2. Reform Programs, China and Russia, 2008: Who Won, Who Lost?

Shanghai, China[a]	Saint Petersburg, Russia[b]
Those who won	*Those who won*
—High-ranking officials	—High-ranking officials
—Senior corporate executives	—Senior corporate executives
—Entrepreneurs	—Entrepreneurs
—General officials and state employees	
—People with high levels of education	
—Scientists	
—Creative professionals	
Those who relatively won	*Those who relatively won*
—Qualified workers	—Qualified workers
	—Residents of large cities
	—Creative professionals
Those who neither won nor lost	*Those who neither won nor lost*
—Residents of large cities	—General officials and state employees
—Residents of small towns	—People with high levels of education
—Peasants	—Refined scholars
—Men	—Men
Those who relatively lost	*Those who relatively lost*
—Unqualified workers	—Unqualified workers
	—Residents of small towns
	—Scientists
Those who lost	*Those who lost*
—Refined scholars	—Peasants

Source: Surveys of Social Identity of Reforms (2008), jointly conducted by the Institute of Sociology, Shanghai Academy of Social Sciences, and the Institute of Sociology, Russian Academy of Sciences.
a. $N = 1,604$.
b. $N = 1,300$.

general officials and state employees, highly educated people, scientists, and creative people. A majority of these are middle class, which is quite different from the situation in Russia.

In addition, the results show that peasants, accounting for over half of the Chinese population, were also beneficiaries. The vast majority of unskilled workers (most of them employees of state-owned factories under the planned economy) were hurt by the reforms (as was the case in Russia), but their overall living conditions vastly improved. Therefore, most Chinese people shared in the benefits of the reforms. Some scholars point out that Russia lacks any semblance of a middle class.[28] In Russia's largest cities it is hard to find a medium-price restaurant. In China, however, low- to medium-price restaurants are everywhere. As Cui Zhi-yuan argues, China's *xiaokang* (getting rich together) can be interpreted as the "generalization of the petite bourgeois."[29] This echoes Phillips Huang's point: that Chinese society cannot be explained fully by either Marxist proletariat theory or American middle-class theory.[30]

The result of this win-win situation is that while inequality is on the rise, the level of tolerance for socioeconomic differences is also increasing. Market reforms have provided citizens of different classes the opportunity to seek a *xiaokang* life. In a society full of opportunities, people tend to think more about how to grasp them and better their lives than about what other people get and whether they acquired it fairly. This is also why some Chinese look down upon the *xiaokang* family, because a typical *xiaokang* family often only tends to its own affairs. The pursuit of a *xiaokang* life fits human nature, but at the same time it can cause people to lose a sense of social and public responsibility. Therefore, when we discuss the impact of the notion of middle class on occupational and economic structures in China, we must recognize that Chinese socialism is aimed at becoming a *xiaokang* society with a predominant *xiaokang* class. This process is characterized by "everyone caring about themselves," which may have bearing on the middle class's relation to the future of China. If the middle class has an unfair advantage in the market, then its social responsibility may be weakened.

The well-known Chinese scholar Liang Shuming published *Themes for Chinese Culture* immediately after the establishment of the PRC in 1949.[31] He argues that, historically, Chinese society had occupational divisions but no class divisions. This is a sensible argument if we examine China from a social theoretic perspective. When the CCP was founded in 1921 its mission was to be the champion of the working class. However, there were only 2 million industrial workers at that time, less than 5 percent of the national population.[32] They mainly worked in five industries: railroads, mining, ocean shipping, textiles, and ship manufacturing. In his *China Social Class Analysis*, Mao Zedong mentions the semiproletariats, which included most semi-self-employed peasants, poor peasants, small manufacturing workers, retail assistants, and street vendors. The semi-self-employed and poor peasants accounted for a vast majority of the rural population. After the CCP takeover in 1949, China quickly "finished" the socialist transformation of rural areas and private capitalists. By the end of 1956, while the entire country was celebrating the beginning of a new socialist era, statistics show that the working class was only 46.51 million people, or less than 8 percent of the national population of 600 million.[33]

Therefore, China's revolution was a poor people's revolution and great practice for the Chinese collective culture. Today we are interested in the middle class in China, which could be a new engine for China's progress. However, *xiaokang* is also generally accepted. Therefore, the impact of China's growing middle class should be measured by the country's changing social structure, not simply by its market power.

A Dynamic Model of Social Stratification in Reform-Era China

After China abandoned its class struggle ideology and implemented *gaige kaifang* (reform and opening up), Chinese society began to develop in a normal way. More and more, China's social structure tends to be classified by profession rather than class struggle. British scholar John Goldthrope's approach to classify according to occupation has been widely accepted. His studies show that in modern societies social stratification is mostly a categorizing phenomenon, rather than a system of hierarchy.[34] While occupation demonstrates people's status and their level of importance in economic activities, every occupation can provide a sense of achievement and value.

However, because China experienced socialism for over half a century, the social hierarchy idea is still not widespread.[35] For example, my survey with Bian Yanjie (conducted over the 1980s and 1990s) on social status perception shows that the majority of respondents believe they are of middle socioeconomic status (lower middle 25.5 percent, middle 41.2 percent, upper middle 7.7 percent). Moreover, some worker respondents chose upper class as their subjective status identity class. Apparently, this reflects the still lingering ideological premise that the "working class is the leading class."[36] Occupational status reflects the characteristics of certain social structures and is also related to people's living conditions and lifestyles. Research suggests that the perceptions of occupational prestige are about the same between developed and developing countries. A survey conducted in 1993 also shows that Chinese respondents rank occupational status in a similar way as people in developed countries, although at the time China was still reliant on a very strong planned economy.[37] After the establishment of the market economy, differences to China's social structure began to be reflected in the country's occupational structure and socioeconomic life conditions. Figure 5-1

FIGURE 5-1. The Five-Class Structure in China's Social Stratification[a]

(4) Rich class: capital owners, profiteers	(1) Elite class			(5) Poor class: the poor, the unemployed
	Party and government leaders	Business executives	Senior professionals	
	(2) Midlevel class (knowledge service groups)			
	Government and office clerks	White-collar workers in corporations	General professionals	
	(3) Direct producer class			
	Self-employed business owners	Manual/ semimanual workers	Retail service assistants/ self-employed workers	Peasants	
Small business owners				Unable to be self-sustainable
Rich	Well-off			Poor

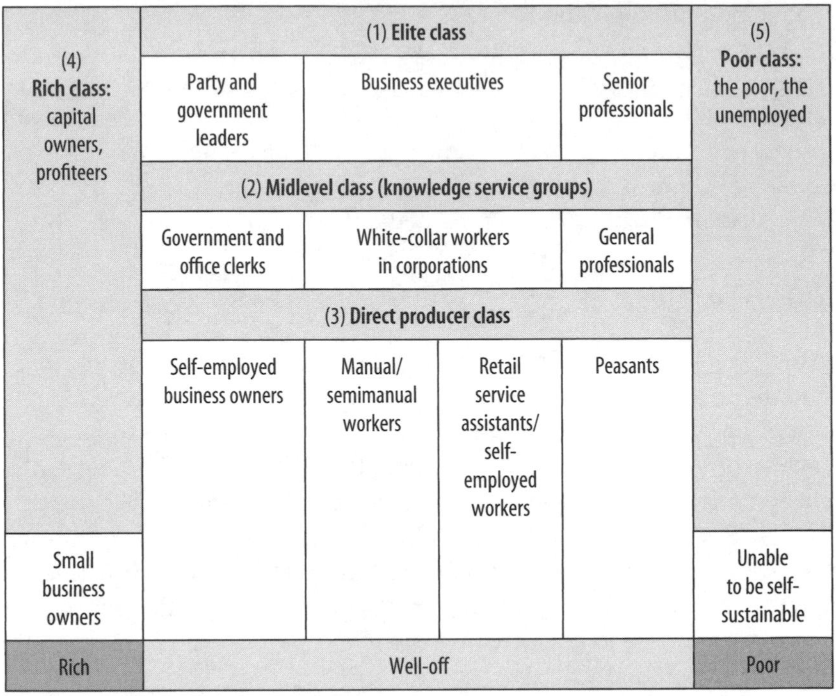

Source: Lu Hanlong, "Human Capital, Social Stratification, and Capacity of Development," paper prepared for the Sino-French conference Economic Development and Transformation of Human Capital, co-organized by the Institute of Sociology, Shanghai Academy of Social Sciences, and the French Center for Research on Contemporary China (Hong Kong), March 27–28, 2003. Also see *Research on Mao Zedong Thoughts and Deng Xiao Ping Theory journal* (Shanghai) 4 (2005): 61–66.

summarizes the current social structure in China, which includes five classes. It is a simplified picture of the stratification of Chinese society based on occupations and life conditions.

The three classes in the center of the figure—the elite class, the midlevel class, and the direct producer class—are composed of professionals. They are mainly employees or the self-employed. China's efforts to build an all-around *xiaokang* society are making these three classes enter the middle stratum.

The elite class includes mid- to high-level senior officials in Communist Party and government departments (above the director level; this may vary in different areas), senior business executives in corporations and enterprises, and senior professionals and intellectuals who have specialized skills. To put it simply, the elite class includes political, corporate, and intellectual (skilled) elites. After years of reform of the human resources system, most people in the elite class are well educated and have specialized skills. They have not only acquired relatively high levels of human capital but have also achieved social success through their professional experiences. They usually boast a high income and a stable job. The three groups in this class participate in the same prestigious human resources market. There is mobility among the three groups, and there are personal relationships, such as being fellow alumni, sharing a hometown, and being colleagues. They are considered elites because they have significant impact on the local society, with their knowledge, personal characters, career achievements, and lifestyles.

The midlevel class is composed of knowledge service groups and is in between the elite class and the direct producer class. As shown in the figure, it includes general clerks in the government and business and skilled technical professionals. They have received at least a midlevel education and some professional training. They often play important roles in the job market. Their occupations are mostly management and knowledge service. They have relatively high levels of human capital, and their incomes are higher and more stable than those of direct producers. In summary, they are the middle-stratum class, in between the elites and the direct producers. Some of them are outstanding individuals from the direct producer class. The class as a whole is usually considered the main body of the middle class.

The direct producer class includes manual or semimanual laborers in agriculture, business, and high-tech industries.[38] This class includes the majority of the Chinese population. We probably do not need to differentiate peasants from workers in towns and cities, because there is currently little difference in their living conditions, although there are some differences in their occupational prestige, income, and education. So many peasants have left the countryside to work in towns and cities that urban residents now account for nearly half of China's population. According to the latest statistics, peasant workers account for 58 percent of all employees in the industry sector; and 68 percent of manufacturing employees and almost 80 percent of construction and mining employees are peasant workers. In the service sector, which includes wholesale, retail, and the restaurant business, peasant workers account for more than 52 percent. According to a report from the McKinsey Global Institute, the urban population in China will be nearly 1 billion in 2025.[39] If we look at it from the occupational market structure perspective, in every area we can find direct producer counterparts for the elite and midlevel classes. The direct producer class is obviously different from the other two classes in the center, but it shares similar status and life conditions. For example, the social differences between a peasant and a county head are similar to the social differences between a supermarket cashier and an urban district head.

The fourth category is the rich class, which relies primarily on capital returns. In China, the mixed economic ownership system will continue for a long period. Within this system private capital ownership is protected, which therefore creates a group of profiteers. It includes large and medium-size business owners, large stockholders, profiteers in the stock market, property owners (making profits through real estate), and people making huge profits through trust funds and bank interests. We consider these people an independent class because they share three distinguishing features: they do not directly take part in production or service, they enjoy relatively high incomes, and they are not necessarily well educated.

We list class 4 on the figure separate from classes 1, 2, and 3 because it is a new group to have emerged in the course of China's reform and opening up. It came from the other three classes. For class 4, grasping opportunities, cultivating connections, and managing effectively are the keys to success. We include small business owners in class 4, as well. In the current situation, small business owners directly manage their companies and are somewhat similar to the midlevel class (class 2). However, their life goals mostly include acquiring a large return on capital and increasing the scale of their businesses. Class 2 people generally hope that they will become their own boss rather than work for someone else. Therefore, some of them have the chance to join the rich class through their own efforts.

The fifth class includes disadvantaged social groups who are either long-term unemployed or have no realistic hope of being self-sustainable. This class is also listed next to the three main classes, which means that it can be derived from them (especially from the direct producer class). The poor class is made up of those who are not able to be independent in society for physical reasons or because they are psychologically unprepared for a rapidly changing world. It is also possible that they are not able to survive in a system of market competition. Society should provide welfare support to those who are seriously disabled, mentally ill, or elderly, and those who lack stable incomes.[40] These groups, with few exceptions, constitute the poor population of China.

We should note that the five-class structure shown in figure 5-1 is a formula for demonstrating inequality but does not necessarily represent a hierarchy. It shows that the five classes have differences in income, social prestige, power, and education. People within the same class tend to identify with one another, have frequent contact, and enjoy similar life opportunities. We can find the five-class structure of inequality both in the remote countryside and in prosperous metropolitan areas such as Beijing, Shanghai, and Shenzhen, with various degrees of inequality. Needless to say, the three classes in between the rich and the poor constitute the middle class, or *xiaokang*. This trend has been evident in many developed countries, but the process has just begun in China.

Notably, human capital is playing an increasingly important role in the formation of China's middle class. Educational levels and work experience have become the key factors in determining the social status and mobility of the three classes in the middle. China's censuses and many research projects have established the correlation between occupation and education. Therefore, China is paying more and more attention to education and equal access to education. This is an important reason for the emergence of China's middle class. In terms of living conditions, the income gaps and consumer behavior gaps are deepening in China. For example, to buy a lunch in Shanghai, the choices range from an average lunch box for $1–$3, to a fast-food combination for $3–$8, to a business meal for $10–$15. While a fast food combo at $3 to $8 is regarded as a typical lunch for white-collar workers, those who eat from lunch boxes and those who eat business meals also consider themselves to be leading a *xiaokang* lifestyle. Chinese people at all levels have improved living conditions for themselves, and they want to further improve their living conditions and realize their own *xiaokang* lifestyle. This phase of Chinese development is a time full of hope and anxiety.

A Middle Class without Class Consciousness

There are several views regarding the definition, scope, and size of the middle class. Terms such as *old middle class, new middle class, marginal middle class,* and so on, referring to a wide spectrum of middle classes, are all supported by the evidence. The estimated size of China's middle class ranges widely, from 4.1 percent to 32.9 percent.[41] However, it seems that a unified middle-class standard, or class self-identification, has not yet formed in China.

The theory of the middle class originated in a society with two classes. However, in today's world, social classes are interdependent and cooperate with one another. I would argue that the middle class is one that directly creates wealth, is less vulnerable to social unrest, and greatly benefits from a competitive yet cooperative society. Its members would be a mainstream body of rational citizens, working professionally and living in substantial *xiaokang*. In a differentiated and unequal society, such as China, capital and power are the two resources most worth pursuing. In addition, knowledge is a resource closely linked to both capital and power. Knowledge can be considered human capital and material capital, and it can also counter brute power. The group in between pure capital and power is composed of the private enterprise class (midsize and small business owners) and the knowledge service class. These two groups are the core part of China's middle class (or core middle class). Their lifestyle has a symbolic meaning and sets the tone for the *xiaokang* lifestyle. The following passages examine the lifestyles and social attitudes of these two groups.

Middle and small business owners (private entrepreneurs) are an emerging class in China since reform and opening up. In the past, under the planned economy, the majority of this group was marginalized. It included capable yet unnoticed peasants, heads of village and country businesses, unemployed urban dwellers, the restless staff of state-owned enterprises, and even a few former prisoners or people reeducated through labor. They had a lower social status at the time, but this prepared them to acquire an entrepreneurial spirit similar to the Protestant ethic in the West. They work very hard and are good managers. Their success stimulated the second wave of so-called "diving into the ocean of business" among entrepreneurs. In the mid-1990s, the sudden dissolution of certain state enterprises prompted a few capable former employees to found their own companies. Having had plenty of production and management experience, they were able to channel their social and political resources into these new pursuits.

The Fifteenth National Congress of the CCP in 1998 formally recognized that the private economy is a component of the socialist market economy (the PRC's temporary policy on private companies, issued in 1988, defines the private economy as a "complimentary component" of the public economy). The social and political status of private entrepreneurs has improved markedly, and the private economy plays an increasingly important role in the national economy. Even though private enterprises still face many challenges—such as attracting financing, improving product technology, and implementing corporate social responsibility—in the past three decades of reform and opening up, China has nurtured a spirit of entrepreneurship and a generation of new entrepreneurs. This appears to be social progress. The success of private entrepreneurs directly challenges state industries to demonstrate the advantage of their public nature.

However, China's private entrepreneurs have not yet developed their own social identity. They are still in the stage of capital accumulation and have yet to walk onto the sociopolitical stage. In a survey conducted by the All-China Federation of Industry and Commerce in 2004, the top consideration for Chinese entrepreneurs was "talking about business when we are in the business and trying our best to build a good company."[42] The second consideration was "building a good personal and corporate image in daily life and becoming a responsible and respectable person in the society." They care about their reputation as private entrepreneurs and wish to coexist harmoniously with other groups in society. They are generally eager to become members of the People's Congress or Political Consultative Conference and aspire to be portrayed positively in the media. Finally, they attempt to maintain a good relationship with the Communist Party and government officials and often wish to join the party.

The survey also indicates that when private entrepreneurs ranked their status from 1 to 10 (1 being the highest, 10 the lowest), they rank their economic status at 4.58, their social status at 5.01, and their political status at 5.19.[43] Therefore, they generally believe their overall status is around the midlevel, political status is lower than social status, and social status is lower than economic status. Their self-evaluation of political status reflects their desire to participate in politics. This desire is based on achieving *xiaokang* and then getting rich. Very few are able to obtain political positions and become members of the People's Congress or the Political Consultative Conference. In general, they can achieve higher social status and receive benefits by being assimilated into the existing political framework. Most private entrepreneurs, then, are apolitical and concentrate on showing off their wealth and planning how to leave it to their children.

The knowledge service class is much more complex than the private entrepreneur class because it is in the midlevel of human capital. Knowledge-based skills, and their capital value, can change with individuals, events, and times. Therefore, it is hard to provide specific definitions. Like the elite class, the knowledge service class can be categorized into the realms of politics, economics, and society and the ways they contribute to politics, business, and social sectors. The class usually includes general clerks in Communist Party and government departments, management and technical staffs (including technicians) in corporations, and staff in various social organizations that specialize in certain fields, such as education, health care, technology, and culture. In short, this class includes what we normally call general public service people, including office affairs staff, white-collar employees in corporations, and professionals. While their power and capital place them in the middle, they have different characteristics and functions as part of the middle class.

China's public service workforce encompasses various subgroups, not only leaders of party-state departments and cadres at various levels but also senior management and leaders of state social enterprises at the elite level. Their power is highly institutionalized. Membership in China's elite club, so to speak, is mostly determined by the party organization department (party-managed cadres). It is a power selection process from the top to the bottom, rather than a structure of authority emanating from the bottom up. This is the main reason that China's elite class is not widely identifiable by the public. For example, although recent senior officials, state enterprises managers, and leaders of social organizations (university presidents, hospital heads, science academy directors, chairman of Red Cross) have high educational levels, educational background has little to do with their work. These leaders are mostly technocrats, with a few who specialize in politics, law, and management. Some cadres' advanced degrees were granted through executive studies after they were already confirmed as leaders, and it is hard for normal statistical analysis to detect such a phenomenon, thereby creating the false impression that when they became elites they had high levels of human capital.

In recent years the requirements for general public service jobs have become stricter. In August 1993 China issued the "State Public Service People Temporary Policy," requiring that "hiring public service people below the director level in state administrative departments should use open examinations and strict screening and select under the principle of both good education and good virtue" (item 13). After an open examination and strict screening for hiring public service people, it became increasingly difficult to find work in the public service field. The admission rate in 2009 for national public service positions was 78:1, which is much more selective than college admissions. Therefore, the overall quality of people working in public service is improving. Of course, they still must rely on connections to reach the elite level, but for more ordinary promotions the government management system is increasingly based on law and acknowledgment of merit. Although the professional capabilities and social attitudes of these workers are important for future sociopolitical changes in China, a majority of them still lack an understanding of service and believe that "being a leader means being an aristocrat." The popularity of public service jobs is mostly because the jobs are considered stable, well paid, and of high status, thus qualifying as a *xiaokang* job.

Similar to those working in public service are professionals, including doctors, lawyers, and accountants. These people have benefited relatively well from the market reforms and are generally regarded as middle class. However, because of the market transition and the lack of financial government support for education, health care, and legal services, these professionals sometimes have ethical issues. For example, schools over-charge parents, doctors receive extra bonuses from patients, and judges and lawyers abuse their power. While these social phenomena sometimes lead to public resentment, the professionals complain that the lack of government support and commitment forces their hand. Some scholars argue that these professionals have become the scapegoats for the disadvantaged groups to vent their grievances.[44]

Since China entered the WTO corporations have been conducting reforms of their governance structures, blurring the borders of their various ownerships. The reforms also introduced the market management system to social organizations, and the social sector continues to develop. White-collar workers are increasing rapidly. Many multinational corporations have entered China's market, along with international NGOs and NPOs. The open economy has introduced modern management skills to China, and Chinese white-collar workers have become increasingly international and modern.

The family background of these white-collar workers influences their work and life. In multinational corporations and direct foreign investment corporations, China's local white-collar workers usually occupy the middle and lower levels. Senior management positions are hard to attain. For general positions, there are obvious differences between local city people and transplants from other towns and villages. Out-of-town people lack the family and network basis that urbanites have, but they are more willing to work extra hours. They have to work harder than urbanites to settle down in the city. They sometimes make jokes that they are just like migrant workers.

Job stability and stress are enduring problems for white-collar workers. Housing, education, and health care are the three most difficult problems for white-collar workers. There is always a distance between their material desires and what they can get from society. However, they have higher incomes than average workers. In general, they enjoy comfortable material lives. Having a house, a car, and a stable job is generally regarded as the criteria for middle-class life. In addition, these workers are mostly young (they are often called "little white collars").

The life tastes of these white-collar workers are those of the petty bourgeoisie. The group is considered "slaves" to consumer goods and is the main population that indulges in travel and entertainment. In 1993 China's travel department started *Vogue* magazine. Since 1998 the department has acquired copyrights from U.S. fashion magazines such as *Cosmopolitan*, *Esquire*, and *Harper's Bazaar*. It now publishes more than seventeen magazines, with a readership of more than 10 million, most of them white-collar employees.[45] More and more of these people are using credit cards issued by China Merchants Bank, living in apartments built by the Wanke real estate group, using China Eastern Airlines for traveling, booking hotels on Xiecheng Net, shopping on taobao.com, watching Hong Kong-based Phoenix TV, and reading *Vogue* magazine.

China's white collars are generally not passionate about politics. This is not because they lack the enthusiasm to participate in public life. In 2005 they were the main force in the demonstrations against Japan becoming a permanent member of the United Nations Security Council. In 2008 many white-collar employees volunteered at the Beijing Olympics and participated in the relief efforts for the Sichuan earthquake.

A major theme of China's middle class and its effect on Chinese society is that its use of consumer rights affects political rights. This effect may not be on purpose, but it has great implications. For example, after the commercialization of housing, the Real Estate Ownership Committee began to speak for residential management, posing a direct challenge to the government's control of residential committees. In another example, the very popular idol TV programs created by Hunan Satellite TV in 2005, *Super Girls* and *Happy Girls,* encourage grassroots efforts, fair competition, and a spirit of cooperation and friendship. In addition, through the programs' well-designed selection procedure, the audience—most of them belonging to the white-collar middle class—participate in a democratic process. This particular kind of participation is of course only useful for self-interest or entertainment, but it can create political sensitivity. For example, the government often regards the Real Estate Ownership Committee as a troublemaker and approaches it with caution. The mainstream official media look down on programs like *Super Girls* and sometimes even block the selected star.

The Internet, of course, is an important arena for the white-collar class's socialization and expression. The number of Internet users in China has been increasing significantly in recent years: the 2008 survey report shows that China had 253 million Internet users at that time. The absolute size is already the largest in the world, although general coverage (19 percent of China's population) has not yet reached the world average.[46] Besides college students, white-collar workers make up the majority of China's Internet users. According to a survey conducted in Shanghai, the main activities that young white-collar employees pursue on the Internet are researching, browsing news and information, and sending e-mails.[47] In recent years, a lot of major news information has been first distributed through the Internet. The Internet is becoming a major channel for distributing information and mobilizing behind public causes. Blogs, in particular, provide a public platform for white-collar employees to exchange their views and life experiences, make friends, and vent complaints.

Sometimes the Internet can even affect public policy and social management. For example, an information technology manager named Wang Qing in a company in Nanyang, Henan, collected information from the Internet and filed petitions with 181 government administrative departments asking them to be transparent in seven areas important to the public, including three major government expenditures: banquets, consumption, and travel.[48] However, his behavior was regarded as espionage, and he even saw "strangers" strolling in front of his home. He was very candid during an interview and commented that he only wanted to know how taxpayers' money was being spent.

Members of the middle class are the main taxpayers under the market system, underwriting government spending. While not yet widely accepted in China, this concept of government "consumers" is beginning to emerge. The role of the Internet in promoting government reforms has begun to increase. Of course, as a new medium in the knowledge economy era, the Internet is not only a supervisor and monitor of use to the government but also a possible creator of violent opinions. Therefore, it would be a significant development if the middle class, especially its white-collar members, could play an important role in directing the trajectory of the web because it is the most important production force in the knowledge economy. Moreover, the government is increasingly tightening its control over the Internet. The mainstream official media (which is controlled by the Communist Party) have become a major creator of web content, trying to "direct" a "healthy" development of the Internet that fits the party's will and promotes political stability. Therefore, it remains to be seen how large an impact the white-collar, middle-class population can have on Internet activities. The so-called angry youth and nationalistic sentiment, as demonstrated on the Internet since the late 1990s, is a case in point. It has both constructive and destructive potential.[49]

Conclusion

As China is a developing nation in the midst of ongoing industrialization, it is important to identify an appropriate referential context regarding economic capital and political power when studying its middle class. It must be measured by level of social stratification and public perception or toleration of social inequality. Researchers should also pay close attention to the impact of the Chinese *xiaokang* idea and the legacies of socialism on grassroots society.

During the process of market reforms and continued integration into the global system, it is without doubt that middle-class occupational groups are rapidly growing in China. However, the precise nature of the Chinese middle class, its characteristics, and its future trajectory, remain unclear. The following three observations are critically important for assessing this future.

First, China's state-owned enterprises are still strong, and the Communist Party dominates them. Midsize and small privately run businesses are developing, but they have to compete with the powerful state-owned enterprises. In addition, among successful entrepreneurs are many Communist Party members, some of them former high-ranking cadres. Their present successes are more or less related to their success in using their political power to embezzle resources under the state-planning system. Moreover, their success also continuously depends on their social network in the Communist bureaucratic system and the capital generated therein. Therefore, up to now they have mainly cared about their own survival and *xiaokang*. It is hard for private entrepreneurs to develop an independent character or identity.

Second, along with economic growth and globalization, the management and professional service sectors of the economy are rapidly developing. Human resources capital is increasingly important vis-à-vis political capital and monetary capital. However, professionalism in China is still in a nascent stage. What might be called professional authority, professional order, and professional ethics are far from well established. The pattern is that, on the business spectrum, the higher the level, the more bureaucratic it is. On the other end of the spectrum, lower levels tend to be more commercial. The result is that although management skills and professionalism are important, they are still wanting. Management and professional service people have a strong desire to pursue a *xiaokang* life relatively lacking in public awareness and social responsibility. They have become the focal point of concern over social inequality and have become the target for grievances.

Third, by being situated between political power and monetary capital, the Chinese middle class is an emblem of *xiaokang* culture. On the one hand, the notion of *xiaokang* is helpful in promoting individualism and family values. It also helps promote the pursuit of a comfortable standard of living and a fair society. On the other hand, the notion of *xiaokang* prompts people to be acquisitive and materialistic and indifferent to the public good. We might call this *xiaokang* dualism. It is particularly obvious among young middle-class people.

Xiaokang culture, based on the Confucian notion of *zhongyong* (the golden mean), dovetails with Communist *datong* idealism. It has served as the cultural foundation for China's market economic reforms. Completely achieving the goal of a *xiaokang* society means to form a vast middle class. It can also catalyze the Chinese government into working harder to reduce, if not eliminate, social inequalities. In recent years China has faced unprecedented challenges regarding education, housing, social welfare, urban community, civil organizations, and other areas of the public weal. The success of China's aspiration to build an all-around *xiaokang* society may depend on whether the middle class can connect to the vaster direct producers and, at the same time, effectively engage in dialogues with monetary capital and political power.

At present, however, China is still a developing country and the majority of its people still serve as direct producers (workers, peasants, and low-end service people). Everyone hopes to achieve *xiaokang* life, but they do not have a collective class-consciousness. In other words, the Chinese middle class has achieved midlevel wealth but does not yet demonstrate a clear middle-class awareness.

Notes

1. The Sixteenth National Congress of the CCP in 2002 proposed the goal of "expanding the proportion of middle-income people." The National Development and Reform Commission and the Macroeconomic Research Institute have sponsored a research project on increasing the middle-income population.

2. Hegel and Marx were among the first scholars to use the concept of a middle class, but they used different frames of reference. Hegel's use of middle class (*mittelklasse*) made reference to nobles and civilians of the bourgeoisie, which was initially used by Engels as well. Four German words have been translated into *middle class* in English: *Bürger* (citizens), *Bürgerliche* (citizens, property owners), *Bürgertum* (citizen class), and *Mittelstand* (middle class).

3. Hsin-Huang Michael Hsiao and P. S. Wan, "The Collective Sociopolitical Awareness of Middle Classes in Taiwan, Hong Kong, and Singapore," in *Market, Class, and Politics in Changing Chinese Societies*, edited by S. K. Lau and others (Chinese University of Hong Kong Press, 2000), pp. 459–92.

4. Deborah Davis and Lu Hanlong, "Consumer Culture and Consumer Revolution," *Social Studies*, no. 5 (2001): 117–18.

5. The concept of human capital was first proposed by Jacob Mincer in his doctoral dissertation, "Human Capital Investment and Personal Income Distribution" (Columbia University, 1957); and Jacob Mincer, "Investment in Human Capital and Personal Income Distribution," *Journal of Political Economy* 66, no. 4 (1958): 281–302. Also see Theodore W. Schultz, "Capital Formation by Education," *Journal of Political Economy* 68 (1960): 571.

6. Robert A. Nisbet, "The Decline and Fall of Social Class," *Pacific Sociological Review* 2, no. 1 (1969): 119–29; and John H. Goldthrope and others, *The Affluent Workers*, vol. 3 (Cambridge University Press, 1968).

7. *Xiaokang*: the literal translation is moderate prosperity or well-off; that is, a relatively comfortable life. See *The Liji* 27–28 (1885). Also see Deborah Davis, ed., *The Consumer Revolution in Urban China* (University of California Press, 2000), p. 124.

8. The classic literatures on the middle class are by American scholars, including C. Wright Mills, *White Collar: The American Middle Classes* (Oxford University Press, 1951).

9. Phillip C. C. Huang, "Chinese Petit-Bourgeois and Zhongjian Jieceng: A Social Paradox" (Chinese), *China Rural Studies*, no. 6 (2008).

10. William L. Parish, "Destratification in China," in *Class and Social Stratification in Post-Revolution China*, edited by James L. Watson (Cambridge University Press, 1984), pp. 84–120.

11. Lu Hanlong, "Consumer Revolution and Consumer Autonomy," preface to the Chinese version of Deborah Davis, ed., *The Consumer Revolution in Urban China* (Shanghai Academy of Social Sciences Press, 2003), p. 11.

12. Roderick MacFarquhar and John King Fairbank, *The Cambridge History of China*, vols. 14, 15 (Cambridge University Press, 1991); Roderick MacFarquhar and John King Fairbank, *China Watch* (Harvard University Press, 1987).

13. *Datong*: the literal translation is *commonwealth*, which means getting rich together. It is a rose-colored egalitarianism. See Lu Hanlong, "To Be Relatively Comfortable in an Egalitarian Society," in Davis, ed., *The Consumer Revolution in Urban China*, pp. 124–41.

14. In 1992 the Fourteenth National Congress of the CCP confirmed that China's reform goal was to establish a socialist market economic system. In 1993 China issued *Corporate Law*, which indicated the beginning of an economic system based on market and law.

15. Lu Hanlong, "Property Rights and Organization Culture Transition in China," paper prepared for the Conference on Chinese Capitalism, Cornell University, April 22–24, 2007.

16. Zhou Xiaohong, "The Shaping of Globalization and Middle Class: Theory and Reality," in *Comparative Studies on the Formation of Middle Class*, edited by Li Chunling (Beijing: Social Sciences Articles Press, April 2009).

17. According to data released by the World Bank in 2008, the new categorizing standard for gross national income (GNI) is as follows: $975 and lower is low income; $976 to $3,855 is lower middle income; $3,856 to $11,905 is upper middle income; higher than $11,906 is high income. In 2008 China's average GNI was $2,770. National Statistics Bureau, September 11, 2009 (www.stats.gov.cn/tjzs/t20090911_402586498.htm).

18. There are statistical differences with regard to the poverty population. According to the World Bank report (April 8, 2009), the 2005 data show that China still had 254 million people living below the international poverty line ($1.25 per person per day), based on purchasing power. But China's statistics show that the poverty population has been reduced to one-tenth of the 1978 level over the past thirty years.

19. PRC National Administrative Bureau of Industries and Commerce, *Statistics: 2008 Report on the Overall Development of the National Market* (March 20, 2009).

20. It is generally considered that social income equality level reaches an alarming level when the Gini index is above 0.4. The Gini index for most developed countries is around 0.3.

21. *Gini Index, 15 Inequality Incomes and Expenditures*, Human Development Report 2007–2008 (United Nations Development Program, 2008).

22. John Logan and Yanjie Bian, "Inequalities in Access of Community Resource in Chinese Cities," *Social Force* 72 (1993): 555–76.

23. Deng Xiaoping initially spoke of *xiaokang* during his meeting with former premier of Japan Masayoshi Ohira (1979). According to data from the National Statistics Bureau, the average GDP for Chinese was $800 in 2000. The Engel indexes for urban and rural resident consumption are 40 percent and 50 percent, respectively. Overall, the goal of *xiaokang* is realized. Reports by Xinhua, September 20, 2000.

24. Deng Xiaoping, "Achieving the Unification of All Chinese Ethnicities," June 18, 1986, in *Selected Works of Deng Xiaoping*, vol. 3 (Beijing: People's Press, 2009).

25. The discussions about *datong* and *xiaokang* were quoted from archives in Xihan Dynasty, *The Liji: Liyun Chapter*. For related research, see Chen Zhengyan, *Studies on Ancient China's Datong Idea* (Hong Kong: China Books Press, 1988).

26. Lu Hanlong, "Well-Off Society: Modern Development Model with Chinese Characteristics," in *Well-Off Society from Goal to Model*, edited by Yin Jizuo (Shanghai Academy of Social Sciences Press, 2004), pp. 1–18.

27. Victor Nee found that the market mechanism would reduce the inequality. See Victor Nee, "A Theory of Market Transition from Redistribution to Market in State Socialism," *American Sociological Review* 54 (1989): 663–81.

28. Cui Zhiyuan, "How to Understand Today's China: Interpreting *Xiaokang* Society," *Reading*, no. 3 (2004).

29. Cui Zhiyuan, "A Petite Bourgeoisie Manifesto," in *The Chinese Model of Modern Development*, edited by Tian Yucao (New York: Routledge Taylors/Francis Group, 2005), pp. 157–73.

30. Phillip C. C. Huang, "Chinese Petit-Bourgeois and Zhongjian Jieceng." The major reason for Huang's argument is that China includes a large majority of peasants and small capitalists.

31. Liang Shuming, *Themes for Chinese Culture* (Beijing: Luming Books Press, 1949).

32. The number was mentioned in Mao Zedong's *China Social Class Analysis* (December 1, 1925).

33. Zhang Wei, "Sixty Years of China's Working Class," special report for *Outlook Weekly* 18 (2009).

34. John H. Goldthrope, *Social Mobility and Class Structure in Modern Britain* (Oxford: Clarendon Press, 1987).

35. Historically China has favored the "officials first" idea of the communist system; this idea continues today. Therefore, the hierarchy system is still in effect in the government.

36. Yanjie Bian and Lu Hanlong, "Economic Reform and Socioeconomic Inequality: Status Perceptions in Shanghai," in *In Search of a Chinese Road Towards Modernization*, edited by Hu Jixuan and others (Lampeter, Ceredigion, Wales: Edwin Mellen Press, 1996), pp. 109–42.

37. Nan Lin and Xie Wen, "Occupational Prestige in Urban China," *American Journal of Sociology* 4 (1993): 793–832.

38. Note that in the emerging information and high-tech industries there is a lot of manual or semimanual work that requires proficiency, including typing, scanning, copy-editing, computer repairing, and biological lab assistance. The work environment for these employees is different from traditional agriculture, manufacturing, and business industries, but the knowledge level and their roles in the economic chain are similar to traditional workers and service assistants.

39. Jonathan Woetzel and others, *Preparing for China's Urban Billion* (McKinsey Global Institute, 2008).

40. China currently has welfare plans for "three not-haves" in urban areas and "five protections" in rural areas. However, welfare for the disabled and the mentally ill lacks public support. According to the census, the number of these people is more than 50 million, affecting more than 150 million family members.

41. Li Cunling ed., *The Formation of Middle Class in a Comparative Perspective: Process, Influence, and Socioeconomic Consequences* (Beijing: Social Sciences Academic Press), pp. 53–54.

42. Sixth National Private Enterprises Survey, conducted by the All-China Federation of Industry and Commerce in 2004 ($N = 2,952$). Also see Wang Xiaoyan, *The Political Participation of Private Business Owners* (Beijing: Social Sciences Academic Press, 2006), p. 33.

43. This is based on raw data from the survey.

44. Sun Liping, "Preventing the Middle Class from Becoming Scapegoats," *Economic Observer*, May 8, 2007.

45. Zong He, "He Uses 'Fashion' to Define a Class," *East Morning Post*, August 22, 2009, p. 11. The co-copyrights for famous Western fashion magazines, such as *Vogue*, *Cosmopolitan*, and *Esquire*, directly use the magazine names (the Chinese translations are *Fashion Women* and *Fashion Men*). Ten percent of the contents are from the English-language edition, and the rest is created in China.

46. The world average was around 22 percent by the end of 2007. China Internet Network Information Center (CNNIC). The update survey shows that by the end of June

2010, Internet users in China reached to 420 million. The general coverage is 31.8 percent of China's population. See *Twenty-Sixth Survey Report,* CNNIC.

47. This survey of young people was conducted by Shanghai Union League. See Shanghai Union League, ed., *Open-Up, Reforms, and Modern Youth: 2008 Youth Development Report.*

48. *Henan Business News,* August 3, 2009.

49. Wang Jun, "Analyzing Nationalism on Chinese Internet," *World Economy and Politics* 2 (2006).

PART III

Issues of Definition: Compositional Differences and Internal Divisions in China's Middle Class

Characterizing China's Middle Class: Heterogeneous Composition and Multiple Identities

LI CHUNLING

Since the beginning of this century a social group with higher levels of income, education, and occupational prestige has been emerging in Chinese cities. In the popular media it is known as the middle class. Even though people dispute the exact definition of the term *middle class,* there is no doubt that this group exists in China and is expanding quickly.

The group has attracted increasing attention from the public, business leaders, and policymakers, as well as from researchers in sociology, economics, and politics. Sociologists especially have had a long-standing interest in the group and have discussed many aspects of it. However, because this middle class is newly emerging and its boundaries and attributes are unclear, these discussions provide very different, sometimes contradictory, descriptions of China's middle class. This chapter, based on data from several national surveys, attempts to present a general profile of China's middle class by elucidating the competing Chinese definitions and assessments of the middle class.

Based on a general description of China's middle class, the chapter deals with two important issues concerning the Chinese middle class. The first is definitional. The existing literature on the Chinese middle class contains various definitions of middle class, which provide very

I am indebted to Yinsheng Li for his research assistance. I would also like to thank Jordan Lee and Robert O'Brien for suggesting ways in which to clarify the chapter.

different pictures.[1] These disparate understandings of China's middle class reflect the uncertain condition and ambiguous boundary of this newly emerging group. Further, this definitional confusion has seriously disrupted research into China's middle class. The chapter distinguishes the various definitions, illustrates their exact meanings, and proposes a sociological concept of the middle class that can be accepted by a consensus of Chinese sociologists.

The second issue involves a sociological debate over the Chinese middle class. Is the Chinese middle class only a statistical category based on certain criteria such as income, education, and occupation? Or is it a real class in the sociological sense with sociopolitical homogeneities? This would mean that its members have developed a coherent identity, a class culture, and sociopolitical attitudes and values and have probably taken some class action. By defining the components of the Chinese middle class and describing its characteristics, this chapter examines the homogeneities or heterogeneities of the alleged middle class so as to assess the possibility of the formation of a true class.

This study is based on data from a variety of sources, including the national census (1982, 1990, and 2000) and a 1 percent population survey (2005) conducted by the National Bureau of Statistics; a household income survey of Chinese cities (1988, 1995, and 2002) conducted by the Institute of Economics at the Chinese Academy of Social Sciences; a national survey on social structure change (2001); the China General Social Survey (2006); and the Beijing Middle Class Survey (2007) carried out by the Institute of Sociology at the Chinese Academy of Social Sciences.[2]

Emergence of the Middle Class

Discussion of the middle class in the Chinese academic community first began in the mid-1980s, but few people considered it to be a truly existing entity until the beginning of this century.[3] Only over the last decade have most Chinese people begun to recognize the emergence of a middle class, owing to the cumulative effects of the fast socioeconomic development of recent decades.

Economic and Income Growth

Stable and fast economic growth over the last few decades provided a foundation for the emergence of China's middle class. Figure 6-1

FIGURE 6-1. GDP and Family Income, China, 1978–2006

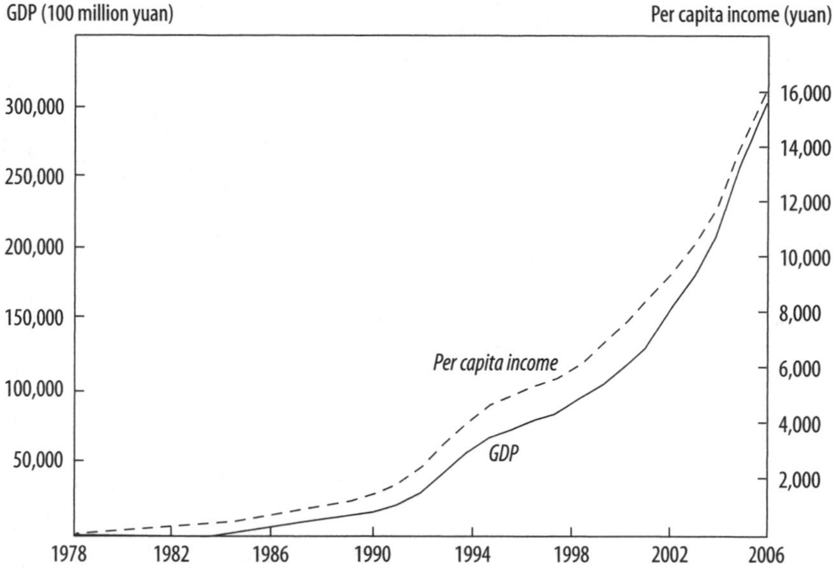

GDP (100 million yuan)   Per capita income (yuan)

Source: Statistics Bureau of China, *Zhongguo Tongji Nianjian* [China statistical yearbook] (Beijing: China Statistics Press, 2009), p. 53.

illustrates China's GDP growth and income growth in recent decades. In 1978 China's GDP was only 364.5 billion Chinese yuan, but it reached 21,087.1 billion yuan by 2006, nearly fifty-eight times the 1978 figure. The average annual economic growth over these twenty-eight years was more than 13 percent. Alongside this fast economic growth, per capita family income also increased significantly. In 1978 per capita family income for urban areas was only 342.4 yuan, but by 2006 it had increased to 11,759.5 yuan, a thirty-four-fold increase.

Urbanization

Urban expansion and an increase in the urban population afforded favorable conditions for the emergence of a middle class in China. In 1978 there were only 193 cities in China. By 2007 the number had increased to 651. The urban population increased steadily during this period, as shown in figure 6-2. It increased from 173 million in 1978 to 594 million in 2007. However, the rural population in China still remains very large. Today about 55 percent of the population lives in rural areas. Most of this group have low incomes, low educational

FIGURE 6-2. Urbanization of China, 1978–2007

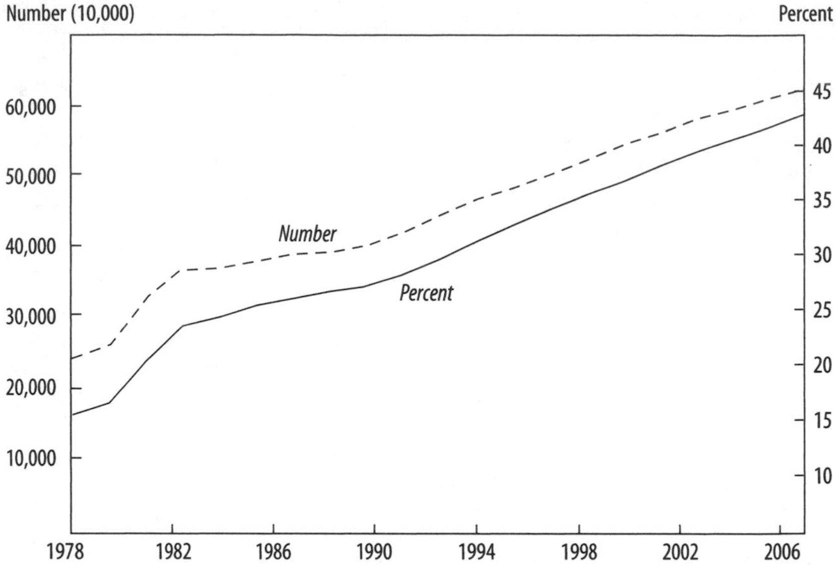

Number (10,000)   Percent

Source: Bureau of China, *Zhongguo Tongji Nianjian* [China statistical yearbook] (Beijing: China Statistics Press, 2009), p. 95.

levels, and disadvantageous living conditions. Because of such a huge rural population, the middle class is still a small proportion of China's national population despite growing very quickly in cities.

Higher Education and White-Collar Jobs

The expansion of higher education and the growth in white-collar jobs have also stimulated the rise of the middle class in China. Figure 6-3 shows the trend of expansion of higher education in China between 1990 and 2007. Since 1999, when the government announced a policy to vastly expand higher education enrollment, the number of college students and the opportunities to pursue higher education have increased sharply. Over the five years following 1999, the number of college students increased four times, and the opportunity to pursue higher education almost doubled.

At the same time, the number of persons with higher education among the population has been increasing significantly. In the 1980s, among the population over eighteen years old, only about 1 percent nationwide and 11 percent in cities had received higher education. In 2005

FIGURE 6-3. College Students Before and After 1999 Policy Change, China, 1990–2007

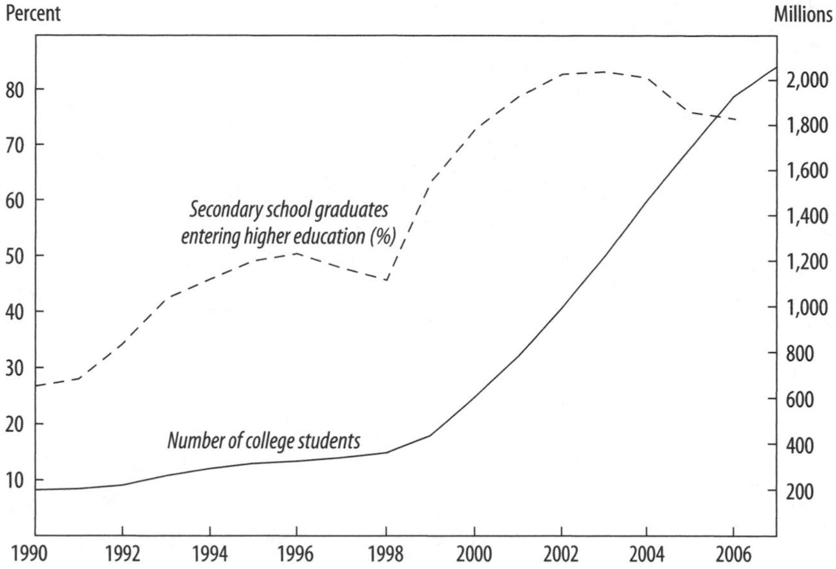

Source: Bureau of China, *Zhongguo Tongji Nianjian* [China statistical yearbook] (Beijing: China Statistics Press, 2009), p. 651.

the percentages had increased to 7 percent and 17 percent, respectively. Moreover, China has witnessed a corresponding increase in the number of white-collar employees. In 1982 about 7 percent of the national population over eighteen years old held white-collar jobs. By 2005 this percentage had increased to 12 percent. Figure 6-4 shows the increase of the population with white-collar jobs and higher education. These people constitute the major part of the new middle class, and expansion of this group implies an enlargement of the middle class.

Definitions of Middle Class

Who makes up the middle class? What is the actual definition of *middle class*? These are highly controversial questions in China. There are many different and conflicting definitions. Usually four criteria are used to define the middle class in China. The first is income. A member of the middle class should be a person with relatively high and stable income. The second criterion is occupation. A member of the middle class should be a person holding a professional or managerial job. The third criterion

FIGURE 6-4. Number of Persons with White-Collar Occupations and Higher Education, China, 1980–2010

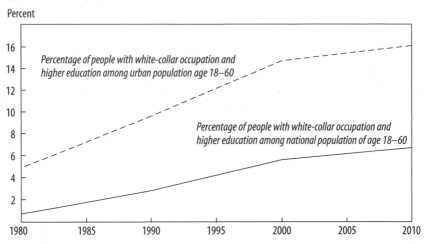

Percent

Source: Census data of 1982, 1990, 2000; 1 Percent Population Sample Survey of 2005.

is education. A middle-class person should have received a higher education. The fourth criterion is consumption. A member of the middle class should be able to afford a comfortable lifestyle and should enjoy a relatively high standard of living.

At present, there are at least three major perspectives of the middle class in China: the public image of the middle class, the government's official description of the middle class, and sociologists' definition of the middle class. Each version highlights one or two of the criteria mentioned above. Different concepts of middle class can denote quite diverse social groups. In addition, there is large disparity in the size of China's middle class depending on the definition.

Public Image of the Middle Class

The public image of the middle class was initially derived from advertisements for real estate, automobiles, and other expensive commodities.[4] These advertisements, printed in newspapers and magazines, featured beautiful pictures of these commodities and the people enjoying them. Expensive commodities thereby became a symbol of the middle class. TV dramas, novels, and other mass culture phenomena further elaborated and enriched this image of the middle class predicated upon the consumer behaviors and lifestyles of the rich.[5] This contributed to a Chinese impression of the middle class consisting of business people, managers, and intellectual elites with very high incomes and consumer habits.

By this definition, consumption is the decisive criterion to distinguish the middle class from other classes. The members of the middle class are expected to be able to afford large houses, luxurious cars, and other expensive goods. They wear name-brand suits, work in modern office buildings, go abroad for holidays, invest in the stock market, and send their children to study abroad. This image of the middle class created by the public media and businesspeople has become the dominant definition of middle class in China.

It is very different from the concept of middle class in Western societies, where middle class usually means regular people in the middle of the socioeconomic hierarchy. In China, however, the middle class is considered by the public to be a special group with quite high socioeconomic status. By the sociological definition, discussed below, these people belong to the upper class or upper middle class. According to the public definition, the size of China's middle class is very small, usually thought to be less than 8 percent of the total population.

Government's Definition of the Middle Class

China's authorities have long disliked the term *middle class* for political reasons. The term was almost prohibited from formal publications during the 1990s. This was because the term had acquired political connotations when it was referenced by liberal scholars during the 1980s. At the time, middle class mainly denoted private entrepreneurs, a newly emerging social group in the 1980s, which developed quickly in the 1990s. Liberal intellectuals thought the growth of this social group would bring about political changes, such as political democratization. Accordingly, authorities have continued to deem the middle class a threat to the existing political system.[6]

In the late 1990s a few influential sociologists argued that a large middle class was one of the general characteristics of modern societies and could be a stable force, not an unstable force, for society.[7] These sociological arguments have become more prevalent since the late 1990s and seem to have gradually convinced Chinese policymakers that a rising middle class could be a positive element in maintaining political stability. These sociologists especially stressed that the growth of the middle class would help to reduce the income gap, which the state considered to be one of Chinese society's most serious problems, one that could even trigger political unrest.

Although political leaders seemed to partly accept this view, they have remained distrustful of the middle class. They continue to prefer the term *middle-income stratum* to the term *middle class*. In November 2002 Jiang Zemin, then secretary general of the Chinese Communist Party (CCP), stated in his report to the Sixteenth National Party Congress that "expanding the middle-level-income group" was one of the policy targets of the government. Some analysts considered this statement to be a signal that the government would make an effort to develop the middle class, or middle stratum, as defined by the income criterion. But the question arose, How much income makes a person a member of middle class? It is difficult to reach a consensus view. Some believe that if a person has an annual income of $5,000 or higher he or she is a member of the middle class. But others think $30,000 should be the baseline. This is clearly a huge difference. Large disparities of income between urban and rural areas and among regions have made it impossible to arrive at a nationwide standard of income to define the middle class.

Sociological Concept of the Middle Class

Chinese sociologists tend to favor a definition of middle class different from the public and government definitions. They think the public's image of the middle class only describes the upper stratum of the middle class. Ordinary members of the middle class in China do not have high incomes and costly consumption habits; they cannot afford luxurious cars and large houses. Sociologists think that the concept of a middle stratum defined by income alone differs essentially from the concept of a middle class. They point out that such an income group includes diverse people, for whom it is impossible to develop a shared class identity, class consciousness, or class culture.

Thus sociologists usually define the middle class based on occupational classification and employment status. Following the traditional class theories of neo-Marxism and neo-Weberism, sociologists tend to highlight the divisions between employers and employees, as well as those between manual labor and mental labor.[8] The distinction between white-collar workers and blue-collar workers is believed to be a critical division between the middle class and the working class.[9]

Property ownership is another important criterion to divide the middle class from the upper, capitalist, class. Large owners fall in the upper class. Midsize or small property owners and self-employed people are middle class. The problem for sociologists is that if all white-collar workers are members of the middle class then the size of China's middle class should be very large. Indeed, it would encompass up to 30 percent of the total national population. Obviously, nobody believes the Chinese middle class is this large. Furthermore, most white-collar workers deny that they belong to the middle class because they feel they are far from experiencing the socioeconomic conditions a member of the middle class should enjoy.

To solve this problem, sociologists propose adding another criterion—such as education, income, or consumption—to the definition of the middle class. However, different criteria adopted by different sociologists result in huge disparities in the estimated size of the middle class, which ranges from 4 percent to 25 percent. Corresponding percentages of the urban middle class range from 8 percent to 50 percent.[10]

Composition of the Middle Class

Although Chinese sociologists have not arrived at a consistent definition of the middle class, most of them think that it includes various subclasses. They find the subclasses of the middle class to have differing economic conditions, living standards, and sociopolitical attitudes. Some sociologists prefer the plural, middle *classes,* to the singular, middle class. They argue that distinguishing different middle classes is as important as distinguishing the middle class from the working class or from the upper class. When talking about the economic conditions and sociopolitical characteristics of the middle class, we should be mindful of these differences. A framework outlining the heterogeneous composition of the Chinese middle class will help to clarify its characteristics.

Four Subclasses of the Middle Class

There are four social groups that most Chinese sociologists consider to be the major components of China's middle class.[11] One group is private entrepreneurs, whom some refer to as the capitalist class.[12] Another group consists of professionals, managers, and government officials; it is sometimes called the new middle class. A third group, known as the old middle class, is composed of small employers, small business owners, and the self-employed. The fourth group, or the marginal middle class, consists of low-wage white-collar and other workers.

TABLE 6-1. Four Subclasses of the Middle Class, Two Classification Methods

Goldthorpe's middle-class subclasses	Author's middle-class subclasses for China
I Higher grade professionals	1. Capitalists (employers with 20 or more employees)
II Lower grade professionals	2. New middle class
IVa Small employers with employees	3. Old middle class
IVb Small employers without employees	
IIIa Routine nonmanual employees	4. Marginal middle class
IIIb Personal service workers	
V Technicians and supervisors	*Addendum*
VIa Skilled workers	Working class
VIIa Semiskilled and nonskilled workers	
IVc Farmers	Farmers/farm labor
VIIb Agricultural workers	

Source: John H. Goldthorpe, *Social Mobility and Class Structure in Modern Britain* (Oxford: Clarendon Press, 1987); also see Hsin-Huang Michael Hisao, ed., *East Asian Middle Classes in Comparative Perspective* (Taipei: Institute of Ethnology, Academia Sinica, 1999).

This classification of the middle classes is derived from John H. Goldthorpe's class scheme, one of the most popular classifications of contemporary societies.[13] Table 6-1 illustrates the similarities between Goldthorpe's class scheme and that of the author.

The new middle class is the subclass of the middle class that might have the most significant influence on the direction of sociopolitical change in China. Its members occupy important positions in the social, political, and economic fields. Their institutional affiliations provide them with access to policymakers and elite groups. However, the institutional segmentation between the public and private sectors continues to divide the new middle class into two parts. One part is the group of officials, professionals, and managers in the public sector, including state-owned enterprises, governmental organizations, and institutions funded or controlled by the government. Another part are professionals and managers in the private sector. The public sector group differs from its counterpart in the private sector in terms of its social, economic, and political characteristics.

Private entrepreneurs, or the capitalist class, are active actors in the economic field and might become political actors in the future. Actually, this group has been increasing in its political influence, especially at the local level. But its influence has been restrained by the central government, because top CCP leaders remain suspicious of this group's political loyalty. Both sociologists and the public consider the new middle class and the capitalist class to be typical of China's middle class.

As for the other two subclasses—old middle class and the marginal middle class— although most of the public does not think they count as middle class, sociologists deem them to exist between the working class and the typical middle class. Although the socioeconomic status of these two groups appears to be lower than that of the new middle class and the capitalist class, some of their members will probably join the new middle class or the capitalist class in the future. The marginal middle class is considered to be younger than other middle-class subclasses and to have higher educational attainment, more democratic consciousness, and greater capacity for political participation. This subclass has lately gained a high profile in the media, mass culture, and on the Internet. Its members are the most active participants in grassroots social movements and display much more political liberalism than the new middle class. Some analysts imply that China's middle-class mainstream, a relatively politically conservative group, might change when these young people become more dominant.

Growth of the Middle Class

Table 6-2 lists the percentages of the urban population aged sixteen to sixty composing the four subclasses of the middle class— the capitalist class, the new middle class, the old middle class, and the marginal middle class—over the period 1982 to 2006. Even though the different methods of classification used across these various data sets mean that one cannot reach a perfectly precise estimation, the overall growth trend is clearly reflected in these data.[14]

From 1982 to 2006 the new middle class increased by roughly 10 percentage points. The old middle class was almost nonexistent in the early 1980s but by 2006 was nearly 20 percent. This fast growth of the old middle class is one of the most significant characteristics of the development of the Chinese middle class. In most Western countries expansion of the new middle class has been followed by a diminution of the old middle class. In Mainland China, however, the old middle class and new middle class have expanded simultaneously. Actually, the size of the old middle class in many midsize and small cities, especially towns, is larger than that of the new middle class.

The marginal middle class has also developed quite rapidly. It increased by about 10 percentage points during this period. The capitalist class first emerged during this period, but its percentage remains small compared to other classes. The rise of the middle class has resulted in a

TABLE 6-2. Share of the Four Subclasses of the Middle Class, Urban China, 1982–2006

Percent

Year	Capitalist	New middle	Old middle	Marginal middle	[Working][a]
1982	0.0	13.9	0.1	19.7	66.3
1988	0.1	17.2	3.2	23.8	55.7
1990	0.5	19.6	2.2	19.9	57.8
1995	0.6	22.1	5.5	26.6	45.2
2001	1.5	16.6	10.3	33.2	38.4
2002	1.1	23.6	11.1	29.1	35.1
2005	1.6	21.0	9.7	31.4	36.3
2006	0.6	18.8	19.6	25.4	35.7

Source: Percentages for 1982, 1990, and 2005 are calculated from census data and the 1 percent population survey. Percentages for 1988, 1995, and 2002 are derived from the household income survey of Chinese cities. Percentages for 2001 and 2006 are from the national survey of social structure change and the China General Social Survey (2006); these data include cities and towns (with a lower percentage of new middle class and a higher percentage of old middle class). Others are data of cities.

a. The working class is not, according to the criteria, part of the middle class.

significant shrinking of the working class, which decreased by about 30 percentage points over the period.

The middle class accounted for about 64 percent of the urban population in 2006. If we exclude about 5 percent of the elite class and add in the farmer population in rural areas, the urban middle class is about 60 percent; the country's middle class is about 30 percent. However, if we use the more strict definition of middle class—that composed of only the new middle class and the capitalist class—the percentages of middle class among the urban population and the national population are, respectively, about 18 percent and 9 percent.[15]

Distribution of the Middle Class

As a newly rising class, China's middle class has some distinct characteristics in terms of its demography and socioeconomic situation.

Sector and Occupation. China's middle class has been emerging amid tremendous changes in the country's economic conditions, namely, the transformation from a planned economy to a market economy. Previously almost all employees worked in the public sector. In 1982, for instance, all members of the new middle class and the marginal middle class worked in the public sector, and the capitalist class and old middle

TABLE 6-3. Share of the Middle Class, Two Subclasses and Occupation, Urban China, 1982–2006

Percent

	New middle class		Marginal middle class		New middle class		
	Public	Private	Public	Private	Professional	Administrator	Manager
1982	100.0	0.0	100.0	0.0	...	...	...
1988	99.6	0.4	99.6	0.6	70.2	21.7	8.1
1995	99.1	0.9	98.2	1.8	63.7	12.3	23.9
2002	87.0	13.0	76.9	23.1	66.7	12.2	21.1
2006	62.2	37.8	54.2	45.8	71.2	10.3	18.5

Source: See table 6-2.

class did not exist (table 6-3). As a result of the economic marketization since the 1980s, the capitalist class and the old middle class began to appear in the private sector. They became the new elements of the middle class.

At the same time, members of the new middle class and the marginal middle class gradually transferred into the private sector. However, most of the new middle class (62.2 percent) and the marginal middle class (54.2 percent) still work in the public sector. This has resulted in an important feature of China's middle class: public sector members have a closer relationship with the state than private sector members because they depend on the state for their socioeconomic well-being. Some of them, especially the upper new middle class, exert strong influences on policymaking and public opinion.

Professionals, managers, and administrators of governmental organizations are the three major occupations of the new middle class, but their respective percentages have changed over time. Professionals have accounted for the highest percentage consistently, although the exact figures have fluctuated. The percentage of administrators, however, has declined over time. The percentage of managers was the lowest of the new middle class in 1988, increased sharply in 1995, but has since decreased slightly. Its sharp increase in 1995 might be the result of the rapid development of township and village enterprises in the late 1980s and early 1990s. The slight decrease after 1995 was probably due to the shrinkage of these enterprises as well as to the bankruptcy of many state-owned enterprises.

T A B L E   6 - 4 .   Years of Education and Age, Middle-Class Subclasses, China, 1988–2006

Years

Subclasses of the middle class	Education				Age			
	1988	1995	2002	2006	1988	1995	2002	2006
Capitalist	5.8	9.7	10.9	13.8	41.5	41.2	43.1	35.1
New middle	10.4	12.3	13.2	14.9	42.5	45.6	41.6	36.0
Old middle	6.4	8.1	9.2	9.8	35.1	35.6	39.7	38.3
Marginal middle	8.8	10.6	12.2	13.9	38.7	40.7	39.0	34.9
[Working][a]	7.3	8.5	9.4	9.3	34.8	41.9	40.7	37.25

Source: See table 6-2.
a. The working class is not, according to the criteria, part of the middle class.

Education, Age, and Sex. China witnessed a fast expansion of secondary and tertiary education over the years 1988 to 2006. As a result, the educational level of the middle class also advanced rapidly (table 6-4). The years of schooling for the capitalist middle class increased by 8.0 years, that of the new middle class by 4.5 years, that of the old middle class by 3.4 years, and that of the marginal middle class by 5.1 years. In 1988 the capitalists and old middle class had the lowest educational levels, even below that of the working class. By 2006, however, years of schooling increased greatly, especially those of the capitalist class, which was also the class with most economic capital and least cultural capital in the 1980s and 1990s. Now this class possesses not only economic capital but also cultural capital. Its average educational level is now close to that of new middle class.

As for age, the middle class seems to become younger over time, and this is especially true of the capitalist class, the new middle class, and the marginal middle class. The average ages of these three groups decreased by about six years from 1988 to 2006. One plausible reason is that China's overall workforce has become younger as the age of retirement has lowered and a tide of new labor has arrived. However, the average age of the old middle class increased by about three years over the same period.

The sex ratio of the middle class seems to have remained fairly stable over time. Men have consistently been more represented than women across all subsets of the middle class. For example, the female percentage of the new middle class was 38.2 percent in 1988, 39.9 percent in 1995,

TABLE 6-5. Share of Middle-Class Subclasses by Gender, China, 2006

Percent

	Capitalist	New middle			Old middle	Marginal middle	[Working]ᵃ
		Professional	Administrator	Manager			
Male	86.7	48.0	87.5	82.1	55.0	57.9	55.9
Female	13.3	52.0	12.5	17.9	45.0	42.1	44.1

Source: National Survey of Social Structure Change (2001).
a. The working class is not, according to the criteria, part of the middle class.

38.4 percent in 2002, and 38.8 percent in 2006. That suggests that it is difficult to overcome the advantaged place of men in the middle class.

The figures in table 6-5 show that classes with more power or authority tend to have higher percentages of men. Indeed, the capitalist class has the highest percentage of men (86.7 percent). The gender gap in the new middle class is much smaller than that of the capitalist class because a higher percentage of females than males are professionals. More than 60 percent of the new middle class is male. However, the new middle class groups with most authority (administrators and managers) have higher percentages of men than groups with less authority (professional).

Multiple Identities of the Middle Class

Simultaneously possessing multiple status identities is a very important feature of China's middle class. Very few people self-identify as members of the middle class. According to the Beijing Middle Class Survey of 2007, among all subsets of Chinese middle classes—the capitalist class, the new middle class, the old middle class, and the marginal middle class—only about 10 percent admit that they are members of the middle class. Furthermore, less than one-third of the new middle class identify themselves as members of the middle class. Indeed, most of the people whom sociologists define as middle class deny this status. However, they are more willing to admit being members of a middle stratum.[16] In their view, middle class and middle stratum are different concepts. As mentioned earlier, members of the middle class are supposed to be persons with high levels of income and consumption. And members of the middle stratum are thought of as regular people and not at the extremes of wealth or poverty.

TABLE 6-6. Share of Middle-Class Subclasses by Father's Class and First Occupation, China, 2001

Percent

	Capitalist	New middle	Old middle	Marginal middle	[Working][a]	[Farmer][a]
Father's class						
Capitalist	0.0	7.9	3.8	8.5	21.1	58.7
New middle	0.0	37.1	2.5	7.7	21.0	31.7
Old middle	0.0	6.6	10.0	2.7	24.3	56.4
Marginal middle	0.0	16.5	1.5	22.6	26.5	32.9
[Working][a]	0.0	7.1	2.2	4.8	39.5	46.4
First occupation						
Capitalist	2.1	9.1	8.5	13.2	31.2	35.9
New middle	0.9	37.1	2.0	23.7	22.2	14.1
Old middle	0.0	5.1	5.9	5.2	47.6	36.1
Marginal middle	0.0	15.8	1.5	28.2	34.7	19.8
[Working][a]	0.0	1.8	1.8	7.2	49.8	39.4

Source: National Survey of Social Structure Change (2001).
a. The working class and the farmer class are not, according to the criteria, part of the middle class.

Family Class Background and First Occupation

As the first generation of the middle class, today's group includes heterogeneous family backgrounds and diversified occupational experiences, which prevent an identical status identity or class-consciousness from forming. Table 6-6 lists middle-class members by their fathers' class background and by their first jobs.[17] Most members of the capitalist class and the old middle class are from modest family backgrounds. Nearly 60 percent of these two classes came from farmer families and more than 20 percent from working-class families. Although many of the new middle class come from better-off family backgrounds, more than half of them are from farmer and working-class families. Of the middle class as a whole, 65.3 percent are from farmer or working-class backgrounds.

Most members of the middle class (56.5 percent) held blue-collar jobs before they entered the middle class. The first jobs of two-thirds of the capitalist class (67.1 percent) were as farmers or blue-collar workers. For the old middle class, the share is 83.7 percent. For the marginal middle class, 54.5 percent were farmers or blue-collar workers before they became middle class. Even among the new middle class, 36.3 percent were first farmers or blue-collar workers.

These two factors—heterogeneous family background and diversified occupational experience, often having a close relationship to farmers and the working class—have had significant impacts on the formation of class identity of China's middle class. They have also erected barriers to the development of a middle-class identity and a common consumption culture.

Inconsistency between Social Status and Economic Status

One cause of a lack of middle-class status identity is an inconsistency between members' social status and their economic status, since income and consumption are the two most important criteria by which the public defines middle-class membership. The public—and the middle class itself—tends to think that the middle class should be composed of high-income earners.

A 2007 study by Li Peilin and Zhang Yi developed a method for determining high income.[18] According to their method, persons with an income more than 2.5 times the average income of an urban area are members of the high-income group. This high-income group is in closer accord with the public image of the middle class. Using the China General Social Survey data to calculate income, the baseline of the high-income group is a yearly income of 28,272 yuan. In other words, according to this income definition, persons with a yearly income of 28,272 yuan or greater are middle class. Based on sociologists' definition, a very low percentage of the middle class has an income higher than this baseline. Table 6-7 lists the average yearly incomes of the middle class's four subclasses and the percentage of each that is above this threshold.

Except for the capitalist class, only a low percentage of the middle classes meet this income criterion. Less than one-third of the new middle class, less than one-fifth of the old middle class, and slightly more than one-tenth of the marginal middle class have yearly incomes of more than 28,272 yuan. Among the middle class as a whole, only 18 percent reaches the income threshold. In addition, only the average income of the capitalist subclass is higher than this income baseline; the other three subclasses all have lower average incomes than this baseline. Based on this proportion, we may estimate that only 11 percent of the urban population and 6 percent of the entire population meet both criteria of middle class, that is, the sociological criterion and the public criterion.

T A B L E 6 - 7 . Average Yearly Middle-Class Income by Middle-Class Subclass, China, 2006

Unit as indicated

Class	Average yearly income (yuan)	Persons with yearly income of more than 28,272 yuan (percent)
Capitalist	46,495[a]	75.0
New middle	26,422	28.3
Old middle	18,630	16.7
Marginal middle	16,971	11.7
[Working][b]	11,371	3.7

Source: China General Social Survey (2006).
a. Amount is much less than actual income because capitalist class data are based mostly on small-size entrepreneurs.
b. The working class is not, according to the criteria, part of the middle class.

This dichotomy between social and economic status has resulted in a bizarre phenomenon. Most members of the middle class, as defined by sociologists, deny that they belong to the middle class and complain about their inability to achieve middle-class living standards. At the same time, this is a strong motivating force for the middle class to pursue their economic interests and strive for such a standard of living. Indeed, more and more members of the middle class have moved into the high-income group in recent years. Table 6-8 shows an increasing percentage of persons and families reaching this income criterion over time. In 1988 only 0.5 percent of the adult population had incomes higher than 28,272 yuan, and 0.7 percent of urban families had per capita incomes higher than 20,715 yuan. These figures increased in 2006 to 8.6 percent and 5.8 percent, respectively, in cities and towns. Nationwide percentages also increased over time.

Conclusion

The middle class is expanding very rapidly in China. Its expansion has been especially obvious in income and consumption, but has also recently expanded in the sociopolitical domain. Since no consensus exists on the definition of middle class, it is hard to estimate the size of China's middle class in a definitive way and to clearly describe its characteristics.

There are many different definitions of *middle class*. In the public and government's view, the middle class is mainly considered an income

TABLE 6-8. Share of Urban Middle-Class Individuals and Families Making
the Average Income, China, Selected Years, 1988–2006

Percent

Year	Income, middle-class individual[a]		Per capita income, middle-class family[b]	
	Urban area	Nationwide	Urban area	Nationwide
1988	0.5	...	0.7	...
1995	0.8	...	0.8	...
2001	3.4	2.1	3.4	1.7
2006	8.6	4.6	5.8	3.0

Source: See table 6-2.

a. Percent having yearly income of more than 28,272 yúan. The calculation includes the price index for each year.

b. Percent having per capita yearly income of more than 20,715 yuan (2.5 times of average per capita family income). The calculation includes the price index for each year.

group and defined by income and consumption criteria. Sociologists prefer to define the middle class based on occupation and employment. There is a major divergence between the income-defined middle class and the occupation-defined middle class. From a sociological perspective, the income-defined middle class is the upper part of middle class. But as the middle class emerges, the income-defined middle class has become the image most representative of a middle-class lifestyle and culture—and will likely remain so.

This diversity of definitions and the vague boundaries may be inevitable when a middle class emerges in a society undergoing such rapid changes to its social structure. How can one estimate the size of this class under such complicated circumstances? Perhaps the pragmatic choice is to do so using a mixture of quantitative and qualitative methods, while incorporating multiple dimensions and different perspectives.

The sociological definition undoubtedly overestimates the real size of China's middle class. Based on occupational classification, it considers all white-collar employees, employers, and self-employed people to be members of the middle class. However, many white-collar workers and self-employed people lack the socioeconomic status that one would expect of members of the middle class. Some have lower incomes, less education, and unstable employment.

The public definition of the middle class, defined by high income and consumption, usually underestimates the size of the middle class. The two definitions have narrowed the gap between their estimations of the size of middle class, so perhaps combining them will yield a definition that is broadly accepted. Thus the middle class includes these people: private entrepreneurs (the capitalist class); professionals, managers, and officials with stable middle or high incomes (the new middle class); and some small business owners or self-employed persons with stable middle or high incomes (the old middle class). This definition is closest to the real meaning of the concept of middle class. According to such a definition, the size of the Chinese middle class is 10–12 percent of the national adult population and 20–25 percent of the urban adult population.

The size of the middle class estimated by sociologists, and based on the four-subset classification (capitalist class, new middle class, old middle class, and marginal middle class), is about 30 percent of the national adult population and 60 percent of the urban adult population, much higher than the percentages of the combined definition. However, such high percentages may not be completely unfounded. They may overestimate the current situation but may become true in the coming years as long as the economy continues to grow steadily. The income of these four groups, after all, has been increasing significantly in recent years. It will not take long for most members of these four groups to reach the alleged economic status of the middle class.

Additionally, the sociological classification of the middle class introduced by this chapter is a useful framework within which to understand the present situation of China's middle class, although it does admittedly overestimate its size. China's middle class is made up of four major social groups with different socioeconomic characteristics. As a new and emerging class, it is a heterogeneous group that lacks a shared identity. Most members of the middle class have close relations with the working class. It seems impossible for such a varied group to become a real class with a coherent identity, culture, and sociopolitical attitudes and values.

In other countries, the new middle class has led middle-class culture, which sometimes dominates the entire society's values. In China likewise, the new middle class has played a key role in helping to develop a leading culture and certain values and political views. But the capitalist class and the old middle class (which run micro enterprises and small enterprises and are private entrepreneurs and small property owners, most of whom have modest backgrounds and low educational levels) have a very different culture and value system than the new middle class.

In addition, the new middle class itself is separated into two groups: public sector and private sector. These two parts of the new middle class have differing sociopolitical attitudes, especially concerning the state and its policies. More than half of the new middle class is located in the public sector. This part of the middle class has the most influence on the government's policies because of its close relationship to the government, but it is sometimes criticized by members of the middle class because of this perceived dependence on the authorities.

In summary, multiple orientations coexist among China's middle class today, and it has a long way to go before it forms a homogeneous middle-class identity and culture.

Notes

1. Li Chunling, "Zhongguo zhongchan jieji yanjiu de lilun quxiang ji guanzhudian de bianhua" [Theoretical orientation and change of focus in the study of the middle class in China], in *Bijiao shiyexia de zhongchan jieji xingcheng: guocheng, yingxiang yiji shehui jingji houguo* [Formation of the middle class in comparative perspective: process, influence, and socioeconomic consequences], edited by Li Chunling (Beijing: Social Sciences Academic Press, 2009), pp. 53–54.

2. These data form the major database for the study of social stratification and also are the best data for research into China's middle class. The census is conducted each decade; the 1 percent population survey is conducted middecade. Household income surveys of Chinese cities are usually conducted every five or seven years; they comprise 7,000–9,000 household cases and 21,000–32,000 individual cases selected from a nationally stratified sample. The national survey of social structure change and the China General Social Survey data have about 6,000–10,000 individual cases selected from the nationally stratified sample. The Beijing Middle Class Survey is a small survey of 800 cases selected by random sample from fifteen middle-class communities in Beijing. This author participated in three of these surveys: the national survey of social structure change, the China General Social Survey, and the Beijing Middle Class Survey.

3. Li, "Zhongguo zhongchan jieji yanjiu de lilun quxiang ji guanzhudian de bianhua," pp. 47–48.

4. Chen Xiaoya, "Zhongguo zhongcen jieji fuchu shuimian" [Emergence of China's middle class], *Business Culture* 2 (2002): 42–45; Xu Jiang, "Xin zhongcen jieji jueqi: Zhongguo fuyu shidai de kaishi" [The emerging new middle class: a beginning of the wealth age of China], *Economy and Trade World* 8 (2001): 4.

5. He Pin, "Dangxia wenxue zhong de 'xiaozi qindiao' he 'zhongcen jieji quwei'" [Sentiments of the petty bourgeois and the middle class in contemporary literature], *Literature Review* 6 (2005): 50–55; Xiang Rong, "Xiangxiang de zhongcen Jieji yu wenxue de zhongcenhua xiezuo" [The imaging of the middle class and the writing of the middle class], *Literature Review* 3 (2006): 24–27; Zhang Qinhua, "Women shidai de zhongcen jieji quwei" [Emotion and taste of the middle class in the modern age], *Southern Literature Forum* 2 (2006): 13.

6. He Jianzhang, "Woguo suoyouzhi jiegou de tiaozheng he shehui jiegou de bianhua" [Adjustment of ownership system and change of class structure in the country], *Sociological Research* 3 (1987): 2; "Woguo xianjieduan de jieji jiegou" [Class structure of China in the present period], *Sociological Research* 5 (1988): 4; "Lun 'zhongcen jieji'" [A comment on middle class], *Sociological Research* 2 (1990): 1.

7. Qiang Li, "Guanyu zhongchan jieji he zhongjian jiecen" [Middle class and middle stratum], *Transaction of Renming University* 2 (2001): 19; Xueyi Lu, *Dangdai Zhongguo shehui jiecen yanjiu baogao* [Report on social classes of contemporary China] (Beijing: Social Science Academic Press, 2002), p. 62.

8. Li Chunling, *Duanlie yu suipian: Dangdai Zhongguo shehui jiecen fenhua shizheng fenxi* [Cleavage and fragment: an empirical analysis on the social stratification of contemporary China] (Beijing: Social Sciences Academic Press, 2009), pp. 54–58.

9. Zhou Xiaohong, *Zhongguo zhongchan jieji diaocha* [Survey of the Chinese middle class] (Beijing: Social Sciences Academic Press, 2005).

10. Li, "Zhongguo zhongchan jieji yanjiu de lilun quxiang ji guanzhudian de bianhua," p. 53.

11. This classification of middle class is a revised version of class scheme developed by East Asian Middle Class Project. Hsin-Huang Michael Hisao, ed., *East Asian Middle Classes in Comparative Perspective* (Taipei: Institute of Ethnology, Academia Sinica, 1999), p. 9.

12. The capitalist class is not classified as a part of the middle class in classifications of other societies. However, capitalists, named as private entrepreneurs, are supposed to be an important part of the middle class in China. That is because the Chinese capitalist class is a new class, and its appearance is changing the original class structure and symbolizes the rise of the middle class.

13. John H. Goldthorpe, *Social Mobility and Class Structure in Modern Britain* (Oxford: Clarendon Press, 1987); Li, *Duanlie yu suipian: Dangdai Zhongguo shehui jiecen fenhua shizheng fenxi*, pp. 71–73.

14. Calculation of the sizes of classes mainly depends on occupation and a few other, related variables (such as the employment situation). However, different data have different categories of occupation and different definitions of the employment situation. In addition, census data (1882, 1990, 2000), the 1 percent population survey (2005), and the household income survey (1988, 1995, 2002) provide less detail. But the national survey of social structure change (2001) and the China General Social Survey (2006) have more detail for classifying classes. That makes it impossible to precisely estimate the exact size of subclasses. Though the percentages in table 6-2 fluctuate, the trend—expansion of the middle class—is quite clear.

15. Although the old middle class and the marginal middle class are classified by the criterion of occupation into middle class, most people think of these two groups as between middle class and working class because their socioeconomic status is lower than that of the regular middle class and higher than that of the working class.

16. The surveys of 2001, 2006, and 2007 all ask about social stratum. Social strata have five categories: upper, upper-middle, middle, lower-middle, and lower. More than 90 percent of members of the middle class classify themselves as upper-middle stratum, middle stratum, and lower-middle stratum; about 60 percent classify themselves as middle stratum. However, only a few identify themselves as middle class. This confuses researchers who use the criterion of subjective identity to estimate the size of the Chinese middle class. If they use social stratum to calculate the size of middle class, about 60–70 percent of the total population is middle class. But the percentage becomes lower than 10 percent if they use class ("middle class") as the category.

17. The earliest class of a person is determined by his first occupation in the labor market. Present class position is probably different from the early position if his occupation changed. Sociologists study social mobility by observing changes of occupation and class position of individuals.

18. Li Peilin and Zhang Yi, "Zhongguo zhongchan jieji de guimo, rentong, he shehui taidu" [The scale, recognition, and attitudes of China's middle class], in *Daguoce tongxiang Zhongguo zhilu de Zhongguo minzhu: Zengliang shi minzhu* [Strategy of a great power: incremental democracy and Chinese-style democracy], edited by Tang Jin (Beijing: People's Daily Press, 2009), pp. 183–201.

CHAPTER SEVEN

China's New Upper Middle Classes: The Importance of Occupational Disaggregation

JIANYING WANG and DEBORAH DAVIS

In the course of thirty years of unbroken economic growth China's class structure has experienced fundamental changes. While workers and peasants were the dominant classes before 1978, the structural and institutional transformation that followed has led to the rise of new social groups, which have subsequently changed the class maps of contemporary China. These new social groups, ranging from private entrepreneurs to professionals and managers in the nonstate sector, often fall into the broad category of middle class.

The emergence of a new middle class in contemporary China inspires important questions concerning its social and political impact. Nevertheless, to answer these questions one has to go beyond the general characterization of these different social groups as one middle class. Rather, studying the emerging middle class in China requires a closer look at the similarities and differences among the various segments of the middle class and what underlies these commonalities and distinctions.

For sociologists interested in social stratification, class analysis is important because it helps to explain variability in individual life chances and attitudes.[1] To achieve these goals, scholars employ a variety of analytical methods to examine the structure of social classes. The conventional approach to class analysis focuses on a small number of big classes defined by a particular variable (such as authority or employment relations) that is deemed especially useful in understanding the classes' structure. Recent scholarship, however, argues that smaller social groups, such as occupational groups, have become so deeply institutionalized in the labor market that they serve as better metrics to explain individual behaviors and attitudes. The latter thus proposes a more disaggregated approach to class analysis, or analysis of social stratification in general, that provides greater explanatory power than big class models.[2] Following this approach, we attempt in this chapter to disaggregate the broad category of middle class and focus on one specific group, the upper middle class, to understand the changing class maps in postreform China. Our study shows that even within the upper middle class there is considerable variation among its subgroups in terms of their life chances and attitudes.

After winning the civil war in 1949, the Chinese Communist Party (CCP) not only stigmatized the bourgeoisie ideologically but also implemented policies that blocked the reproduction of a distinctive upper middle class.[3] By 1953 all college students were assigned jobs as state cadres (*guojiaganbu*) upon graduation, and the private sector disappeared as a viable job choice for young managers and professionals.[4] Outside the workplace, the state's rationing of daily necessities and its political attacks on conspicuous consumption discouraged the upper middle classes from developing distinctive lifestyles. At the same time, the state's concerted effort at suppressing occupational associations prevented urbanites from mobilizing politically around class interests independent of the CCP. Thus those who by profession or education might have come to constitute a distinct social class and act collectively in politics lost this capacity.

However, as market rules have come to set wages and a globalized trade regime offers first-world salaries to professionals and managers with scarce skills, occupational differences have translated into increased inequality and a more differentiated class hierarchy.[5] In this chapter we investigate the impact of these macrolevel shifts by asking two questions:

—Has economic inequality between different segments of the middle class increased over time?

—Can we identify consequences beyond greater material inequality between manual laborers and other workers?

To address these questions we rely on two urban samples drawn from the Chinese Household Income Project (CHIP), a national survey conducted in 1995 and 2002 by the People's Republic of China's (PRC's) National Bureau of Statistics under the direction of a team of researchers from the Institute of Economics, the Chinese Academy of Social Sciences, and several foreign institutions. Designed to provide a comprehensive estimate of the distribution and determinants of household income, the survey also includes probes of individual attitudes toward social and economic trends.[6]

These materials reveal both variation in income and attitudes about China's increasing inequality and about life satisfaction. To investigate the question of increasing economic inequality we compare the distribution of economic assets, family income, and property ownership of more than 12,000 male household heads with urban household registrations. To assess the impact of class position on attitudes we analyze the responses of 5,718 men who were asked about the fairness of the income distribution and their overall satisfaction with the status quo in 2002.[7] Overall, we find that economic inequality increased and that attitudes toward current social issues varied across class positions. Thus rather than finding one middle class distinguishable from blue-collar workers, we find a pattern of increasing differentiation that suggests a reversal of the process of class leveling initiated after the Communist victory in 1949.

Defining the Middle Classes and Estimating Their Sizes

As other contributors to this volume note, *middle class* is a fuzzy or ambiguous term that, depending on the definition, will give varying estimates of its size.[8] If one relies on income distribution alone, the middle class includes all those who fall into the middle quintile of an income distribution. By that metric, however, the middle class would never expand beyond the middle 20 percent.

An alternative, which allows us to capture changes in the size of a middle class, is to use income levels deemed adequate to provide a middle-class lifestyle, usually one that presumes a steady income, ownership of a home, and the ability to afford higher education for the children. If we assume that in urban China an annual per capita household income of 10,000 yuan marks entry into this lifestyle, the trend lines displayed in figure 7-1 indicate that in 1990 China had no middle class, that by 2000 roughly 20 percent of urban households were middle class, and that by 2007 fully 60 percent had crossed this threshold.[9]

Because of our interest in disaggregating the middle class, we depart from this purely income-based definition and follow the sociological convention of defining *middle class* by occupation and education, drawing specifically upon the microclass framework of Kim Weeden and David

FIGURE 7-1. Mean Annual Urban per Capita Household Income, 1990–2007[a]

2005 yuan

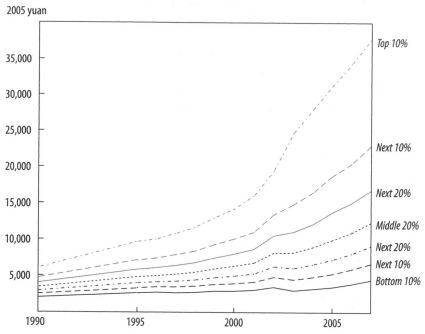

Source: *Zhongguo lianxiao jingying nianjian, 1990–2008* (Chinese retail business yearbooks, 1990–2008).
a. The seven deciles or quintiles are adjusted to the value of the yuan in 2005.

Grusky. They argue that class homogeneity is generated at the occupational level through three mechanisms: the allocative processes of self-selection and differential recruitment; the transformative effects of the objective conditions of work and the social practices characteristic of an occupation; and the institutionalization of the processes by which work is typically structured and rewarded.[10] Because we are particularly interested in exploring how market reforms have affected college-educated professionals and managers who were absorbed in the undifferentiated category of state cadre during the socialist era, we adopt the following eight-class schema, which combines occupational status and educational attainment:

—Workers: these are unskilled or skilled manual workers and sales and service workers.

—Clerks: these are ordinary office workers.

—Lower managers: these are noncadre managers without a college education.

TABLE 7-1. Distribution of Male Household Heads by Occupation, China, 1995 and 2002[a]

Percent

	1995		2002	
Occupation	Share of total	Share in state jobs	Share of total	Share in state jobs
All classes	...	98	...	81
Worker	34	98	40	76
Clerk	20	99	16	87
Lower manager	11	99	13	89
Lower professional	17	100	15	86
Upper manager	1	98	2	81
Upper professional	7	99	6	91
Cadre	9	100	6	100
Self-employed	1	45	4	6

Source: Chinese Household Income Project, 1995, 2002.
a. 1995, $N = 6,236$; 2002, $N = 6,185$.

—Lower professionals: these are professionals without a college education.

—Upper managers: these are noncadre managers with a college education.

—Upper professionals: these are professionals with a college education.

—Cadres: these are managers who are party members and work in government/state institutions.

—The self-employed.[11]

Table 7-1 shows the relative size of each occupational class based on the above schema in 1995 and 2002. In addition, we further subdivide each occupation for which there are private employers into state and private sector jobs. Comparing the distribution of jobs in these two years, one discovers two major shifts. First, the overall percentage of male household heads working in the state sector declined from 98 percent to 81 percent. This decline is not surprising, given the expansion of the nonstate sector in the reform era since the late 1990s, when the reform of state-owned enterprises accelerated, but it is a potentially significant distinction that a broader definition of the middle class fails to elucidate. Second, the relative share of different occupations also changed. The percentage of working-class men increased from 34 to 40 percent, while the percentage of men in lower-middle-class occupations such as clerks, lower-level managers, and lower-level professionals decreased from 48 percent to 44 percent, and the percentage of cadres declined from 9 percent to 6 percent. Somewhat surprisingly the share of college-educated managers and professionals, or what we would call the upper middle classes, remained stable at 8 percent. As expected, the share of the self-employed rose (from 1 percent to 4 percent).

Taking into account that the CHIP survey did not include rural migrants, a group that constituted an increasing percentage of the urban labor force between 1995 and 2002, the rising percentage of urban men in manual and service work further reinforces our findings that over time the upper middle classes of upper managers, upper professionals, and cadres have become an increasingly privileged group that stands apart from the majority. We now turn to a closer examination of this growing inequality in income and assets.

Income Distribution across Occupations

Table 7-2 displays the median per capita household income across eight occupational classes in 1995 and 2002. In both years, the three upper-middle-class groups enjoyed noticeably higher income than all the others. Moreover, their income advantages increased over time. In 1995, for example, the annual median per capita household income of upper managers was 1.53 times that of workers, and that of upper professionals was 1.45 times as high; by 2002 the median income of upper professionals and upper managers reached 1.87 and 1.69 times that of workers. Box plots representing dispersion around the mean per capita household income graphically illustrate the growing inequality among the eight occupational groups over time (figures 7-2 and 7-3). Thus in comparing the distributions of annual per capita income, we see that whereas in 1995, 75 percent of households headed by workers, clerks, or the self-employed had a per capita income of less than 5,000 yuan, among the upper middle class the figure was only 50 percent. By 2002 almost 50 percent of workers and the self-employed still averaged less than 5,000 yuan a year, whereas among the upper middle class half exceeded 10,000 yuan a year.

The above results indicate that the overall income level of the upper middle class, as a whole, stands apart from other groups and that income inequality between the upper and lower class strata in China has increased over time. Moreover, tests of median difference show that

TABLE 7-2. Median per Capita Household Income by Occupation, China, 1995 and 2002[a]

Yuan

	1995		
Occupation	Current yuan	Adjusted to 2002 yuan	2002
Worker	3,690	4,096	5,797
Clerk	3,785	4,201	7,276
Lower manager	4,522	5,019	8,196
Lower professional	4,337	4,814	7,639
Upper manager	5,367	5,957	9,768
Upper professional	5,631	6,250	10,836
Cadre	5,022	5,574	9,233
Self-employed	3,577	3,970	5,180
Addendum			
Anova test of median difference (*p* value):			
Between all groups		0.000***	0.000***
Between three upper middle groups		0.007**	0.001**

Source: Chinese Household Income Project, 1995, 2002.
**Significant at 1 percent level, ***significant at 0.1 percent level
a. 1995, $N = 6,236$; 2002, $N = 6,185$.

the median income differs significantly not only among the eight occupational groups but also among different segments of the upper middle class (see table 7-2). In both 1995 and 2002 college-educated professionals had the highest median income level, followed by college-educated managers and cadres, which suggests that when measured by income alone well-educated professionals as a whole have benefited most from market reforms.

Assets of China's Urban Professionals and Managers

The increasing advantages enjoyed by those in upper-middle-class occupations can also be demonstrated by comparing changes in the value of their homes and financial assets. Because comprehensive housing reform did not start until after 1997, we do not see a clear advantage among college-educated managers and professionals in 1995 (table 7-3). In fact, in 1995 the 32 percent homeownership rate among upper managers was

FIGURE 7-2. Per Capita Household Income, China, 1995

Yuan

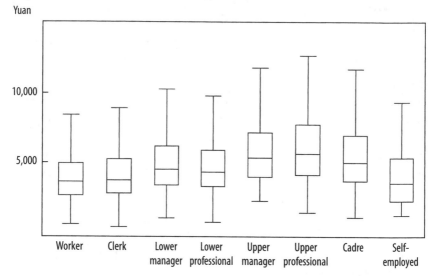

Source: Chinese Household Income Project, 1995.

FIGURE 7-3. Per Capita Household Income, China, 2002

Yuan

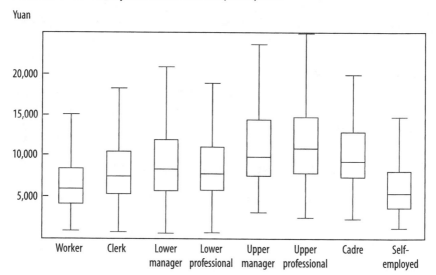

Source: Chinese Household Income Project, 2002.

TABLE 7-3. Home Ownership and Home Value by Occupation, China, 1995 and 2002[a]

Units as indicated

Occupation	Home ownership (percent)		Median home value (yuan) in 2002
	1995	2002	
Total	42	79	
Worker	39	74	50,000
Clerk	45	80	60,000
Lower manager	41	81	61,000
Lower professional	42	83	55,000
Upper manager	32	84	73,764
Upper professional	39	81	70,000
Cadre	48	88	80,000
Self-employed	59	75	50,000
Addendum			
Anova test of median difference (*p* value):			
Between all groups			0.000***
Between three upper middle groups			0.163

Source: Chinese Household Income Project, 1995, 2002.
***Significant at 0.1 percent level.
a. 1995, $N = 6,236$; 2002, $N = 6,185$.

the lowest of all groups, an anomaly that we attribute to the fact that before housing reform upper managers in state enterprises routinely paid very low rents for some of the best urban housing.[12] However, since the full commodification of real estate between 1998 and 2000, income advantages have come to correlate quite closely with both higher levels of homeownership and higher home values.

That said, income alone is not decisive. Thus the highest-level ownership (88 percent) and the highest median value (80,000 yuan) are among households headed by a male cadre; those headed by upper managers rank second, with 84 percent ownership and a median home value of 73,764 yuan. Although upper professionals have the highest median income (as shown in the previous section), they fared less favorably than cadres and upper managers in terms of property ownership. These results suggest that while cadres do not have an obvious advantage in income, they have benefited disproportionately from the housing reforms

FIGURE 7-4. Estimated Home Value, 2002

Yuan

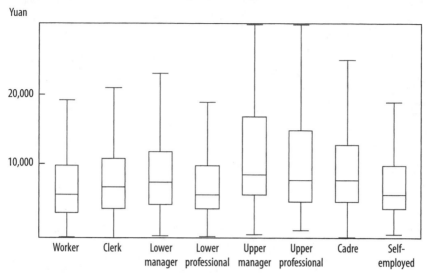

Source: Chinese Household Income Project, 2002.

launched in the late 1990s. This property advantage is not trivial, yet it could not have been observed if one looked at income alone.

When we use box plots to illustrate the dispersion of home values across and within the occupations in 2002, after homeownership had become the norm, we find a pattern that generally maps onto that observed for overall income dispersion. In figure 7-4, for instance, we see that in 2002 almost three-quarters of workers, clerks, lower professionals, and the self-employed owned homes worth less than 100,000 yuan and that even among those in the upper quartile, home values ranged between 100,000 and 200,000 yuan. By contrast, the upper quartile value of homes owned by upper managers, upper professionals, and cadres ranged between 150,000 and 300,000 yuan. In other words, the upper middle class as a whole stands apart from other groups in terms of property values. On the other hand, the interquartile ranges of home value are largest among upper managers, followed by upper professionals and cadres, suggesting that in addition to their advantages over the families of workers and the lower middle class, there is also great inequality within the upper middle classes.[13]

In terms of such financial assets as certificate of deposits and stocks and bonds, we also observe rising values and increasing inequality.

T A B L E   7 - 4 . Median Value of Financial Assets by Occupation, China, 1995 and 2002[a]

Yuan

Occupation	1995	2002
Worker	3,100	8,250
Clerk	4,000	10,000
Lower manager	5,150	17,000
Lower professional	5,000	11,000
Upper manager	8,000	20,000
Upper professional	8,000	30,000
Cadre	7,940	20,000
Self-employed	4,500	50,00
Addendum		
Anova test of median difference (*p* value):		
Between all groups	0.000***	0.000***
Between three upper middle groups	0.681	0.011*

Source: Chinese Household Income Project, 1995, 2002.
*Significant at 5 percent level,***significant at 0.1 percent level.
a. 1995, $N = 6,236$; 2002, $N = 6,185$.

As shown in table 7-4, the median financial assets possessed by upper managers, upper professionals, and cadres in 1995 were similar to each other and higher than all other groups. By 2002 the upper-middle-class groups continued to enjoy significant advantages over other groups in terms of financial assets. Moreover, there is a pronounced differentiation among the three upper-middle-class groups. In particular, the upper professionals stand out from the others. Given that such financial assets as stocks are relatively new instruments, we hypothesize that because of their college education, upper professionals are more likely to know about these options than members of other classes and thus own more financial assets.

Occupational Class and Attitudes

The CHIP data do not allow us to directly engage the questions raised by Han Sang-Jin (chapter 12), Ethan Michelson and Sida Liu (chapter 14), and Jie Chen (chapter 15) relating to authoritarianism, democracy, and political reform. However, because the 2002 CHIP survey did ask respondents to assess both the fairness of the national income distribution and their own life satisfaction, we can create a dialogue with other contributors and speak to the editor's overarching question about the political implications of a growing middle class in China. Moreover, because the CHIP data provide complete information on such individual attributes as age, income, state employment status, and health and marital status, multivariate analysis of the 2002 data allows us to test explicitly for the independent effect of occupational class on attitudes toward fairness and happiness that may have implications for predicting long-term political values and behavior.

We turn first to questions that asked respondents to rate the fairness of the national income distribution. For convenience, we recoded the answers into two categories: fair versus unfair. As we see in table 7-5, across all occupations a large majority believes that the current situation is unfair, suggesting that rising income inequality in the postreform era is widely recognized among urban residents. However, upper managers are twice as likely (23 percent) as workers (11 percent) to consider the income distribution fair, and workers are the most likely to find the current situation unfair, indicating the generally worsening position of workers in the reform era.

When we examine responses to the question concerning overall life satisfaction, only a small minority of any class is unhappy (see table 7-5). However, variation across classes for this question is more marked than for attitudes to income distribution. Upper managers have the highest level of satisfaction, with 77 percent reporting that they are happy about their lives and only 1.5 percent reporting negatively. By contrast, only half of workers report they are happy and 16 percent report that they are unhappy. Cadres and upper professionals also exhibit relatively high levels of life satisfaction, whereas the self-employed report a satisfaction level as low as that of workers. To the extent that class status is closely associated with attitudes and life conditions, the variation among these occupational classes along these dimensions demonstrates the centrality of occupation in determining class status.

To test whether occupational class independently affects perceptions of fairness and happiness, we conducted multivariate logistic regressions that control for the effects of age, employment in the state sector, self-perceived health, marital status, and household income. To estimate the differences between the upper middle class and other groups, as well as the differences among the three occupational groups (upper manager,

TABLE 7-5. Perception of Fairness in National Income Distribution and of Own Life Satisfaction, Male Household Heads by Occupation, China, 2002[a]

Percent

Occupation	Perceives income distribution as fair	Life satisfaction		
		Happy	Just so-so	Unhappy
Worker	11	49	35	16
Clerk	12	56	32	12
Lower manager	14	62	29	9
Lower professional	13	63	29	8
Upper manager	23	77	22	1.5
Upper professional	15	68	25	6.5
Cadre	19	76	20	5
Self-employed	16	50	31	19

Addendum

Anova test of mean difference (p value):

Between all groups	0.000***		0.000***	
Between three upper middle groups	0.257		0.125	

Source: Chinese Household Income Project, 2002.
***Significant at 0.1 percent level.
a. $N = 5,718$.

upper professional, and cadre) within our omnibus upper-middle-class category, we examine three different disaggregations of class.

First, we collapse all but workers into one white-collar class to assess the degree to which the boundary between blue-collar and white-collar employment distinguishes attitudes. In our second model we test for variation between the lower and upper middle classes, and in the third we test the distinctions among the component members of the upper middle class, with the reference group being upper managers. We keep the self-employed as a separate category from both lower middle class and upper middle class because of their distinct position in the urban labor market of postreform China. The majority of the self-employed operate outside of the state sector but are severely constrained by state policies.[14] The institutional environment for self-employment changes over time, as does its political status. The origins and economic outcomes of the self-employed also vary greatly. Thus we expect the self-employed to have distinct attitudes from other occupational groups.

TABLE 7-6. Selected Characteristics of Male Household Heads Surveyed on Attitudes Questions, 2002[a]

Units as indicated

Variable	Worker	Clerk	Lower manager	Lower profes- sional	Upper manager	Upper profes- sional	Cadre	Self- employed
Age (years)	48	47	56	49	50	46	46	43
Marital status (% married)	96	97	97	98	100	97	99	98
Health condition[b]	1.48	1.42	1.48	1.44	1.32	1.36	1.26	1.34
Annual per capita household income (yuan)	6,686	8,416	9,524	8,617	12,124	12,382	10,865	6,942
Log of per capita household income (mean)	8.64	8.89	8.99	8.93	9.26	9.28	9.16	8.61
Type of work unit (% state)	76	86	89	86	81	92	100	6
N	2,266	915	736	838	97	331	340	195

Source: Chinese Household Income Project, 2002.
a. N = 5,718.
b. Health condition was given values of 1, 2, or 3, with 1 being good or very good, 2 being average, and 3 being bad or very bad.

Perceptions of Fairness

We use logistic regression models to distinguish the effect of class status from other variables on perceptions of fairness of the income distribution. The dependent variable for the model is a dummy variable, with 1 representing "fair" and 0 representing "unfair." The independent variables are age, log of annual per capita household income, marital status, self-reported health status, and state employment. Table 7-6 lists the mean scores for each variable in the model for each of the eight occupations. As we can see, the average age of these respondents varies from forty-three years among the self-employed to fifty-six years among lower managers. Almost all are married, and the majority report somewhat better than average health. Except for the self-employed, most work in the state sector.

Table 7-7 presents the results of logistic regression models on perceptions of fairness in the national income distribution. In model 1 we see that those with higher income, good health, and employment in the state sector are more likely to find the income distribution fair. However, after controlling for these attributes, as well as for age and marital status, working-class respondents are significantly less likely than nonworkers to find the distribution fair (model 1). Specifically, the odds of workers regarding

TABLE 7-7. Three Logistic Regression Models, Attitude toward Fairness of National Income Distribution, China, 2002[a]

	Model 1			Model 2			Model 3		
Variable	Coefficient	Standard error	Odds ratio	Coefficient	Standard error	Odds ratio	Coefficient	Standard error	Odds ratio
Age	0.003	0.004	1.0	0.004	0.004	1.0	0.004	0.004	1.0
Marital status	−0.101	0.230	0.9	−0.102	0.230	0.9	−0.113	0.23	0.89
Health	−0.267***	0.072	0.77	−0.262***	0.072	0.77	−0.259***	0.072	0.77
Annual per capita household income (in log form)	0.167*	0.071	1.18	0.163*	0.072	1.18	0.165*	0.072	1.18
State sector	0.363**	0.114	1.44	0.511***	0.13	1.67	0.518***	0.13	1.68
Occupation									
Worker	−0.196*	0.087	0.82						
White collar	...	...	...						
Worker				−0.096	0.093	0.91			
Lower middle class				...	...	...			
Upper middle class				0.204†	0.117	1.23			
Self-employed				0.777**	0.229	2.17			
Worker							−0.647*	0.261	0.52
Lower middle class							−0.551*	0.256	0.58
Upper manager							...	...	...
Upper professional							−0.497†	0.293	0.61
Cadre							−0.321	0.287	0.73
Self-employed							0.23	0.332	1.26
Constant	−3.297***	0.689		−3.547***	0.704		−3.001***	0.763	
Log likelihood		−2,177.44			−2,171.06			−2,169.65	
Pseudo R^2		0.01			0.01			0.01	

Source: Chinese Household Income Project 2002.
†$p < .10$, *$p < .05$, **$p < .01$, ***$p < .001$.
a. $N = 5{,}718$. Measure: 1 = fair.

the income distribution to be fair are 82 percent of the odds of nonwork-ers finding it fair. Given the loss of benefits and the basic insecurity of working-class jobs in the postsocialist economy, it is not surprising that the blue-collar/white-collar distinction is consequential. However, as we and others argue, the middle class or middle classes are much more than simply those who are not working class. To address this issue, in model

2 we juxtapose the lower middle class to workers and the upper middle class, and in model 3 we juxtapose the upper managerial class to all others.

As shown in model 2 of table 7-7, those with higher incomes, good health, and employment in the state sector are more likely to find the income distribution fair, but when we control for these attributes we find no significant difference between workers and the lower middle class. However, at the same time we do observe a significant difference between the lower middle class and the self-employed as well as between the lower middle class and members of an omnibus upper middle class (managers, professionals, and cadres). Specifically, the self-employed are 2.17 times as likely as those in the lower middle class to say that the national income distribution is fair, and those in the upper middle class are 1.23 times as likely. These findings demonstrate that within the broad category of middle class the lower and upper strata exhibit distinctive attitudes toward the social reality.

When using upper managers as the reference category (model 3, table 7-7) we again find that higher incomes, state employment, and good health predict a more favorable response, but we also find differences within the upper middle class. For example, upper professionals are significantly less likely than upper managers to consider the national income distribution fair, whereas the attitudes of cadres and the self-employed do not significantly differ from those of upper managers. More specifically, the odds of workers, the lower middle class, and upper professionals to say that the national income distribution is fair are, respectively, 52 percent, 58 percent, and 61 percent the odds of upper managers.

In sum, there are divergent attitudes not only between the upper and lower strata of the middle class but even among upper-middle-class groups. This is partly due to the distinctive occupational paths taken by the upper middle class during the reform process. In particular, the incremental approach to reforms has meant that managers are likely to maintain a strong link to the state, whereas upper professionals are more likely to find jobs in the private sector or hold state jobs that follow market rules. To the extent that the state remains socially and politically dominant and constitutes a constraining force on the market, those who benefit from close association with the state are more likely to hold a favorable view toward the status quo.

Happiness

To examine the impact of class status on life satisfaction, we use ordered logit models. The dependent variable is recoded into a

T A B L E 7 - 8 . Three Logistic Regression Models, Life Satisfaction, China, 2002[a]

Variable	Model 1			Model 2			Model 3		
	Coefficient	Standard error	Odds ratio	Coefficient	Standard error	Odds ratio	Coefficient	Standard error	Odds ratio
Age	0.011***	0.002	1.01	0.012***	0.002	1.01	0.012***	0.002	1.01
Marital status	0.308*	0.156	1.36	0.303†	0.156	1.35	0.296†	0.156	1.34
Health	−0.572***	0.045	0.56	−0.567***	0.045	0.57	−0.565***	0.045	0.57
Per capital annual household income (in log form)	0.812***	0.050	2.25	0.783***	0.05	2.59	0.785***	0.05	2.19
State sector	0.274***	0.068	1.32	0.234**	0.073	1.26	0.235**	0.073	1.27
Occupation									
Worker	−0.252***	0.056	0.78						
White collar	...	...	...						
Worker				−0.205**	0.06	0.81			
Lower middle class				...	...	...			
Upper middle class				0.317**	0.093	1.37			
Self-employed				−0.079	0.158	0.92			
Worker							−0.837**	0.256	0.43
Lower middle class							−0.632*	0.255	0.53
Upper manager							...	...	...
Upper professional							−0.466†	0.279	0.63
Cadre							−0.248	0.281	0.78
Self-employed							−0.71*	0.294	0.49
Log likelihood	−5,019.05			−5,012.8			−5,011.07		
Pseudo R^2	0.06			0.06			0.06		

Source: Chinese Household Income Project, 2002.
†$p < .10$, *$p < .05$, **$p < .01$, ***$p < .001$.
a. $N = 5,718$. Measure: 1 = unhappy, 2 = just so-so, 3 = happy.

three-category ordinal variable, with 1 representing "unhappy," 2 representing "just so-so," and 3 representing "happy." Table 7-8 presents the results of three ordered logistic regressions on life satisfaction: model 1 juxtaposes blue-collar and white-collar respondents, model 2 juxtaposes the lower middle class with others, and model 3 permits disaggregation of the upper middle classes into managers, professionals, and cadres.

Results in model 1 of table 7-8 show that workers are significantly less happy than everyone else. The odds of workers reporting that they are happy rather than just so-so or unhappy are 78 percent the odds of a non-worker feeling happy, again indicating that workers were generally losers in the market reform. In model 2 we see that distinctions go beyond the white-collar/blue-collar divide. Workers continue to be less happy than both the lower and upper middle classes, but within the middle classes the upper middle classes are significantly happier than the lower middle class after controlling for age, health, income, and state employment. The odds of someone from the upper middle class feeling happy are 1.37 times the odds of someone from the lower middle class feeling happy. This further illustrates the differentiation within the middle class.

In model 3, where the upper middle class is disaggregated into upper professionals, upper managers, and cadres, we see that workers, men in the lower middle classes, and the self-employed are all significantly less happy than upper managers. The odds of workers, the self-employed, and the lower middle class saying they are happy instead of the just so-so or unhappy are, respectively, 43 percent, 49 percent, and 53 percent the odds of upper managers.

Here, however, we also discover that after controlling for income and everything else, the upper middle class is not homogeneous. Instead, upper professionals are significantly less happy than managers (the odds of upper professionals reporting that they are happy are 63 percent the odds of upper managers). However, there is no gap in the level of satisfaction between upper managers and cadres. That upper managers enjoy the greatest life satisfaction further confirms their favored position in the urban political economy of 2002. The equally favorable assessment by cadres also suggests that not only have cadres not been marginalized in postsocialist China but that a dual elite of upper managers and officials may characterize the urban social structure for some time to come. More generally, the results indicate that when looking beyond economic transformations, scholars gain precision when they disaggregate the middle class into constituent segments rather than treating it as one homogeneous social category.

Conclusion: Class and Occupation

In this chapter we rely exclusively on two surveys of male household heads who were officially registered residents of Chinese cities and towns. Because we were necessarily limited by the original investigators' primary interest in economic outcomes, we could not explore the full range of possible topics raised by this volume's editor and by other contributors. Nevertheless, the data did allow us to move beyond the simple dichotomy of blue collar and white collar and to identify the relative winners and losers of economic reform across a range of occupations.

The results also speak to a broader debate in sociology between those led by John Goldthorpe and his colleagues, who advocate "big class" analysis, and those led by David Grusky and Kim Weeden, who advocate "microclass" analysis.[15] For Grusky and Weeden, specific occupations are considered the key location for the formation of class, because they believe that it is at the occupational level that individuals form class identities and class interests through the shared experiences of recruitment, promotion, and ongoing socialization. Although our disaggregation of the urban middle classes and upper middle classes could not capture the refinement that Weeden and Grusky advocate, our multivariate models do illustrate how disaggregating macroclasses can help to identify significant variation among segments of white-collar employees as well as confirming the importance of the split between those in manual and those in nonmanual jobs.

Finally, as Wang Feng shows in his book on inequality and stratification in urban China, disaggregation by occupation is particularly important in analyzing Chinese politics, because in China the boundaries and categories created around political position, professional rank, and geographic location create opportunities for hoarding and the extraction of surplus.[16] Thus to understand or predict what will result "beyond economic transformation," it is essential that scholarship moves beyond models that presume an undifferentiated middle class to work with more refined categories that capture the gradients of power and authority among occupational positions.

Notes

1. Kim Weeden and David Grusky, "The Case for a New Class Map," *American Journal of Sociology* 111, no. 1 (2005):141–212.

2. Robert Erikson and John H. Goldthorpe, *The Constant Flux* (Oxford: Clarendon Press, 1992); and Weeden and Grusky, "The Case for a New Class Map."

3. Deborah Davis, "Self-Employment in Shanghai," *China Quarterly* 157 (March 1999): 22–43; Deborah Davis, "Social Class Transformation: Training, Hiring, and Promoting Urban Professionals and Managers after 1949," *Modern China* 26, no. 3 (2000): 251–75.

4. Yanjie Bian, "Urban Occupational Mobility and Employment Institutions," in *Creating Wealth and Poverty in Post-Socialist China*, edited by Deborah Davis and Wang

Feng (Stanford University Press, 2009), pp. 172–92; Deborah Davis, "Skidding: Downward Mobility among Children of the Maoist Middle Class," *Modern China* 18, no. 4 (1992): 410–37.

5. Davis and Wang, *Creating Wealth and Poverty in Post-Socialist China.*

6. Azizur Rahman Khan and Carl Riskin, "Income and Inequality in China: Composition, Distribution, and Growth of Household Income, 1988 to 1995," *China Quarterly* 154 (June 1998): 221–53. Through the Chinese Household Income Project (CHIP), the National Bureau of Statistics of China conducted comprehensive national surveys in 1988, 1995, 2002, and 2005. For this chapter we use 6,236 male household heads from the urban sample of 1995, which covers a total of 21,698 individuals in 6,931 households; and 6,179 male household heads from the urban sample of 2002, which covers a total of 20,628 individuals in 6,836 households.

7. The survey asked household heads questions on their perceptions of income inequality and life satisfaction. In this study we focus on three questions: Do you think current national income distribution is fair? (Answers range from very fair, relatively fair, relatively unfair, and very unfair.) In general, do you feel happy? (Answers range from very happy, relatively happy, just so-so, not so happy, and very unhappy.)

8. See Homi Kharas and Geoffrey Gertz, chapter 2, this volume.

9. In the statistical yearbooks the National Bureau of Statistics provides the mean per capita household figure for households that fall in the top two and bottom two deciles and in the three middle quintiles. Using these mean estimates in each of the seven groups, one can derive a rough estimate of the increase in middle-class households.

10. Weeden and Grusky, "The Case for a New Class Map."

11. The CHIP asked respondents to identify their own occupational status. The unemployed reported their last occupation before unemployment. The retired reported their occupation before retirement. The original occupations include owners of private enterprises; the self-employed (*getihu*); professionals; directors of a government agency, an institution, and an enterprise; department directors of a government agency, an institution, and an enterprise; clerical/office staff; skilled workers; unskilled workers; sales and service workers; farmers; and others. Respondents were asked whether their work units were enterprises, government agencies, or institutions, which was used to identify cadres.

12. Deborah Davis, "Urban Chinese Homeowners as Citizen Consumers," in *The Ambivalent Consumer*, edited by Sheldon Garon and Patricia Maclachan (Cornell University Press, 2006), pp. 281–99.

13. Interquartile range is the number of cases that fall 25 percent above and below the median. It is useful to visualize the dispersion, and thus degree, of inequality.

14. Jianying Wang, "Self-Employment in Urban China," Ph.D. dissertation, Yale University, 2009.

15. Erikson and Goldthorpe, *The Constant Flux;* Weeden and Grusky, "The Case for a New Class Map."

16. Wang Feng, *Boundaries and Categories* (Stanford University Press, 2008).

PART IV

Expanding China's Middle Class: Housing Reform and Educational Development

CHAPTER EIGHT

China's Housing Reform and Emerging Middle Class

JOYCE YANYUN MAN

Over the past decade China's housing policy and housing market have experienced dramatic changes. Since the 1990s housing reforms have focused on the privatization of state-owned housing stock, and this market-provided housing has contributed significantly to the emergence and growth of a middle class in China. These reforms have led to profound changes in the distribution of housing and in homeownership in urban China, both of which greatly affect Chinese peoples' social and economic lives.

As a result, China has totally abandoned the old system of linking housing to one's employment, as a welfare benefit. Government policies aimed at promoting the provision of housing as a commodity through the market, especially in urban areas, have contributed to the rapid development of the housing sector, which has become a significant segment of economic activity and of the Chinese government's tax base. It has also greatly improved urban residents' housing conditions, whose floor area per capita increased from 6.7 square meters (about 72 square feet) in 1978 to 28.3 square meters (about 305 square feet) in 2007.[1] In Chinese society today homeownership is one of a household's most important economic goals, partly owing to its status as a symbol of wealth and social standing. It is also an invaluable analytical perspective from which to assess the characteristics of the middle class in urban China.

The definition of middle class is still controversial among scholars, and there is no official government definition across nations. However, many studies seek to define *middle class* both qualitatively and quantitatively. The middle class may be viewed as the broad group of people in contemporary society who fit socioeconomically between the working class and the upper class. The members of this socioeconomic class tend to have received tertiary education, hold professional qualifications, have secure jobs, own homes, and have a special social status and cultural identification.

Quantitative studies tend to be based on surveys of household income and expenditures. Nancy Birdsall, Carol Graham, and Stefano Pettinato define the middle class as those households falling between 75 and 125 percent of a country's median per capita income.[2] Based on a household survey of thirteen developing countries, Abhijit Banerjee and Esther Duflo define the middle classes as those whose daily consumption per capita is $2 to $4 for the lower middle class and $6 to $10 for the upper middle class.[3] Combining household income quintile data from the Census Bureau with survey responses, Brian Cashell narrowly identifies the U.S. middle class as households with income in the middle quintile, between $36,000 and $57,660, and more widely (based on the three middle quintiles) as households with income between $19,178 and $91,765.[4] William Easterly defines the middle class as those lying between the 20th and 80th percentiles on a country's consumption distribution.[5] *The Economist* magazine characterizes the middle class as people for whom about one-third of their income is disposable, after paying for basic food and shelter.[6]

An extensive literature on the subject provides us with a quantitative frame of reference within which to identify the middle class in China. *Middle class* is different from *middle income,* despite the two terms being used interchangeably by many scholars. In general, middle-income households are those in the middle of the overall distribution of household income. Middle class is a much broader category; it describes a segment of the population that not only has a median or average income but also has achieved a certain social status, as reflected in education levels, occupations, aspirations, and even political views. Either way, a household's place in the household income distribution should be one factor that contributes to inclusion in the middle class.

Using data from the large-sample Urban Household Survey of 2007 conducted by the National Bureau of Statistics of China, this chapter seeks to define the middle class according to household income distribution and to investigate how well the Chinese middle class has fared relative to other classes as a result of Chinese housing reform.[7] It focuses on the middle class's homeownership and housing consumption and on housing affordability issues. This analysis has implications for housing policies that could lead to a strong housing market and sustainable economic growth in China.

Income Distribution in Urban China

This study analyzes Urban Household Survey data for 256 prefecture-level cities in 2007 and finds great variation in income among urban households. By ranking nearly 250,000 urban households in the survey sample by income and placing them in deciles, this study finds that the average annual income ranges from 9,288 yuan in the lowest 10th percentile to 137,679 yuan in the highest percentile, with an overall average of 43,350 yuan for the entire sample size of 249,777 observations of the urban households reported in the survey. The median household income varies from 9,600 yuan in the lowest 10th percentile to 109,600 in the highest 10th percentile, with an overall median household income for 2007 at 32,400 yuan. The average income for the ten income deciles in 2007 was as follows:

—Lowest, 9,288 yuan
—Second, 14,902 yuan
—Third, 19,842 yuan
—Fourth, 24,526 yuan
—Fifth, 29,765 yuan
—Sixth, 35,649 yuan
—Seventh, 42,117 yuan
—Eighth, 51,640 yuan
—Ninth, 67,167 yuan
—Highest, 137,679 yuan

However, China has demonstrated a geographic disparity in economic bases and growth rates across regions. The eastern coast and big cities have exceeded the midwestern and northeastern regions in terms of economic performance and income growth since the early 1980s. Figure 8-1 reveals that median household incomes among 256 cities do not show a classical normal distribution. Instead, they range from 13,200 yuan in Hegang City to 80,000 yuan in Dongguan City, with an average of 27,600 yuan and a median of 30,333 yuan for the sample cities. Nearly 60 percent of these 256 prefecture-level cities had median household

FIGURE 8-1. Median Household Income, 256 Prefecture Cities, China, 2007

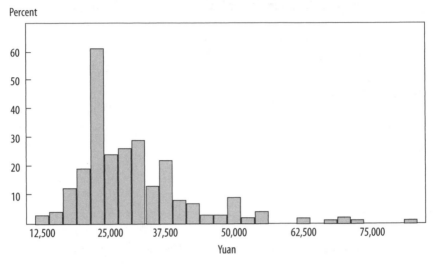

Percent

Source: Large-sample Urban Household Survey, 2007.

incomes below 30,000 yuan. Only 7 cities in the sample had a median household income of 60,000 yuan or above. This demonstrates that geographic differences must be addressed when one discusses income distribution, consumption, and wealth patterns in China. This regional disparity is especially important to keep in mind for an emerging economy like China. Any government policy addressing social, economic, or political issues must take into account regional differences and accommodate the variations that exist across local governments.

Who Are the Middle Class in China

What constitutes the middle class is relative, subjective, and not easily defined. This study follows Nancy Birdsall, Carol Graham, and Stefano Pettinato in defining the middle class in China by income in a relative sense, based upon the distribution of household incomes.[8] This study employs two definitions of the Chinese middle class, the first of which is to define the middle class as the households in the 50th and 60th percentiles (the middle-quintile definition) of annual household incomes; we call this definition A. This is the narrowest view of who might be considered middle class. Definition B includes households earning 75–125

TABLE 8-1. Characteristics of the Urban Middle Class, China, 2007[a]

Unit as indicated

	Definition A	Definition B
Age in years	41.5	41.6
Annual income	32,734 yuan ($14,232)	32,741 yuan ($14,235)
Household floor area	83.6 square meters (900 square feet)	83.6 square meters (900 square feet)
Average market value of housing	227,000 yuan ($98,790)	228,000 yuan ($99,000)
Annual expenditure	23,257 yuan ($10,111)	23,417 yuan ($10,181)
Daily expenditure per person	$9.2	$9.3
Number of households in sample	48,457 (20 percent of sample)	66,859 (26.7 percent of sample)

Source: Large-sample Urban Household Survey, 2007.
a. Definition A includes only the households between the 50th and 60th percentiles in income distribution; definition B includes all households between the 75th and 125th percentiles of median per capita income. Dollars are adjusted by purchasing power parity.

percent of median per capita income. Using these two definitions in tandem, one should be able grasp the characteristics of the middle class in China, especially its housing consumption.

Table 8-1 shows that both definitions result in similar characteristics for China's middle class. The head of a middle class household is about forty-one years old, and household income is about 32,700 yuan, or approximately $14,200 after purchasing power parity (PPP) adjustment. The floor area of a typical middle-class household is about 84 square meters (900 square feet), and the average market value of its housing is roughly 227,500 yuan, or about $99,000. Annual household expenditure is 23,257–23,417 yuan for an average of three persons per household, amounting to $9 per person per day.

The above calculation is based on the two definitions used in this study. Applying either the standard of the 50th and 60th percentile of the income distribution or the median per capita income of 75 percent and 125 percent, this study finds that the middle class in urban China has a per capita annual income of 10,950 yuan. For this group, daily per capita consumption is $3.12 or $3.15, using the current exchange rate of 6.8 yuan to $1. If this figure is adjusted by the commonly used PPP factor of 2.3 yuan to $1, as the *McKinsey Quarterly* has calculated, then daily per capita consumption expenditure might reach $9.23.[9]

These figures also meet the standards proposed by Banerjee and Duflo in their study of thirteen developing countries, in which members of the middle classes have daily consumption per capita between $2 and $4 or between $6 and $10 per day.[10] Based on the literature on the middle class in other developing countries, one can reasonably believe that this group of China's urban population is fairly commensurate with middle-class groups in most other developing countries, at least in terms of income and daily consumption.[11] Based on the sample size of these survey data, one can calculate that in 2007 between 39 million and 52 million urban households in China fell into the category of middle class. These numbers translate to 117 million to 156 million people.

If a consensus is reached that households whose income is in the 50th percentile or above in the income distribution can be labeled middle class in China, then one can conclude, based on Urban Household Survey data, that this group accounts for about 60 percent of urban households, with average incomes between 29,765 yuan and 137,679 yuan and daily per capita consumption expenditures between 19.8 yuan and 64.4 yuan. After the adjustment of renminbi purchasing power parity, it is equivalent to household incomes of $12,941 to $59,860, respectively. Daily consumption per capita is between $8.60 and $28.00 after adjusting for PPP. Based upon this standard, there were about 117 million urban households, or nearly 350 million members of the urban population, that fell into the middle-class category in 2007.[12]

Housing Reform and China's Emerging Middle Class

Housing policies are closely linked with the fate of China's middle class and have had a significant impact on the size and characteristics of it. Housing polices have gone through dramatic changes over the past six decades, which can be divided into five periods: 1949–57, 1958–77, 1978–97, 1998–2004, and 2005 to the present.[13]

1949–57: Heavily Regulated Urban Housing Markets

During these years the urban private housing market was heavily regulated by the Chinese government, which practiced rent control and confiscated private property owned by capitalists and warlords. Shortly after the People's Republic of China (PRC) was founded in 1949, the Chinese government started to incorporate the largely urban private housing market into the socialist system by assuming state ownership of almost all economic assets, including housing. The central government used rent control to prevent speculation and to ensure housing affordability.

Private ownership of housing, however, was still dominant in most Chinese cities.[14] Leasing of privately owned properties was still allowed, and the private sector supplied housing to a majority of urban dwellers.[15] However, the share of housing provided by the private sector fell from nearly 100 percent in 1949 to 52 percent in 1957.[16] The state's housing policies during this era led to limited housing investments, a shortage of housing, deteriorating housing conditions, and shrinking housing markets.

1958–77: Work Unit, or Danwei, Housing System

The transition from private to public ownership of housing was gradually accomplished through the establishment of work units, or *danwei*. The establishment of the residence registration system, commonly known as *hukou*, enabled the government by 1958 to divide the entire population into urban and rural groups. Urban residents were linked to their work unit, an economic institution in the socialist system. The housing sector became part of the centrally planned economy, like all other sectors of the economy (such as major industries, infrastructure, education, and health care). Consequently, *danwei* became the vehicle for the central government to control housing investment, construction, and maintenance and to distribute housing as welfare to employed urban residents.

Before the economic reform program of 1978, urban housing in China was allocated to urban residents as a part of a welfare package offered by their employer (the work unit) according to the employee's office ranking, occupational status, work experience, and other merits. Housing construction was largely initiated and financed by various work units, and residential land was allocated through administrative transfer within the central planning system. Under this system, in which a housing market was absent, it was the financial conditions and workplace policy of employees' work units instead of workers' income and other household characteristics that determined the quality and quantity of their housing. As a result, the share of housing provided by the private sector dropped to 15 percent in 1977.[17] Private housing construction was almost wholly eliminated in practice, and the central government assumed full responsibility for housing through its central planning system and the distributional channel of *danwei*. The socialist welfare housing policy was firmly established.

1978–97: Reform Experiments of Marketization in the Housing Sector

Since the beginning of economic reform in 1978, the Chinese government has brought market forces into the housing sector to reform the state-controlled public housing system. In 1980 Deng Xiaoping pushed for a housing reform that promoted private ownership and the sale of public housing to urban residents. Rent was raised to market level, and private and foreign investments in housing were encouraged. The sale of existing public housing stocks and newly built housing was introduced nationwide starting in 1988.[18] As a result, the nature of housing was transformed from public goods and services, as a part of the social welfare package enjoyed by employed urban residents, to commodities that were privately owned and largely provided by the private sector, with rights to be traded in the market.[19]

1998–2004: Development of Housing Markets

This period witnessed the rapid development of the urban housing market in China. State Council Document 23, issued in 1998, finally terminated direct public housing distribution to workers—the *danwei* housing system—and introduced cash subsidies for housing to newcomers entering the urban workforce. The government also provided subsidized housing or public rental housing to selected low- and middle-income families and relied on commercial housing to meet the needs of groups with access to mortgage financing. As a result, a vigorous urban housing market rapidly developed. Employers were allowed to offer housing subsidies to their new employees but could not involve themselves directly in housing construction, distribution, or management.[20]

The housing reform initiated in 1998 prescribes an urban housing system that promotes homeownership and a variety of housing services. It encourages the development of social rental housing (*lianzu fang*) that targets families with a monthly per capita income below the municipal poverty line and families with per person living space less than the minimum standard set by municipal governments. The central government also heavily subsidizes affordable housing (*jingji shiyong fang*), targeting low- to middle-income urban households. At the same time, the Chinese government relies on the private sector to provide commercial housing (*shangpin fang*) to satisfy the needs and demand for housing of higher-income households.

2005 to the Present: Addressing Housing Affordability and Low-Income Housing

The privatization of public housing and the reliance on the market for the provision of housing, unleashed by a series of reforms in the housing sector, have significantly increased the homeownership rate, increased the supply of housing and its quality, and improved the living conditions of a large number of urban households in China. But demand for housing has begun to outpace supply in the eastern coastal areas and in big cities, driving housing prices up drastically. Housing has become less and less affordable to low- and middle-income families, the urban poor, and the generation that entered the workforce after 1998.

Housing problems are gradually becoming a social issue, with the potential to threaten urban social stability and to hinder the establishment of a harmonious society. As State Council Document 24 indicates, the Chinese government has started to provide housing for low- and middle-income urban residents and to encourage the provision of smaller housing units, with price ceilings, and the construction of rental housing.

Housing Reform and the Middle Class: A Summary

Housing reform in recent years has had a profound effect on the formation and development of the middle class in China. Combined with increased income, expenditure levels, and educational levels, the middle class in China has also acquired housing and other assets and become an increasingly important factor in urban China's social, economic, and political development.

Homeownership, Housing Consumption, and Housing Value in China

Since 1998 the privatization of the housing sector has benefited a large number of households, and many families can now purchase houses from their work units or in the housing market. As a result, the homeownership rate, an important measure of the housing market in a country, has increased considerably in China.

This study follows the international standard, defining the homeownership rate as the ratio of owner-occupied housing units to total housing units. Survey data show that the owner-occupied homeownership rate in China reached 82.3 percent in 2007, exceeding the rate of many developed countries, such as the United States (in which the rate was 67.8 percent in 2008).[21] Like many other countries, the owner-occupied homeownership rate in China is highly correlated with household income. The middle-income class has an owner-occupied homeownership rate of 83.5 percent according to definition A and an 83.6 percent rate according to definition B. These numbers are 1.2 and 1.3 percentage points higher than the average ownership rate for all households in the sample.

In addition, housing size averaged about 83.6 square meters (about 900 square feet) of floor space per household, according to both definition A and definition B, indicating a significant increase in housing consumption since the beginning of economic reform in 1978.

Middle-class households also have benefited from a rapid increase in urban housing values. The median housing value of all households in the sample ranges from 130,000 yuan for the lowest 10 percent of household income to 644,000 yuan for the highest 10 percent, with a median value of 228,000 yuan (equivalent to $99,000 adjusted for PPP). This shows that housing has become a significant share of the wealth and assets of many households in urban China. The housing value of a dwelling occupied by the middle class ranges from 227,000 yuan to 228,000 yuan, depending upon the definition of middle class. These figures are a bit below the average housing value for all the households (281,000 yuan). It is likely that high-income groups are more likely to own a house, and so its market value is disproportionally much higher. As a result, the middle class as defined in this chapter may have a lower average market value of housing than the average for all households in the sample, largely owing to the large deviations among housing values across income groups.

Housing Affordability and the Chinese Middle Class

The housing reform that began in 1998 has resulted in rapid growth for the commodity housing market in China, a high homeownership rate, and high housing consumption measured by housing floor areas in a typical city. But reform has also led to a rapid increase in housing prices, particularly in China's eastern coastal region and big cities. The consequence is that many urban households, and lower-income families in particular, find housing to be unaffordable. In fact, housing prices have risen rapidly in many large cities in China since 1998, and many families, young people in particular, have been priced out of the market. To measure housing affordability, this study applies the price-to-income ratio (PIR), the commonly used method to compute the ratio of a house's value to household income. PIR, often calculated as the ratio of median house prices to median household income, is the basic affordability measure for housing in a given area.

The Global Urban Observatory of UN-HABITAT conducts an annual housing affordability survey that covers more than 200 markets in Australia, Canada, Ireland, New Zealand, the United Kingdom, and the United States.[22] The survey uses PIR as an indicator of housing affordability. Housing affordability is rated using four categories based upon the value of PIR:

—A PIR equal to or greater than 5.1 gives a housing rating of "severely unaffordable."

—A PIR of 4.1–5.0 gives a housing rating of "seriously unaffordable."

—A PIR of 3.1–4.0 gives a housing rating of "moderately unaffordable."

—A PIR of equal to or below 3.0 gives a housing rating of "affordable."

Based on the survey data, this study calculated the PIR ratio for the middle class under both definition A and definition B and finds that the PIRs for the middle class, using the two definitions, are 5.11 and 6.97, respectively. Both figures fall into the category of "severely unaffordable." In other words, the PRI exceeds the international standard of affordability, which means that the middle class in China is experiencing a housing affordability problem. Its members would have to spend more than five times their annual income to purchase a house.

This finding indicates that housing conditions in China are hurting the middle-income group, lowering the standard of living for the middle class as well as the urban poor, affecting the future prospects of the emerging middle class, and hindering the further growth of a strong middle class.

Major Findings and Conclusions

This chapter analyzes the size and characteristics of the middle class and its housing consumption in China. It uses two definitions of the middle class, definition A and definition B, using an approach based on income.

Using these two definitions, the middle class is defined either as the 50th and 60th percentiles of household income among the nearly 250,000 households in the 2007 large-sample Urban Household Survey (definition A) or as the group earning 75–125 percent of median per capita income (definition B). The study finds that the head of a middle-class household is about forty-one years old and that the average household size is three people.

The household's annual income is about 32,700 yuan, equivalent to $14,200 adjusted for PPP. The owner-occupied homeownership rate in China reached 82.3 percent in 2007 for all households in the sample, while the middle class in China fares a bit better, with a homeownership rate of 83.5 to 83.6 percent. The Chinese homeownership rate exceeds many developed countries, a significant outcome of successful housing reform. This study also finds that the average floor area of a middle-class dwelling is about 84 square meters (about 900 square feet). This is equivalent to about 63 square meters (about 675 square feet) of usable living space. By calculation, average floor area and usable living area per capita is about 28 square meters (about 300 square feet) and about 21 square meters (225 square feet), respectively, a significant improvement over the late 1970s figure of about 7 square meters (about 72 square feet) per capita. It hints at the success of the privatization of China's housing market in 1998.

Many middle-income households have also enjoyed the benefits of accumulated wealth derived from their homeownership. In 2007 the average market value of housing for this group was about 228,000 yuan (equivalent to $99,000), with an annual total household expenditure of about 23,400 yuan. Per capita daily expenditure in a typical urban household among China's middle class reached $9.20, meeting the international standard for the middle class in many developing countries. If this group of households belongs to the middle class, as this study argues, then it consists of 117 million to 156 million people, representing 20–27 percent of China's urban population. If one accepts the daily spending per capita standard of $8 to $10, then China's urban households whose income is above the 50th percentile all belong to the middle class. One can extrapolate that its size might even reach 350 million people in urban China.

The rapid growth of the housing market has also led to high housing prices in many cities. The price-to-income ratio for the Chinese middle class ranges from 5.1 to 6.9, suggesting that a majority of middle-class households in many cities in China face "severely unaffordable" housing, even though affordability is calculated using housing stock data. If the data on newly constructed housing are also considered, the housing affordability problem may be even more severe.

If as this study suggests housing has become severely unaffordable for much of the Chinese middle class in urban areas, and particularly for younger entrants to the market, then China's housing conditions have become an obstacle to the further growth of a strong Chinese middle class. Housing is already negatively affecting the standard of living for the middle class, whose members are often burdened with large mortgages. Without an effective and coherent policy promoting affordable housing and a strong commitment by various levels of government to promote and strengthen a middle class in China, the prospects of a vibrant, stable, and affluent middle class may be less than encouraging. The failure to establish a strong middle class in China may also negatively impact economic growth, the goal of a more consumption-based domestic economy, and the hope of building a harmonious and civil society in China.

This study favors a narrow definition of middle class, in a relative sense, based upon income level. Further research using other definitions may help us understand the middle class in China and its consumption patterns and preferences. Sound policies encouraging the growth of the middle class are necessary to ensure sustainable development in any country. This is particularly important for a populous country like China.

Notes

1. Joyce Yanyun Man, Siqi Zheng, and Rongrong Ren, "Housing Policy and Housing Markets in China: Trends, Patterns, and Affordability," in *China's Housing Reforms and Outcomes*, edited by Joyce Yanyun Man (Cambridge, Mass.: Lincoln Institute of Land Policy Press, forthcoming).

2. Nancy Birdsall, Carol Graham, and Stefano Pettinato, "Stuck in the Tunnel: Is Globalization Muddling the Middle Class?" Working Paper 14, Center on Social and Economic Dynamics (Brookings, 2000).

3. Abhijit V. Banerjee and Esther Duflo, "What Is Middle Class about the Middle Classes around the World?" (Department of Economics, Massachusetts Institute of Technology, 2007).

4. Brian W. Cashell, *Who Are the "Middle Class"?* Report for the Congress, March 20 (Congressional Research Service, 2007).

5. William Easterly, "The Middle Class Consensus and Economic Development," Policy Research Working Paper 2346 (World Bank, 2000).

6. "The New Middle Classes in Emerging Markets," *The Economist*, February 12, 2009.

7. The large-sample Urban Household Survey of 2007 covers more than 600 cities in China, with 520,000 responses to questionnaires. This data set is unique, because it reveals the conditions of the housing stocks in China instead of new construction, which accounts for only a portion of the total housing stock.

8. Birdsall, Graham, and Pettinato, "Stuck in the Tunnel."

9. Diane Farrell, Ulrich A. Gersch, and Elizabeth Stephenson, "The Value of China's Emerging Middle Class," *McKinsey Quarterly,* special edition, *Serving the New Chinese Consumer,* 2006.

10. Banerjee and Duflo, "What Is Middle Class about the Middle Classes around the World?"

11. See ibid.; and Birdsall, Graham, and Pettinato, "Stuck in the Tunnel."

12. This finding is close to the figure estimated by McKinsey Global Institute in 2009, which suggests China's lower middle class reaching 290 million people, and accounting for 44 percent of the urban population, by 2011.

13. See X. Q. Zhang, *A Study of Housing Policy in Urban China* (Commack, N.Y.: Nova Science Publishers, 1996); Y. P. Wang and A. Murie, "The Process of Commercialization of Urban Housing in China, *Urban Studies* 33, no. 6 (1996): 971–89; Y. P. Wang and A. Murie, *Housing Policy and Practices in China* (New York: St. Martin's Press, 1999); Yan Song, G. Knaap, and C. Ding, "Housing Policy in the People's Republic of China: A Historical Review," in *Emerging Land and Housing Markets in China,* edited by Chengri Ding and Yan Song (Cambridge, Mass.: Lincoln Institute of Land Policy Press, 2005); Man, Zheng, and Ren, "Housing Policy and Housing Markets in China."

14. Yang, Knaap, and Ding, "Housing Policy in the People's Republic of China."

15. Zhang, *A Study of Housing Policy in Urban China;* Wang and Murie, "The Process of Commercialization of Urban Housing in China"; and Wang and Murie, *Housing Policy and Practices in China.*

16. Zhang, *A Study of Housing Policy in Urban China.*

17. Ibid.

18. State Council, *The Notice on Further Reform of Urban Housing System and Speeding up Housing Development,* Document 23, July 3, 1998.

19. M. Zhou and J. R. Logan, "Market Transition and the Commodification of Housing in Urban China," *International Journal of Urban and Regional Research* 20, no. 3 (1996): 400–21; Y. P. Wang, "Social and Spatial Implications of Recent Housing Reform in Chinese Cities," in Man, ed., *China's Housing Reforms and Outcomes.*

20. Wang and Murie, *Housing Policy and Practices in China.*

21. Chinese homeownership rate was calculated by author using data from the large-sample Urban Household Survey of 2007, National Bureau of Statistics of China. The U.S. figure is drawn from U.S. Census Bureau, "Homeownership by Area," 2008. Also see "EU Homeownership Rates, 2002" (www.en.wikipedia.org).

22. UN-HABITAT (ww2.unhabitat.org/programmes/guo/guo_analysis.asp).

CHAPTER NINE

The Housing Effect: The Making of China's Social Distinctions

LUIGI TOMBA

It is not unusual for the social classifieds in urban Chinese newspapers and websites to include, when describing the qualities of a potential life partner, the following assertion: "Must own apartment and car." In the largest remaining socialist country in the world, real estate has become a common signifier of middle-class status among urban families, and homeownership is widespread. Colorful apartment blocks and tall buildings, often with outlandish designs or sequestered behind gates, have almost entirely replaced the grey, inexpensive, low-rise edifices (inspired by Soviet functionalism) that were the dominant residential form during the first three decades of the People's Republic of China. Scores of urban Chinese residents have been, in a mere two decades, transformed from employees and subsidized tenants of public housing to private investors and homeowners. In 2006 the Ministry of Construction announced that the homeownership rate in urban China had reached 82 percent, "the highest in the world."[1] These changes in residential space have been accompanied by changes in social spaces, by new hierarchies and governance modes, and by the remaking of social relations.

Research on housing reform in China has taken different directions. In some cases the emergence of a housing market has been seen as a problem

Funding for different aspects of this research was provided by an Australian Research Council Discovery Project grant (DP0662894) and by a German Research Foundation grant (TO638 1-2).

of real estate development, with increasing numbers of Chinese participating in the growth of an asset market previously accessible only through the redistributive system. Increasingly, however, researchers also point out the effects that this change is having on China's social and political arenas. Housing has been studied as an important element of the contemporary rearrangement of social stratification; as a spatial phenomenon through the domination of such forms as gated communities; as a territorial marker for the reorganization of urban governance, a manifestation of the increasing segregation of urban spaces; and finally, as an indication of more sophisticated "taste," a sign of the new ways in which consumption choices and consumption ability are affecting social structures.[2]

Arguments on the effect of housing often originate in the widely held assumption that, as was the case in other countries, mass private ownership of housing is one of the crucial engines behind the emergence of a middle class. In the case of China, through the combined effect of the redistribution of state-controlled assets and the marketization of such production factors as land (use rights), the privatization of public housing stock happened very rapidly. This in turn has suggested that propertied groups could achieve rights awareness and societal autonomy and, as a consequence, could bring pressure for democratization. Research on private housing and community building in residential compounds over the last decade has thus been looking for signs of this evolution; this research, however, has produced contradictory results, ranging from optimism to outright pessimism on the prospects of such a trajectory.[3]

Whatever the consequences for political participation, housing privatization has already had a major impact on other dimensions of Chinese society. In different parts of the country, however, this impact appears substantially different and is likely to affect the structures of opportunities of social groups in different ways. A focus on local experiences can therefore highlight the fragmentation within this newly formed propertied class in China, one that is spatially segregated, opportunity driven, and dependent on local political economic structures. Reform policies have not led to more certain, market-driven rules of social mobility but rather have greatly increased variations, depending on local conditions and the developmental models implemented by local elites.

My aim in this chapter is not to provide a rather unlikely unified theory of the impact of China's housing boom and privatization on the formation of a middle class and its characteristics but rather to paint a picture (through different cases) of the housing effect in light of the substantial variations and contradictions in the relationship between the middle classes and housing in China.[4] It should be said as a disclaimer that the housing boom of the last two decades—with the substantial land grab by local governments, the unprecedented urbanization of rural areas, and the reconstruction of broad swaths of traditional cities—also produced enduring and dramatic consequences for a new strata of urban, or peri-urban, poor, although this topic is beyond the bounds of this chapter.

The very existence of variations points to two important considerations that are crucial to our search for the middle class. First, the formation of new elites and the middle strata is path dependent and often driven by policies. The path, however, is drawn largely on the basis of local conditions of state-society relations and on the specific nature of the local political economy. This observation, rather than pointing to a national project to produce a unified middle class, suggests the need for a localized explanation of the emergence of a middle class/bourgeoisie. I thus place emphasis on the different impacts of local housing practices and policies on the emergence of a propertied middle class.[5]

Second, a propertied class seems to emerge out of vastly different structures of interests and opportunities, often in apparent contradiction with one another (public servants, educated highly skilled professionals, private entrepreneurs, newly affluent farmers). This suggests that unified, middle-class-based, action toward certain goals of political and structural change in China will not necessarily follow from the simple emergence of a better-off cluster of urban citizens.

This chapter argues that access to housing has been a crucial factor in the social mobility experienced by different groups over the last twenty years. It has also been a crucial lever, which local governments have activated differently, for the upward social mobility of various social groups, depending on the conditions of the local political economy. Some of these privileged groups had a bureaucratic background and enjoyed administrative advantages in their access to resources. Others, however, were unlikely winners, finding themselves the unexpected beneficiaries of a situation produced by the transformation of land and housing rights in their own locality. The common denominator among these groups remains, nonetheless, the ability to take advantage of their position in the local political economy to become homeowners.

To unravel these differences, I first present a short background on the housing reform policies of the last twenty years. I then focus my analysis on three dimensions of the housing effect:

—The building effect (the effect of the actual physical construction, ownership, and management of housing)

—The lifestyle effect (the effect of the various forms of housing on such issues as segregation, stratification, interest formation, and community)

—The governing effect (the impact that housing is having on the way in which the Chinese population is governed and administered).

By interweaving analysis along these three dimensions, this chapter provides a holistic picture of the impact of housing reform and its relationship to the emergence and nature of China's urban middle class. This multidimensional analysis aims to explain how differing forms of authority and power intervene in the construction of social distinctions through material and economic incentives, discourses of moral and ethical value, and flexible forms of governance.

From Tenants to Owners: China's Urban Housing Reform

The initial steps in the reform of housing allocation were taken in the early 1980s. Housing had long been considered part of the welfare provisions that enterprises and work units were required to make available to their employees. Despite the lack of a market and an emphasis on egalitarian redistribution, by 1978 the socialist distribution of housing had produced significant differences in the quality of housing available to urban workers. Better resourced *danwei*s, generally those with a higher status in the hierarchy of public enterprises, had been allocated larger and higher quality apartments for their employees. For the same reason, certain groups—including cadres, party members, and managers—had secured higher quality dwellings.[6]

When the housing reform started, first in the early 1980s and more systematically after 1988, the first step was to progressively privatize existing public housing and work-unit housing. The sale of these units to sitting tenants occurred between the end of the 1980s and the end of the 1990s and at substantially discounted prices (seniority, family composition, and position within the organization were often cause for further discounting). The consequence of this system was to turn the lifestyle advantages that certain tenants had acquired during the socialist period into concrete market advantages in the form of private assets. When during the 1990s the real estate market entered a period of rapid development, with the construction of large quantities of commercial housing (*shangpin fang*), these early birds could use their property as collateral to buy new commercial housing.

During the 1990s larger-scale local governments and state developers cooperated in making real estate one of the largest sources of revenue for municipal governments and housing the hottest commodity for urban consumers. Numerous policies contributed to stimulate homeowner-ship, including the subsidization of private housing purchased by urban middle-income earners through such programs as economy housing (*jingji shiyong fang*); the introduction of housing provident funds (*zhu-fang gongjijin*) among large enterprises and public employers; the pro-gressive opening up of a previously nonexisting mortgage market, with banks becoming heavily involved in the funding of the housing boom; and finally, the 1998 final step in housing reform, which prevented state-owned work units from providing housing to their employees. This last resulted in a substantial gap in opportunities between generations, as the youngest employees were unable to benefit from the subsidization that their older colleagues had enjoyed.

As a result of the construction boom and these long-term ownership-oriented policies, homeownership rates in urban centers are now among the highest in the world, banks devote almost 10 percent of their lending to residential mortgages (3.9 trillion yuan in mid-2009), and per capita residential space grew fourfold, to 26 square meters (about 280 square feet) in 2006.[7] Large projects characterized the construction of housing in urban centers (the average size of residential developments in Beijing was 53,000 square meters—or thirteen acres–in 2002), and gated com-munities with private guards controlling access and security have become the new architectural norm. Favored by local government regulations that encourage the erection of walls in new and old compounds, metro-politan areas have come to be dominated by highly segregated residential spaces. Miao Pu estimates that by the year 2000 almost 83 percent of Shanghai's neighborhoods had undergone some form of gating, while Guangdong Province already had 54,000 gated communities.[8] The amount of high-quality housing (*gaodang gongyu*) also grew steadily: in 2007 alone over 5 million square meters—or about 12,000 acres—of prestigious communities were sold in Shanghai and 3.2 million square meters (about 741 acres) in Beijing.[9] Development companies are among the biggest winners in this process, with skyrocketing profits. In 2007, for example, these profits reached 73.6 billion yuan in Shanghai.[10]

These reforms also brought about a separation between workplace and place of residence. With employers less likely to distribute housing, employees began to have more choice about where they lived. With the disappearance of the work unit as an agent of population management, the local state was forced to overhaul its neighborhood governance. Since 1999, in numerous Chinese cities, many of the governing and service functions previously performed by work units were transferred to neighborhood committees, which in many places were beefed up and renamed communities. Communities are subordinate to Street Offices (the lowest level of government) but are so-called self-governance institutions. Their role tends to depend on the type of neighborhood: they are more active and visible in poorer neighborhoods than in middle-class, gated communities. With the development of a culture of self governance at the neighborhood level, new institutions representing homeowners and residents have emerged, including homeowner committees (*yezhu weiyuanhui*), which are elected by the homeowners and are entitled to represent the residents' interests in disputes with the management companies.[11]

The Building Effect

The existence at the beginning of the 1980s of decaying residential units controlled by the state or its agents (by publicly owned work units, in particular), plus public ownership of urban land, ensured that the state remained at the center of the new housing market throughout its rapid development.[12] The construction industry was, no doubt, increasingly privatized: in 2007 development companies formally under state ownership amounted to only 6.7 percent of the total number, while companies with state participation accounted for about 8 percent of total investment in the industry.[13] Nonetheless, both state and public employers have continued to use housing as a perk for public employees and to reap the advantages derived from their control over land. By 1999, one year after the latest housing reform, about 48.4 percent of China's urban populations already owned privatized reform housing (*fanggai sifang*), that is, housing they had purchased from their work unit at a highly subsidized price. By then, public housing (*gongfang*) still housed over 28 percent of the urban population, while only about 5 percent had purchased commodity housing (*shangpin fang*).[14]

In the following decade, as mentioned earlier, permanent urban residents benefited from the combined effects of subsidized housing and of the original advantage of cheap entry into the housing market.[15] The housing policies of urban administrations were aimed at producing a substantial number of homeowners through specific low-income subsidization schemes rather than at providing public housing for the less well off. High rates of homeownership was a target consistent with other Asian urban experiences (Taiwan and Singapore have among the highest homeownership rates in the world) and contributed substantially to link the provision of housing subsidies to a population traditionally urban and employed in the public sector. Housing reform and the privatization of the real estate market not only produced more and better-quality housing but also enhanced the original advantages of those who benefited from the first redistribution of public housing.

Migrant workers and temporary residents (Beijing and Shanghai both house more than 7.7 million people without a permanent registration), as well as younger generations of urban workers excluded from the pre-1998 redistribution, became the groups most likely to rent apartments. Data from the Ministry of Public Security suggest, for example, that only a very small number of nonresidents have succeeded in purchasing apartments in the city, while 50 percent of them (61 million nationwide) lived in rented apartments in 2008.[16]

Further, only registered residents are entitled to the subsidized prices offered in such programs as *jingji shiyong fang* (economy housing). These apartments, generally of a quality similar to commercial properties (although generally of a smaller size), are sold at a significant discount to urban residents (generally middle-income, first-home buyers).[17] Nationwide, the program amounted to about 6 percent of the total sales of urban residential floor space in 2007, or about 33.4 million square meters (360 million square feet). In certain cities this advantage is more marked. In the same year, for example, the average market price per square meter for high-quality apartments was about 5.5 times higher than the average subsidized economy housing price in Beijing (15,740 and 2,869 yuan, respectively), but only two times higher in Shenyang (5,612 and 2,696 yuan).[18]

Despite increasing separation of workplace and housing, reform and privatization have not completely eliminated the impact that workplaces have on the ability of individuals to achieve homeownership, as public employment still provides significant advantages. As a matter of fact, during the 1990s the ability of different groups in society to access housing diverged even more dramatically, with people more linked to the state enjoying the bulk of the subsidization effort, even while the significance of public housing diminished. Enterprises also continued to include housing subsidies in their salary packages, thus favoring those who had managed a smooth transition from the *danwei* system to one of the new forms of stable employment.

That said, employment in public enterprises still provided an advantage: large and relatively wealthy nonproductive units, such as universities, were in a good position to subsidize homeownership, as they maintained control over land and capital. According to Beibei Tang's elaboration on a 2005 nationwide survey, employees in state-owned enterprises (68.2 percent), government offices (53.18 percent), and institutions (62.48 percent) have a much greater likelihood of achieving full or partial ownership rights to their own residence than employees in the private sector (31.02 percent).[19] Also, one's father's employment in the public sector remains, despite these reforms, an important predictor of better housing conditions and homeownership.[20]

During interviews in Beijing between 2002 and 2004 the role played by this housing subsidization in the upward mobility of the new middle classes was also evident. The housing careers of new homeowners had often been kick-started by the subsidized acquisition of a *danwei* dwelling, by access to subsidies to buy a second or even third apartment, by access to credit through the "housing provident fund," or again, through the use of the *danwei* apartment as collateral in a mortgage agreement. Despite relatively low average incomes and salaries, homeownership and even investment properties became a real possibility, especially for people within the system. Beijing is probably among the clearest cases in which the local government has used housing policies to boost consumption and build a broad-based, high-consuming, professional middle class.[21]

Not in all cities, however, were housing construction and the middle class so causally connected. In Shenyang, a city affected by rapid and substantial industrial decline, the building effect was very different.[22] Starved for cash and besieged by hundreds of thousands of unemployed, chiefly from its once-thriving state-owned heavy industrial plants, the local government had to strike a delicate balance: on the one hand it could not simply evict the already angry and disgruntled jobless from the central locations their old dwellings were built on. On the other hand, deprived of the income and status previously provided by the industrial enterprises and left with large welfare bills for its ailing, unemployed, and aging population, the local leadership was also forced to make the most out of the only asset it had available locally: land for real estate development in convenient locations. Of the over 50 million square meters of floor area under construction in Shenyang in 2007, 80 percent was residential, and the value of high-end commercial housing sold in the city more than tripled between 2006 and 2007. In 2005 alone the Shenyang municipality realized 8.3 billion yuan in land sales.[23] Despite relatively slow growth in average housing prices in Shenyang, the market price of better quality apartments in commercial housing easily surpasses 6,000 yuan per square meter.[24] A typical 80-square-meter apartment at this price costs 480,000 yuan, equivalent to more than twenty-nine years of an average Shenyang salary in 2005 (16,393 yuan).[25]

The stable incomes and hunger for property of the local professional middle class came to the rescue of such districts as Tiexi. Here an industrial tradition—established during the Japanese occupation and continued during the Soviet-funded industrialization—appeared to be invulnerable. But economic restructuring turned that expectation on its head, and most of Tiexi's factories were torn down.[26] Now, after being perceived for decades as a living industrial hell by residents of Shenyang's other areas, Tiexi is targeting a postindustrial urban middle class of professionals and educated employees to fill the new real estate developments, whose gardens and high rises are rapidly replacing factory yards.

This situation is producing a state-driven gentrification of the district, while the middle-aged *xiagang* (laid-off workers) are increasingly squeezed into smaller and more crowded residential areas, managed by committees of low-level cadres, and chronically dependent on public welfare. Thus middle-class values have helped the local government to appropriate its share of the 26 billion yuan in commercial apartment sales recorded in Shenyang in 2007.[27] The dream of high-quality homeowners (*gao suzhi yezhu*) is crucial to a project that has all but annihilated the industrial heritage of Tiexi and raised the economic value of the area.[28] Besides polarization, here the building effect is producing clear-cut segregation, driven by prices and living standards and a separation between the groups deemed residual and those deemed advanced.

Whereas in Beijing housing subsidization was a strategy to produce wealth among middle-income earners, in Shenyang the idea of a middle class created value for assets that the state already controlled. This production of value is made possible by a system that deems educated, wealthy, and successful citizens as a measure of civilization and modernization, as opposed to "backward" migrants and "stubborn" workers.

Developers convert inhospitable or highly polluted areas into what they term middle-class paradises, while the local media call the new residents pioneers in the development and conversion of dilapidated parts of the city and the government cooperates in the promotion by, for example, calling Shenyang a "forest city."[29]

If one steps away from the more traditional and postindustrializing cities of China, the picture of the building effect changes again. Traditional urban centers are shedding their industries or moving them to newly urbanizing peripheries, so that industrialization is now affecting the countryside. In Guangdong Province, for example, rapid industrialization has produced a great variety of local arrangements of housing. Different from most other places in China, the power of the state to grab land from local communities has here had to face the resilience of rural collectives. This has not only produced such sociospatial phenomena as "villages in the cities," where villagers have maintained land rights even after its redevelopment and preserved village practices in highly urbanized settings, it has also positively affected the upward social mobility of specific groups (in this case, farmers).[30] This newfound and unexpected wealth has been the consequence of the specific conditions of the local political economy, characterized by rapid industrialization, availability of land, a favorable geographic location, the existence of informal governance structures such as lineages, and most important collective land ownership and villagers' ability to resist the local state and to bargain with it.

Urbanization in the Pearl River Delta has come with an unexpected bonus for traditional farmers, as industrialization has produced substantial increases in the value of the land they used to farm and the value of the housing they build. When village-held agricultural land is reallocated to industrial production or to real estate projects, local villagers realize the advantages of economic growth not through jobs but through land leases and the construction and renting of private housing. While urban land is leased for seventy years to real estate developers, who build gated communities, in the Pearl River Delta township-level governments maintain control over building permits, and housing is therefore mainly self-built. Townships and villages have strict regulations on the size of the lots (*zhaijidi*) allocated to families for housing construction (generally 80 square meters, or 861 square feet) and on the height of buildings (14 meters, or 46 feet). However, with the population density rapidly growing, the more industrialized areas often allow much higher houses to be built by local families.

The construction of rural housing in Guangdong Province has continued to grow steadily; and per capita floor space rose from 17 square meters to 27 square meters between 1990 to 2007. *Loufang* (or multistory buildings) are rapidly replacing the traditional *pingfan* (traditional one-story dwellings). The per capita floor space in the latter steadily declined over the last decade, from 7.8 square meters to 5.4 square meters.[31] Only resident villagers are allowed to build new houses, a monopoly that provides villagers with the exclusive profits of a booming rental market. These peculiar conditions of the local political economy in a time of rapid industrialization and urbanization are turning farmers into a local bourgeoisie, which protects its interests by occupying the local political hierarchies. Marketization has favored the position of certain communities (paradoxically, this is reinforced by the existence of both traditional and socialist norms) over the proverbial innovation of market entrepreneurs. Thus the building effect is, here, contributing to the emergence of a different type of middle class, one that is oddly enough the outcome of both industrialization and the resilience of socialist collective practices, which make local villagers the beneficiaries of economic growth and urbanization.

In each of the examples above—Beijing, Shenyang, and Guangdong—the building of houses appears intrinsically connected with the emergence of new wealthy groups. The building effect and its beneficiaries are, however, very different. In Beijing the middle class is the result of a conscious intervention of the local bureaucracies, aimed at producing through housing a new high-consuming and high-quality middle class. In Shenyang the middle class is used as a marker of civilization, one that contributes to the rebranding of an old industrial city with immense social problems into a postindustrial city with a profitable real estate market. In Guangdong traditional communities' positional advantages and the resilience of collective and lineage practices turned local villagers into winners in the process of industrialization. The three groups and the three cases suggest that the experience of upward mobility is driven by the developmental and modernization projects of the local states.

The Lifestyle Effect

Another important argument relating to the contemporary housing boom is that reform-era China's new living arrangements are having a substantial impact on what China's middle class will look like in the near future. The impact of housing privatization, in this respect, has at least three dimensions. First, privatization has produced a separation between individuals' living and working environments, thus providing an alternative arena for status formation.[32] No longer dependent for its status on the work unit, the Chinese citizen is finding new interests to protect and is exploring grassroots participation inside the residential community, where it develops identities as both a consumer and a political actor. Second, especially through the social inclusion and exclusion of private gated residential areas (now the dominant living environment in large cities), new housing is producing new solidarities and communities among people with similar interests and therefore potentially contributing to the formation of a middle-class identity.[33] Third, the lifestyles offered by private housing are providing an opportunity for the middle class to experience and establish a specific "taste," which not only drives consumption patterns, behaviors, and desire for political participation but also immerses the Chinese middle class in the global stream of middle-class consumerism.[34]

It is open for question whether or not the privatization of residential communities and housing property is indeed producing a middle-class identity, more autonomy from the state, and more potential for political participation—elements that would suggest a political role to be played by these new homeowners. I do, however, suggest that these three processes are not straightforward and that their impacts on the political system are not as much a matter of quantity (that is, how much identity, autonomy, and political participation the middle classes have developed) as they are a matter of quality (the types of identity, autonomy, and participation that are developing). My own observations suggest a much more complex and contradictory picture than the one presented in today's mainstream narratives describing China's possible political futures.

To begin with, the identity developed through engagement in community activities is not the marker of a new class identity. Housing-related interests are very localized, and the autonomy that homeowner communities gain through their engagement in community matters is limited by the physical and normative boundaries of their own living environment. The conflicts in urban residential communities could suggest the possibility of a united front of homeowners that might effect social change. These conflicts, however, are atomized, concern mainly private players, and have yet to develop into a force for social change. There are indeed cases of individual activists becoming involved in the political process at a level higher than their own community (*weiquan* lawyers and independent candidates for local people's congresses have sometimes come from the ranks of homeowners), but homeowner unions have never materialized. Participation is also geographically, functionally, and numerically limited. The legal status of homeowner committees allows them to intervene only in members' relationships with management companies in their own compounds. Elections of homeowner representatives can indeed become an exercise in participation, but these elections are often run by the management company and encourage only limited participation.

In communities characterized by numerous conflicts, like Beijing and Shanghai, grievances over localized and practical problems have indeed produced significant potential for socialization and for community-level action and participation, but these have a rather limited scope. In my interviews, even the most active of homeowners in the middle of a conflict generally described themselves as angry consumers and used the language of patriotism, responsibility, and human quality, rather than that of autonomy.[35] They often mentioned the imperative of building a stronger nation as a frame for their grievances as well as the responsibility attached to their roles as the elites of the country.[36] The standard governmental discourse of harmony and human quality has found a fertile ground among these homeowners, who are often the loudest supporters of social stability. While these attitudes might be treated as strategic frames, which homeowners mobilize to legitimize their claims vis-à-vis the state and other stakeholders, they also limit the systemic impact of such very common conflicts and contain them within the private sphere.

Homeowners are also divided among themselves. Since, as I mentioned earlier, the present generation of homeowners is the result partly of market reforms and partly of public subsidization, the path toward homeownership often produces clear distinctions within their ranks. In Shenyang's gated communities homeowners from the public sector often see themselves as radically different from the private entrepreneurs who live in the same compound, and vice versa. The two groups often despise one another: public servants see the market-driven new rich as the result of corruption and immoral behavior, while entrepreneurs often see public servants as parasites, privileged by their reliance on (and knowledge of) state policies.

While homeownership is a shared experience for many in late socialist China, it is not an undivided identity. Belonging and group loyalty seem to attach to social status and to a particular group rather than to the abstract idea of a proactive middle class. The diffusion and sharing of values and interests that are necessary for a new class to solidify its identity do not appear to be a consequence of homeownership. The issue of housing consumption and the protection of interests and rights remains largely a localized one, taking different shapes in different cities. One's relationship to the state, for example, remains an important defining element of belonging, with life histories, professions, and educational background as other possible markers of identity formation. Although it is much more complex and divided than it used to be, the structure of representation of collective interests still allows the state to maintain control over which identities are possible and which are not, which interests deserve representation and protection and which are likely to produce social unrest. In such a hierarchy of interests, homeowners, as a category rather than a class, are encouraged to represent their own interests, but their autonomy remains limited by their nature as consumers, by the physical environment in which they live, and by the narrow scope of their representative bodies.

The private nature of the new residential compounds and the exclusive lifestyles offered by developers and management companies are also sometimes seen as important elements of the emergence of middle-class taste and increasingly sophisticated forms of consumption. One should not, however, forget that lifestyles in these newly built and privately managed compounds are almost invariably decided upon at an early stage of large-scale real estate development. They are, in other words, often built in rather than the product of communities adapting their living environment to their own needs or desires (as is sometimes the case in the gentrification in Western metropolises). The potential for subcultural outcomes or alternative lifestyles (that in other environments is creeping through the interstices of Chinese society) is very limited in these highly policed and highly sanitized new housing complexes. The market of lifestyles is largely segmented a priori, so that people must choose among compounds aimed at singles, with small apartments and a focus on entertainment and socialization; those aimed at families, with facilities and services for kids; or those aimed at professionals, with services to favor uninterrupted productivity. Or the choices might be characterized as high security, education-intensive, or even harmonious.

Thus the domination of large housing complexes makes lifestyle (*shenghuo fangshi*) a part of the commercial offering that developers attach to their real estate projects, to the point that some developers and managers even try to patent their own lifestyle. Large, gated compounds promote a segmentation of lifestyles, what Jing Wang calls hairsplitting marketing strategies.[37] Cities like Beijing and Shenyang are not experiencing gentrification (understood here as a process that requires a certain agency by the creative and wealthy classes) so much as a hierarchy of lifestyles sanctioned by the city's planning agencies.

In other words, at least in the realm of housing, the emergence of so-called middle-class taste is largely the result of the entrepreneurship of both local governments and real estate developers. Local governments see conservative and value-producing middle classes as preferable to the troublemaking but hard-working migrants and disenfranchised workers. Developers seek to maximize their returns by reaping long-term profits from managing a homeowner's existence. Both groups buy into the same moral discourse promoted by the government about ethical communities and moral principles. One of the most successful and profitable private developers in China, for example, describes its business as "building a boundless life" based on "humanism," where "morality and ethics are more important than commercial profit." The company claims to "persist in its moral value principles and refuse the temptation of profits" and highlights in its new neighborhoods the principle of "civility" (*wenming*).[38]

The organic view of the middle class that I have presented so far is not intended to deny the social change that China is experiencing or the potential agency of these new social groups. Rather, I wish to point out that the identity of the new, propertied middle class is being shaped by an institutional and market environment still largely dominated by state-produced discourses and by market agents acting largely in the interest of social order and the developmental strategies of the local state. In other words, I want to raise the possibility that because of the hegemonic involvement of state actors in housing privatization, the emergence of new identities that are generally associated with the new private living environment and with market reforms might, in fact, be less about autonomy and more about a new form of governing social change.

The Governing Effect

The privatization of housing also had important consequences for how urban China is governed, both by redefining the tools of grassroots government and by producing spaces of limited autonomy where the middle class can become more involved in (and made more responsible for) the harmonious (*hexie*) management of its interests and the preservation of social order.[39]

With the decline of the role of socialist work units, the literature on urban governance has focused on several aspects of this governmental reform. Through so-called community building (*shequ jianshe*, a campaign to reform the lowest level of community governance started around 2000 in many cities) local administrations transfer the governmental jurisdiction of resident populations from work units to territorial units. These communities (*shequ*) are an evolution of the existing residents committee (*jumin weiyuanhui*), manned by a mix of elected cadres and hired employees.[40] This strategy, divided and flexible, is perceived by the population in different ways depending on people's level of dependence on (or autonomy from) the state. The differentiation in the typologies of housing that resulted from privatization has thus also produced a fundamental segmentation of governance strategies.

In older compounds, where the older and worse off population is generally found, governance is still a matter of visibility, intervention, control over the territory, and dependence on public welfare. Community committees are still seen as the government. In private compounds, however, the state relies on private agents (private management companies and guards in particular) to maintain social order. The proliferation of private agents suggests a progressive privatization, or subcontracting, of governance functions. I encountered numerous examples of local governments that subcontract such activities as family planning and security to private management companies. In some conflict-ridden middle-class compounds it was relatively common for homeowners to organize public protests inside the premises of the residential areas, which were patrolled by private guards rather than by the police. Only demonstrations that left the compound would attract the attention and presence of the local police.

The governing effect produced by housing privatization is thus twofold. First, at a time when work units have lost their function of controlling both territory and a given population, community-based governance improves the legitimacy of the city's social hierarchies. By increasing segmentation and segregation among social groups, local states are able to put in place governing mechanisms that are substantially different depending on where people live. The same segregation sold by real estate companies as a characteristic of their compounds' lifestyle becomes a useful tool to modulate the intensity of direct governing activities. Second, the privatization of housing and related services makes it possible for the Chinese state to govern through a number of agents (real estate developers, management companies, security guards, Internet providers, for example), performing tasks that used to be carried out directly by state institutions.

These two processes cut to the heart of the relationship between China's new homeowners and the authoritarian state: a growing flexibility in the ways people are governed. In middle-class neighborhoods the contacts that citizens maintain with the state are very limited and often mediated through private agents. The visibility of the state and its institutions in the daily activities of socialization is restricted. Here residents hardly know the location, let alone the function and composition, of their community committees. In older compounds, however, community cadres play a central role among neighbors in conflict resolution and social campaigns and in monitoring social problems. In Shenyang's working-class compounds, where residents often still depend on the welfare distributed by community committees, the visibility of the state and contact with it are very high, with all daily activities and services at the level of the community still provided by cadres. Services that the communities provide include the distribution of subsidies, reemployment services, family planning, sanitation, security, and even recreation.

Where private actors, like management companies, perform public functions, their relationship with public actors is generally a collaborative one. In some of Shenyang's middle-class areas the privately hired head of the management company is also the elected director of the state-controlled community committee, thus enabling a paradoxical situation in which private employees perform public functions. In the same way, it is not uncommon for private managers to take upon themselves the role of implementing public campaigns inside the compounds. Gated communities have sometimes been accused by state media of being a safe haven for violations, as in the numerous reported infringements of the one-child policy among upper-class urban families.[41] This ability to avoid the daily interference of the government creates, indeed, a possibility for the middle and upper classes to "buy" some autonomy from the state. This autonomy, however, remains limited to the sphere of private behaviors and private conflicts and is spatially demarcated by the spaces under the control of the management company.

The development of a wealthy, educated, consuming, and above all "responsible" urban middle class serves what seems to be the present purpose of the Chinese government: the gradual transition to an orderly and efficient state capitalism that protects the legitimacy and supremacy of the existing regime. Also, the apparent acquiescence and self-discipline of this group appear to be a consequence of its long-term involvement in the developmental strategies of the state, first as members of a privileged urban workforce and then as members of an upwardly mobile educated elite. An urban middle class possessing what one Chinese sociologist calls a "well trained ethical and civil awareness and self-discipline" is a facet of China's governmental strategy, relying on co-optation, agency, and an ethos of self-discipline.[42] The institutions of the state have not just retreated in the face of an advancing market, they have participated actively by creating a justification for the existence of a middle class in a technically classless society and by helping to give rise to new, diffused, and responsible economic elites.

Housing reform (privatization and the sale of public housing) and the reform of neighborhood institutions have contributed to a zoning of urban populations based on consumption as opposed to the earlier cell-structured spatial pattern organized around the work unit. In other words, China has drastically moved away from the ideal of a democratic urban space divided into self-reliant work units to a situation in which residential and productive areas occupy completely separate suburbs and in which different social groups live in different parts of town.[43] Both official rhetoric and popular discourse justify this arrangement by placing those with better *suzhi* on a higher step on the ladder of the civilization. *Suzhi* therefore becomes the foundation of a new rationality of government that the middle class (for which it is a component of social capital and is set as a self-affirming benchmark) is willing to endorse and act upon. The outcome is a classification of society into those who are exemplars of modernity and can be trusted to govern themselves (*zizhi*) and those who need to be improved and governed: these latter include the low-*suzhi* migrants and the downwardly mobile urban working class.

Social spaces have become essential tools for the enforcement of this hierarchy, arenas for the cooperation of governmental and nongovernmental actors interested in shaping the outcomes of urban modernization. Pro-growth coalitions have emerged among local governments, real estate developers, and speculators to address the new middle class's demand for modernity (lucrative for the developers and empowering for the administrators).[44] As a result of this collective effort, residential spaces and the traditional social arrangement of cities have been radically transformed since the 1990s.

The involvement of the state in land allocation and the privilege accorded by developers to large projects has also led not to a more open planning of private spaces but to the dominance of the gated community. The form of the segregated community has, to use Ann Anagnost's words, spatially "concretized" the "rhetoric and practice of separation" employed in the strategies of middle-class positioning.[45] According to Aihwa Ong, the "graduated citizenship" resulting from China's zoning technologies is an attempt to maximize return for global capital. Graduated citizenship is, in her words, "an effect of states moving from being an administrator of a watertight national entity to regulators of diverse spaces and populations that link with global markets."[46] However, the active classification undertaken through the gating of urban spaces and the resulting flexible governance patterns does not reduce the Chinese state to a simple tool of global capital. It facilitates, rather than compromises, the state's legitimacy as the administrator of a national entity.

The policy of community self-government has also affected the making of a middle class. Despite the new governance system having been renamed community self-government (*shequ zizhi*), the democratic content of grassroots governance and elections remains limited. Participation is low, and elections are indirect and noncompetitive.[47] Inside privately owned gated communities, however, where rights consciousness is generally higher, homeowners are alert to even minor infringements of their rights, and private interests can coalesce in a more homogenous form to determine higher rates of participation. But autonomous participation within these spaces is limited by the physical and administrative boundaries of the community. Gates therefore work both as inclusive and exclusive technologies (creating social spaces but limiting autonomy to clearly delineated social and consumption groups). However, because these groups enjoy self-administration and relative autonomy, homeowners' activism is often imbued with an ethos of social and political responsibility. An ethos of this kind leads the newly propertied, loan-repaying groups to share elements of the civilized discourse of the political and intellectual elites. Thus popular perceptions of middle-class status and social roles often intersect with and reinforce the discourses of *suzhi*—civic and moral self-cultivation—rather than challenge the legitimacy of the authoritarian government.

Making Sense of the Housing Effect

The housing effect is much more than simply the effect of housing privatization. It includes the effects of economic reform and state policies on social stratification, of social organization on the remaking of social hierarchies, and of new private spaces on the legitimacy of urban areas and the new forms of governance. The social distinctions that characterize the emergence of China's middle class are thus a complex construction involving the agency of governments, private actors, and economic communities.

Housing has been a central facet in this process during the last two decades. Its effects vary, however, and are shaped by local conditions. To assume, for example, that only certain groups would benefit from housing privatization would be to ignore the fact that elites are shaped by the local political economy. Local middle classes that took advantage of differing housing policies differ greatly; they evolved under different political economic conditions and according to a variety of developmental strategies adopted by local governments.

I take housing to expose a central paradox in our understanding of the role of the middle class in China's current social and political changes. On one side the privatization of housing and homeownership are shared experiences among a generation of urban residents and are likely to produce shared private interests among a broad group of urbanites who might favor an increase in autonomy. On the other side, however, such privatization is also producing a more conservative middle class with a stake in the preservation of the social order and whose frames of reference are informed by the moral discourses of quality and responsibility.

In other words, while housing has indeed improved the economic opportunities of certain social groups (in particular those able to benefit from their proximity to the state), it has not produced the kind of proactive middle class that we might expect, in the short term, to promote political change.

Notes

1. "'Zhufang siyoulü shijie di yi' bu shi zhengji shi weiji" ["The highest homeownership rate in the world" is not an achievement but a risk], *Renmin wang,* October 7, 2006 (politics.people.com.cn/GB/30178/4577745.html).

2. There is a growing literature on all these themes that is almost impossible to summarize here. On the development of a real estate market, see Yaping Wang and Alan Murie, "Commercial Housing Development in Urban China," *Urban Studies* 36, no. 9

(1999): 1475–94; S. M. Li and D. K. W. Fung, "Housing Tenure and Residential Mobility in Urban China: Analysis of Survey Data," occasional paper, Center for China Urban and Regional Studies (Hong Kong Baptist University, 2001); X. Q. Zhang, "The Restructuring of the Housing Finance System in Urban China," *Cities* 17, no. 5 (2000): 339–48. On housing and social stratification, see L. Wang, "Urban Housing Welfare and Income Distribution," in *China's Retreat from Equality: Income Distribution and Economic Transition,* edited by C. Riskin, R. Zhao, and S. Li (Armonk, N.Y.: M. E. Sharpe, 2001), pp. 167–83; J. Li and X. Niu, "The New Middle Class(es) in Peking: A Case Study," *China Perspectives* 45 (2003): 4–20; L. Tomba, "Creating an Urban Middle Class: Social Engineering in Beijing," *China Journal* 51 (2004): 1–26; Y. P. Wang, "Housing Reform and Its Impacts on the Urban Poor in China," *Housing Studies* 15, no. 6 (2000): 845–64. On China's gated spaces, see F. Wu, "Rediscovering the 'Gate' under Market Transition: From Work-Unit Compounds to Commodity Housing Enclaves," *Housing Studies* 20, no. 2 (2005): 235–54; G. Giroir, "The Purple Jade Villas (Beijing)," in *Private Cities: Global and Local Perspective,* edited by G. Glasze, C. Webster, and K. Frantz (London: Routledge, 2006); C.-P. Pow, "Securing the Civilised Enclaves: Gated Communities and the Moral Geographies of Exclusion in (Post)-Socialist Shanghai," *Urban Studies* 44, no. 8 (2007): 1539–58; Choon-Piew Woo, *Gated Communities in China: Class Privilege and the Moral Politics of a Good Life* (London: Routledge, 2009). On housing and urban governance, see D. Bray, "Building 'Community': New Strategies of Governance in Urban China," *Economy and Society* 35, no. 4 (2006): 530–49; D. Bray, *Social Space and Governance in Urban China: The Danwei System from Origins to Reform* (Stanford University Press, 2005); L. Tomba, "Residential Space and Collective Interest Formation in Beijing's Housing Disputes," *China Quarterly* 184 (2005): 934–51. On residential segregation, see Wang, "Housing Reform and Its Impacts on the Urban Poor in China"; X. Hu and D. H. Kaplan, "The Emergence of Affluence in Beijing: Residential Social Stratification in China's Capital City," *Urban Geography* 22, no. 1 (2001): 54–77. On the consumption of housing and its impact on social structures, see D. S. Davis, ed., *The Consumer Revolution in Urban China* (University of California Press, 2000); L. Tomba and B. Tang, "The Forest City: Homeownership and New Wealth in Shenyang," in *The New Rich in China: Future Rulers, Present Lives,* edited by D. S. G. Goodman (London: Routledge, 2008), pp. 171–86.

3. Among the optimists, see Bruce Gilley, *China's Democratic Future: How It Will Happen and Where It Will Lead* (Columbia University Press, 2004); Ronald M. Glassman, *China in Transition: Communism, Capitalism, and Democracy* (New York: Praeger, 1991). For more cautious views, see D. S. G. Goodman, ed., *The New Rich in China: Future Rulers, Present Lives* (London: Routledge, 2008); Kellee S. Tsai, *Capitalism without Democracy. The Private Sector in Contemporary China* (Cornell University Press 2007); Tomba, "Creating an Urban Middle Class."

4. Over the last five years I have conducted fieldwork (including participatory observation and in-depth interviews) in housing compounds of different types in Beijing, Chengdu, Shenyang, and Shunde (Foshan) in the Pearl River Delta. This chapter uses some of the findings to highlight a more comprehensive evaluation of the different impacts of housing reform.

5. Tomba, "Creating an Urban Middle Class."

6. B. Li, "Zhongguo zhufang gaige zhidu de fenge xing [The unequal nature of China's housing reform]," *Shehuixue yanjiu* [Research in the social sciences] 2 (2002): 80–87.

7. For mortgage lending, see "OECD Economic Surveys: China 2010" (www.oecd. org/eco/surveys/China); for residential space, see Mark Duda, Xiulan Zhang, and Mingzhu Dong, *China's Homeownership-Oriented Housing Policy: An Examination of Two Programs Using Survey Data from Beijing,* W05-7, Joint Center for Housing Studies (Harvard University, 2005); L. Tomba, "Gating Urban Spaces: Inclusion, Exclusion, and

Government," in *Gated Communities: Social Sustainability in Contemporary and Historical Gated Developments,* edited by S. Bagaeen and O. Uduku (London: Earthscan, 2009).

8. P. Miao, "Deserted Streets in a Jammed Town: The Gated Community in Chinese Cities and Its Solution," *Journal of Urban Design* 8, no. 1 (2003): 45–66.

9. State Statistical Bureau, *2008 Zhongguo fangdichan tongji nianjian* [Statistic yearbook of China's real estate] (Beijing: China Statistical Press, 2008), p. 435.

10. Ibid., p. 444.

11. Tomba, "Residential Space and Collective Interest Formation in Beijing's Housing Disputes"; B. Read, "Democratizing the Neighbourhood? New Private Housing and Home-Owner Self-Organization in Urban China," *China Journal* 49 (2003): 31–59.

12. X. Q. Zhang, "Governing Housing in China: State, Market, and Work Units," *Journal of Housing and the Built Environment* 17, no. 1 (2002): 7–20.

13. State Statistical Bureau, *2008 Zhongguo fangdichan,* pp. 346–47.

14. Yunqing Zhou, *Zhongguo chengzhen jumin zhufang juzhu zhiliang* [Residential quality of Chinese urban household] (Beijing: Shehuikexue wenxian chubanshe, 2008), p. 121.

15. See Zhang, "The Restructuring of the Housing Finance System in Urban China"; Tomba, "Creating an Urban Middle Class."

16. The rest of the nonresidents are reported living either at their workplace or with their employing family. Gonganbu zhian guanli jubian, *2009 nian quanguo zanzhu renkou tongji zailiao huibian* [2009 statistic collection on temporary residents in China] (Beijing: Qunzhong chubanshe, 2009).

17. Tomba, "Creating an Urban Middle Class."

18. State Statistical Bureau, *2008 Zhongguo fangdichan.*

19. Beibei Tang, "The Making of Housing Status Groups in Postreform Urban China: Social Mobility and Status Attainment of Gated Community Residents in Shenyang," Ph.D. dissertation, Australian National University, p. 102.

20. Ibid., p. 105.

21. Tomba, "Creating an Urban Middle Class."

22. J. Chen and A. Barrientos, "Extending Social Assistance in China: Lessons from the Minimum Living Standard Scheme," Working Paper 67 (Manchester: Chronic Poverty Research Centre, 2006); E. P. W. Hung and S. W. K. Chiu, "The Lost Generation: Life Course Dynamics and Xiagang in China," *Modern China* 29, no. 2 (2003): 204–36; C. K. Lee, *Against the Law: Labor Protests in China's Rustbelt and Sunbelt* (University of California Press, 2007).

23. State Statistical Bureau, *2008 Zhongguo fangdichan,* p. 521.

24. The average price per square meter rose from 2,686 yuan in 2000 to 3,118 yuan in 2007, or slightly more than 15 percent. Prices of higher quality housing have, however, been growing much faster. State Statistical Bureau, *2008 Zhongguo fangdichan,* p. 437.

25. Shenyang Statistical Bureau, *Shenyang Statistical Yearbook, 2006.*

26. Tomba and Tang, "The Forest City."

27. State Statistical Bureau, *2008 Zhongguo fangdichan,* p. 441.

28. The most impressive graphic documentation of the final years of Tiexi's industrial and social decline is a nine-hour documentary by the Beijing-based director Wang Bing: B. Wang, "Tiexi qu" [A l'ouest de rails: west of the tracks] (MK2, Allumettes Films, 2004).

29. I describe some of these strategies in Luigi Tomba, "Of Quality, Harmony, and Community: Civilization and the Middle Class in Urban China," *Positions: East Asia Cultures Critique* 17, no. 3 (2009): 591–616. Also see Tomba and Tang, "The Forest City."

30. For villages in the cities, see T. Li, "The Chengzhongcun Land Market in China: Boon or Bane? A Perspective on Property Rights," *International Journal of Urban and Regional Research* 32, no. 2 (2008): 282–304. For an example of upward social mobility

in a Guangdong village, see Anita Chan, Richard Madsen, and Jon Unger's updated edition of *Chen Village: From Revolution to Globalization* (University of California Press, 2009).

31. Guangdong Statistical Bureau, *Guangdong Nongcun Tongji nianjian, 2008* [Agricultural statistical yearbook of Guangdong, 2008] (Beijing: Zhongguo Tongji Chubanshe, 2008), p. 457.

32. Li and Niu, "The New Middle Class(es) in Peking"; Hu and Kaplan, "The Emergence of Affluence in Beijing"; T. Heberer, "Die Reorganisation Staedtischer Wohnviertel Im Lichte Kommunitarischer Und Partizipativer Vorstellungen," *China Aktuell* (2003): 1223–240.

33. Read, "Democratizing the Neighbourhood?"

34. Goodman, ed., *The New Rich in China: Future Rulers, Present Lives;* Read, "Democratizing the Neighbourhood?"; Gilley, *China's Democratic Future.*

35. On the discourse of *suzhi* in contemporary China, see Ann Anagnost, "The Corporeal Politics of Quality (*Suzhi*)," *Public Culture* 16, no. 2 (2004): 189–208; Tomba, "Of Quality, Harmony, and Community"; A. Kipnis, "Suzhi: A Keyword Approach," *China Quarterly* 186 (2006): 295–313; H. Yan, "Neoliberal Governmentality and Neohumanism: Organizing Suzhi/Value Flow through Labor Recruitment Networks," *Cultural Anthropology* 18, no. 4 (2003): 493–523.

36. On the use of a patriotic frame in the creation of identities among professionals, see L. Hoffman, "Autonomous Choices and Patriotic Professionalism: On Governmentality in Late-Socialist China," *Economy and Society* 35, no. 4 (2006): 550–70.

37. Jing Wang, "Bourgeois Bohemian in China? Neo-Tribes and the Urban Imaginery," *China Quarterly* 185 (2005): 532–48.

38. *Qiju: Wanke de fangzi* [Poetic dwelling: Vanke's house] (Wuhan: Huazhong keji daxue chubanshe, 2007), p. 8.

39. Creeping democracy has been discussed as a potential consequence of institutional reform at the local level both in the countryside and in the cities. Read, "Democratizing the Neighbourhood?"; Z. He, T. Heberer, and G. Schubert, eds., *Citizen Participation in Rural and Urban Areas and Political Legitimacy* [Chengxiang gongmin canyu he zhengzhi hefaxing] (Beijing: Zhongyang bianyi chubanshe, 2007); R. Benewick, I. Tong, and J. Howell, "Self-Governance and Community: A Preliminary Comparison between Villagers' Committees and Urban Community Councils," *China Information* 18, no. 1 (2004): 11–28.

40. The word *shequ*, meaning a spatially delimited social area, is generally translated as community. While this use was first introduced by Fei Xiaotong as a translation of *Gemeinschaft*, its use today in public jargon generally refers to institutions that administer a residential estate. F. Xu, "Gated Communities and Migrant Enclaves: The Conundrum for Building 'Harmonious Community/*shequ*,'" *Journal of Contemporary China* 17, no. 57 (2008): 633–51. On the evolution of community committees from resident committees introduced in Communist China since the 1950s, see among others Bray, "Building 'Community'"; R. Benewick and A. Takahara, "Eight Grannies and Nine Teeth between Them: Community Construction in China," *Journal of Chinese Political Science* 7, nos. 1–2 (2002); B. Read, "Revitalizing the State's Urban 'Nerve Tips,'" *China Quarterly* 163 (2000): 806–20.

41. One such example is Yan Ping, "Dalian gaodang xiaoqu cheng le 'chaosheng bifeng gang'" [Dalian high-quality neighborhoods become safe havens for illegal births], *Renmin wang,* June 15, 2003 (past.people.com.cn/GB/shehui/47/20030615/ 1016299.html).

42. X. Lu, ed., *Dangdai zhongguo shehu jieceng yanjiu baogao* [Research report on contemporary China's social stratification] (Beijing: Shehuikexue wenxian chubanshe, 2002), p. 254.

43. Bray, *Social Space and Governance in Urban China;* Hu and Kaplan, "The Emergence of Affluence in Beijing"; Z. Li and F. Wu, "Sociospatial Differentiation and Residen-

tial Inequalities in Shanghai: A Case Study of Three Neighbourhoods," *Housing Studies* 21, no. 5 (2006): 695–717.

44. L. Zhang, "Contesting Spatial Modernity in Late Socialist China," *Current Anthropology* 37, no. 3 (2006): 461–84. See also You-tien Hsing, *The Great Urban Transformation: Politics and Property in China* (Oxford University Press, 2010).

45. Anagnost, "The Corporeal Politics of Quality (*Suzhi*)," p. 190.

46. Aihwa Ong, *Neoliberalism as Exception: Mutations in Citizenship and Sovereignty* (Duke University Press, 2006), p. 78.

47. He, Heberer, and Schubert, *Citizen Participation in Rural and Urban Areas and Political Legitimacy.*

CHAPTER TEN

Higher Education Expansion and China's Middle Class

JING LIN and XIAOYAN SUN

This chapter discusses China's higher education expansion, which enables 23.3 percent of the college-aged population to attend universities. Twenty-six million students are enrolled in Chinese universities, and in 2009 the number of graduates reached 7 million. In the next ten years, China will increase enrollment by another 10 percent, according to Minister of Education Zhou Ji.[1] In the not so distant future, 50 percent of the age cohort will be studying in significantly revamped and upgraded universities.

We argue that a potential massive middle class is being created through this breathtaking expansion of higher education, although the impact may take some years before it becomes obvious. The expansion of higher education allows the new middle class to come from all sectors of society, which affects every family and community in China. It is also ushering in a generation of young people with distinct characteristics, those who grew up in a one-child family and in the middle of China's rapid and profound social and economic transformation, with its wide and rich access to sources of information via the Internet.

One of the authors conducted extensive fieldwork with her colleagues between 2004 and 2008, studying the expansion of elite public universities and the emergent private universities. In 2006–09 Ruth Hayhoe, Jing Lin, Qiang Zha, and Jun Li studied twelve universities, examining their expansion between 1995 and 2005.[2] University leaders, faculty, and students were interviewed. Using mainly this fieldwork, we here examine the two parts of the new middle class: graduates of private universities and ordinary public universities, on the one hand, and graduates of elite public universities, on the other. This difference divides these graduates into blue-collar, grey-collar, and white-collar workers.[3]

Our subject is the generation born during the 1980s and 1990s, those who are current university graduates or students. We examine the characteristics of this generation, look at their civic awareness and participation in social affairs, and reflect upon them becoming a massive new middle class in China.

Higher Education and the Formation of a Middle Class: Review of the Literature

Higher education has been a major force driving the rise of a middle class.[4] Harold Kerbo states that instead of people being placed in a stratified system because of qualities beyond their control (for example, because of their race, sex, or class at birth), education is seen as relying on qualities that can be controlled by individuals, which can be called placement by achievement.[5] Kerbo further notes that class division is based on a person's position in the occupational structure and in the authority structure and on whether or not the person owns property. In this structure, *middle class* signifies those with relatively little property but with high-to-middle positions in the occupational (nonmanual labor) and authority hierarchies.[6] Skills acquired through education tend to produce higher income. In Max Weber's view, skills and educational credentials are one of two basic elements of class formation.[7] Based on Weber's concept of status groups, credentialists argue that education is important because it indicates membership in a status group that controls access to higher-paying jobs.[8]

In today's world, education is a key factor in upward social mobility. In China this is increasingly the case. In the 1980s and 1990s a large number of people who made it into the middle class had low educational attainment, often working as contractors or owners of industrial private enterprises.[9] Then foreign direct investment began to pour into the country, catapulting China's economy forward and giving rise to many more white-collar jobs, all of which contributed to the arrival of new entrants to the middle class through higher education.

Li Qiang, a professor of sociology at Tsinghua University, states that since the mid-1980s there has been a sharp decrease in the rural population and an increase in the midlevel class, especially in major cities such as Beijing, Shanghai, and Guangzhou, where white-collar workers have exceeded the number of blue-collar workers. He notes that the formation of a middle class requires a transformation from the second (manufacturing) industry to a third industry (the service sector). It is in this transition, from the second to the third, that a middle stratum appears, consisting of managers, technicians, engineers, business people, and clerks. This process of occupational change has a direct connection with education, especially higher education. He states, "Universities are the machines manufacturing the midlevel strata; a very important function of the university is to enable people to embrace mainstream norms and midlevel strata norms."[10]

Indeed, higher education can be said to be a huge engine of middle-class growth in China. The 1978 restoration of the national university entrance exam ushered in unprecedented occupational mobility through higher education. Many who received higher education then and afterward were promoted to leadership positions in the government or took up positions as professionals. In the 1990s millions of people with university educations became rich by joining the world of business. They, along with newly rich private business owners, formed the main group that, by late 1990, sent its children to the newly established elite private schools.[11]

In the 1990s Jing Lin conducted fieldwork in several dozen schools in China, with a special focus on elite private schools.[12] She found that in the 1980s and up to mid-1990s a good proportion of the so-called middle class came from the private entrepreneurial ranks, who might have little education but became wealthy through establishing small businesses, contracting the construction of buildings, and engaging in international trade. A small portion of them were intellectuals who were promoted to leadership positions or who benefed from the reform through their professional expertise. However, by the late 1990s higher education became one of the required conditions for joining the ranks of the middle class. By the twenty-first century government officials and professionals almost all had received a higher education, not necessarily from famous universities. They have often relied on their higher education background to gain their positions and live a decent and comfortable life. Furthermore, using the power in their hands they have acquired a lot of perks and gray income. Meanwhile, people in "hot" fields, such as real estate and entertainment, have begun to attract a great deal of attention as scholars and people increasingly speak of a rising middle class in China.

In 2006 the China National Research Association, under the National Bureau of Statistics, did a survey about the rising middle class in an effort to shed light on the reality of this group and to help the government grapple with the proper terminology to describe its members. The survey results confirm the conventional criteria of middle-class membership: they received a good education, enjoy a prestigious career, have a decent income, and enjoy social influence. These people are civil servants, company managers, technicians, or private business entrepreneurs, and they are a driving force in the country's modernization and stability.[13]

It is said that wealth, occupation, and education are required criteria for being middle class. In China these are all interrelated, and with the expansion of higher education the linkage of occupation and education is closer than ever. Yanjie Bian claims that Chinese class stratification has transformed from a rigid status hierarchy under Mao to an open, evolving class system in the post-Mao period.[14] Socioeconomic inequalities have also altered. State redistributive inequalities are giving way to patterns increasingly generated by the way individuals and groups succeed in a growing market-oriented economy; occupational mobility, a rare thing under Mao, is becoming a lived experience for many Chinese.

How much income qualifies one for being middle class? In 2005, after surveying more than a quarter of a million people, and taking into consideration the standard set by the World Bank and the exchange rate and purchasing power, the National Statistical Bureau chose a yearly income between 60,000 and 500,000 yuan.[15] Zheng Xinli, the then vice minister of the Communist Party's Central Policy Research Office, said that after taking price changes into consideration, 55 percent of the population will be middle class by 2020, with 78 percent of city dwellers and 30 percent of those in rural areas reaching that status. Zheng defines middle class as having an annual household income of between 60,000 ($8,200) and 200,000 yuan. Expansion of the middle class is seen as part of the country's efforts to quadruple its per capita gross domestic product by 2020, a target set at the Seventeenth National Congress of the Communist Party of China in October 2007. In 2006 per capita income was $1,500.[16]

In another study, by Diana Farrell, Ulrich Gersch, and Elizabeth Stephenson, the bar for lower-middle-class households was an annual income of 25,001 to 40,000 yuan, and the range for upper-middle-class incomes was 40,001 to 100,000 yuan (taking into consideration the purchasing power of households).[17] Using the criteria set out by the authors above, we can consider a large number of university graduates as potential members of the middle classes, whether upper, middle, or lower middle. We think the criteria outlined by the National Statistical Bureau, by Zheng Xinli, and by Farrell, Gersch, and Stephenson all make sense. Which is more suitable depends on where you live, so a few thousand yuan or even 10,000 yuan more or less make relatively little difference. (An examination of the income of university graduates later on in this chapter establishes that, some years after their graduation, many of them join the ranks of middle class. Higher education expansion is therefore a force for bringing a large number of people into the ranks of the middle class.)

China's Higher Education Expansion, 1999–2009

Due to the political turmoil of the Cultural Revolution, enrollment of high school graduates in Chinese universities dropped dramatically during the period 1966–76. The college entrance exam was canceled. When it was restored in 1977, 5.7 million candidates competed for only 220,000 places in the nation's institutions of higher learning. From 1977 to 1999, nearly 60 million Chinese students took the college entrance exam; 1 million actually enrolled.[18] The number of people able to gain access to higher education was further limited by the fact that a large number of rural and urban children were not even offered a high school education.[19]

The extreme competitiveness of the college entrance exam was sometimes compared to a stampede of "thousands of soldiers and tens of thousands of horses across a single log bridge" (*qianjun wanma guo dumuqiao*).[20] In 1999, to provide greater access to higher education, the Chinese government started expanding university enrollment. Table 10-1 provides an overview of higher education expansion between 1990 and 2005.

The table demonstrates that from 1990 to 2005, a mere fifteen years, China's higher education enrollment increased by almost 800 percent. This is a spectacular development indeed. China's higher education expansion now enables 23.3 percent of the age cohort to attend universities: 26 million students are now enrolled in Chinese universities, and more than 7 million graduated in 2009. According to an official government estimate, by 2030, 50 percent of the age cohort will study in significantly revamped and upgraded universities.[21]

TABLE 10-1. Institutions of Higher Education, Number, Enrollment, and Graduates, China, Selected Years 1990–2005

	1990	1995	2000	2001	2005
Number of universities	1,075	1,054	1,041	1,225	1,792
New students (10,000)	60.9	92.6	220.6	268.3	504.5
Total enrollment (10,000)	206.3	290.6	556.1	719.1	1,561.8
Graduates (10,000)	61.4	80.5	95.0	103.6	306.8

Source: National Bureau of Statistics of China, 2006.

As previously indicated, if judged by income level, a potentially massive middle class is being created through higher education expansion. The expansion allows the new middle class to come from all sectors of the society, broader in scale than ever before and potentially affecting every family and community in China.

Case Studies of Higher Education Expansion

The following case studies draw on a project carried out by Jing Lin and her colleagues Ruth Hayhoe, Qiang Zha, and Jun Li between 2006 and 2008. The project highlights the way Chinese universities have expanded and the various institutional arrangements they have adopted. Five universities representing the spectrum of Chinese universities are presented. Peking University is a national icon, representing elite, comprehensive universities; Huazhong University of Science and Technology represents universities with a focus on engineering and science; East China Normal University represents teacher education institutions; Yanbian is a university for ethnic minorities; and Xi'an International Studies University is a typical private university.

Peking University: A National Icon of Cultural Leadership

Peking University's undergraduate enrollment increased from 9,280 in 1995, to 13,328 in 2000, and to 15,125 in 2005.[22] However, the number of students in the humanities and social sciences changed little, totaling 4,276 in 1995, 4,484 in 2000, and 4,914 in 2005. Similarly, the number of students enrolled in basic sciences was 4,247 in 1995, 4,380 in 2000, with a slight jump to 5,449 in 2005. The increase in undergraduate numbers between 1995 and 2000 was mainly due to the school's merger with

Beijing Medical University in the autumn of 2000, which added 3,818 medical students. The further increases in enrollment between 2000 and 2005 reflect new programs in engineering, with the number of engineering students increasing from 550 in 2000 to 1,787 in 2005.

Huazhong University of Science and Technology

Growth in student enrollment at Huazhong has been dramatic since the national policy decision of 1999.[23] Figures provided by the university for the years 1990, 1995, 2000, and 2005 indicate that total undergraduate enrollment in 1990 was 8,895, rising only gradually to 9,407 in 1995, but jumping to 21,195 by 2000 and 35,586 by 2005. Graduate enrollment rose from 1,448 in 1990 and 2,434 in 1995 to 6,558 in 2000 and 25,484 in 2005.

The percentage of female students at the undergraduate level has shown a significant increase over the period, with 20 percent in 1990, 19 percent in 1995, 28 percent in 2000, and 27 percent in 2005. At the graduate level, female percentages increased from 16 percent in 1990, to 20 percent in 1995, 25 percent in 2000, and 26 percent in 2005. Breakdowns on enrollment in social sciences and the humanities show 48 percent of students in the social sciences were female in 2005 and in the humanities, 71 percent.

About 50 percent of students came from rural families, a percentage that remained constant. Minority students constituted a very small percentage of the total in 1995, just 447 of 9,407 (4.7 percent), then dropping to 408 in 2000 (under 2 percent); but this number rose to 2,337 in 2005 (7 percent). This reflects support policies for minority students, including two special classes for Tibetan and Uighur students, as well as those minority students who come in through regular channels but are given some priority in admissions.

East China Normal University: A Female-Dominated Teacher Education School

In 1990 East China Normal University had an enrollment of 5,318 undergraduate students, showing only modest growth since the mid-1980s.[24] By 1995, however, undergraduate enrollment had reached 5,913, by 2000 it was 9,913, and by 2005 enrollment was 12,256. Meanwhile, graduate enrollment increased from 1,088 in 1990, to 1,320 in 1995, to 2,415 in 2000, and to 6,898 in 2005. As a normal university with the primary goal of training high school and college teachers, women students tend to predominate. However, this was the period when a large number of new programs were developed that did not lead to teaching careers. In spite of this new orientation, women continued to dominate enrollment, constituting 52 percent of undergraduate students in 1995, 60 percent in 2000, and 65 percent in 2005. Parallel figures at the graduate level are 33 percent in 1995, 49 percent in 2000, and 60 percent in 2005.

Yanbian University: An Ethnic Minority Regional University

In the early 1990s Yanbian University experienced a slight drop in undergraduate student enrollment, from 1,939 in 1990 to 1,890 in 1995.[25] But the numbers soon surged to 8,451 in 2000, with a growth rate of 347.1 percent, partly due to the merger of five institutes in 1996. In 2005 it surged again, to 15,485 (a growth rate of 83.2 percent). In terms of graduate education, Yanbian University had a very small graduate student body in the early 1990s, but the number grew rapidly with the national expansion policy, particularly in the early 2000s. In 1990 there were only 48 graduate students in the university, but this number grew to 184 in 1995, 562 in 2000, and 1,902 in 2005, with growth rates of 283.3 percent, 205.4 percent, and 238.4 percent every five years, respectively.

Xi'an International Studies University: A Private University

New entrants taking courses at Xi'an International Studies University in preparation for the National Examination of Qualification and Certification of Higher Education (*gaodeng jiaoyu xueli wenping kaoshi*) more than doubled in one year, from 2,400 students in 1994 to 5,600 in 1995.[26] By 1999 enrollment was 12,000, and by 2007 it was 36,000. Among these students, 60 percent were from rural areas. After Xi'an International Studies University was accredited as a degree-granting institution for undergraduate programs in 2005, it began to recruit students who planned to study in a bachelor's program. A total of 1,675 students enrolled that year in bachelor's programs, 763 male and 912 female. By that year 13,375 students were enrolled in programs preparing for the National Examination of Qualification and Certification of Higher Education and 15,000 students enrolled in programs for the self-learning examination in higher education (*gaodeng jiaoyu zixue kaoshi*).[27] The total enrollment goal is 45,000 students.

Summary of Case Studies

In sum, given the pattern of expansion illustrated in these case studies, 26 million students are currently studying in universities. More than 6 million graduate from universities every year, mostly becoming white-collar and grey-collar professionals. Many will fill government positions, and many others will become entrepreneurs or managers of enterprises. The large majority will become professionals in law, accounting, engineering, and so on.

Stratification of Higher Education and a Stratified Middle Class

There is another side to the creation of the new middle class through higher education: the different outcomes for graduates of private universities and ordinary public universities, on the one hand, and those for graduates of elite public universities, on the other. These outcomes will likely divide graduates into white-collar, grey-collar, and blue-collar workers, and their differing incomes will place them on different rungs of the social ladder. This is especially true of the universities explored in two government projects, Project 211 and Project 985.

Project 211 was initiated by the Ministry of Education of China in 1995 and sought to build a hundred comprehensive research universities for China's development in the twenty-first century. Universities included in the project receive national and local funding to build up their overall institutional capacity and their key disciplines. The aid they receive is meant to enhance their academic competitiveness so as to meet international standards for scientific research, for teaching, and for training of professionals.[28] Between 1996 and 2000 some $2.2 billion was distributed among Project 211 universities.[29] Since inception, Project 211 universities have enrolled top students through nationwide selection. They are heavily supported by local governments and sometimes by the central government as well.

Project 985 was launched in 1999 to promote China's higher education system. The digits 98 represent the year 1998, and 5 is the month of May: on May 4, 1998, the Chinese president of that time, Jiang Zemin, gave a speech at Peking University's centennial celebration, declaring that "China must have . . . first-rate universities at the international advanced level."[30]

Hence in China's higher education system, prestige is based on whether or not an institution is included in either Project 985 or Project 211. The lower level in the hierarchy includes ordinary public universities, private universities, and second-tier colleges. In terms of government policy support and funding, there are vast differences between these two levels.

Project 985 universities comprise the forty-three top universities in the country, and they receive massive funding from the government. Tsinghua University and Peking University alone received 1.8 billion yuan in the first phase of Project 985, and now they are at the end of the second phase of the project, having been granted another 1.8 billion yuan each in 2006. These universities, along with the hundred universities in Project 211, train leaders, managers, and professionals (white-collar workers). Table 10-2 shows the beginning monthly salary of the highest paid graduates in 2007, by university. The list contains mostly universities included in Project 985 or Project 211. These are beginning salaries, and usually after one to two years, once the graduates have passed their probation period, they see their income increase by 30 percent or more. Moreover, those who do well can increase their income many times over in a short period of time. As time goes on, many of them move to higher pay brackets and qualify for middle-class rank.

Lower-level universities train staffs, clerks, midlevel professionals, and technicians. Private universities, being at the bottom of this level, train grey-collar workers, defined as those who have more skills than blue-collar workers but who are narrowly trained in practical skills. In our interviews, although elite university students tended to have high expectations for their careers, aiming to work in major cities and for government organizations or major national and international corporations, private university students hoped first and foremost to be able to support themselves, and many indicated that they would be content with a monthly salary as low as 600–1,000 yuan, the income of babysitters.[31] Generally, these students do not aspire to be high-income earners but rather hope for a stable job that will allow them to be self-sufficient. Many private university graduates establish their own businesses, which means that some of them could become very rich and eventually enter a higher social class. Table 10-3 reports the top monthly earnings of private university graduates in 2006.

Data in table 10-3 are from the best private universities. The average monthly income for all private university graduates, however, is 1,000–1,500 yuan; 86 percent of those surveyed make less than 2,000 yuan.[32] Another report, though, says that the income gap among university graduates will narrow or disappear after three to five years. Although

T A B L E 1 0 - 2 . Ranking of Fifty Universities Based on Graduates' Monthly Salaries, China, 2007

Yuan

University	Starting median monthly salary
1. Dalian University of Foreign Languages	5,050
2. University of Electronic Science & Technology of China	4,900
3. Central University of Finance & Economics	3,916
4. Central Academy of Drama	3,875
5. Fudan University	3,863
6. Beijing Foreign Studies University	3,717
7. University of Science & Technology of China	3,700
8. Xi'an Jiaotong University	3,682
9. Shanghai International Studies University	3,633
10. Shanghai Jiao Tong University	3,596
11. Shanghai University of Finance & Economics	3,591
12. Huazhong University of Science & Technology	3,550
13. Tongji University	3,517
14. Shanghai University	3,453
15. East China University of Science & Technology	3,332
16. China Agricultural University	3,289
17. Beijing Film Academy	3,250
18. University of International Business & Economics	3,169
19. Tsinghua University	3,167
20. Beijing University of Posts & Telecommunications	3,129
21. Sun Yat-sen University	3,083
22. East China Normal University	3,033
23. Central Conservatory of Music	3,027
24. Beijing International Studies University	3,024
25. Renmin University of China	2,900
26. Communication University of China	2,846
27. Peking University	2,833
28. Wuhan University	2,759
29. Xidian University	2,723
30. Beijing Jiaotong University	2,649
31. South China University of Technology	2,567
32. Nankai University	2,465
33. China University of Political Science & Law	2,434
34. Beihang University	2,357

(continued)

TABLE 10-2 (*continued*)

University	Starting median monthly salary
35. Northwestern Polytechnical University	2,352
36. Southeast University	2,350
37. East China University of Political Science & Law	2,324
38. Beijing Normal University	2,300
39. Chongqing University	2,291
40. Xiamen University	2,233
41. Northeast Normal University	2,220
42. Lanzhou University	2,212
43. Wuhan University of Technology	2,152
44. South China Normal University	2,088
45. Sichuan University	2,065
46. Zhejiang University	2,058
47. Tianjin University	2,047
48. Nanjing University of Aeronautics & Astronautics	2,032
49. Central South University	2,030
50. Harbin Engineering University	2,021

Source: Retrieved September 5, 2009, from http://news.qq.com/a/20070515/001804.htm.

employers report that private university graduates have less overall ability than public university graduates, they also comment that private university graduates have good hands-on skills.[33]

Yue Changjun, chair of the Department of Economics of Education at Peking University, conducted a national survey in 2005 on the employment of China's college graduates.[34] The survey covered thirty-four universities and colleges in sixteen provinces. Of the 21,220 graduates surveyed, 78.5 percent were regular college students and 16.6 percent were graduates of vocational and adult training colleges. The survey finds that the average monthly income for students from professional vocational and adult training colleges was 1,333 yuan ($166.60), compared to that of university graduates of 1,549 yuan ($193.60). Students with a master's or a doctoral degree could expect an average monthly income of between 2,674 and 2,917 yuan ($334.30 and $364.60). As a result, Yue came to the conclusion that individual graduates' level of education is directly correlated with their salary.

Farrel, Gersch, and Stephensen make a very interesting point about the significance of higher education expansion indirectly:

TABLE 10-3. Ranking of Eleven Private Universities Based on Graduates' Monthly Salaries, China, 2006

University	Starting median monthly salary (yuan)	Standard score
1. Xi'an Fanyi University	2,856	1.00
2. Beijing Renwen University	2,792	0.90
3. Nanchang Institute of Technology	2,632	0.63
4. Anhui Xinhua University	2,614	0.59
5. China Management Software Institute	2,547	0.47
6. Beijing Geely University	2,531	0.46
7. Xi'an International University	2,410	0.25
8. University for Science &Technology Zhengzhou	2,380	0.20
9. Xiamen Nanyang University	2,324	0.10
10. Jiangxi City University	2,260	0.00
10. Shandong Yingcai University	2,260	0.00

Source: Chinese Academy of Management Science and Zhongqing Shijia Education Resource Organization, "Zhongguo Minban Gaoxiao Biyesheng Jiuye Xianzhuang Diaocha Baogao" [Investigation on undergraduates' employment from the private colleges in China], in *Zhongguo Jiaoyu de Zhuanxing yu Fazhan* [Transformation and development of China's education 2006], edited by Yang Dongping and Zhu Yinnian (Beijing: Social Sciences Academic Press, 2007), pp. 339–405.

As the economic tide rises, two phases of steep growth in the middle class are anticipated, with waves of consumers in distinct income brackets emerging and receding at specific points. The first wave, in 2010, will be the lower middle class, defined as households with annual incomes of 25,001 to 40,000 yuan. A decade later comes the upper middle class, with annual household incomes of 40,001 to 100,000 yuan. By around 2011 the lower middle class will number some 290 million people, representing the largest segment in urban China and accounting for about 44 percent of the urban population, according to our model. Growth in this group should peak around 2015, with a total spending power of 4.8 trillion yuan. A second transition is projected to occur in the following decade, when hundreds of millions will join the upper middle class. By 2025 this segment will comprise a staggering 520 million people—more than half of the expected urban population of China—with a combined total disposable income of 13.3 trillion yuan.[35]

What is also evident is that China's greatly expanded higher education system will be the main engine producing this projected new middle class.

Employment Challenges for the Post-Eighties Generation

With higher education expansion has come criticism that students are receiving lower quality education, as universities have become less selective and class size has grown from one faculty member per three or four students in the early 1990s to the current ratio of one faculty member to twenty, thirty, or even forty students. However, others argue that the quality of the graduates has been sufficient to meet the needs of China's modernization: the students have learned both general and specialized knowledge, including computer skills, social skills, and English proficiency. In short, today higher education cultivates the masses rather than the elites for the potential rank of middle-class status.

There are unique challenges facing young people today. First, they face an extremely competitive job market. With only about 70 percent of graduates finding jobs each year, students we interviewed, even those from the most elite universities, often harbored strong anxieties. Further, they face rising prices and costs of services. There is great uncertainty, therefore, as to how many of them can make it into the ranks of the middle class. One survey indicates that the average monthly starting salary in Beijing is 2,655 yuan. After paying for rent, transportation, food, and clothing, little is left. The graduates surveyed felt they could hardly survive on this salary, and in the soaring housing market the dream of buying their own house felt very remote.[36]

Faced with cutthroat competition for employment and struggling to survive in a big metropolis, when dreams meet harsh reality many young people find themselves with no choice but to turn to their parents for help. They become the so-called NEET group ("Not in employment, education, or training") and are dubbed the "gnawing the old clan" (*kenlao zu*), which must depend on their parents. Even those who buy an apartment after working for a few years often rely on their parents to help with the down payment.

Zhang Hongyi, an associate professor at the School of Business Management of Shandong University of Finance, conducted a survey targeting 2008 graduates of six colleges (including two Project 211 universities, two common colleges, and two vocational colleges) in Shandong Province.[37] Zhang found that 33 percent of graduates found it hard to look for jobs before graduation and 65 percent thought it hard to get satisfying jobs. Of all the graduates surveyed, 42 percent found jobs, but only 10 percent found their job offer satisfactory. The majority agreed that they faced greater difficulties in job hunting than their elders did in previous years. Zhang's study concludes that although it is hard for college graduates to find jobs right after graduation, it does not necessarily mean protracted unemployment, as more opportunities come along in time. Zhang's findings correspond to the results of the survey on employment of Chinese college graduates done by Li Chunling and Wang Boqing. Based on a survey of 445,000 graduates, these researchers find that the employment rate of college graduates improves in the first half year after graduation.[38]

Because it is hard to get jobs, many graduates choose further study and go to graduate school. In 2009, 1.25 million undergraduate degree holders took postgraduate entrance exams, and more than 1.28 million students are currently pursuing graduate degrees. The trend of delaying entry into the workforce is on the rise, which also means more and more young people will marry late. Our fieldwork suggests that a large number of graduate students are having difficulty finding mates and are delaying marriage, which will have significant demographic implications for China in the long term.[39]

Postgraduate unemployment causes a lot of anxiety and frustration. A TV series on the subject, *Striving,* attracted more than 30 million viewers.[40] The global financial crisis, which began in 2008, has affected university students' job prospects and futures. It is reported that universities and students try all measures to find jobs and that government officials are required to pursue concrete measures to help university graduates find jobs. One of the universities in the case studies, Yanbian University, has enjoyed a relatively high employment rate for its graduates, as many companies owned by South Korean enterprises prefer to hire graduates who know Korean; however, with many Korean companies pulling out of China, this has changed.

One private university included in the case studies long enjoyed a top rank in terms of graduate employment but under huge market pressure has boosted the number of companies it collaborates with from 500 to 2,000 so as to maintain this advantage.

Characteristics of the Post-Eighties Generation

Who are the members of the post-eighties generation? What kind of environment have these people grown up in? What are their unique features as the potential future members of the middle class?

Little Emperors and Empresses

China began the one-child family planning policy in the late 1970s. This policy of family planning was introduced to avoid social, economic, and environmental problems caused by overpopulation. It has been credited with a significant slowing of China's population growth. The Chinese government claims that the policy prevented more than 250 million births from 1980 to 2000.[41] The adoption of the one-child policy has created a distinct demographic pattern of urban families with only one child and a fertility rate of 1.3 in in 2004.[42] According to official statistics, 200 million babies were born between 1980 and 1989. About 65 percent of the nation's overall post-eighties generation is from single-child families; the figure is as high as 85 percent for urban areas.[43]

This generation of single children has long been branded "little emperors" and "little empresses," who, commanding the sole attention of their parents and grandparents, are spoiled, self-centered, and lacking a sense of social responsibility. A sarcastic label for them is the strawberry generation (*caomei zu*), meaning, on the one hand, that they are well-dressed, confident, and energetic and, on the other, that they cannot bear the hardship of the real world or do any hard work. They have also been called the lost generation and the crashed generation.

The other side of the debate argues that while most born in the 1980s have been provided with unprecedented material comforts, they grew up in an intense atmosphere where competition at school for higher grades was fierce and the pressure from parents grave. The expectations placed on them were high, and the schools still used the prevailing methods of indoctrination while ignoring students' creative abilities.[44]

However, the many new channels of information open to those of the post-eighties generation has rendered them very open-minded (willing to try new things and more open to foreign cultures), and a large majority of them are Internet literate and very vocal in voicing their opinions. Faced with the derogatory labels and prejudices against their generation, their indignant refutations are often seen online. Moreover, a survey indicates that those who were born in the 1950s through the 1970s are critical of the newer generation, while the generation itself is optimistic about its ability to shoulder social responsibilities and pursue careers and life choices.[45]

Morality and Challenges

The post-eighties generation is said to work in a diverse and multidimensional world. Economic development, globalization, and Western influence have ushered in cultural clashes and generated tension between the global and the local and between history and the present. The new generation grew up being aware of a diversity of moral principles. Further, in the course of the marketization and globalization of the economy, concepts of equality, competition, and autonomy are accepted by the younger generation, which wishes to change and rebel against traditional moral indoctrination. There is no longer one single authority or one dominant moral belief system. Having said this, the post-eighties generation has also been the most manipulated and overwhelmed by parents' excessive care and unrealistic expectations. Hence some suggest that Chinese society shed its indoctrination methods and guide its young people with open, explorative, and participatory methods to establish moral principles.[46]

Volunteerism

Members of the post-eighties generation have also demonstrated a sense of responsibility. They have shown it through their enthusiasm for volunteering during the 2008 Beijing Olympics and through their efforts to help during the Sichuan earthquake.

The Beijing Olympics inspired a number of initiatives to foster a greater sense of civic service. On December 5, 2008, Beijing put into effect a regulation promoting volunteer work by describing hundreds of types of volunteer work available, raising public awareness of opportunities for civic service, and making it more convenient for citizens to become involved. These initiatives were meant to popularize volunteer service among Chinese youth and thereby make it part of everyday life for civic-minded Chinese.[47] During the 2008 Beijing Summer Olympics, at least 100,000 young volunteers offered their services, with 70,000 on the event sites and the remaining 30,000 spread across the city. Mostly college students of the post-eighties generation, these young volunteers, friendly and competent, made a good impression on foreign athletes and visitors.

During the disaster relief efforts in the aftermath of the 2008 Sichuan earthquake, the military personnel, the armed police forces, and the engineering troops who headed to the front lines of the quake zone at the earliest possible moment and who conducted rescue missions in the hardest-hit areas were mostly young people of the post-eighties generation. Young faces were also frequently seen among the medical staff and their names on disaster relief donation lists.

Volunteering is one of the important forms of civic engagement. The volunteerism of China's post-eighties generation is closely connected with civic awareness. "The young people have channeled their patriotism in a passionate but controlled manner into volunteering activities," said Peng Fuchun, NPC deputy and professor at the School of Philosophy, Wuhan University. "We see hope in those young people."[48]

Netizens

The new generation of university students and graduates are also active participants in the cyber world, the so-called netizens. The China Internet Network Information Center (CNNIC) defines a netizen as any Chinese citizen age six and above who has used the Internet for at least half a year. According to the "2009 Report on the Behavior of China's Young Internet Users," released by CNNIC on April 26, 2010, the number of young Chinese Internet users reached 195 million in December 2009, and China's Internet penetration rate reached 54.5 percent among young people, much higher than the national average of 28.9 percent.[49] Close to 70 percent of netizens were born after 1980. The CNNIC report also points out that Chinese netizens tend to have higher than average levels of education: most urban netizens have tertiary education and most rural netizens have completed high school.

In 2009, 69 percent of Chinese netizens used government websites (central and local) at least several times a year, compared to 61 percent in 2007 and 62 percent in 2008.[50] Chinese netizens are also keen on using cyber power for civic participation; they are twice as likely as Americans to use chat rooms; three times as likely to microblog and to blog and video conference; "more likely to share information broadly and openly"; and more likely to use social media.[51]

Such information sharing at a social level comprises cyber power. One example that illustrates Chinese netizens' cyber power is the "human flesh search engine." The term is a literal translation of the Chinese *renrou sousuo*, which was coined in 2001 when an entertainment website asked users to track down film and music trivia.[52] Nowadays human flesh search engines have become a Chinese phenomenon: they are a form of online vigilante justice in which Internet users hunt down and punish people who have attracted their wrath; with the goal of getting the targets fired from their jobs and shamed in front of their neighbors or run out of town, online searches of this kind are crowd-sourced detective work with offline results.[53] With 210 million Chinese netizens wiring up to the Internet, its influence can be powerful. Over the years, the human flesh search engine has been frequently used against socially unacceptable behaviors, including political corruption, extramarital affairs, animal cruelty, and perceived betrayal (or hostility) toward the Chinese nation.

One of the recent victims of the human flesh search engine is Zhou Jiugeng, a government official in charge of real estate development in Nanjing, Jiangsu Province. Certain netizens spotted photos of Zhou wearing a Vacheron Constantin watch worth 100,000 yuan (around $15,000) and sitting at a table with cigarettes that go for 150 yuan ($22) a pack.[54] Upon further investigation, netizens found that Zhou drove a Cadillac to work. When the information was released online, many were angered by the apparent corruption and some went so far as to file complaints with the local authorities. Thanks to netizens' activism, Zhou was dismissed from his position. In October 2009 he was sentenced to eleven years in prison for taking bribes.

According to Clay Shirky, who has written and been interviewed extensively about the Internet since 1996 and whose columns and writings have appeared in the *New York Times*, the *Wall Street Journal*, and the *Harvard Business Review*, online tracking demonstrates how dramatically interconnected we have become. The old limitations of media have been radically reduced, with much of the power accruing to the former audience. It also demonstrates the ease and speed with which a group can be mobilized for the right kind of cause.[55] In terms of defining what cause is right, netizens now have a powerful voice.

Notably, as our interviews indicate, nearly all college students are Internet literate, perhaps showing the effect that higher education has on the Internet savvy of the post-eighties generation.

Patriots

The post-eighties generation has earned another nickname, *fenqing* (literally, angry youth). As noted in a seminar on understanding China's angry youth, Kai-Fu Lee, the then vice president of Google and president of Google Greater China, commented that these young Chinese "often use the Internet to vent their frustrations, and that frustration often comes from either their patriotism or their desire to seek what is right, fair, true, and transparent. They care about social issues. They're concerned. And they feel they need to be outspoken, to have their voices heard. And they often use the Internet to gain knowledge and to have their voice heard."[56]

FIGURE 10-1. Channels through which Students Learn of Social Events, by Gender, China

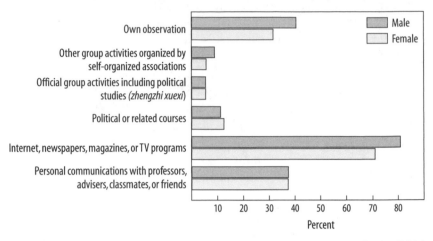

Source: Jun Li, "Fostering Citizenship in China's Move from Elite to Mass Higher Education: An Analysis of Students' Political Socialization and Civic Participation," *International Journal of Educational Development* 29 (2009): 382–98.

Our Research Findings

The fieldwork conducted by Jing Lin and her colleagues also examines the civic awareness of the post-eighties generation, the sources from which it acquires information about society and the world, and its sense of social responsibility and civic participation.

We collected data in May and June of 2007 through a nationwide questionnaire administered in twelve case study universities. The twelve universities include nine public and three private institutions, including comprehensive, teacher education, language, engineering, and agricultural universities. The nine public universities are all part of Project 211, and seven of them are part of Project 985. The twelve institutions are in representative geographic regions of China, both the developed Eastern region and the underdeveloped Western and Central regions. The number of questionnaires disseminated was 2,332; 2,321 valid copies were returned, for a return rate of 99.5 percent.

The survey finds that students gather information mainly from public sources and that they search for information independently. For example, as figure 10-1 shows, 31.6 percent of the female students and 40.5 percent of the male students rely on their own observations to learn about social events; and both male (80.9 percent) and female (70.9

FIGURE 10-2. Voting Arenas Students Participate in, by Gender, China

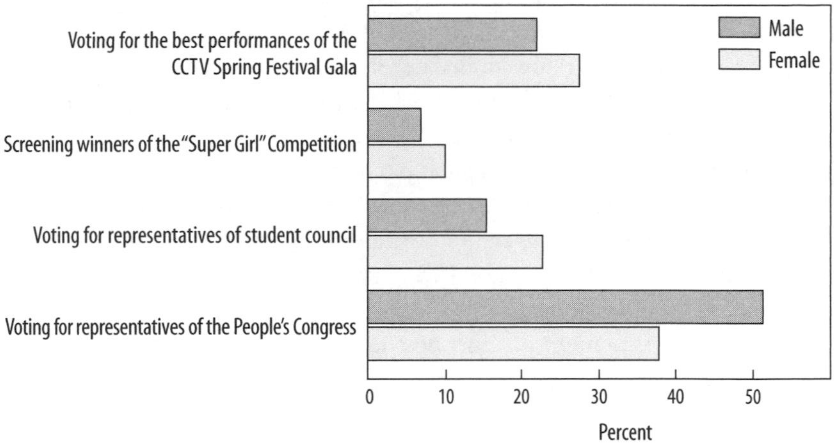

Source: Jun Li,"Fostering Citizenship in China's Move from Elite to Mass Higher Education: An Analysis of Students' Political Socialization and Civic Participation," *International Journal of Educational Development* 29 (2009): 382–98.

percent) students rely heavily on unofficial sources such as the Internet, newspapers, TV programs, and magazines for information.

In terms of associations, more than half of the students (52.9 percent of males and 51 percent of females) are involved in associations of peers from the same region, close to half are part of sports organizations or teams, and more than 60 percent join student councils. Between a quarter and a third of students are engaged in activities for the social good, more than 80 percent being engaged in activities of the Communist Youth League.[57] Students feel they would have a voice mainly through voting for representatives of the People's Congress (figure 10-2). In recent years, the People's Congress has put forward many bold proposals for laws and has seen many powerful laws passed, which may give students a belief in the role of the People's Congress.

Our interviews correspond with the data provided in Jun Li's study, that is, that students are actively engaged in all kinds of activities, such as providing care to the elderly, collecting money for children who drop out of school, and doing volunteer work for environmental protection. Genuine enthusiasm is evident on the part of students in organizing and participating in activities that they feel are part of their duty. The universities we studied all give high priorities to supporting student-initiated activities, especially those for the social good. Also, students feel they learn a lot and benefit from participation in civic activities. For example, they benefit through social learning (71.9 percent of males and 80.4 percent of females), leadership ability development (67.6 percent of males, 73.8 percent of females), and networking and socializing (89.3 percent of males, 93.3 percent of females). Further, close to two-thirds of the students find leisure and joy in such participation.

In sum, our fieldwork and secondary sources indicate that members of the potential new middle class in China are participatory, have diverse sources of information, are good at networking, and participate in the causes they believe will help to better society, although they also face dire challenges in employment, a shifting social morality, and criticism from the older generation.

Conclusion

China's higher education expansion has important implications for the creation of a massive new middle class. It means that education will be the key credential for people to obtain white-collar (professional) and grey-collar jobs. Government officials are among the first groups to become middle class, and nowadays to become a public servant requires passing extremely competitive examinations and having received superior higher education.

Higher education will be the most important criterion for middle-class status. Successful businesswomen and -men, professionals, government officials, managers, entertainment stars, and consultants all need to have higher educational credentials in order to do well in today's China. In the 1980s only 2–4 percent of the age cohort could attend universities; today, more than 23 percent can attend. The expansion of higher education, coupled with rapid urbanization and the growing number of white-collar jobs, will lead to the rapid growth of the middle class in the decades to come.

The young people of the post-eighties generation will become the backbone of China's middle class. Despite certain stereotypes of the post-eighties generation as spoiled little emperors and empresses or as those who chase ephemeral fashion trends and treat marriage and sex casually, our fieldwork and research indicate that these young people are very resourceful in terms of information access, that they actively participate in activities for the social good, and that they often band together to champion justice and equality. The expansion of university enrollment may have lowered the quality of higher education, but the form of higher education provided today is meeting the expectations of the masses if not the elites: the new generation of students will have specialized knowledge, communication skills, computer skills, and a wide exposure to information from not only official channels but also unofficial channels.

In conclusion, the expansion of higher education in China is playing a crucial role in lives of the post-eighties generation, which is likely to eventually constitute a massive new middle class. This well-educated generation will have economic and political ramifications for China's future. In the Chinese government's view, these ramifications will be positive. Hence the expansion of education will continue, and the prediction could come true—that in the next several decades more than half of the Chinese people will qualify as middle class.

Notes

1. Zhou Ji, "College Enrollment Will Increase by Another 10%, Due to the Decrease in Primary and Secondary School Enrollment" [Daxue maoruxuelü jiangzeng baifenzhishi deyiyu zhongxiaoxuesheng jianshao], *Sohu Education*, September 11, 2009 (http://learning.sohu.com/20090911/n266656081.shtml [September 2009]).

2. See Ruth Hayhoe and others, eds., *Portraits of Twenty-First-Century Chinese Universities: In the Move to Mass Higher Education* (New York: Springer, forthcoming).

3. Although in the West the term *grey collar* is used to describe an aging population within the workforce, in China it refers to neither white-collar nor blue-collar workers but people in between, such as technicians. For a more detailed analysis of Chinese grey-collar workers, see Kate Hutchings and others, "Perception of the Effectiveness of Training and Development of 'Grey-Collar' Workers in the People's Republic of China," *Human Resource Development International* 12, no. 3 (2009): 279–96.

4. C. Wright Mills, *White Collar: The American Middle Classes* (Oxford University Press, 1956).

5. Harold R. Kerbo, *Social Stratification and Inequality: Class Conflict in Historical and Comparative Perspective* (New York: McGraw-Hill, 1991), p. 12.

6. Ibid., p. 13.

7. Max Weber, *Economy and Society: An Outline of Interpretive Sociology*, edited by Guenther Roth and Claus Wittich (University of California Press, 1978), p. 302.

8. M. D. R. Evans and Jonathan Kelley, *Australian Economy and Society 2001: Education, Work, and Welfare* (Sydney: Federation Press, 2002), p. 21.

9. Jing Lin, *Social Transformation and Private Education in China* (New York: Praeger, 1999).

10. Li Qiang, "Zhongguo Zhongdeng Shouru Jieceng de Goucheng" [The composition of China's midlevel income strata], *Journal of Social Science of Hunan Normal University* 4 (2003): 7–9.

11. Lin, *Social Transformation and Private Education in China*.

12. Jing Lin, "Educational Stratification and the New Middle Class in China," in *Education and Social Change in China: Inequality in a Market Economy,* edited by Gerard Postiglione (Armonk, N.Y.: M. E. Sharp, 2006), pp. 179–98.

13. "Defining 'Middle Class,'" *China Daily,* September 26, 2006 (http://english.peopledaily.com.cn/200609/26/eng20060926_306436.html).

14. Yanjie Bian, "Chinese Social Stratification and Social Mobility," *Annual Review of Sociology* 28 (2002): 91–116.

15. *Zhongguo Zhongchan Jieji: Nianshouru Liuwan de Menkan Hai Bugou* [China's middle class: an annual income of 60,000 yuan as the threshold], *China Times* (http://news.sina.com.cn/cul/2005-01-21/3346.html).

16. "50 Percent of People to Be Middle Class," *China Daily,* December 27, 2007 (http://english.peopledaily.com.cn/90001/90776/6328124/html).

17. Diana Farrell, Ulrich A. Gersch, and Elizabeth Stephenson, "The Value of China's Emerging Middle Class," *McKinsey Quarterly*, special edition, *Serving the New Chinese Consumer,* 2006, pp. 60–69.

18. "Massive Expansion of University Rolls Causes Problems for China," *People's Daily Online,* June 6, 2007 (http://english.people.com.cn/200706/06/eng20070606_381598.html).

19. Jing Lin and Yu Zhang, "Educational Expansion and Shortage of Secondary Schools," *Journal of Contemporary China* 15, no. 47 (2006): 255–74.

20. Sharon LaFraniere, "China's College Entry Test Is an Obsession," *New York Times,* June 13, 2009 (www.nytimes.com/2009/06/13/world/asia/13exam.html).

21. Zhou Ji, "College Enrollment Will Increase by Another Ten Percent, Due to the Decrease in Primary and Secondary School Enrollment."

22. Ruth Hayhoe, Qiang Zha, and Yan Fengqiao, "Peking University: Icon of Cultural Leadership," in *Portraits of Twenty-First-Century Chinese Universities: In the Move to Mass Higher Education,* edited by Ruth Hayhoe and others (New York: Springer, forthcoming).

23. Ruth Hayhoe and others, "A Microcosm of New China's Higher Education Development," in Hayhoe and others, *Portraits of Twenty-First-Century Chinese Universities.*

24. Ruth Hayhoe, Qiang Zha, and Li Mei, "East China Normal University: Will It Become China's Ecole Normale Supérieure?" in Hayhoe and others, *Portraits of Twenty-First-Century Chinese Universities.*

25. Jing Lin, Jun Li, and Piao Taizhu, "Yanbian University: A Multicultural Approach in China's Northeast," in Hayhoe and others, *Portraits of Twenty-First-Century Chinese Universities.*

26. Jun Li, Jing Lin, and Wang Guan, "Xi'an International Studies University: Transforming Fish into Dragons," in Hayhoe and others, *Portraits of Twenty-First-Century Chinese Universities.*

27. The national examination was abolished by the Ministry of Education in 2004.

28. "Project 211: A Brief Introduction" (www.edu.cn/HomePage/english/education/highedu/211/index.shtml [January 2001]).

29. Li Lixu, "China's Higher Education Reform 1998–2003: A Summary," *Asia Pacific Education Review* 5, no. 1 (2004): 14–22.

30. Ministry of Education of the People's Republic of China, *Action Scheme for Invigorating Education toward the Twenty-First Century* (Beijing: Department of International Cooperation and Exchange, 2000), p. 17.

31. Interviews were conducted during from 2004 through 2008.

32. Chinese Academy of Management Science and Zhongqing Shijia Education Resource Organization, "Zhongguo Minban Gaoxiao Biyesheng Jiuye Xianzhuang Diaocha Baogao" [Investigation on undergraduates' employment from the private colleges in China], in *Zhongguo Jiaoyu de Zhuanxing yu Fazhan* [Transformation and development

of China's education 2006], edited by Yang Dongping and Zhu Yinnian (Beijing: Social Sciences Academic Press, 2007), pp. 339–405.

33. UNIVERSUM, *2009 Zhongguo Minban Gaoxiao Biyesheng Jingzheng Li Diaocha Baogao* [Survey report on the competitiveness of graduates from private universities in China 2009], released at the National Symposium on the Competitiveness of Chinese Private University Graduates, hosted by Xinhua news agency's magazine *Liaowang* [Outlook], Beijing, June 13, 2009.

34. See Wang Ke, "New Trends in Employment of China's Graduates," *China.org.cn,* February 15, 2006 (www.china.org.cn/english/2006/Feb/158126.htm).

35. Farrell, Gersch, and Stephenson, "The Value of China's Emerging Middle Class," pp. 60–63.

36. "Daxue Biyesheng Gongzi Diaocha" [Poll: the average monthly salary for college graduates] (www.cjol.com/main/ArticleResource/view_new.asp?articleId=31053 [August 2009]).

37. Zhang Hongyi, "A Survey of Graduates' Employment and New Venture Creation in China in 2008," *International Education Studies* 2, no. 1 (2009): 64–69 (http://ccsenet.org/journal/index.php/ies/article/viewFile/301/365).

38. Li Chunling and Wang Boqing, "Zhongguo Daxuesheng Jiuye yu Gongzi Shuiping Diaocha Baogao" [Survey on employment and wage level of college graduates], in *2009 Nian Zhongguo Shehui Xingshi Fenxi yu Yuce* [Society of China: analysis and forecast, 2009], edited by Ru Xin, Lu Xueyi, and Li Peilin (Beijing: Social Sciences Academic Press, 2009).

39. The other extreme is the emergence of the marry-upon-graduation group (*bihun zu*). The term refers to those young people who marry immediately after graduating from college. Many of the female graduates in this group consider marriage to a financially stable partner a solution to the tight job market. But whether it is marriage upon graduation or late marriage, behind both phenomena is the fact that graduation may mean unemployment in present-day China.

40. Ma Feima, "An Investigation into the Livelihood of Chinese Scriptwriters," *Phoenix Weekly,* December 24, 2007 (www.zonaeuropa.com/20071225_1.htm).

41. "China Steps Up 'One Child' Policy," *BBC News Online,* September 25, 2000 (http://news.bbc.co.uk/2/hi/asia-pacific/941511.stm).

42. Therese Hesketh, Li Lu, and Zhu Weixing, "The Effect of China's One-Child Family Policy after 25 Years," *New England Journal of Medicine* 353, no. 2 (2005): 1171–76.

43. Wang Linyan, "Post-80s: The Vexed Generation?" *China Daily,* May 27, 2009 (www.chinadaily.com.cn/cndy/2009-05/27/content_7945266.htm).

44. These complaints were repeatedly mentioned in our interviews.

45. Dong Haijun and Gao Fei, "80 hou shehui pingjia de daigou" [Generational gap on social judgment of the post-80s generation], *Research on Youth,* no. 6 (2009).

46. Feng Chao and Wang Yishan, "Uncertainty of Moral Beliefs of the Post 80s Generation College Students: Causes and Analysis of Solutions," *Frontiers of Education* (theory edition) 3 (2009).

47. "Volunteers: Growing Social Force in China Ascends Olympic Stage," *Xinhua,* July 25, 2008.

48. Quoted in ibid.

49. "Young Chinese Netizens Number Nearly 200 Million," *People's Daily Online,* April 27, 2010.

50. China Internet Network Information Center, "Statistical Survey Report on Internet Development in China," January 2010, p. 83.

51. Netpop Research LLC, "Nations: The Great Social Wall of China," August 2009 (http://netpopresearch.com/node/26601).

52. "Human Flesh Search Engines: Chinese Vigilantes that Hunt Victims on the Web," *Times Online,* June 25, 2008 (http://technology.timesonline.co.uk/tol/news/tech_and_we/article4213681.ece).

53. Tom Downey, "China's Cyberposse," *New York Times,* March 3, 2010.

54. Sky Canaves, "Human Flesh Search Engines Set Their Sights on Official Misbehavior," *China Real Time Report,* December 19, 2008 (http://blogs.wsj.com/chinarealtime/2008/12/29/human-flesh-search-%20engines-set-their-sights-on-official-misbehavior).

55. Clay Shirky, *Here Comes Everybody: The Power of Organizing without Organizations* (New York: Penguin, 2008).

56. "Understanding China's 'Angry Youth': What Does the Future Hold?" Brookings Institution seminar, April 29, 2009 (www.brookings.edu/~/media/Files/events/2009/0429_china_youth/20090429_china_youth.pdf).

57. Jun Li, "Fostering Citizenship in China's Move from Elite to Mass Higher Education: An Analysis of Students' Political Socialization and Civic Participation," *International Journal of Educational Development* 29 (2009): 382–98.

PART V

The Chinese Middle Class in Comparative Perspective

CHAPTER ELEVEN

Placing China's Middle Class in the Asia-Pacific Context

HSIN-HUANG MICHAEL HSIAO

The rise of the middle class in East Asia first began to attract attention in the 1980s, followed in the 1990s by a similar discovery in Southeast Asia. Based on East and Southeast Asia's experiences of the middle class, one can begin to characterize this newly born class as a whole. The middle classes of countries in the Asia-Pacific region are the direct structural creation of state-led industrialization strategies, the result of unprecedented upward mobility and affluence. These classes, though distinctive and distinguishable from other classes, are internally differentiated, diverse, and even segmented. More significant, the power relations between the middle classes and authoritarian regimes tend to be dialectical over the long term.

Since 2000 a middle class along these lines has also been found in China. This chapter intends to place China's emerging middle class in the Asia-Pacific context, so as to delineate the similarities and differences between the middle-class experience in China and the experiences in other Asian countries. Several central theses concerning the composition, the economic and social features, and the political-democratic roles of middles classes in East and Southeast Asia are tested and assessed against China's emerging middle class.

Changing Perspectives on the Rise of the Middle Class in China

In orthodox Chinese Communist ideology—which takes a leaf from orthodox Marxism—the middle class is not a legitimate or independent social class. As late as 1990, twelve years after the Chinese Communist Party (CCP) under Deng Xiaoping initiated the reform and opening policy era, discussion of the middle class in mainstream Chinese sociology was still prohibited and denounced as a fabricated and politicized concept developed by capitalist countries' "bourgeoisie sociology." Therefore, it was openly declared that a middle class could not be allowed to exist or to emerge in socialist China.[1] For example, even though Deng's state-led pursuit of market reforms was resulting in three emerging "strata" within the private business sector, including individual entrepreneurs and private enterprise owners, they could not be considered a middle class. Furthermore, intellectuals were exempted from an independent middle-class position by the suggestion that they should not be separated from the working class. On the other hand, those belonging to the higher-ranking professional-managerial strata were also ruled out of a middle class because communist orthodoxy considered them part of the monopolistic capitalist class and upper class.[2]

Consequently, the concept of a middle class was not only taboo in the Chinese Communist lexicon but also the newly emerging social and economic groups, such as small individual entrepreneurs, private business owners, intellectuals, and managerial professionals, were incapable of being properly and objectively analyzed in China's sociological studies during the early 1990s. In other words, the above-mentioned four newly emerging occupational groups, or employment positions, were not given any class meaning or seen as the collective constituents of China's emerging middle class.[3]

Rather, the economic (in income measures) situations of the four occupational groups were dealt with separately. Only urban middle-income families and certain occupations were briefly referred to as the middle strata.[4] However, these newly created employment groups were outside of the state and public sectors (they had gone down to the "seas of market competition," like the four strata mentioned above, and were also called the "early rich groups" [*xianfuqunti*]). The early rich groups were actually considered to be at the top and part of the privileged stratum within an emerging "unequal and unstable dualistic social structure." According to Li Qiang, what was missing was the middle stratum, the one between the two polarized income groups.[5] In this frame of analysis, the early rich groups could not be seen as the middle class. Therefore, it stands to reason that in the absence of this middle stratum, the issue of the situational placement of a middle class in Chinese society still lacked an answer.

Moreover, a discernable collective social attitude for those new occupational groups was hardly discussed, and their potential political character and propensity were never mentioned in the early literature. It is important to note that these kinds of unspoken yet clear political limits on how to perceive and analyze the changing occupational and class structures in China, the result of the "four modernizations with market forces brought into socialism," dictated the research and policy discourse over the whole decade of the 1990s.

From Denial to Ambivalence

The early 2000s marked a point of departure in the central government's perspective toward the situational placement of the middle class in official academia. An official publication written by eighteen Chinese scholars was released by the CCP's Central Party School, the highest institution for training party officials, titled *Class Stratification in Present China*.[6] While the report avoids directly mentioning a distinctive middle class, or middle stratum, it does acknowledge separate new occupational groups. Moreover, intellectuals, private business owners, individual small entrepreneurs, and business executives and managers are depicted as being independent of one another—instead of being grouped together as a collective class—and a separate chapter is devoted to these "early rich groups," with a detailed analysis of how they became rich. Interestingly, a section also centered on the negative social consequences of these suddenly rich groups.

Finally, four out of six sources or features of current class contradictions found in China are related to those strata in the middle class, such as the early rich, nonmanual white-collar workers, individual entrepreneurs, private business owners, and party or state bureaucrats. These depictions suggest an ambivalent yet somehow negative attitude toward these new occupational groups and class elements, even though they do not explicitly refer to them as middle class.

From Acceptance to Expectation

The position of the Chinese academy on the middle class has experienced a significant and noticeable shift since 2002. This trend is embodied in a book written by a group of ten sociologists, titled *Report on*

Social Strata Research in Contemporary China.[7] The report, a pioneering study of China's increasingly differentiated social stratification, delineates ten major strata brought about by the wave of reforms that reorganized China's economic institutions and spearheaded the country's "modernization" since 1978. The ten resulting social strata identified by the research and their respective proportions are as follows:

—State and private executives 2.1 percent

—Managers, 1.5 percent

—Professionals, 5.1 percent

—Private business owners, 0.6 percent

—Clerical workers, 4.8 percent

—Individual small entrepreneurs, 4.2 percent

—Commercial and service workers, 12.0 percent

—Industrial workers, 22.6 percent

—Agricultural workers, 44.0 percent

—The unemployed, 3.1 percent.

The authors also use five socioeconomic rankings (upper, middle upper, middle middle, middle lower, and lower) to classify the above ten strata into five socioeconomic brackets. However, the criteria used in this reorganization are unclear, and no percentage is provided for each ranking.

Although the report makes no deliberate attempt to define the middle class within the current Chinese social class structure, a separate chapter is devoted to a thematic analysis of the "middle strata." China's middle strata is determined to include those "mainly engaged in nonmanual work with salary as the means of living, earning higher income, better work conditions and having certain autonomy as well as control over their work and co-workers, equipped with adequate household consumption ability and leisure life quality, possessing civic virtues and consciousness."[8] The report clearly outlines the criteria for making some individuals members of the middle strata in both objective and subjective terms. The following occupational individuals and groups are specifically identified as examples of the middle strata: engineers, technicians, professionals, office managers, individual small entrepreneurs, commercial salespeople, intellectuals, cadres in state enterprises, private business owners, village or township entrepreneurs, business executives, professional managers and white-collar state employees, private or foreign enterprise employees, scientists, and technical and professional personnel in agricultural, medical, or social science research or teaching

TABLE 11-1. Three Segments of the Middle Class, by Occupation, China

Percent

Segment	Percent
New	11.4
Professional	5.1
Managerial	1.5
Office and administrative	4.8
Old	4.8
Private business owners	0.6
Individual small entrepreneurs	4.2
Marginal	12.0
Sales and service	12.0
Total	28.2

Source: Lu Xueyi and others, eds., *Report on Social Strata Research in Contemporary China* (Beijing: Social Science Documentation Publishing House, 2002), p. 9.

institutions. In short, the report covers almost all of the newly created occupations and owners and personnel in the private business sector.

For the purpose of placing these research findings into a sociological framework of middle-class studies, it may be instructive to regroup the above ten social strata classified by Lu Xueyi and his associates and reformulate the relative proportions of different segments of the middle strata in present-day China. The resulting framework is taken from the class scheme constructed and used in the comparative middle-class research projects in East and Southeast Asia by the author and his research teams.[9] Table 11-1 indicates the distribution of the segments of the middle class we call *new* (the professional, managerial, and administrative strata), *old* (the entrepreneurial strata), and *marginal* (the sales and service strata).

By 2009 the most prevalent middle-class segments were the new and the old, or about 16 percent of the population. Another study of present-day China's middle class also highlights the new (managerial-professional and office administrative personnel) and the old (individual entrepreneurs and private business owners) and estimates that China's middle class was about 13 percent of the population.[10] The marginal segment (sales and services personnel) is ignored by most scholars. One rationale for this is that these workers are considered working class.

On the other hand, unique roles and functions are attributed to the middle class in most scholarly and popular writings since 2002. For example, in Lu and his associates' books of 2002 and 2004 the middle class is given the function of providing the coordination, stability, and order required by a modernized society.[11] Specifically, the middle class is to be the model for keeping the socialist market's economic order (such as facilitating the social norm of "fair competition"). The middle class is also expected to uphold certain positive social values, such as achievement motivation, creativity, respect for law and order, search for harmony, and open-mindedness. In public social life, members of the class are thought to be polite, tolerant, civil, and active in public activities conducive to modernizing society, as well as altruistic, helping socially disadvantaged groups after having made money by legal means.

Unlike in the past, the middle class is not criticized for being the cause of increasing income and social inequality but is rather thought to serve as the buffer and mediator between rich and poor, between top and bottom, by offering what could be called the middling values (*zhongjian jiazhi*) of those in the middle economically, politically, and culturally. Similarly, Li Qiang also cites the stability-promoting function of the middle class in the West and expects that China's middle class will also mediate social contradictions.[12]

Analysts and commentators in China agree that the marginal segment of the middle class could not fulfill all of the social functions listed above. Only the professional-managerial and entrepreneurial segments could manage the role of being the solid and stabilizing middle in China's rapidly developing economy and changing society. These two segments of China's emerging middle class have, as a result, become the focal point of a new social and political discourse that centers on their politically conservative and stabilizing propensity and their civilizing social character. And that is probably why the official and academic perspectives on the middle class have shifted from rejection and denial to acceptance and ambivalence and, finally, to a fairly welcoming embrace.

By the mid-2000s the social emergence of the middle class, and especially that of the above two core segments, was no longer viewed by the regime as a challenge to an increasingly outdated ideology that might force a reluctant recognition of differentiated class structures. The period's relatively open discussion of Chinese society's diverse strata and classes and their consequent social inequality and class conflicts marked the end of Chinese communism's class orthodoxy.[13] Along with sociologists and party-state elites recognizing the reality of social transformations, the middle class has been given, by both academia and the state, a unique mission to mediate, narrow, and even stabilize worsening social cleavages and contradictions. This explicitly conservative perspective has not only protected research on the middle class by Chinese academics but has also shaped the way the middle class is studied and characterized.

China's Middle Class in the Asia-Pacific Context

It is no surprise to see that most studies of China's middle class by Chinese scholars, and most public statements by politicians, concentrate on the economic aspect, income and consumption specifically, to demonstrate the distinctiveness of the emerging middle class. This focus has allowed the party-state to be convinced that the higher the number of middle-income individuals in society, the more mild and ideologically conservative the public's attitudes would become, and the more manageable social conflicts would become. At the Sixeenth Congress in 2002 Jiang Zemin even made it a government objective to expand the middle-income portion of Chinese society.[14] Given the public's minimal understanding of the terms, and the difference among the terms, the government chose *middle-income groups* over *middle class* or *middle strata*. In retrospect, middle-income groups was the politically safe classification, because it did not directly challenge Chinese Communist intellectual orthodoxy. Therefore, the sociological studies that have developed from this framework have a bias in favor of emphasizing income and consumption. Yet this does not mean that sociologists in China were not aware of the sociological difference between middle-income groups and middle class or between middle class as portrayed in the media and middle class as discussed in sociology.[15]

This uniformity of perspective—looking at the middle class from the prostate, prostability, and conservative standpoint—is unique in comparison with the discourses on middle-class discovery found in other countries in Asia. Since the early 1980s the emergence of the middle class in various newly industrialized societies in East and Southeast Asia—Taiwan, South Korea, Hong Kong, and Singapore—has caught the attention of academics, governments, and the media. The resulting debates over how to conceptualize the new social phenomena have been interesting. In each of these societies the political effect of the rising middle class on democratization was always at the center of the debates.[16] In Taiwan and South Korea, both of which were under martial law at various points after World War II, the 1980s saw the flowering of social movements and increasing demand from the public for political liberalization. The conservative authoritarian regimes that ruled these societies argued that the middle class had opted for economic growth and political stability and, therefore, should be on the side of the ruling regime. On the other hand, rising opposition groups were able to capture the hope for progressive reforms and democracy in the collective mind of the middle class and expected the middle class to support the pro-democracy opposition. Actually, in both Taiwan and South Korea, the political role of the middle class was determined primarily by the ways in which its liberal or radical segments were politically mobilized.[17]

In Hong Kong the crisis of the 1997 handover triggered a vibrant public discussion of what middle-class professionals and intellectuals should do to safeguard the political freedom and capitalist lifestyles of Hong Kong residents after the Communist takeover. In other words, the political pressure of having to face a change in Hong Kong's future facilitated the rise of a middle-class awareness, or consciousness. The Singaporean case is another story, though still colored by politics. In academic circles there were not many studies of the public discourse of the middle-class issue, but the ruling People's Action Party's (PAP) loss of votes in elections since the early 1980s had begun to alarm the Singapore state. The reaction of the rising middle class was taken to be the main cause of the PAP's losing absolute domination in elections. To fix the new political reality, the Singaporean government went so far as to define who belonged to the middle class in order to lure them back to the conservative camp.[18]

In contrast to Taiwan, South Korea, Hong Kong, and Singapore in the 1980s, China's middle class was defined quite differently in the 2000s. In the 1980s, as the middle class was emerging in these societies, it took on a multifaceted and pluralistic political character. One decade later, in the 1990s, the middle classes in the Philippines, Malaysia, Thailand, and Indonesia also showed such diverse and nonuniform characteristics. The dual political features of these middle classes were heatedly discussed in both academic and political circles. However, two decades later, in the 2000s, in the case of latecomer China a one-dimensional, prostate, status quo and apolitical conservative orientation dictates the whole discourse on its middle class.

The empirical findings of two comparative research projects on East and Southeast Asia's middle classes (the EAMC and SEAMC projects) in the above-mentioned eight societies also demonstrate that the spectrum of political attitudes and behaviors among their emerging middle classes has ranged from progressive and reform oriented to conservative and status-quo centered. The diverse characteristics can be observed not only in their subclasses or in certain sectors of society but also under specific yet different historical and political contexts.[19] There is no way that one can pinpoint whether or not middle classes in the Asia-Pacific are overall politically conservative, liberal, or radical. Rather, as illustrated above, they are contingent and situational.

The politics of the rising middle class in China has been controlled from its birth and has developed under the supervision of authoritarian political rule. Preliminary studies that characterize China's middle strata as "depoliticized" or "progressive consumption, regressive politics" testify to this truth and could in fact only perpetuate an a priori image ascribed to them.[20] Such apolitical attitudes among China's middle strata were also actually one of the direct social-psychological consequences of Communist rule.

In terms of the group's economic character (manifested by its higher income, greater consumption, and possession of more material goods as well as an eagerness to chase fashion and brand-name products), the composition of China's middle strata is in large extent no different from its counterparts in Asia during the previous decade. The popularization of the term *the new rich,* which was applied to the middle classes of East and Southeast Asia in the 1990s, is now widely used to portray China's emerging middle strata, the prime beneficiaries of China's economic growth.[21] Income, wealth, spending, and consumption are the crucial indicators in measuring the middle class in China today. This was also the case when middle classes were referred to and defined in Taiwan, South Korea, Hong Kong, Singapore, the Philippines, Malaysia, Thailand, and Indonesia. Yet what made the eight other Asian societies different from China is that the notion of a middle class in public consciousness implied something more than money, material possessions, and consumption. Self-improvement, knowledge, sophistication in taste and lifestyles, social awareness and concerns, conduct toward the betterment of collective social and political life, and a global way of thinking, looking, and visioning one's own national affairs were also considered key qualities of the middle classes in Taiwan, South Korea, and Hong Kong and to a lesser extent in Thailand, Malaysia, and Singapore. The middle classes in these societies were seen to represent a mix of global and local values, a digest of new and old ways, a balance of stability and change.[22]

In addition to the major contrasts found in the politics and culture of the middle class in China vis-à-vis their counterparts in other societies in the Asia-Pacific, there are several other significant differences worth noting. From the theoretical foundation used in the general comparative perspectives derived from the research findings of the EAMC and SEAMC projects, four theoretical propositions on the formation and characterization of Asian middle classes are relevant:

—The Asian middle classes are in fact the first generation of their kind and are the result of unprecedented intergenerational upward mobility.

—The middle classes in the industrialized Asia-Pacific are also unique, ascending new classes.

—The Asian middle classes, though distinct and distinguishable from the capitalist and working classes, are differentiated, diverse, and even segmented in their internal composition.

—The power relations between the middle classes and authoritarian political regimes are dialectical over the longer term.

In most cases the middle classes in the Asia-Pacific, especially the new middle-class stratum, originated in working-class and farmer families. They were indeed the upwardly mobile first generation of the middle class. This is particularly true for Taiwan, South Korea, Hong Kong, and Singapore and to lesser extent for Malaysia and Thailand. They were the product of intergenerational mobility, and some even changed their class positions through intragenerational mobility. The primary sources of intergenerational mobility were higher education and the acquiring of skills required by modern industrial societies; such intergenerational mobility occurred mainly through business opportunities provided by the state-led, export-oriented industrialization.

Turning to China, the studies done by Lu and his associates in 2004 and Li Chunling in 2009 discovered that intergenerational upward mobility did exist for different segments of the middle strata and that many were the direct beneficiaries of the market reform policies.[23] In many cases they were in fact former state or party or national business cadres or other elites who became managers. Some came from second-generation business families and others from the party or state bureaucracies. All in all, those who inhabit the Chinese middle class in today's society are not necessarily the real first-generation middle class, which comes from a lower-class family background such as laborers and farmers. One's social origins and family background matter a lot when it comes to attaining middle-class status. The role of *guanxi* (connection) is important for those managerial professionals who were directly shifted from their previous leadership positions in state-financed sectors. Therefore, the dynamics of this transformation are more closely modeled on intragenerational horizontal mobility than on intergenerational vertical mobility. It is very important to note that many current middle-class members actually benefited from the market economy reforms and undeniably inherited benefits from their organizational resources, connections, education, and political power.

The initial rise of the middle class in China therefore stemmed from three major sources: the transfer of previously held political power, market exchange, and personal social networking. Thus the origins of, and the mechanisms behind, the development of China's middle class are more complex and complicated than their counterparts in other capitalist industrial societies, and the first theoretical proposition generated from other Asian experience cannot fully explain the origins and structural nature of the segments of China's emerging middle class. It is not completely a new class structure in and of itself; rather, it is made over by the changing political economy, having taken advantage of the evolving political opportunities while inheriting political and social privileges from positions in the prior political structure.

Even though the middle classes in the industrialized capitalist Asia-Pacific are still composed of the upwardly mobile first generation, they aim higher. What they have achieved socially and financially has been through the possession of professional and managerial skills or specialist services that they believe are irreplaceable. The collective sense of self-ascendancy is a mix of pride and anxiety as well as an awareness of making a contribution to the betterment of social and political life; it goes without saying that they regard themselves as the defenders of democracy and supporters of social movements. These ascending middle classes have a unique position between the capitalists and the workers. They are not necessarily procapital or prolabor but tend to identify themselves as the class in the middle. This is particularly true of the professional-managerial new middle-class segment. Also, it is this new segment that has expressed support for political reforms and democracy. All in all, the middle classes in Asian industrialized nations desire to be a class of their own as they ascend within society.[24]

The individuals and groups in China today who belong to the middle class are often just situated in the middle in terms of income, education, and occupation. They also are more likely to consider themselves in the middle in society, especially in the cities. In a study by Li Peilin and Zhang Yi, middle class is also labeled the *social middle,* to include those who belong to the middle on all three criteria: income, education, and occupation.[25] The notion of middle is taken quite literally: the middle class is the people in the middle, between rich and poor and between high and low. Such numerical definition is a straightforward and convenient way to convey the meaning to the government and the public, but it may be too narrow and not sociologically rigorous. Taking this definition and measure as it stands, the social middle refers to the situation in which an individual's income, education, and occupation are all in the middle (although the Chinese word for middle class contains *chan,* meaning ownership). Li Lulu and Li Xeng, in their 2009 article, further stress the middle position occupied by the middle class in social structures.[26]

Yet it is quite shocking to detect from the survey findings by Lu and his associates and Li and Li that members of the middle class are also likely to be members of the CCP.[27] They tend to support the status quo by regarding most government policies as fair and just, they are in favor of getting rich by any possible means, and they would not oppose the government even if some policies were proved to be wrong. Therefore, the emerging middle class in China seems to be less politically independent and more socially conservative than middle classes elsewhere. Members are also less inclined to openly advocate for social reforms or democracy. As they themselves are part of the vested interest class—closely associated with political and bureaucratic power—the middle class does not make collective decisions without first accommodating party-state power brokers. Material possessions have become their primary goal.[28] In comparison with their counterparts in other societies in Asia, China's middle class members aim to climb the social ladder for themselves alone, following their own individualistic incentives and mostly in concert with the old power structure.[29]

One very important finding of the EAMC and SEAMC projects is the internal differentiation and diversity within the middle classes. As the result of ongoing class transformation, multiclass families have been on the rise in today's newly industrialized societies in East and Southeast Asia. From the 2002 and 2004 studies by Lu and his associates on China's social strata and social mobility, it is no surprise to observe a similar trend.[30] Also the study points out that between 1978 and 1991 social mobility, led by economic transformation, produced great social differentiation, and only after 1992 did an initial formation of China's new social stratification begin. Social class transformation implies greater social differentiation, with an increase in class categories. The classification of the ten social classes as constructed by Lu's team is a typical expression of the differentiated social class structure. Meanwhile, the further differentiation of the middle class into old, new, and marginal—or into individual small entrepreneurs, private business owners, managers and professionals, and lower clerical personnel—appears to be evidence of internal diversity. So in this sense China shares the same social differentiation trend found in other societies.

A recent national survey also establishes some important aspects of the collective mindset of the "climbing" middle class.[31] Its members tend to be pleased with their present living conditions as compared to the past and are optimistic about these conditions improving. Amid such contentedness and optimism there also exists a sense of "uncertainty," "lack of safety," and even "insecurity" surrounding income and wealth, physical well-being, transportation, medical condition, dietary health, work status, personal communication, and privacy. It is particularly important to note that among the professional-managerial segment of the middle class, the level of security is far lower than that of business elites and private business owners; in fact, their insecurity is similar to that of blue-collar workers. The marginal segment suffers the highest level of insecurity of all groups.[32] Such varying degrees of anxiety and insecurity experienced by different middle-class segments—behind the overall high contentedness—adds some nuance to our perspective on the psyche of China's highly differentiated middle strata.

In a few of the new democracies in the Asia-Pacific, such as the Philippines, South Korea, and Taiwan, where the middle classes were produced largely by authoritarian state-led proindustrial strategies and were therefore partly dependent on the regime, the middle classes eventually began to express criticism of authoritarianism. Liberalization and democratization eventually began to take hold, suggesting a dialectical power relationship between the authoritarian states and the middle classes they created. Of course, such dialectical power did not occur in a short time; it usually took place after the middle classes developed more conscious attitudes toward social and political affairs. The phenomenon of "critical citizenship" is detected in such newer democracies as Taiwan, the Philippines, and South Korea, and to a lesser extent Malaysia,

Indonesia, and Thailand.[33] This phenomenon of growing demand and an increasingly dissatisfied public is also on display in nondemocratic, or partially democratic, Hong Kong.[34]

The China case tells a different story, though it generally supports the observation that under less democratic political systems, the middle classes tend to be more conservative and proestablishment for fear of political oppression and economic suppression. The "myth of the democratic private entrepreneurs and business owners" is the succinct phrase of Kellee Tsai.[35] Tsai's study of the rising private sector in contemporary China finds that these private entrepreneurs and capitalists would not be expected to bring about democratic change. She concludes by saying, "We can have capitalism without democracy, political change and indeed capitalists in a communist party."

According to Li Chunling, all classes in China tend to have a very high level of trust in their central government (over 90 percent of the population), less so in their local government (over 70 percent).[36] The middle class does not demonstrate any significant divergence from other classes. It is also trustful of institutions owned or controlled by the government, such as state media (around 60 percent), and of statistics released by the government (also roughly 60 percent). It feels a similar way toward judges and police (60 percent). Such overwhelming public trust cannot be found in any established democracy nor in the three new democracies of Taiwan, the Philippines, and South Korea.

To push the argument further, it is found that the middle class tends to have a positive evaluation of social stability in China, though the marginal segment, along with the working class, is a bit more negative about it. The same can be said about the collective assessment of the most popular social conditions in present-day China, namely social harmony. Again, only about 18 percent (the old segment) and 21 percent (the new segment) consider Chinese society today to be lacking social harmony. Workers again are more pessimistic (with about 23 percent expressing dissatisfaction with the level of social harmony).[37] The overall attitude of the middle-class members reflects the better conditions they enjoy in comparison with workers and farmers. So far, no real critical or demanding attitudes can be found among the middle class toward the authoritarian Communist government.

However, another set of attitudinal data on how to perceive citizen and government relations presented by Li Chunling is of great interest for further assessment of the dialectical relations between the middle class and the Chinese state. It is found that there is an emerging sense of citizens' autonomy vis-à-vis the government. When asked if "democracy is where the government decides for the people," the middle class tends to be the least supportive of all classes, with the new segment of the middle class expressing greater contention (almost half in disagreement, 49 percent), followed by the marginal segment of the middle class (39 percent in disagreement). Again, the new middle-class segment tends to be more opposed to the statement "Ordinary people should simply listen to the government; the subordinated should obey the superior," with more than half of the respondents expressing their discontent (54 percent), also followed by the marginal segment (46 percent). Finally, the new, the old, and the marginal segments all demonstrate a significant level of awareness of political efficacy. About 79 percent of the new segment, 75 percent of the marginal segment, and 62 percent of the old segment oppose the assertion "Let the government take care of big things the ordinary people do not need to be bothered with."[38]

Are these reliable signs of the growth of a "demanding public" or "critical citizenship" with a kind of antiestablishment and pro-democracy constituency within the Chinese middle class? The answer to this question is a small yes and a big no. The small yes is that at least the middle class can now openly express its differing views. The big no is that individual expression of not-so-conservative attitudes does not really constitute the coherent and consistent pro-democracy mindset necessary for becoming a critical citizen. In other words, based on the various empirical evidence presented by the current research findings cited above of how the middle class thinks and its ability to act on various social and political issues, there is definitely no clear indication of contested relations between critical middle-class attitudes and the practice of state authoritarianism in present-day China. All available data collected by Chinese sociologists so far point to middle-class conservatism rather than middle-class liberalism.

Assessing the Link between the Middle Class and Civil Society in China Today

This concluding section addresses the supposed link between the affluent and privileged middle class to another, also much-discussed social phenomenon, namely, the activism of civil society for social and political reforms in present-day China. The critical question is, then, whether or not the middle class under review in this chapter has something to do with the emergence of a civil society. Once again, the comparative experiences of the middle classes in other East and Southeast Asian countries, especially in newly established democracies, can be instructive.

From the two comparative research projects, EAMC and SEAMC, one very important finding is that there existed an identifiable portion of the middle-class, usually from the new middle-class segment, that not only openly expressed its belief in the principles of democracy but also explicitly considered itself the vanguard of democracy in its country's political changes. In the cases of three new Asian democracies—Taiwan, the Philippines, and South Korea—this middle-class group has stood behind various social reform movements on behalf of consumers, the environment, women, indigenous cultures and peoples, human rights, laborers, farmers, urban housing prices, media and judiciary reforms, and congressional watching.

Some members of this class initiated, supported, organized, and sustained some of these advocacy-oriented civil society organizations in the form of NGOs, NPOs, membership associations, and foundations. The link between the middle class and civil society is therefore not nominal, simplistic, or linear; rather, it is complex and dynamic. The profound social and political transformations attending Asia-Pacific democratization show that neither the emergence of the middle class nor the rise of civil society is an end in itself. In the newly established democracies of the Philippines, South Korea, and Taiwan the sequential and causal links are evident and direct: the middle-class-backed and -supported progressive and pro-democracy civil society organizations played a notable role in the liberalization and democratization of their countries. Further, different stages of democratization involved different segments of the middle class. The importance of the social movements organized by workers and farmers, of course, should not be ignored either, nor the dynamics of class coalitions involving the pro-democracy segments of the middle class and the working and capitalist classes.[39] In transitional democratic countries like Indonesia, Malaysia, and Thailand the role of pro-democracy civil society movements has also been documented, as has the active participation of some progressive elements of these societies' new middle-class segments, though the links among the middle class, civil society, and democracy building are not so noticeable.

Two lessons can be drawn from the democratization experiences examined here. One is that in the long course of the democracy-making process, it is civil society through organized advocacy and pro-democracy social movements that tends to initiate and push for democratic reforms. A bottom-up political process is essential to force democratization to start. None of the authoritarian regimes initiated top-down democratization.

The second lesson is that it is not the middle class as a whole that serves as the vanguard of democracy, and the numerical relations between a sizable middle class and the transition to democracy cannot possibly predict civil activism and democratization, as some political modernization theories may lead us to believe. Specific members of the middle class, especially of the new segment of the middle class (liberal or radical intellectuals and pro-democracy professionals), must commit their energy and efforts to the cause of democratization, because it is only they who have contributed to the birthing of democracy. Furthermore, the organizational mechanisms through which this middle-class segment was able to institutionalize democracy were found in civil society organizations, not at home, in the office, in the market, or even at polling stations. It requires struggle on the part of the progressive middle class. To be specific, it involves organized struggles by a pro-democracy civil society. The theoretical-empirical proposition that follows from the two lessons is that the links among the progressive middle class, proreform civil society organizations, and the prospect of a democratic future are dynamic and complex. From this proposition stem four general observations about the middle class in China and, specifically, its relation to democratization:

—In China there is a lack of progressive elements within the middle strata as measured by economic and income indicators or occupational criteria.

—In China there is no indication that a true sector of nongovernmental civic organizations has developed into a viable social force. There is very limited political room for pro-democracy NGOs to emerge.

—In China there are clear signs that the authoritarian Communist regime has been deliberately monitoring civic organizations (most of them are in fact government-organized nongovernmental organizations) and preventing the growth of grassroots organizations focusing on civil rights and legal reforms.

—In China there is a disconnect rather than a link between the emerging middle class and the growth of civil society.

Therefore, it is very uncertain how recent changes in Chinese society, with a growing number of disaffected in the middle strata, can catalyze and sustain any democratic reforms in China. Judging from past experience in Asia, and given China's present situation, one should be cautious about being too optimistic about the future of democracy in China.

Notes

1. Ho Jien-Zhang, "On Middle Class," *Sociological Research* 2 (1990): 1–7.

2. Ibid.

3. Li Qiang, *Social Stratification and Mobility in Contemporary China* (Beijing: Chinese Economic Publishing House, 1993).

4. Ibid.

5. Ibid.

6. Yen Zi-Ming, ed., *Class Stratification in Present China* (Beijing: Chinese Communist Party Central Party School, 2002).

7. Lu Xueyi and others, eds., *Report on Social Strata Research in Contemporary China* (Beijing: Social Science Documentation Publishing House, 2002).

8. Ibid., p. 252.

9. Hsin-Huang Michael Hsiao, ed., *East Asian Middle Classes in Comparative Perspective* (Taipei: Institute of Ethnology, Academia Sinica, 1999); Hsin-Huang Michael Hsiao, ed., *Exploration of the Middle Classes in Southeast Asia* (Taipei: Program for Southeast Asian Area Studies, Academia Sinica, 2001).

10. Li Qiang, *China's Social Stratifications in Transitional Era* (Shenyang: Liao-ning Educational Publishing House, 2004), pp. 310–11.

11. Lu and others, *Report on Social Strata Research in Contemporary China;* Lu Xueyi and others, eds., *Social Mobility in Contemporary China* (Beijing: Social Science Documentation Publishing House, 2004).

12. Li Qiang, *China's Social Stratifications in Transitional Era*, pp. 282–83.

13. Li Peilin and others, *Social Conflict and Class Consciousness* (Beijing: Social Science Documentation Publishing House, 2005); Shigeto Sonoda, *Unequal Nations: China* (Tokyo: Chuokoron-Shinsha, 2008).

14. Li Chunling, ed., *Formation of Middle Class in Comparative Perspective: Process, Influence, and Socioeconomic Consequences* (Beijing: Social Sciences Academic Press, 2009).

15. Zhou Xiaohong, "Chinese Middle Class: Reality or Myth," *Social Sciences of Tianjin* 3 (2006).

16. H. H. Michael Hsiao, ed., *Discovery of the Middle Classes in East Asia* (Taipei: Institute of Ethnology, Academia Sinica, 1993).

17. H. H. Michael Hsiao and Hagen Koo, "The Middle Classes and Democratization," in *Consolidating the Third Wave Democracies*, edited by Larry Diamond and others (Johns Hopkins University Press, 1997), pp. 312–33.

18. Mak Lou-Fong, "The Rise of the Singapore Middle Class: An Analytic Framework," in Hsiao, ed., *Discovery of the Middle Classes in East Asia*, pp. 307–36.

19. Hsiao, *East Asians Middle Classes in Comparative Perspective;* Hsiao, *Exploration of the Middle Classes in Southeast Asia.*

20. Cited in Li Chunling, *Formation of Middle Class in Comparative Perspective.*

21. David S. G. Goodman, ed., *The New Rich in Asia* (London: Routledge, 1996); David S. G. Goodman, ed., *The New Rich in China: Future Rulers, Present Lives* (London: Routledge, 2008).

22. H. H. Michael Hsiao and Po-San Wan, "The Experiences of Cultural Globalizations in Asia-Pacific," *Japanese Journal of Political Science* 8, no. 3 (2007).

23. Lu and others, *Social Mobility in Contemporary China*; Li Chunling, *Formation of Middle Class in Comparative Perspective.*

24. H. H. Michael Hsiao, ed., *The Changing Faces of the Middle Classes in Asia-Pacific* (Taipei: Academia Sinica, 2006).

25. Li Peilin and Zhang Yi, "The Size, Identity, and Social Attitudes of China's Middle Class," in Li Chunling, ed., *Formation of Middle Class in Comparative Perspective,* pp. 99–116.

26. Li Lulu and Li Xeng, "Divergent Approaches, Different Types: A Typological Analysis of Middle Classes in China's Cities," in Li Chunling, ed., *Formation of Middle Class in Comparative Perspective,* pp. 195–215.

27. Lu and others, *Report on Social Strata Research in Contemporary China*; Li Lulu and Li Xeng, "Divergent Approaches, Different Types."

28. Li Lulu and Li Xeng, "Divergent Approaches, Different Types."

29. Hsiao, *East Asian Middle Classes in Comparative Perspective*; Hsiao, *Exploration of the Middle Classes in Southeast Asia.*

30. Lu and others, *Report on Social Strata Research in Contemporary China*; Lu Xueyi and others, *Social Mobility in Contemporary China.*

31. Li Chunling, "The Growth and Current Conditions of China's Middle Class," in Li Chunling, ed., *Formation of Middle Class in Comparative Perspective,* pp. 117–46.

32. Ibid.

33. Pippa Norris, "Introductions: The Growth of Critical Citizen," in *Critical Citizens: Global Support for Democratic Government,* edited by Pippa Norris (Oxford University Press, 1999), pp. 1–27.

34. Hsiao, *Exploration of the Middle Classes in Southeast Asia*; H. H. Michael Hsiao and Po-San Wan, "Collective Socio-Political Consciousness of the Middle Classes in Taiwan, Hong Kong, and Singapore," in *Market, Class, and Politics in Changing Chinese Societies,* edited by S. K. Lau and others (Hong Kong: HKIAPS, CUHK, 2000), pp. 459–92; T. Ka-Ying Wong, H. H. Michael Hsiao, and Po-San Wan, "Comparing Political Trust in Hong Kong and Taiwan: Levels, Determinants, and Implications," *Japanese Journal of Political Sciences* 10, no. 2 (2009): 147–74.

35. Kellee S. Tsai, *Capitalism without Democracy: The Private Sector in Contemporary China* (Cornell University Press, 2007).

36. Li Chunling, *Formation of Middle Class in Comparative Perspective,* pp. 138–39.

37. Ibid., p. 139.

38. Ibid., pp. 139, 140–42.

39. H. H. Michael Hsiao, ed., *Asian New Democracies: The Philippines, South Korea, and Taiwan Compared* (Taipei: Taiwan Foundation for Democracy and Center for Asia-Pacific Area Studies, Academia Sinica, 2008); Hagen Koo, "Globalization and the Asia Middle Classes," in Hsiao, ed., *The Changing Faces of the Middle Classes in Asia-Pacific,* pp. 9–24.

CHAPTER TWELVE

Middle-Class Grassroots Identity and Participation in Citizen Initiatives, China and South Korea

HAN SANG-JIN

The theme of this volume, beyond economic transformation, calls our attention to a potential political significance of China's emerging middle class.[1] It invites us to see members of the middle class as actors or agents with value orientations and capable of making lifestyle choices rather than simply a statistical category convenient for social scientific analysis. Conventionally, the middle class has been seen as the product of macroeconomic forces, such as a country's income distribution, occupational trends, and rate of urbanization. In this chapter, however, a social class is not treated simply as a class in itself but instead as a class *for* itself. The former description may describe objective characteristics presumably shared by certain categories of people that we call a class. The latter description delves deeper, implicating the concrete patterns of understanding and action that these actors manifest, often in direct confrontation with other classes.

It is well known that of all class categories the middle class is the most ambiguous and difficult to grasp.[2] This is particularly so when the middle class is in an early stage of its historical formation, as in China today. The Chinese context of economic development, cultural traditions,

The author thanks Cheng Li, the editor of this volume, Shim Young-Hee, professor of sociology at Hanyang University, Korea, and anonymous reviewers for their careful reading and for their valuable comments on this chapter. Thanks also are owed to Kim Min-Hye and Jo Myong-Ok, who provided statistical and computer work.

contemporary politics, and social relationships is quite distinctive and therefore deeply consequential for the manner in which the middle class will develop. This requires us to be sensitive to the dynamic fluidities of the Chinese middle class in this early stage of formation.

A useful case of reference is England, where in her early stage of modernization researchers first described the emerging middle class as "the middling sort of people."[3] The term *middling* here refers to a dynamic process of upward mobility that opened up a middle space in the course of early economic modernization. Noticing these changes, researchers were eager to learn how this new phenomenon, an emerging middle class, would come to affect society. As we discuss present-day China's emerging middle class we would do well to preserve this kind of historical sensibility and sociological imagination.

Likewise, an attempt is made here to explain the characteristics of the emerging middle class in China from the vantage point of the Korean experience.[4] The author does not dispute the utility of Western conceptual schemes and classification models; the point at issue is simply that when we study the middle class in China, we need to pay attention to the hidden function of the conceptual strategy we use. In other words, imposing on China the conceptual framework borrowed from the West, where the middle class is well established, may hinder us from grasping the subtle dynamics of China's middle class in its early stage.[5] This is particularly so when we investigate the sociopolitical role of the middle class. In China, as almost everywhere, information, discourse, desire, and aspiration are cutting across class boundaries conventionally assumed. Thus there seems to be no compelling reason to believe that the sociopolitical attitudes and practical capacities for action are divided by such objective variables as occupation or income.

It is instructive in this regard that Li Peilin and his associates at the Chinese Academy of Social Science have attempted to test the extent to which the "objective" Western models of middle-class classification are able to grasp the more idiosyncratic sociopolitical aspects of China's middle class.[6] Their studies have significant methodological implications because they use the same data from the China General Social Survey. They approach the middle class with the same questions but employ different conceptual frameworks. In this way, they demonstrate clearly that sociological knowledge of the middle class depends on how one defines the class, to whom the class is compared, and what strategy one adopts when examining specific aspects of the middle class. These discussions

can help us to see how problematic it can be to simply state the findings of empirical research without explicating the hidden function of the
framework employed.

This chapter is an attempt to advance a more nuanced approach,
drawing attention to the role of identity as an independent variable
in explaining the middle class's political attitudes and behaviors. The
emphasis of my argument is not to compare the middle class with other
classes such as farmers and the working class but to compare two distinctive segments of the middle class, which differ from each other in terms
of their identities. They share many characteristics, such as high levels of
education, yet differ in their political orientation. This focus on internal
differentiation may be more fruitful than the conventional strategy of
comparing the middle class with the nonmiddle classes. Furthermore, the
author wants to explore whether it is possible to go beyond Erik Olin
Wright's conception of the middle class by dividing the middle class into
two identity-based segments of equal significance.[7]

How to Study Identity

Before we examine the research design and outcomes, it is necessary to
specify how to study identity methodologically. Two points need to be
mentioned. First, identity, as defined in this chapter, does not refer to the
subjective category as conventionally understood but to a sociocultural
category that emerges out of the processes of discursive social construction and functions as a sorting mechanism of meaning and orientation
in everyday life.[8]

Second, it is limiting to treat identity as an auxiliary concept or a
mediating variable attached to class structure objectively defined. The
key question is whether and how members of an objective class obtain
their class identity in struggle. This strategy may work well in the case of
working-class formation, as can be seen in the works by E. P. Thomson.
In the case of middle-class formation, however, this strategy is problematic because it excludes the working class and farmers as a whole from
the middle class, which cannot be fixed by such objective factors as
occupation, the labor market, job skills, and institutional positions but
is formed within the fields of discursive formation in Foucault's sense.

Once socially constructed, the identity of the middle class significantly
affects how one sees the world and how one acts in it, transcending
class boundaries objectively defined. Therefore, it is important to pay

due attention to the relationship between identity and the middle class's attitudes and actions.[9] Such formative processes of the middle class may be more visible in South Korea and Japan than in China.

Just as *the middling sort of people* was the first term used to describe the emerging middle class in England, the notion of *zhongchan cheng* (middle propertied stratum) has been widely used by the mass media and social scientists in South Korea and China to refer to upwardly mobile people in rapidly modernizing economies.[10] The identity of the emerging middle class as *zhongchan cheng* is subject to social construction, through which its meaning, standards, and characteristics are formed. *Zhongchan cheng* is not identical with the new or the old middle class since it can, in principle, include at least some workers and farmers. Furthermore, those who share this identity may change depending on circumstances. In Korea, for instance, up until the middle of the 1990s, over 60 percent of the population accepted this explicit identity. Since then, however, Korea has faced repeated economic crises, and as a result the share has drastically declined to 30–40 percent.[11]

One way of seeing the impact of identity is consumption, already a hot topic for many researchers on the middle class in China. The thesis is that members of China's middle class, no matter their origins, construct their life world from the vantage point of consumption, as is evident in their purchases of housing, cars, leisure activities, food, foreign travel, arts, and other cultural activities. As the notion *zhongchan cheng* already captures the importance of the middle class's economic well-being, there is no doubt that consumption provides a key to understanding the middle class in the age of globalization.

Yet this chapter is primarily concerned with the sociopolitical aspect of the middle class in China. Two axes of identity formation deserve our careful attention. One is the economic aspect of the middle class, and the other is related to the social aspect of middle-class identity. Important for the latter is the family background of the emerging middle class. Many members of the middle class are, in fact, in the process of upward mobility in their life span from their parent's status of farmer or worker. For this reason, they can be more sympathetic and sensitive to the situation of ordinary people than the middle class in the West, which is shielded by its distinctive cultures. No less important than the family background is, of course, the social construction of the middle class identity through mass media, politics, and social movements. Combined, these social factors may give rise to the formation of a grassroots identity, enabling part of the middle class to see the world from the viewpoint of ordinary people. This social dimension of middle-class identity, especially in the class's early stages of historical development, is as significant and consequential as its economic dimension.

It is important, therefore, to examine the discursive process of identity formation within the overall trend of economic modernization and political change. Though *zhongchan cheng* refers primarily to those who have benefited greatly from economic modernization, the notion also implies characteristics such as a certain public morality, civic virtues, a capacity for reasonable argument, certain cultural tastes, and so on. On the whole, it is an open question, theoretically, how members of the middle class relate to other social groups in a rapidly transforming society. In a nutshell, some may develop a grassroots identity and be inclined to support reform and change. Others may be more interested in joining the upper class and thus develop a mainstream identity, favoring the rule of law and state authority. In this context, the author argues that it is limiting to define the determining factor as interests, in the conventional sense. Instead, it should be understood as identity, which involves moral and aesthetic dimensions of human subjectivity in addition to self-interests.

In South Korea, for instance, the middle class's identity was an important issue during the 1980s as the country democratized. This transition was enabled by three key factors:

—The state, despite overseeing economic modernization, began to suffer from the lack of legitimacy due to its repressive practices, creating public frustration and disillusionment.

—The legitimate interests of suppressed people began to find expression in the broader society.

—The mass media and politicians began to pay attention to the role of the middle class in such sensitive historical conjunctures.

These conditions gave rise to the grassroots identity of the middle class, which played an important role in subsequent democratic change. In this context, the author has developed the concept of the middling grassroots identity.[12]

Though the case of China is different in many ways, because of similar cultural traditions, a grassroots identity may be possible. As in South Korea, China has developed a rich normative tradition of people-centered politics. The normative idea *minben* (people centered) is still an important component of Chinese political culture and most people's mind-set, which makes it possible to explore whether or not part of the emerging middle class may be inclined to develop a grassroots identity.[13]

Why China and South Korea?

Despite many differences between China and South Korea in terms of the size of their territories and populations, their ruling ideologies, their ethnic compositions, and the timing of their development trajectories, there seem to be three reasons why we need a comparative study of these two countries with respect to their middle classes.[14]

The first reason is related to the leading role of the bureaucratic authoritarian state in the process of capitalist economic development. Both South Korea from 1961 to 1987 and China since the 1980s represent a model in which a bureaucratic authoritarian regime, characterized by unprecedented success in facilitating economic growth, exercised systematic control over civil society so as to secure political and social stability.[15] The dual aspects of this type of regime have given rise to the extraordinary power of economic institutions like the Economic Planning Board in South Korea and the National Development and Reform Commission in China, as well as the two countries' public security apparatuses. There are important differences between South Korea and China with respect to the internal processes of policy formation, the role of the ruling party vis-à-vis the administration, the extent of power concentration, and the relationship between central and provincial governments. Yet South Korea and China both are successful models of a bureaucratic authoritarian regime.

The second reason for this comparative study is the shared experience by the two countries of a rapidly expanding middle class resulting from state-centered economic development. In particular, an increase in large-scale enterprises and the expansion of the state's economic activities made possible the rapid increase in cities of both the new middle class and the working class. In this context, the emerging middle class began to draw public attention, inviting a diversity of approaches, via, for example, occupation, education, and consumption.[16] This is simply because researchers define the middle class in terms of occupation, education, income, or consumption. Whichever criteria are used, however, there is a broad consensus holding that the Chinese middle class is in the process of rapid expansion.

The third reason concerns the efficacy of examining the effect of cultural traditions on the formation of a middle-class identity. The normative politics of *minben* has been deeply rooted in China and Korea, producing many significant attempts in modern history to reinvent this tradition by linking it to Western ideas such as democracy, popular sovereignty, national self-determination, the Communist revolution, the people's right to self-rule, and so on.[17] All variations within this spectrum, however, converge on the fundamental tenets that political power should serve the interests of the people, that the people are sovereign, and that the people are free to express their opinions and to participate in broader community. Since division between the power bloc and the people is unavoidable, and since the idea of *minben* is inherently critical of an illegitimate regime, the question becomes, What does the grassroots identity of the middle class mean when confronting this situation?

An interesting fact is that this normative tradition has given rise to numerous social campaigns led by public intellectuals, who as members of the middle class existing during historical conjunctures have acted on behalf of the people, defending their rights against foreign aggression, the moral decay of a ruling monarch, or the misuse of power by bureaucrats. Consequently, the tradition of a loyal opposition became quite strong in China and Korea from very early on, especially among the knowledge-based middle class. An obvious example is the student movements in modern China and Korea. During the 1980s college students in South Korea developed a distinctive *minjoong* (politically suppressed grassroots) culture, breaking away from traditional elitism.[18] Though this is not as conspicuous in China, the normative cultural potential still exists in the hearts of the people.

Therefore we can ask how cultural tradition becomes embedded in the middle-class identity and whether the middle class in its early stage of identity formation aligns with the power bloc above it or with the ordinary people below—and from whom they originated. The issue is all the more significant if the opposition between the power bloc and the people remains a deep, underlying developmental pattern for the country and if the power bloc is seen as lacking legitimacy. This was the actual course of events in South Korea during the 1980s. This normative tradition of *minben* politics can be fruitfully utilized to explore the critical potential of China's middle class.

It must be stated that this chapter is not intended to be a discursive analysis of the formation of middle-class identity as a historical project. On the contrary, the social construction of identity is assumed in the background, while the lion's share of the analysis focuses on the influence of identity on the middle class's attitudes and actions. Two options are used in this regard. The best option is to use the explicit reference of *zhongchan cheng* as middle-class identity if it is included in the nationwide survey data. If not, the conventional variable of socioeconomic status is used as the second-best alternative.

Data and Major Findings

The main data used in this chapter include the 2006 China General Social Survey (CGSS), the South Korean survey of 1987, and the World Value Survey (WVS) conducted in South Korea in 1995 and 2006. The Korean data of 1987 and CGSS of 2006 are also used to compare demographic characteristics of the middle classes in China and Korea. These two sets of data reflect the social situation after three decades of rapid economic development in these two countries: Rapid transformation began in Korea in 1960 and in China in 1979.

The basic model of classification is composed of the two axes of middle-class formation mentioned above. One axis deals with the question of whether concerned individuals identify themselves as included in the socially constructed category of *zhongchan cheng*. This axis is interpreted primarily to mean the economic aspect of middle-class formation. The other axis deals with the question of whether concerned individuals identify themselves as oriented either toward the common people or toward the upper class. This axis is primarily interpreted to mean the political aspect of middle-class formation.

South Korea: Zhongchan Cheng versus Minjoong

In South Korea, when the massive mobilization of various social forces for democracy took place during the 1980s, the concepts of *zhongchan cheng* and *minjoong* appeared widely in the mass media and political discourse.[19] Heated debates had been unfolding since the middle of the 1980s revolving around questions of, for example, where the middle class stood in economic modernization and political democratization. Given the fact that college students took the advocacy role—that is, were more *minjoong*, becoming the most decisive force driving toward political democratization—it was frequently asked whether the emerging middle class, that is, the *zhongchan cheng*, was likely to act as a progressive force or a conservative force.

TABLE 12-1. Four Identity Groups, South Korea[a]

		Minjoong	
		Yes	No
Zhongchan cheng	Yes	Middling grassroots	Propertied mainstream
	No	Bottom grassroots	Double outsiders

Source: Han Sang-Jin, "The Dynamics of Middle-Class Politics in Korea: Why and How Do the Middling Grassroots Differ from the Propertied Mainstream?" *Korean Journal of Sociology* 43, no. 3 (2009): 1–19.

a. Typical questions used to elicit identity were, "We use the notion of *zhongchan cheng* in our everyday life. Do you consider yourself to belong to the *zhongchan cheng* or not?" And "We use the notion of *minjoong* in our everyday life. Do you consider yourself to belong to the *minjoong* or not?" Answers could only be yes or no.

It was in this historical context of identity construction that the author made the first attempt to use the notions of *zhongchan cheng* and *minjoong* in a nationwide survey. The term *zhongchan* was originally thought to be more economic than political in nature, while *minjoong* was the opposite. It was assumed that the *zhongchan cheng* were well off economically and politically conservative, while the *minjoong* were economically poor and politically progressive. However, since these two concepts are not mutually exclusive, it was an open question if, and to what extent, members of the *zhongchan cheng* might share the identity of the *minjoong*, and vice versa. In fact, various white-collar groups had a clear *minjoong* identity and actively joined democratic movements during the 1980s.[20] The combination of these two axes resulted in the four categories shown in table 12-1: middling grassroots, propertied mainstream, bottom grassroots, and double outsiders.

The Korean data from 1987 to 2006 include two explicit identity variables referred to above; thus it is possible to examine the longitudinal trends of identity distribution and its impact on the sociopolitical attitudes of citizens. As can be seen in table 12-2, the decrease in the middle class (middling grassroots plus propertied mainstream) from 1999 on is striking. This reflects what the popular mass media and magazines have called the collapse of the middle class in Korea. Until the middle of the 1990s more than half of Korean adults identified themselves as *zhongchan cheng*, but this fell radically, to 30–40 percent, after the economic crisis (except in 2002, when there were high hopes for an economic recovery). In contrast, the percent of those who identified with the bottom grassroots sharply increased between 1995 and 1999, suggesting increased potential for social conflict. The middling grassroots do not appear to have been as seriously affected by the

TABLE 12-2. Size of the Four Identity Groups, South Korea, Selected Years 1987–2006

Number (percent)

Identity group	1987	1995	1999	2001	2002	2005	2006
Middling grassroots	260 (20.8)	322 (26.0)	310 (25.9)	436 (36.0)	483 (48.3)	289 (28.7)	228 (22.7)
Propertied mainstream	418 (33.4)	468 (37.8)	106 (8.8)	98 (8.1)	65 (6.5)	75 (7.5)	84 (8.3)
Bottom grassroots	213 (17.0)	163 (13.2)	479 (39.9)	409 (33.8)	294 (29.4)	392 (39.0)	388 (38.6)
Double outsiders	359 (28.7)	284 (23.0)	304 (25.4)	268 (22.1)	157 (15.7)	250 (24.9)	306 (30.4)
Total	1,250 (100)	1,237 (100)	1,199 (100)	1,211 (100)	999 (100)	1,006 (100)	1,006 (100)

Source: Han Sang-Jin, "The Dynamics of Middle-Class Politics in Korea."

economic crisis as the propertied mainstream. This chapter compares only these two groups.

China: Functional Equivalent Subsets

An important difficulty in comparing Chinese middle-class identity with that of the Korean middle class is that no explicit terms, like those used in South Korea, have been used in China. The alternative is to use the conventional variable of socioeconomic status. The size of *zhongchan cheng* so measured turns out to be significantly bigger than that of South Korea.[21]

In a similar way, a plausible substitute for the concept *minjoong* can be found in an item of the CGSS of 2006. To the statement, "There is no need to worry about democracy if the economy continues to show stable development," possible responses were "Absolutely agree (8.9 percent)," "Agree (36.5 percent)," "Disagree (43.9 percent)," and "Absolutely disagree (10.6 percent)." This question is significant in that it asks respondents to choose one of two positions: one is to prioritize steady economic development, which is close to the basic orientation of the mainstream of the middle class; the other is to value democracy and not condone it being sacrificed for the sake of economic development. This position is close to the concept of *minjoong* in Korea.

The distribution of the four identities in China is presented in table 12-3. The middling grassroots are the largest portion, at 33 percent, while the propertied mainstream measures 26 percent. The large size of these two identities owes much to the fact that about 60 percent of respondents occupy *zhongchan cheng* in terms of their socioeconomic status. What is important for this discussion is the influence of this cohort's identity on the middle class's sociopolitical attitudes and behavior.

TABLE 12-3. Size of the Four Identity Groups, China, 2006[a]

Identity group	Number	Percent
Middling grassroots	2,954	33.0
Propertied mainstream	2,342	26.2
Bottom grassroots	1,924	21.5
Double outsiders	1,731	19.3
Total	8,951	100.0

Source: China General Social Survey, 2006.

a. The standardized question is, Where does your socioeconomic status belong? Upper, middle-high, middle, middle-low, or low? Those who answer from upper to middle-low are counted as *zhongchan cheng.*

Demographic Characteristics of the Middling Grassroots Identity

The dynamics of the middle class have their roots in the demographic profiles of its two identity groups. In the case of Korea, the most persistent factor affecting the internal differentiation of the middle class is education. During the 1980s and until the middle of the 1990s age was as conspicuous as education. This means that the middling grassroots were more likely to be found among the young cohorts than among the old. Since then, however, the influence of age has been significantly reduced though it has not disappeared altogether. This seems to have something to do with the fact that members of the young cohorts have aged. On the other hand, the influence of education has proved consistent. The higher the level of education, the bigger the proportion of the middling grassroots, as can be seen in table 12-4.[22]

Some trends initially spotted in South Korea have been found in China. In both countries, the middling grassroots have tended to increase along with level of education. The 2006 profile of the Chinese middling grassroots suggests that their level of education is far higher than that of the propertied mainstream and the bottom grassroots.[23] In both countries, the middling grassroots significantly decrease as age increases. This means that the middling grassroots tend to be located more among the young cohort.

These demographic characteristics of the middling grassroots reflect an intrinsic affinity to a post-traditional, participation-oriented interpretation of the *minben* tradition. Being younger and more educated, they are inclined to support an active political role for citizens.

TABLE 12-4. Size of Two Identity Groups of the Middle Class, by Education, South Korea, 1995

Number (percent)

Identity group	Middle school	High school	College and above	Total
Middling grassroots	31 (22.5)	123 (39)	168 (50)	322 (40.8)
Propertied mainstream	107 (77.5)	192 (61)	168 (50)	467 (59.2)
Total	138 (100)	315 (100)	336 (100)	789 (100)

Source: World Value Survey, 1995. Han Sang-Jin, "The Dynamics of Middle-Class Politics in Korea."
$x^2 = 31.382, p < 0.001$.

The Middling Grassroots Identity and Citizen Initiatives: A Cross-Country Comparison

The sociopolitical, ideological, and cultural orientations of the middle class, together with its capacity for action, are of crucial significance for understanding the middle class. This issue can be investigated with respect to participation in citizen initiatives by the middling grassroots and the propertied mainstream of the middle class. Those with a grassroots identity can be assumed to be more willing than those with a mainstream identity to take part in citizen initiatives, such as signing petitions and attending peaceful demonstrations or joining in boycotts, labor strikes, and sit-down strikes. As shown in table 12-5, the middling grassroots are much more likely than the propertied mainstream to participate in the citizen initiatives surveyed.

Given the fact that the identity of the middling grassroots is strongly related to higher education, however, one might ask if identity alone can wield independent influence with education controlled.[24] This challenge should be taken seriously. Two types of advanced analysis are required: one is multiple regression analysis and the other is a detailed profile analysis combining education and identity. First, a multiple regression analysis shows that the identity variable is as significant as that of education in independently shaping citizens' participation in politics. The influence of education is greater than that of identity in South Korea (table 12-6). Yet it is important to note that identity works independently.

Second, to go a step further, an attempt has been made to examine how the two independent variables, namely education and identity,

T A B L E 1 2 - 5 . Participation in Citizen Initiatives, by Two Identity Groups, South Korea, 1995 and 2006

Percent

	1995			2006		
Citizen initiative[a]	Middling grassroots	Propertied mainstream	Average	Middling grassroots	Propertied mainstream	Average
Signing petition	91.3	79.8	84.4	84.1	60.7	75.3
Joining boycott	86.1	72.4	78.0	72.8	50.0	65.1
Joining demonstration	64.3	45.5	53.2	73.7	50.0	65.5
Joining labor strike	52.7	33.5	41.4	...	...	...
Joining sit-down strike	33.3	18.5	24.6	...	...	...

Source: World Value Survey, 1995, 2006. Han Sang-Jin, "The Dynamics of Middle-Class Politics in Korea."
a. All of the initiatives were included in the World Value Survey, 1995; only the first three were included in the World Value Survey, 2006. The suggested answers to each question were, Have already done, Might do if chance is given, and Would never do. The first two answers are combined in the present analysis.

interact to shape the parameters of the middle class's civil engagement. The analysis shows that among the four groups (middling grassroots with a university education, middling grassroots with high school or less, propertied mainstream with a university education, and propertied mainstream with high school or less) the middling grassroots with a university education were the most active in political actions in all items surveyed in both 1995 and 2006, without exception. The group that comes in second for 1995 is the propertied mainstream with a university education in all items except sit-down strikes. When the focus is explicitly on the middling grassroots and the propertied mainstream with the same university education, the difference between them is rather stark, particularly in the WVS 2006 data.

Furthermore, table 12-7 demonstrates that in 2006 second place in participation in citizen initiatives is occupied not by the propertied mainstream with a university education but by the middling grassroots with a high school education or less, and this placing is consistent on all three items surveyed. The efficacy of identity is unmistakable in this case, since identity turns out to be more influential than education.[25]

Based on the above, a thesis can be advanced that identity as an independent variable of explanation is as significant as education in shaping middle-class politics. In cases like the 2006 data, identity turns out to be more influential than education over middle-class politics. The participation index of 1995 and 2006 clearly supports this claim, too. The scale is

TABLE 12-6. Multiple Regression Analysis, Participation in Citizen Initiatives, by Six Variables, South Korea, 1995 and 2006

	1995 beta	2006 beta
Age	--0.134***	0.009
Education	0.259***	0.242***
Middling grassroots	0.182***	0.126***
Income	0.053	X
Socioeconomic status	X	−0.037
Male	0.042	0.089**
R^2	0.199	0.087
F	38.159***	18.765***

**p < 0.01, ***p < 0.001
Source:: World Value Survey, 1995, 2006. Han Sang-Jin, "The Dynamics of Middle-Class Politics in Korea."
X: no equivalent item available.

five to fifteen in 1995 and three to nine in 2006. The means of the participation index of the middling grassroots with a university education is 10.0 in 1995 and 6.5 in 2006, significantly higher than the indexes of all other combinations of identity and education. In 2006 the middling grassroots with a high school education or less were more active in citizen initiatives than the propertied mainstream with a university education. Above all, the middling grassroots with a university education were full of significance and, as such, invites our further attention.

The Middling Grassroots Identity and Citizen Initiatives in China

As mentioned above, the identity variables used in the surveys in South Korea and China are not the same, but comparable questions concerning citizen participation were included in both surveys. Five citizen initiatives were included in the WVS of 1995 and three in the WVS of 2006. The CGSS of 2006 includes questions about irrational use of public funds, environmental protection, petitions, collective negotiation and legal suits, labor strikes, collective assembly, and street demonstrations. The survey also asked whether respondents witnessed any of these events over the previous five years, what role they played, whether they took part in the preparation of the events, and whether they provided material assistance or moral support.

Even though participatory citizens were a small group in China as of 2006, occupying only 3.6 percent of the total respondents (N = 8,951),

TABLE 12-7. Participation in Citizen Initiatives, by Identity Group and Education, South Korea, 1995 and 2006[a]

Number (percent)

	University education		High school education or less			
	Middling grassroots	Propertied mainstream	Middling grassroots	Propertied mainstream	Total	x^2
1995						
Signing petition	162 (96.4)	151 (89.9)	130 (85.5)	220 (74.1)	663 (84.5)	46.634***
Joining boycott	160 (95.2)	147 (87.5)	117 (76.0)	190 (63.8)	614 (77.9)	73.321***
Joining demonstration	126 (75.0)	96 (57.1)	81 (52.6)	115 (38.9)	418 (53.2)	57.613***
Joining labor strike	109 (65.3)	69 (41.1)	60 (39.0)	86 (29.1)	324 (41.3)	58.249***
Joining sit-down strike	61 (36.3)	30 (17.9)	46 (30.1)	55 (18.6)	192 (24.5)	24.870***
2006						
Signing petition	113 (90.4)	18 (60.0)	78 (76.5)	33 (61.1)	242 (77.8)	25.817***
Joining boycott	103 (81.7)	14 (46.7)	63 (61.8)	28 (51.9)	208 (66.7)	24.729***
Joining demonstration	103 (81.7)	13 (43.3)	65 (63.7)	29 (53.7)	210 (67.3)	24.910***

Source: World Value Survey, 1995, 2006. Han Sang-Jin, "The Dynamics of Middle-Class Politics in Korea."
a. The suggested answers to each question were, Have already done, Might do if chance is given, and Would never do.
***$p < 0.001$.

the difference between the middling grassroots and the propertied mainstream is still clear: the activist middling grassroots are double the activist propertied mainstream (table 12-8).[26]

It is natural that the bottom grassroots is the most active group in support of citizen initiatives, particularly in urban settings, since this group has been deeply disadvantaged by China's economic development. As in South Korea during the 1980s, the middling grassroots might be situated in between the propertied mainstream and the bottom grassroots in China today. The middling grassroots are sympathetic to the situation of the bottom grassroots, as shown by their engaging in citizen initiatives, but they may not be as radical as the bottom grassroots.

Given the small number of participatory activists in China, logistic regression analysis was used to test the independent influence of the identity variable (table 12-9). The result of the analysis is striking. Of all the independent variables used, only the variable of identity is significant independently. Education, age, gender, and class all turn out to be insignificant. This finding poses questions that require further investigation.

TABLE 12-8. Participation in Citizen Initiatives, by Identity Group
and the Urban/Rural Dichotomy, China, 2006

Unit as indicated

Place	Middling grassroots		Propertied mainstream		Bottom grassroots		Double outsiders		Total	
	Percent	N	Percent	N	Percent	N	Percent	N	Percent	N
Urban	4.13	2,057	2.02	1,389	5.03	1,173	4.68	834	3.75	5,453
Rural	4.46	897	2.10	953	5.06	751	3.01	897	3.87	3,498
Total	4.23	2,954	2.05	2,342	5.04	1,924	3.81	1,731	3.57	8,951

Source: China General Social Survey, 2006.

Comparative Reflection

This chapter seeks to examine the internal differentiation of the middle class, namely between its grassroots and its mainstream identities and their influence on citizen participation. This strategy is more useful than comparing the middle class with nonmiddle classes and helps us to avoid an essentialist claim. The above analysis shows that the middle class in China involves the middling grassroots group, which is not only as large as its propertied mainstream but also has progressive potential, as evidenced by its capacity for engaging in citizen initiatives. This discovery seems to correspond with the thesis of the formation of the grassroots identity being rooted in and supported by the *minben* normative tradition.

At the same time, this discovery is an effect of a specific conceptual strategy. The outcome could differ if *zhongchan cheng* as a whole were compared with other groups. This sensitizes us to the methodological issue touched upon earlier. To substantiate this, the author wants to compare the strategy taken in this chapter to that taken by Jie Chen in chapter 15 of this volume.

Jie Chen describes his major findings as follows: "In terms of political implications, the new middle class in China now is unlikely to serve as an agent or supporter of fundamental change toward democracy."[27] He asserts further that "the middle class as a whole seems to be even less democratically oriented than the nonmiddle class." Before we accept or reject this claim, it is important to draw attention to the following points.

TABLE 12-9. Logistic Regression Analysis, Participation in Citizen Initiatives, by Five Variables, China, 2006

Variable	Beta	Exp beta
Intercept	−4.145***	…
Gender (reference category: male)		
Female	−.254	.776
Age (reference category: age 60+)		
Age 18–39	.508	1.661
Age 40–59	.396	1.486
Education (reference category: middle school and below)		
High school	−.395	.673
College and above	−.088	.916
Class (reference category: farmer)		
Working class	.148	1.159
Middle class or entrepreneur	.316	1.371
Identity (reference category: propertied mainstream)		
Middling grassroots	.727***	2.069
Addendum		
−2 log likelihood	1,493.222	
Likelihood χ^2		30.475***
N	5,290	

Source: China General Social Survey, 2006.
*** $p < .001$.

—Regarding the conceptual framework, he lumps together such occupational groups as managers, professionals, and white-collar office workers into the category of the new middle class and compares it with the nonmiddle class.

—Regarding the political attitudes under examination, he uses the standard components of a liberal democratic political culture, such as individual liberties and multiparty electoral competition. This means that he imposed these cultural points of view upon Chinese respondents when he conducted his survey. Since democracy can mean many things of equal significance, his results may have been different if other issues with more practical relevance for China were addressed.

—Regarding the strategy of testing, he did not include class variables in the multivariate regression analysis. He only compared the middle class with the nonmiddle class in terms of their responses to the questionnaires used.

These considerations may lead one to raise the question of whether Jie Chen offers evidence strong enough to support his thesis of the conservative characteristics of the middle class compared with nonmiddle classes.[28] In the case of China, where the middle class is in a very early stage of formation, conclusions might differ significantly if care were taken to see its internal segments with potentially divergent orientations while properly introducing the variable of identity into Jie Chen's framework.

Li Peilin and Zhang Yi warned that the conceptual framework of the middle class that sociologists construct based on a number of objective indexes may become a "fabrication" in theory, which lacks predictability for explaining the people's actual orientations toward value and behavior.[29] They adopt a dual-track approach in their study of the middle class in China. One track is a mixed-stratification approach combining three dimensions of the middle class: occupation, education, and income. Those who satisfy all three conditions are called the core middle class, and those who satisfy two are called the semi-core middle class. Those satisfying only one condition are called the peripheral middle class. The other track is to use socioeconomic status as a conventional variable of identity. The authors compare the three objective categories of middle class to see whether they make any significant difference with respect to sociopolitical attitudes but find no significant difference. In contrast, socioeconomic status as "the subjective identification of the middle class" is found to be the key factor for determining social attitudes, collective behaviors, and social movements.

Li Chunling classified the Chinese class structure into five categories, in line with the East Asia Middle Class (EAMC) project: the new middle class, the old middle class, the marginal middle class, the working class, and farmers.[30] The new middle class is mainly composed of professionals, whereas white-collar office workers are classified as the marginal middle class. In a multivariate regression analysis she compares the three middle-class groups to the working class to see whether there are significant differences with respect to five indexes for justice, individual living, local government performance, authoritarian political attitudes, and social conflicts.

Although she does not find any consistent patterns, Li Chunling does find that the old middle class with property tends to accept inequality more than the other two groups of the middle class and that the new middle class and the marginal middle class tend to support authoritarian attitudes far less than the working class and the old middle class. Based on this analysis, she claims that the new middle class, together with the marginal middle class, displays more "democratic consciousness" while expecting more "democratic government" in China.

Zhang Yi differs from Li Chunling and Li Peilin in terms of the way he classifies the middle class as well as his strategies of comparison. Zhang developed a sophisticated model of classification in line with Eric Wright and compares all of these categories with farmers. He also finds no consistent patterns, yet he does find that "the new middle class has developed more critical consciousness with greater suspicion on the performance of government and the social system."[31] He also refers to converging trends between the semitechnical working class and the new middle class in terms of their sociopolitical attitudes. He thus rejects the conventional image of the middle class as a stabilizer and claims that the new middle class is "more likely than the old [middle class] to be committed to social reform" because it is equipped with "increasingly evident critical social consciousness."

The outcome of research is inevitably affected by the conceptual model and strategy of comparison chosen. Despite careful efforts to justify the conceptual framework he takes, Jie Chen treats the middle class as an aggregated unified entity when he compares the new middle class with nonmiddle-class categories. This prevents him from exploring the possible differentiations and dynamics of the middle class, as grasped partially by the other sociologists referenced above.

Conclusion

In every economy in the world a middle class tends to emerge and expand as economic growth proceeds. It is a product of modernization. South Korea since the 1960s is a good example, as is China since the 1980s. The trend may be accelerated where the development strategy favors the size of the economy, meaning that resources are heavily channeled into big firms like conglomerates with the assumption that they can better compete internationally. This policy tends to give rise to a large number of trained workers and white-collar employees in a short span of time. In addition, as can be seen in South Korea, the middle class is also the product of political democratization. At least part of its middle class demanded and supported democratic reforms in South Korea, joining in social movements and citizens' campaigns. The Chinese data also show the emergence of a grassroots segment of the middle class that supports citizen initiatives for democratic participation.

One of this chapter's key claims is that the ambiguities and fluidities of the emerging middle class in China, especially with the respect to the sociopolitical role it may play, can be clarified if we pay due attention to the role of middle-class identity in its dual streams. To be more precise, evidence suggests that the grassroots segment of the middle class differs significantly from the middle class mainstream in terms of political orientation and civil engagement. This evidence is basically in line with the major findings of Li Peilin, Li Chunling, and Zhang Yi. Furthermore, the case of the middling grassroots turns out to be much stronger than the conventional subcategories of the middle class in the sense that its orientation in support of change is consistent over all five indexes examined.[32] There is also evidence, like multivariate regression analysis, that the variable of identity yields a strong independent influence over political attitudes.

It is an open question, however, when and how the potential of the grassroots segment of the middle class may be channeled into practical action. In South Korea, it can be suggested that the middling grassroots represent the most significant actor in civil society in support of social change and of reflexive modernization as well.[33] The analysis of the Chinese data also shows that the middling grassroots phenomenon is spreading across the conventional boundaries separating social classes, occupations, and regions. In this context, the historical record suggests that there comes a critical moment when the repressive power of the bureaucratic authoritarian state begins to break down. Simultaneously, it should be emphasized that due to the dual aspect of the middling grassroots as an initiator (or supporter) of change and also as an agent of social integration, transformation tends to unfold not in a chaotic manner but within the framework of political negotiation and when and where the middling grassroots already plays an important role in social transformation.

Notes

1. An overall review of the political role of the middle class can be found in Martin Oppenheimer, "The Political Missions of the Middle Strata," in *Class and Social Development: A New Theory of the Middle Class*, edited by Dale Johnson (London: Sage, 1982), pp. 109–32.

2. Despite numerous discussions in the West no consensus has been achieved concerning the sociopolitical and ideological orientations of the middle class. Some have argued that the middle class has gained from capitalist development and thus tends to be politically conservative. The rise of German Nazism, for instance, was interpreted as strongly supported by the middle class, especially the old middle class, which felt threatened by a radical working class during the economic crisis. A contrasting theory is that of middle-class radicalism, according to which the middle class finds itself disillusioned with the politics of the ruling class and thus confronts this class in an attempt to defend its own interests and values. On this interpretation, see Paul Bagguley, "Middle-Class Radicalism Revisited," in *Social Change and the Middle Classes,* edited by Tim Butler and Mike Savage (London: UCL Press, 1995), pp. 293–309. Focusing on the role of ideology, Nicos Poulantzas, *Classes in Contemporary Capitalism* (London: New Left Books, 1975), suggests that the middle class oscillates between these dual tendencies depending on the historical and structural conjunctures. These ambiguities and controversies have triggered numerous debates throughout the world's scholarly circles and have prompted Erik Olin Wright, *Class* (London: Thetford Press, 1985), to define the middle class more systematically in terms of the contradictory class locations they occupy.

3. Jonathan Barry and Christopher Brooks, eds., *The Middling Sort of People: Culture, Society, and Politics in England, 1550–1800* (Hampshire, U.K.: Macmillan, 1994); Margaret Hunt, *The Middling Sort: Commerce, Gender, and the Family in England, 1680–1780* (University of California Press, 1996). The phenomenon of the middling sort was not limited to England but can be found in the United States too; see Burton Bledstein and Robert Johnson, eds., *The Middling Sorts: Exploration in the History of the American Middle Class* (London: Routledge, 2001). For a systematic inquiry from the perspective of social justice, see Vincent Starzinger, *Middlingness: Juste Milieu Political Theory in France and England, 1815–1848* (University Press of Virginia, 1965).

4. The original formulation can be seen in Han Sang-Jin, *The Search for a Theory of the Middling Grassroots* (Seoul: Moonhakguagiseung, 1992, in Korean). For a most recent argument, see Han Sang-Jin, "The Dynamics of Middle-Class Politics in Korea: Why and How Do the Middling Grassroots Differ from the Propertied Mainstream?" *Korean Journal of Sociology* 43, no. 3 (2009): 1–19.

5. If we take the conventional framework of the middle class for a given in which it is composed of the new and the old middle classes, we already presuppose certain commonalities shared by members of the new or old parts. We then tend to collect empirical data to show either the existence of or the lack of the assumed characteristics for the two categories. Based on this, one may claim that the new middle class is conservative, while another could claim that it is progressive. The point here is not which is correct. The new middle class may look progressive when compared with farmers but conservative when compared with radical segments of the working class. The outcome may also depend on the kind of questions asked. The real problem here is that the new middle class is assumed to be an aggregated, unified entity. Such a conceptual strategy may prevent us from seeing the dynamic trends within the middle class and their relation to historical and cultural developments.

6. The best example is the conference "The Dynamics of the Middle Class in the Age of Social Transformation: China, Korea, and Japan," held at Seoul National University, March 19–20, 2010. Li Peilin and his associates participated in this conference, shedding light on various aspects of the emerging middle class in China.

7. Wright argues that "the process of class formation is decisively shaped by a variety of institutional mechanisms that are themselves 'relatively autonomous' from the class structure and which determine the ways in which class structures are translated into collective actors with specific ideologies and strategies." See Erik Olin Wright, *Class* (London:

Thetford Press, 1985), p. 14. The concept of contradictory class locations is a logical outcome of this translation of class structures into action via institutional mediations. Noting the innovative significance of his argument, this chapter takes up the social constructionist approach to identity formation by regarding identity not as determined or translated by class structures via institutional conditions but as shaped through the discursive processes of communication. The aim is to grasp the active role of the middle class as a historical subject being capable of political action.

8. Identity often reflects the historical experience of social conflict. The identity of the working class, for instance, emerged out of the intensified lived experience of struggle and confrontation in Europe. Likewise, it is an open question how the identity of the middle class is socially constructed in the country under investigation.

9. The author uses a discursive social constructionism with an explicit focus on identity, with the view that the two segments of the middle class differ significantly from each other in terms of their political, social, and moral orientations. In the case of Korean development during the last several decades, the differentiation of the grassroots and the mainstream segments of the middle class, together with the impact of these upon their political orientations, has been well explained and proved. Identity is here understood not as determined by any external (or structural in the conventional sense) factors but as constituted along the processes of the discursive, symbolic, and cultural formation of subjectivity.

10. Three Chinese characters denoting the middle class are pronounced *Joongsan chung* in Korean. However, since this book is about China, the Chinese pinyin *zhongchan cheng* is used in this chapter.

11. When respondents are asked to identify themselves within the scale of socioeconomic status conventionally designed, the majority of them tend to place themselves in either middle-low or middle-middle categories within the middle strata. In East Asian countries, including China, less than 30 percent see themselves as occupying the low strata. The term *zhongchan cheng*, as a socially constructed identity, is not identical with socioeconomic status. Though the former is the best option, the latter can also serve as an identity variable in sociological analysis.

12. See Han, *The Search for a Theory of the Middling Grassroots.*

13. One of the best reinterpretations of this tradition can be found in Xia Yong, "*Minben* and *Minquan*: Historical Foundation of the Chinese Rights Discourses," *Chinese Social Science* 5 (2004; in Chinese). See also Han Sang-Jin, "Confucianism and Human Rights: People-Centered Participatory Communitarian Human Rights and the Kwangju Democratic Self-Rule in 1980," in *What is Confucianism? An Introduction in Pan-Asian Confucianism,* edited by Wonsik Chang and Leah Kalmanson (Seoul National University Press, 2009); Chang Wunsuk and Leah Kalmanson, eds., *Confucianism in Context: Classic Philosophy and Contemporary Issues, East Asia and Beyond* (State University of New York Press, 2010), pp. 121–44.

14. The author has developed the thesis of the dual structure of middle-class politics based on the Korean experience and wants to explore whether it can also be relevant for China, where the rapid increase of the middle class has drawn wide attention. Though it may be difficult to call this study comparative in the rigorous sense, it is still possible to examine the extent to which the two segments of the middle class differ significantly from each other in terms of political and social orientations.

15. Emerging from the military coup d'etat in 1961, the bureaucratic authoritarian regime became consolidated by the *Yushin* reform in 1972 and continued to rule South Korea at least until 1987, when political democracy in the form of a free and direct presidential election was reintroduced.

16. Li Peilin and Zhang Yi have made an explicit attempt to test the three models of the middle class by measuring their impacts on sociopolitical attitudes. See their paper "Middle

Class in China: Measurement, Identity, and Social Attitudes," presented at the conference "The Dynamics of the Middle Class in the Age of Social Transformation."

17. The conventional interpretation is to focus on the leadership of the ruler toward a benevolent politics, whereas the post-traditional one is to emphasize the active role of citizens in defense of their rights as the sovereign subject of politics. The latter has received numerous expressions in modern China and Korea. See works by Xia Yong, especially the essay *"Minben* and *Minqua."*

18. *Minjoong,* as a key outlook of the students during the 1980s, refers to the common people, particularly workers and peasants, who are economically poor, politically suppressed, but potentially capable of expressing their will politically. During the 1980s college students began to construct their identity as part of this *minjoong.*

19. In China and South Korea the term *zhongchan cheng* has been conventionally used by the mass media and politics as identical with *middle class,* but these are not identical from the social-scientific standpoint. The former can include part of the working class and farmers, but the latter cannot. Nevertheless, this chapter uses *zhongchan cheng* as being equivalent to the middle class, following conventional usages.

20. See Han Sang-Jin, "The Political Economy and Moral Institution of the Middling Grassroots in Korea," *Humboldt Journal of Social Relations* 23, nos. 1, 2 (1997): 71–89; also see Han Sang-Jin, "Modernization and the Rise of Civil Society: The Role of the Middling Grassroots for Democratization in Korea," *Human Studies* 24, no. 2 (2001): 113–32.

21. The CGSS of 2006 includes the item "socioeconomic status." The share of middle-strata identity in terms of socioeconomic status was 59.2 percent (upper, 0.2 percent; middle-high, 2.5 percent; middle-middle, 26.8 percent; and middle-low, 29.7 percent). In contrast, the Korean data have included the item *"zhongchan cheng,"* in addition to socioeconomic status. The share of those who accepted this identity was 63.8 percent in 1995, but it dropped to less than half after the economic crisis in 1997. As of 2006 the figure was only 31.0 percent, which differs markedly from the percentage in the socioeconomic middle strata in China (59.2 percent).

22. The overall level of education of the propertied mainstream is also high, though not as high as that of the middling grassroots. From 1987 to 2006 about 35–40 percent of the propertied mainstream were college educated, which is significantly higher than the figure for the bottom grassroots. Within the middle class, however, the two groups show the opposite trend. The portion of middling grassroots increases as the level of education becomes higher, whereas the trend of the propertied mainstream is the opposite.

23. The overall demographic profiles for China in 2006 are similar to those for Korea in 1987. In both countries the middling grassroots increases significantly as the level of education advances. There is also no significant difference in the profiles of the mainstream middle class in two countries.

24. At a conference at Changsha, China, July 21–22, 2007, when I presented an early version of the paper that this chapter is based on, Erik Wright challenged me with the thesis of a dual structure of middle class. But the independent influence of the variable of identity has been confirmed by a regression analysis.

25. Among those with a high school education or less, the middling grassroots are consistently more active than the propertied mainstream in participating in and supporting middle-class politics. To our surprise, the propertied mainstream with a university education is less active than the propertied mainstream with a high school education or less. This may imply that the propertied mainstream with a college education was moving toward an ultraconservative orientation.

26. In this study all of those who responded positively to any question related to direct or indirect involvement in civil engagement are counted as participatory citizens.

27. The quotation is from Ji Chen, "The Orientation of the Middle Class toward Democracy in a Late-Developing Country: Evidence and Insights from Urban China," paper presented at a conference on the middle class in China, Washington, September 2009, p. 21.

28. Evidence seems to be not strong enough to support the independent influence of class categories upon the political attitudes examined. He argues that "most members of the Chinese middle class are vigilant about the individual rights that are closely related to their own interests" (ibid., p. 13). Yet there seems to be no significant difference between the middle class and the nonmiddle class in this respect. He argues that most members of the middle class "are not interested in democratic institutions such as the fully competitive election of leaders without restriction on political parties, nor enthusiastic about participating in government affairs and politics" (ibid., p. 21). Yet it is not clear whether this tendency is more so among the members of the middle class than the nonmiddle class. What he found was the independent influence on political attitudes of such variables as education, household gross income, and party membership, yet he claims that the middle class is more conservative than the nonmiddle class.

29. See Li Peilin and Zhang Yi, "Middle Class in China," p. 23.

30. Li Chunling, "Conservatism and Liberalism of China's Middle Class," paper presented at the conference "The Dynamics of the Middle Class in the Age of Social Transformation," pp. 10–11.

31. Zhang Yi, "The Political Attitude of China's Middle Class," paper presented at the conference "The Dynamics of the Middle Class in the Age of Social Transformation," pp. 14–15.

32. Han Sang-Jin and Li Wei, "Is the Chinese Middle Class Politically Conservative: A Critical Debate," paper presented at the conference "The Dynamics of the Middle Class in the Age of Social Transformation," pp. 17–19.

33. Han Sang-Jin, "Redefining Second Modernity for East Asia: A Critical Assessment," *British Journal of Sociology* 61, no. 3 (2010): 465–88. Also see Han Sang-Jin, "Three Prime Movers in the Contested Civil Society: Why and How Social Transformation Occurs in Korea," in *Social Change in the Age of Globalization*, edited by Jing Tiankui, Masamichi Sasaki, and Li Peilin, vol. 10, *The Annals of the International Institute of Sociology* (Leiden: Brill, 2007), pp. 215–41.

PART VI

China's Middle Class: An Agent of the Status Quo or a Force for Change?

CHAPTER THIRTEEN

China's Cooperative Capitalists: The Business End of the Middle Class

BRUCE J. DICKSON

The central puzzle in understanding contemporary China is that dramatic economic changes are occurring in the absence of regime change. The key insight of modernization theory is that higher prosperity is strongly correlated with the probability of democracy: the richer a country is, the more likely it is to be a democracy. This has made the search for signs of democratic support within China a preoccupation of many China specialists. To date these signs are slight, but the search goes on. At the same time, the leaders of the Chinese Communist Party (CCP) are committed to promoting rapid economic growth and raising living standards. Whereas many observers believe that economic change will eventually trigger regime change, CCP leaders are just as convinced that economic change is a necessity for regime survival. Whose vision of the future will prove to be correct?

This chapter examines recent research published in English on two potential sources of democratic support in China: the growing urban middle class and one of its subgroups, private entrepreneurs.[1] Both have been the subject of sustained speculation and careful empirical research. The middle class is generally seen as essential for the emergence and durability of democracy, but it is also the focus of the CCP's efforts to improve living standards. China's private entrepreneurs have also been a subject of intense interest. Although many outside observers see the emerging private sector as a potential agent of political change, the CCP has seen private entrepreneurs as an important source of popular support. How are the interests of private entrepreneurs and the broader middle class represented in China's political system? Are they a potential threat to the incumbent regime, or pillars of support? The answers to these questions are at the heart of China's political future.

China's Newly Emerging Classes: Definitions, Measures, and Conclusions

Research on China's middle class tends to exhibit two somewhat contradictory commonalities: varied definitions and measures but similar conclusions. Like the concept of the middle class more generally, its application in China has generated a variety of definitions, often based on one or more of the following: occupation, education, income, and values.[2] The middle class generally is said to incorporate white-collar professionals, managers, and private entrepreneurs; those with at least a high school education and, even more important, a college education; those with incomes well above the poverty line, so that the basic necessities of life are not in question and so that real estate and other consumer goods are affordable; and those with modern lifestyles. Because of these different definitions, the size of China's middle class is difficult to pin down. Nevertheless, there is general agreement that China's middle class, although less than 25 percent of the population, is growing.

Although definitions of the middle class vary, conclusions about its political significance are remarkably similar. Most studies published in English agree that the middle class is not yet poised to be the source of political change in China. Instead, its material interests and ties to the state make it supporters of the status quo, favoring stability over uncertainty. With important exceptions, such as opposition to Shanghai's mag-lev train and a proposed chemical plant in Xiamen, political activism by China's middle class is generally limited to housing and "not in my backyard" issues rather than broader social concerns.

As the middle class in China grew and evolved, so too did Western scholarship on this newly emerging class and its political implications. Many early studies, often based on loose comparisons with the experiences of Western democracies, expected that economic growth and especially privatization would create pressure for political change and that the middle class would be the agent of democratization.[3] This viewpoint was based on the insights of modernization theory and on a simplistic theoretical approach to state-society relations, which views social forces as inherently antagonistic toward the state. As noted earlier, modernization theory anticipates that as countries modernize, their social and economic structures change and, consequently, individual values also change. As countries become more urban, more prosperous, and better educated, they also become more likely to democratize.

In the post-Mao reform era, these initial changes were under way, and many expected that the resulting political changes were also imminent. Similarly, the experience of first-wave democracies indicates that the political and economic interests of the urban middle class would lead it to push for institutional arrangements that would constrain the state's capacity to impinge on private property rights and that would represent the interests of this class in the policymaking process. Scholars and journalists began looking for evidence of China's middle class, and private entrepreneurs in particular, asserting its political interests against a reluctant state.

Over time, an alternative perspective emerged. This viewpoint emphasizes that economic development creates material interests that in turn create a preference for stability and, therefore, for support of the current regime. The growth of the private sector, and the middle class more generally, is after all the result of the CCP's own policies. Rather than be antagonistic toward the state, many in the middle class have been co-opted into the state and many others have benefited from its economic policies. In these ways, the beneficiaries of economic reform have become supporters of the current political system. Rather than being in a conflictual relationship with the state, the middle class and private entrepreneurs cooperated in the state's program of promoting economic growth. Improving standards of living, accompanied by a less intrusive state, would provide the basis for popular support of the current regime and preempt demands for political change.

This new conventional wisdom was first articulated by Dorothy Solinger, David Goodman, and others. Beginning in the 1990s and up to the present, these scholars consistently challenged the older conventional wisdom that members of the Chinese middle class were a pro-democracy, anti-CCP vanguard. Instead, their research argues forcefully that the material interests of the middle class made them supporters of CCP rule.[4] More recent works, many based on survey research, confirm their early skepticism that the middle class will be a democratizing force.[5] In short, the current conventional wisdom offers a cautionary note on the political implications of China's growing middle class. Western literature indicates that members of China's middle class are likely to constitute a source of support for the CCP, that the CCP has successfully co-opted some and neutralized others, and ultimately that ongoing social change will not pose a threat to CCP rule.

Several studies reach more sanguine conclusions on what could turn China's middle class into a more influential political force. For example, He Li suggests that the growth in postmaterial values among the middle class may lead them to engage in more pro-democratic activities.[6] However, the spread of postmaterial values is normally measured in generations, not years. We should not expect that changes in the political behavior of China's middle class are dependent on the emergence of postmaterial values. Jie Chen and Chunlong Lu offer an even more optimistic view of the democratic potential of China's middle class. According to their research, members of China's middle class already "think and act in accordance with democratic principles," but these members remain a small part of the population (they estimate no more than 15 percent). They suggest that the growth of the middle class as a whole may be a democratizing factor, because it is already democratically oriented.[7] This is a more optimistic assessment, because the middle class is likely to grow faster than postmaterial values. As Cheng Li's chapter in this volume shows, the middle class's potential to push for political change is commonly found in the Chinese literature. In the English-language literature, however, there is more skepticism that the middle class is now or will soon be a pro-democratic force.

Recent scholarship on China's private entrepreneurs largely mirrors that viewpoint. In the 1990s several studies suggested that China's private entrepreneurs could prove to be agents of political change both by acting within the CCP and by exerting pressure from the outside.[8] These initial expectations were not realized. Research on China's private entrepreneurs consistently shows the conservative nature of their political beliefs, their growing integration into the current political system, and their consequent lack of interest in democratization. Even those who do not support the regime prefer to avoid it rather than confront it. The consensus at present is that China's capitalists have a vested interest in maintaining the current regime and in favoring both economic and political stability. Whether through active support or tacit acceptance, China's capitalists have not posed a political threat to the CCP.[9]

Several studies on the political beliefs of private entrepreneurs exist, and all conclude that their democratic values are not strong.[10] As Kellee

Tsai succinctly concludes, "economic development has not created a pro-democratic capitalist class. . . . Overall, China's business owners are either tolerating the existing political system or leaving the country rather than demanding democratizing changes domestically."[11] However, these studies adopt different measures of democratic beliefs, so we have no reliable way of determining whether the prevalence of democratic values is rising, falling, or remaining constant. All of these studies do conclude, however, that private entrepreneurs are unlikely at present to support democratization and would only do so in the future under very specific circumstances. Although individual entrepreneurs may have an interest in promoting democracy, as a loosely defined group they are more inclined to support the status quo than to risk the uncertainty that democratization would entail. Far from being agents of change, they have become an essential source of political support for the CCP.

The Growing Prominence of China's Private Entrepreneurs

The growth of the middle class and its subgroup of private entrepreneurs was not an unintended consequence of reform policies but rather the intended result of a series of policies that fall under the rubric of *gaige kaifang*—reform and opening. These policies were endorsed and implemented by the CCP over the past thirty years, first under the stewardship of Deng Xiaoping and later refined by subsequent leaders. Jiang Zemin sought to create a "relatively prosperous society" (*xiaokang shehui*) and espoused the theory of the "three represents" (*sange daibiao*) in order to justify his pro-growth policies. More recently, Hu Jintao and Wen Jiabao popularized the goal of creating a "harmonious society" (*hexie shehui*). They also intended to maintain high rates of economic growth but to do so by balancing growth with equity, in this way improving the standards of living for a larger proportion of China's population and, ultimately, keeping the CCP in power.

The expansion of the private sector occurred with the CCP's blessing, first as a small-scale trend that complemented the planned economy, then as the result of active promotion beginning in 1992, and later as a consequence of the reform of state-owned enterprises in the late 1990s and beyond. During the 1980s the private sector was tolerated as a complement to the planned economy. Most private firms were individually owned and operated (and were known generally as *getihu*). For ideological reasons, they were very small in size. According to Marx, firms with more than eight workers engaged in exploitation, and therefore the *getihu* were formally limited to eight or fewer workers, although in practice many grew beyond this limit.[12] Over time the private sector grew in prominence, with more firms and larger firms. During the 1990s the private sector became the main source of economic growth, new jobs, and tax revenue. Because the CCP was committed to rapid economic growth, and because local officials were required to meet annual growth targets, the party moved from simply tolerating the private sector to promoting it.

The CCP's support for the private sector was evident first of all in its changing rhetoric. In the 1988 state constitution, the CCP affirmed the right of the private sector to exist—but only under the guidance, supervision, and control of the state. Rhetorical support for the private sector grew in subsequent years: by 2000 the CCP declared it would support, encourage, and guide the private sector and placed it on equal footing with the public sector.

The second way the CCP showed its support for the private sector was in its growing willingness to admit private entrepreneurs into the party. In the 1980s the CCP's orthodox thinkers pointed out the inherent conflict of interest between capitalists and communists and warned against allowing private entrepreneurs into the party. In the wake of the Tiananmen demonstrations in 1989, the CCP introduced a ban on recruiting capitalists. While it was often ignored in practice, the ban remained the CCP's official policy until 2001, when Jiang Zemin enunciated his "three represents" theory. In his speech marking the eightieth anniversary of the founding of the CCP, Jiang asserted that the CCP represents the interests of private entrepreneurs (the so-called advanced productive forces) as well as workers and farmers, its traditional base of support. While many dismiss the "three represents" as empty rhetoric at best and at worst a betrayal of the CCP's core traditions, the theory indicates the need for party elites to legitimize the shift in party policy with an ideological rationale.

The close ties between private entrepreneurs and the state have evolved into a symbiotic relationship that I dub crony communism.[13] While this cozy and often corrupt relationship has generated ample popular resentment, it has also created the economic and political support that the CCP needs to survive. Because new jobs and economic growth are mainly created by the private sector, it contributes to the CCP's primary task of economic development and thus enhances the CCP's legitimacy. In addition, growing numbers of private entrepreneurs have been appointed to political and advisory groups, giving them a stake in the status quo. The CCP has created an environment in which entrepreneurs can prosper (especially those who are politically well connected), and in return most entrepreneurs have chosen to cooperate with the party rather than attempt to challenge or change it.

Crony communism is first of all characterized by the CCP's dominant role. Party members are encouraged to "take the lead in getting rich," and the ones best able to respond to the call are those deeply embedded in the party-state, especially state-owned enterprise (SOE) managers and local officials. They have easier access to the capital, technology, and markets needed to open and expand their businesses. Others are co-opted into the CCP after becoming successful in business. In both these ways the CCP has integrated with the private sector, and it does so not just to forestall the emergence of a private sector that could pose a political challenge but also to gain material benefits. The private sector produces both the economic growth that local officials need for their annual appraisals and the new jobs and additional tax revenue that come with economic growth. In addition, local officials take advantage of their political power by soliciting bribes, gifts, and favors from the private sector. In order to curry favor with influential officials, entrepreneurs provide jobs for the officials' family members, pay for their children's private school or college educations, or engage in extensive wining and dining.[14]

As the private sector in China has grown, so has the number of "red capitalists"—private entrepreneurs who are also CCP members (figure 13-1). In the early 1990s approximately 13 percent of private entrepreneurs were CCP members. By 2007, 38 percent of private entrepreneurs were red capitalists. Considering that less than 6 percent of the general population belongs to the CCP, the much higher concentration of party members among private entrepreneurs shows the close relationship between the CCP and the private sector. However, most of these red capitalists were already in the CCP before going into business, and the growing percentages shown in figure 13-1 are primarily due to the privatization of SOEs. In addition, red capitalists are concentrated among the largest firms. Very few small-scale entrepreneurs are CCP members.

For those who are not cronies of local officials, there is a glass ceiling: refusals to comply along with too much success can often result either in pressure to join the party or in allegations of illegal business practices. The private sector has grown in China, but it remains under the careful

FIGURE 13-1. CCP Members among China's Private Entrepreneurs, China, Selected Years, 1993–2007

Percent

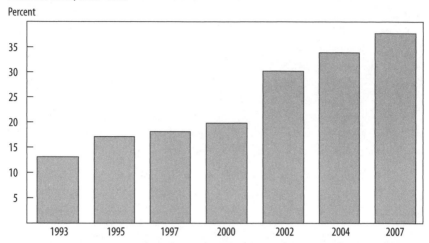

Source: All-China Federation of Industry and Commerce surveys (data available from the Universities Service Center of the Chinese University of Hong Kong); Jie Chen and Bruce J. Dickson, *Allies of the State: China's Private Entrepreneurs and Democratic Change* (Harvard University Press, 2010).

scrutiny if not outright control of the CCP, and those who too aggressively pursue their interests against the state can pay a steep price. Beginning in the 1990s Sun Dawu was one of China's best-known peasant entrepreneurs, founding a successful animal feed company. He publicly criticized the party's interference in his private business activities, especially his inability to get financing from state-run banks. In response, he was arrested and charged with "illegally obtaining public funds," even though the funds had come from his employees. He received a three-year suspended sentence, a personal fine of 100,000 yuan, and an additional fine of 400,000 yuan against his firm. This intimidation signaled to other entrepreneurs the limits under which they could assert their interests.

Private entrepreneurs have been integrated into China's political system not only through membership in the CCP but also through governmental and advisory positions. Private entrepreneurs have been directly elected by voters to local people's congresses and selected for higher-level people's congresses, including the National People's Congress, whose members are selected through indirect elections by lower-level bodies. They also belong to the Chinese People's Political Consultative Conferences, honorary advisory bodies that parallel the people's congresses but that lack their legislative authority. A more direct example of entrepreneurs gaining political power is in elections for village chiefs and representative assemblies. This was a particularly prominent trend in the 1990s, but in more recent years entrepreneurs have shown less interest in serving in village posts. To some extent, they have decided that the business benefits that come with village posts do not match the burdens of office; but to an even larger extent, the decision-making and accounting authority previously enjoyed by villages has been recentralized up to higher bodies, leaving less autonomy and resources for village leaders and further diminishing the utility of serving as a village official.[15]

Along with the direct benefits of these government posts come indirect but still significant benefits. Because local people's congresses and political consultative conferences meet for only a few weeks each year, their direct impact on policy issues is relatively limited. But those who hold these posts have easier access to other local officials throughout the year, allowing them to establish and nurture contacts in the state hierarchy that benefit their businesses in hard-to-measure but still significant ways. Entrepreneurs who are part of the political system, either by membership in the CCP or by selection for government posts (or both), are also more likely to be consulted on policy matters, for instance by being invited to participate in group discussions about local policy. Those with easy access to party and government officials are also better positioned to obtain loans, licenses, and contracts for their business. In multiple ways, the business prospects of private entrepreneurs are dependent on their political ties. Those who benefit from their involvement in China's crony communist system have a strong incentive to uphold it.

As should be expected in a political system that is dominated by a Leninist party, most of the entrepreneurs who hold political posts are also cronies in one way or another. Most of those elected to local people's congresses and village posts are red capitalists; moreover, most of them were already in the CCP before going into business, meaning that the private entrepreneurs entrusted with these kinds of political posts were already well embedded in the political system before they went into business. Only a minority of the entrepreneurs who are political consultative conference deputies are red capitalists, but most deputies are tied to the state by belonging to officially sponsored business associations, especially the All-China Federation of Industry and Commerce. Capitalists who have tried to convert their economic success into political power—especially those who are not CCP members or tied to the state through official business associations—are rarely successful. The growing prominence of private entrepreneurs in China's political institutions is part of the CCP's strategy of co-optation rather than the result of entrepreneurs demanding greater inclusion and representation. In politics, more than in business, CCP approval is still the ultimate prerequisite.

Of course, not all entrepreneurs are cronies of the CCP. Just as in its approach to SOE reform, the CCP has employed a "grasp the large, release the small" strategy when relating to private firms. Large firms are more likely than small firms to be owned and operated by red capitalists and to have party organizations. Even though entrepreneurs who are not cronies do not share in the spoils the way red capitalists do, that does not mean they are inclined to challenge the CCP or the crony communism that its policies have produced. As Kellee Tsai's research shows, most small and medium-size entrepreneurs try to avoid the state rather than confront it.[16] They may not actively support the current regime, but they do not overtly oppose it. Many small-scale entrepreneurs are so occupied with scraping out a living and avoiding the state's scrutiny that they have neither the time nor the inclination to engage in political activities. This tendency is compounded by a classic collective action problem: the number of private firms is growing rapidly, and most of them are small and medium size. The large number and the small scale of private firms make coordination difficult, and many existing business associations are closely tied to the state, if not officially sponsored. Moreover, Tsai argues that the absence of a shared class identity among China's capitalists further inhibits cooperation on the basis of shared interests. The limited resources, the absence of effective organization, and the weak cohesion among these small-scale entrepreneurs are all obstacles to collective political action.

Why Do China's Capitalists Support the Communist Political System?

Although many foreign observers and even some within the CCP thought China's capitalists would pose a challenge to the communist political system, there has to date been little evidence of this. Barrington Moore may have been right in his maxim "no bourgeois, no democracy," but this does not mean that capitalists are inherently or inevitably democrats.[17] In China, rather than confronting the state, they have been increasingly integrated into it. More important, they are highly supportive of the political status quo. What explains this seeming paradox?

In my research with Jie Chen, we found high levels of support for the current regime among private entrepreneurs.[18] This by itself is not too surprising: as described above, the regime's policies directly benefit the private sector. More generally, most studies of public opinion find high levels of regime support despite intense dissatisfaction on specific issues such as corruption and pollution.[19] In this sense, regime support among China's private entrepreneurs should come as no surprise. But the factors that explain the level of regime support are surprising. First of all, party membership by itself has little effect on regime support. The CCP encourages its members to go into business and co-opts other successful businessmen into the party with the expectation that it can count on their support. However, only red capitalists who formerly served as party or government officials express significantly more regime support than non-CCP members. In contrast, regime support among former SOE managers and rank-and-file party members is no different than that of nonparty members. Admittedly, there is a high level of support to begin with, but party membership does not add to this support among most red capitalists. The CCP strategy for integrating with the private sector was undoubtedly designed to generate popular support, but red capitalists are little different from other private entrepreneurs in terms of regime support.

Although party membership alone does not create more regime support, other factors have more significant effects. First of all, those with strong democratic values are less likely to support the regime, all else being equal. This suggests that if democratic values were to become preponderant, support for the regime would likely decline. Second, concern with corruption also reduces regime support. Concern over corruption has caused popular resentment for many years and may be particularly acute among private entrepreneurs, who resent having to wine and dine party officials in order to be successful in business. Ironically, however, most private entrepreneurs believe that corruption was less severe at the time of the survey (2007) than in the recent past, 35 percent think it is about the same, and only 13 percent think it is getting worse. Nevertheless, the worse a person perceives corruption to be, the less likely that person is to support the regime. Both democratic values and concern about corruption therefore have the effect of reducing regime support among private entrepreneurs.

Two other factors, in contrast, serve to enhance regime support. One is evaluation of the government's policy performance. The more satisfied entrepreneurs are with the government's policies for controlling inflation, maintaining social order, promoting enterprise development, and providing other public goods and services, the more likely they are to support the regime. This suggests that the CCP may be able to maintain the support of the entrepreneurs, and the middle class more generally, through improved governance.[20]

The other factor that has a positive effect on regime support is overall life satisfaction. In our survey, 71 percent are satisfied with their material lives and 64 percent are satisfied with their social status, and this satisfaction translates into regime support. Ronald Inglehart argues that life satisfaction is one of the most important factors in creating stability in democratic regimes, and it is likely that the same logic applies to authoritarian regimes like China's.[21] If Inglehart is correct—that satisfaction with material conditions creates the basis for postmaterial values, which then create pressure for democracy—then the positive effect of life satisfaction on regime support may be only temporary. At present, the CCP's efforts to improve both its governance and the material lives of its citizens are generating the support that party leaders undoubtedly hope for.

These findings indicate how popular support for the current political system is contingent on a mix of values and material interests. The CCP is gambling that by improving people's standard of living and quality of life it will generate popular support and preempt demands for political reform, but in order to be successful the state must continue to deliver the goods. Declines in the government's policy performance and popular satisfaction with living standards and increases in democratic values and perceived corruption would threaten regime support. The CCP's current commitment to rapid economic growth and a harmonious society has produced remarkably high levels of popular support and, as a consequence, has reduced pressure for political change. However, maintaining this support will be contingent on the CCP's policy performance, including its ability to rein in corruption.

An End to Crony Communism?

In addition to potential changes in values and material conditions addressed earlier, what other developments could undermine crony communism in China? First of all, because the capitalists' support for the status quo is largely based on a desire to protect their material interests, a decline in the pro-business policies of the CCP would prompt a reconsideration of the capitalists' relationship with the state. This does not seem likely under current circumstances, but new leaders or dramatic changes in the political environment within China could lead to a change of policy that would be detrimental to business interests. However, we should also distinguish between policies that favor business and those that favor the private sector. Efforts to promote growth and stimulate the Chinese economy, especially in the wake of the international economic crisis that began in 2008, favor the state sector over private enterprises.[22] If this trend continues, then the most-favored cronies would be not only well embedded in the CCP but also would be part of the state sector. If prominent private entrepreneurs were then to lose favor with CCP leaders, they might in turn become less supportive of the status quo.

Second, the populist policies of the current leaders might also undermine crony communism. The Hu Jintao and Wen Jiabao administration has moderated the pro-growth strategy pursued under Jiang Zemin by fostering a more balanced pattern of growth so that inland and western provinces do not feel left out of China's modernization. The administration is attempting to reduce regional inequalities with income subsidies and the elimination of rural taxes and has adopted labor laws and environmental policies to ameliorate some of the externalities of rapid growth. At the same time, as noted above, it has supported the state sector at the expense of the private sector. If the current balance between the elitist strategy of development designed to sustain rapid growth and the populist policies designed to improve equity were to tip in favor of populism—and therefore the incentives for growth were curtailed or the size of the private sector began to shrink relative to the state sector—capitalists would be less likely to lend their unqualified support to the state.

Third, as a true market economy emerges, capitalists will be less dependent on the state and, accordingly, less likely to support the political status quo. Even now, this process is under way, however slowly. Private firms are more able to get loans from state banks, though these loans are still highly restricted. Property rights are still weakly and unevenly enforced, but the trend is toward stronger protection, which will make political protection less salient. The state still tightly controls the ability of Chinese firms to list on domestic and foreign stock exchanges, but this control is loosening. As firms become more responsible for their own profitability and less dependent on favors from the state, they will have less incentive to nurture the cozy ties with party and government officials that are now required for firms to be successful.

Finally, crony communism could become the victim of its own success. A variety of consequences of privatization could trigger public resentment. The relationship between the state and business is inherently corrupt, and while at least some capitalists are certainly responsible for their contribution to corruption, it is a cause of tremendous dissatisfaction on the part of other capitalists and the public at large. The rapid growth of China's economy has also been accompanied by a growth in inequality. To the extent that the public comes to perceive that China's nouveau riche attained their prosperity through political ties and not through entrepreneurship and hard work, the public will be less willing to accept the unequal distribution of wealth.[23] The growing number of protests against corruption, land grabs, and other aspects of economic development have to date remained localized and specific, but the potential for more systemic challenges is not out of the question. This would signal the decay of public support for policies of economic reform and openness, posing an exogenous threat to crony communism.

Future Prospects

How much support for democracy is necessary for the middle class or private entrepreneurs to become agents of political change? Is there some undefined tipping point? To be able to properly answer these questions, we need to have a better understanding of what democracy means to the Chinese.

Tianjian Shi argues that a large percentage of the population is already pro-democracy and that it is satisfied with the current level of democracy in China. His analysis of what democracy means in China shows that Chinese survey respondents, although they may have a different concept of democracy from the people asking the questions, have a concept not so different from that of other Asians. For example, almost 30 percent of Chinese respondents in the East Asian Barometer survey offered a populist definition of democracy ("authorities listen to the people's opinions"), which Shi notes is "compatible not only with the doctrine of socialist democracy but also classic Confucian ideas of benevolent dictatorship, since they do not require competitive pluralism to be put into effect."[24] A quarter of the respondents also associate democracy with the increase in personal freedoms that has accompanied the reform and opening policies. In contrast, just under a quarter of respondents define democracy in terms of political rights, institutions, and procedures.

Using these definitions of democracy, almost 85 percent of the respondents in the East Asian Barometer survey believe that China's current political system is either somewhat or very democratic.[25] If these findings are true, then the apparent contradiction between pro-democracy sentiments in China and support for the status quo is much less puzzling: although most outside observers would agree that China's current political system is far from democratic, the Chinese themselves evaluate the level of democracy in China much more favorably, based on their different interpretation of democracy. This suggests that the middle class may become more pro-democracy without necessarily being a threat to the CCP: if they interpret democracy to mean greater personal autonomy and economic opportunity and not the institutional and procedural aspects of political participation and electoral competition for top political posts that the term connotes to most Western observers, then these kinds of democratic beliefs do not necessarily conflict with continued CCP rule.

Moreover, we should also not assume that a decline in support for the current regime necessarily entails a shift toward support for democracy. The middle class, broadly defined, has been supportive of authoritarian and hybrid regimes in a variety of countries. It provided support for fascism in Europe and for bureaucratic authoritarianism in Latin America.[26] Assuming that a transition from communism inevitably entails a transition to democracy ignores the many other alternative regime types that replaced communist governments in the former Soviet Union and Eastern Europe.[27]

Conclusion

Much is made of the middle class's role in political change. Scholars as diverse as Karl Marx, Barrington Moore, and Francis Fukuyama extol the virtues of the middle class (or the bourgeoisie) as the critical foundation for both the emergence and the durability of democratic regimes. It is no surprise, then, that China specialists have been fascinated by the emergence of China's middle class and that they see private entrepreneurs, in particular, as potential agents of political change. The available evidence, however, points to a rather different conclusion: private entrepreneurs defend their new-found wealth not against a rapacious state but against the uncertainty of an alternative regime. They are the products of the CCP's economic reform policies and support the status quo. As long as the CCP remains committed to economic development (and continues its efforts to limit if not eliminate official corruption), it does not seem likely to face opposition from the middle class or the private sector.

Rather than dismiss ongoing research on China's middle class as a dead end, however, I would argue that it remains a useful concept for studying Chinese politics. The emergence and growth of the middle class—and private entrepreneurs in particular—is an important trend but not for the reasons it is normally studied. Looking to the middle class as a force for political change may be wishful thinking, but understanding its contribution to the adaptation and survival of the CCP is important in its own right. If the research question concerns the prospects for democracy, then the middle class may not have a positive effect in the near future; but if we flip the dependent variable around and focus on regime continuity, then the middle class has a more important role to play. Just as the presence of a middle class contributes to the survival of democratic regimes, so too may it contribute to the survival of nondemocratic regimes such as China's.

In other words, it is the quality of governance, not the type of regime, that determines whether the middle class will be a force for political stability or an unruly mob clamoring for change. Just as overall life satisfaction may stabilize authoritarian regimes, so too might a complacent middle class.[28] As long as the CCP is able to deliver the goods—housing, education, health care, roads, and so on—it will retain the support of the middle class. The research question then becomes how well quality public goods are provided in China. Rather than assuming that economic and social change in China inevitably leads to political change, we need to better understand how the country's political institutions are changing to accommodate new challenges and expectations without becoming democratic. It may be a difference of degree rather than of kind, but it remains an important and underappreciated difference.

Notes

1. Strictly speaking, the English-language literature on this topic is not synonymous with Western scholarship, since many of the authors of the studies addressed here are Chinese. Chapter 3 by Cheng Li, this volume, concentrates on works published in Chinese.

2. These studies include He Li, "Middle Class: Friends or Foes to Chinese Leadership?" *Journal of Chinese Political Science* 8, nos. 1, 2 (2003): 87–100; Yongshun Cai,

"China's Moderate Middle Class: The Case of Homeowners' Resistance," *Asian Survey* 45, no. 5 (2005): 777–99; Luigi Tomba, "Creating an Urban Middle Class: Social Engineering in Beijing," *China Journal* 51 (January 2004): 1–26; Jie Chen and Chunlong Lu, "Does China's Middle Class Think and Act Democratically? Attitudinal and Behavioral Orientations toward Urban Self-Government," *Journal of Chinese Political Science* 11, no. 2 (2006): 1–20; Xin Wang, "Seeking Channels for Engagement: Media Use and Political Communication by China's Rising Middle Class," *China: An International Journal* 7, no.1 (2009): 31–56.

3. Robert M. Glassman, *China in Transition: Communism, Capitalism, and Democracy* (New York: Praeger, 1991); Kristen Parris, "Local Initiative and National Reform: The Wenzhou Model of Development," *China Quarterly* 134 (June 1993): 242–63; Gordon White, "Democratization and Economic Reform in China," *Australian Journal of Chinese Affairs* 31 (1994): 73–92. In recent years, this view was best represented by Henry Rowen; see "When Will the Chinese People Be Free?" *Journal of Democracy* 18, no. 3 (2007): 38–62.

4. Dorothy Solinger, "Urban Entrepreneurs and the State: The Merger of State and Society," in *State and Society in China: The Consequences of Reform,* edited by Arthur Lewis Rosenbaum (Armonk, N.Y.: M. E. Sharpe, 1992); Dorothy Solinger, "Business Groups: For or Against the Regime?" in *Political Change in China with Comparisons with Taiwan,* edited by Bruce Gilley and Larry Diamond (Boulder, Colo.: Lynne Rienner, 2008); David S. G. Goodman, "The New Middle Class," in *The Paradox of China's Post-Mao Reforms,* edited by Merle Goldman and Roderick MacFarquhar (Harvard University Press, 1999); David S. G. Goodman, "Why China Has No New Middle Class," in *The New Rich in China: Future Rulers, Present Lives,* edited by David Goodman (London: Routledge, 2008).

5. Wang Zhengxu, "Public Support for Democracy in China," *Journal of Contemporary China* 16, no. 53 (2007): 561–63; Randall Peerenboom, *China Modernizes: Threat to the West or Model for the Rest?* (Oxford University Press, 2007); Wang, "Seeking Channels for Engagement"; Cai, "China's Moderate Middle Class."

6. He Li, "Emergence of the Chinese Middle Class and Its Implications," *Asian Affairs* 33, no. 2 (2006): 67–84.

7. Jie Chen and Chunlong Lu, "Does China's Middle Class Think and Act Democratically? Attitudinal and Behavioral Orientations toward Urban Self-Government," *Journal of Chinese Political Science* 11, no. 2 (2006): 1–20. They are careful to note that their conclusions are based on a survey of only Beijing residents, not a more representative sample, and that the thoughts and actions they base their conclusions on concern local self-government, not the national level (p. 15).

8. See, for example, Parris, "Local Initiative and National Reform"; White, "Democratization and Economic Reform in China."

9. Margaret Pearson, *China's New Business Elite: The Political Consequences of Economic Reform* (University of California Press, 1997); Margaret Pearson, "China's Emerging Business Class: Democracy's Harbinger?" *Current History* 97, no. 620 (September 1998): 268–72; Bruce J. Dickson, *Red Capitalists in China: The Party, Private Entrepreneurs, and Prospects for Political Change* (Cambridge University Press, 2003); Kellee S. Tsai, *Capitalism without Democracy: The Private Sector in Contemporary China* (Cornell University Press, 2007); Bruce J. Dickson, *Wealth into Power: The Communist Party's Embrace of China's Private Sector* (Cambridge University Press, 2008); Jie Chen and Bruce J. Dickson, *Allies of the State: China's Private Entrepreneurs and Democratic Change* (Harvard University Press, 2010).

10. In addition to the works already cited, see Zhaohui Hong, "Mapping the Evolution and Transformation of the New Private Entrepreneurs in China," *Journal of Chinese*

Political Science 9, no. 1 (2004): 23–42; Scott Kennedy, *The Business of Lobbying in China* (Harvard University Press, 2005).

11. Tsai, *Capitalism without Democracy*, p. 201.

12. Wu Jinglian, *Understanding and Interpreting Chinese Economic Reform* (Singapore: Thomson/South-Western, 2005), p. 65, n. 44, and p. 182.

13. Dickson, *Wealth into Power*, esp. pp. 22–27.

14. For more detailed looks at the corrupt ties between business and the state in China, see Yan Sun, *Corruption and Market in Contemporary China* (Cornell University Press, 2004); Shawn Shieh, "The Rise of Collective Corruption in China: The Xiamen Smuggling Case," *Journal of Contemporary China* 14, no. 42 (February 2005): 67–91; Melanie Manion, *Corruption by Design: Building Clean Government in Mainland China and Hong Kong* (Harvard University Press, 2005); Minxin Pei, *China's Trapped Transition: The Limits of Developmental Autocracy* (Harvard University Press, 2006); and Philip Pan, *Out of Mao's Shadow: The Struggle for the Soul of a New China* (New York: Simon and Schuster, 2008), pp. 147–74.

15. Kim Singer and others, "The Forgotten Side of the China Development Model: How Is China Sustaining the Countryside in an Industry-First Development Strategy?" unpublished paper, May 2008.

16. Tsai, *Capitalism without Democracy*.

17. Eva Bellin, "Contingent Democrats: Industrialists, Labor, and Democratization in Late-Developing Countries," *World Politics* 52, no. 2 (2000): 175–205.

18. The following discussion is drawn from Chen and Dickson, *Allies of the State*.

19. *The 2008 Pew Global Attitudes Survey in China* (Washington: Pew Research Center); Wenfang Tang, *Public Opinion and Political Change in China* (Stanford University Press, 2005); Lianjiang Li, "Political Trust in Rural China," *Modern China* 30, no. 2 (2004): 228–58.

20. Tony Saich, "Citizens' Perceptions of Governance in Rural and Urban China," *Journal of Chinese Political Science* 12, no. 1 (2007): 1–28; Jude Howell, ed., *Governance in China* (Lanham, Md.: Rowman and Littlefield, 2004); *Governance in China* (Paris: Organization for Economic Co-operation and Development, 2005).

21. Ronald Inglehart, *Culture Shift in Advanced Industrial Societies* (Princeton University Press, 1990); Ronald Inglehart, *Modernization and Postmodernization: Cultural, Economic, and Political Change in 43 Societies* (Princeton University Press, 1997).

22. Derek Scissors, "Deng Undone," *Foreign Affairs* 88, no. 3 (2009): 24–39. Yasheng Huang offers a much earlier date for the retreat from economic reform. He suggests that the heyday of the private sector was the 1980s, when the focus of reform was on the countryside, and that the shift to an urban focus since the early 1990s brought with it greater state intervention in the economy; see Yasheng Huang, *Capitalism with Chinese Characteristics: Entrepreneurship and the State* (Cambridge University Press, 2008).

23. Martin King Whyte shows that most Chinese do not yet blame the government for rising inequality, and they therefore diminish the potential political impact of this issue. See Martin King Whyte, "Do Chinese Citizens Want the Government to Do More to Promote Equality?" in *Chinese Politics: State, Society, and the Market,* edited by Peter Hays Gries and Stanley Rosen (New York: Routledge, 2010).

24. Tianjian Shi, "China: Democratic Values Supporting an Authoritarian System," in *How East Asians View Democracy,* edited by Yun-han Chu and others (Columbia University Press, 2008), p. 215.

25. Chu and others, *How East Asians View Democracy*, p. 18.

26. Nancy Bermeo, *Ordinary People in Extraordinary Times: The Citizenry and the Breakdown of Democracy* (Princeton University Press, 2003).

27. Michael McFaul, "The Fourth Wave of Democracy *and* Dictatorship: Noncooperative Transitions in the Post-Communist World," *World Politics* 54, no. 2 (2002): 212–44; Larry Diamond, "Thinking about Hybrid Regimes," *Journal of Democracy* 13, no. 2 (2002): 21–35; Steven Levitsky and Lucan Way, "The Rise of Competitive Authoritarianism," *Journal of Democracy* 13, no. 2 (2002): 51–65.

28. Inglehart, *Modernization and Postmodernization*; Dickson, *Wealth into Power*; Chen and Dickson, *Allies of the State*.

CHAPTER FOURTEEN

What Do Chinese Lawyers Want?
Political Values and Legal Practice

ETHAN MICHELSON and SIDA LIU

Searching for vanguards of political reform in China has become a veritable cottage industry among social scientists. Scholars have identified—and disagree about—various sources of popular sentiment in Chinese society supportive of democracy. Regarding China's incipient middle class, some argue that its members are, on the whole, conservative, while others argue the opposite.[1] On the whole, the political values and aspirations of the Chinese middle class appear from some survey data to be highly unified, while other data show them to be mostly incoherent.[2] With respect to their political values, differences between China's "lower" and "middle" classes, which are inconsistently defined using competing occupation and income criteria, are statistically marginal and difficult to interpret.[3]

A separate body of research suggests that the way out of this analytical morass is to disaggregate the middle class into its constitutive elements. More narrowly focused research on specific social groups brings into high relief the limitations of conceptualizing and analyzing the middle class as a monolithic entity. The concept of a middle class obscures internal variation as much as it illuminates internal commonalities. For example, business entrepreneurs appear to be generally politically conservative, whereas support for democratic political reform appears to arise from

We thank Jianling Jiang and Huiguo Liu for their help with survey preparations and Lily Liang for her editorial assistance. Above all, we are grateful to all the people who participated in the survey, whose time and trust made this research possible.

intellectuals, homeowners, students returning from overseas, and Internet users (netizens), groups that do not always map neatly onto income strata or occupational categories.[4] We thus eschew approaches to the study of attitudes that lump together disparate social groups. We instead borrow and build on the microclass approach of sociology, in which the operative unit of analysis is the occupation rather than the "big class." Research in this tradition suggests that attitudes and values are shaped by specific occupational experiences more than by socioeconomic outcomes.[5]

Our aim in this chapter is to use the case of lawyers to contribute to the growing body of research on specific component parts of Chinese society that, taken together, help constitute the middle class. More specifically, we assess the extent to which lawyers, as a part of China's emerging middle class, want political change. Chinese lawyers have grown dramatically in number from only a few thousand shortly after their revival in 1979 to almost 150,000 in 2007.[6] However, recent reports suggest that their thirst for political reform is disproportionate to their still-small population.[7] Using data from a national survey we conducted in the summer of 2009 of about 1,500 lawyers and nonlawyers working in China's legal system, we assess more thoroughly and rigorously than has been done previously the political values of Chinese lawyers. We measure the political values of Chinese lawyers, compare them to various reference populations, and identify some of their sources.

We find that, on the whole, Chinese lawyers are strongly inclined toward political reform, attach greater importance to political rights than to economic rights, and are profoundly discontented with the political status quo. At the same time, their politically radical values are explained in large measure by their economic and institutional vulnerabilities, including deadbeat clients who fail to pay their legal fees, exploitative employers who fail to support their professional work and protect their social security, and state actors who interfere with and obstruct their work. The lawyers who express the most politically radical values are those who are most vulnerable and exposed to these sources of trouble and therefore at the greatest risk of professional failure. In the absence of these sources of vulnerability, Chinese lawyers' political values are no different from those of the general Chinese population.

We conclude that Chinese lawyers' commitment to radical political reform is probably unstable and unlikely to be politically consequential insofar as their overriding priority is to protect and enhance their livelihood. Our findings suggest that their palpable discontent with the political status quo and the importance they attach to political rights and political reform stem less from ideological commitment and more from their desire for institutionalized protection against the sources of vulnerability that compromise their legal practice.

Survey Data and Key Measures

We analyze data from the China Legal Environment (CLE) Survey, a survey we conducted in the summer of 2009. The high rate of Internet usage among Chinese lawyers was the premise that motivated our decision to conduct an Internet survey. Terence C. Halliday and Sida Liu, for example, document the popularity of electronic message boards among Chinese lawyers as a means of sharing information and airing grievances.[8] We collected e-mail addresses from all of the profiles of registered users of four popular electronic message boards frequented by Chinese lawyers: www.acla.org.cn/forum/; www.fl168.com/; www.chinalawyer.org.cn/; and www.law-lib.com/. Because registered users on the four websites also include nonlawyers, our sample includes other actors in the legal system, including judges, prosecutors, law school students and faculty, as well as a few hundred spectators who work outside the law and who thus do not belong to the legal system.

After eliminating redundant e-mail addresses, and after identifying and consolidating multiple e-mail addresses attached to unique users, our database contained the e-mail addresses of 17,276 users. We sent out survey invitations and administered the survey on SurveyMonkey.com (using its alternate URL, Surveymk.com). Each survey invitation contained a unique hyperlink to the survey. We were thus able to track respondents, limit the survey to people we targeted, and prevent people from submitting multiple questionnaires. We launched the survey on July 2, 2009, and closed it on October 4, 2009 (Beijing time).

SurveyMonkey.com reported that 2,660 of the original 17,276 e-mail addresses in our database were "hard bounced," or invalid. Of the remaining 14,616 users with seemingly valid e-mail addresses, 2,335 responded, yielding a response rate of 16 percent. However, the true response rate is undoubtedly much higher for at least two reasons. First, despite our efforts to consolidate e-mail addresses among unique users, some individual respondents reported receiving invitations at multiple addresses. Second, invalid e-mail addresses were undoubtedly far more numerous than the 2,660 reported by SurveyMonkey.com.

Of the 2,335 people who responded to our survey invitations, 1,511 identified themselves as members of the legal system. The remaining 824 individuals either refused to participate in the survey after reading the study information sheet (63), refused to identify their occupation (239), or identified themselves as working outside the law (522).

We should address inevitable concerns about sampling bias. Lawyers eligible to receive our survey invitation—and, among them, lawyers who actually participated—may not represent the true population of lawyers. However, given that many Chinese lawyers work independently of their firms and given that officially published rosters of lawyers contain law firm contact information but not that of individual lawyers, coupled with the fact that such rosters are far from nationally comprehensive, alternatives to an Internet research design offer no obvious advantages. Overall, the benefits of conducting the survey via the Internet—namely, vastly greater geographical coverage at a tiny fraction of conventional survey costs—far outweigh the limitations of this research design. The geographical diversity of our sample is perhaps unparalleled in Chinese survey research: our sample includes lawyers in every province, autonomous region, and centrally administered city. Lawyers reported themselves to be in 194 cities; respondents of every stripe (that is, lawyers and nonlawyers) self-reported from 244 cities.

Although it is not a probability sample (that is, not every member of the Chinese bar had an opportunity to be included), our sample of lawyers is representative of the true population of lawyers in at least two respects. First, the geographical distribution of the 1,019 full-time lawyers who supplied geographical information is almost perfectly correlated ($R = .92$) with the geographical distribution of the 114,253 full-time lawyers in the true population in 2005. Second, the proportion of lawyers who are Chinese Communist Party (CCP) members in our sample (27.5 percent) is practically identical to the proportion of the true population (27.3 percent). However, our sample of lawyers appears to underrepresent women. Whereas the true population of lawyers was 15.8 percent female in 2005, our sample of lawyers is only 11.3 percent female.[9]

Using complex skip patterns, we tailored the instrument to respondents according to their occupations. That is, not every respondent was asked the same set of questions. We first identified members of the legal system ("Are you a legal service provider?"). All survey participants, members and nonmembers of the legal system alike, were asked about their class status, educational background, and political values. Members of the legal system, lawyers and nonlawyers alike, were also asked a battery of questions concerning lawyers' professional challenges. Finally, only lawyers were asked specific questions about their professional practice, including their incomes and various dimensions of job satisfaction.

Class Status

We borrowed measures of class status and political values from the 2005–07 wave of the World Values Survey.[10] Because China was part of the World Values Survey, we were able to use existing Chinese translations and thus to make comparisons between the two surveys with a greater degree of confidence. Although our income data are limited to lawyers, we have subjective measures of class status for all respondents. Moreover, because household income is missing in 40 percent of the 2007 China World Values Survey sample, we would, in any event, still be limited to subjective class measures for purposes of comparison. Our primary measure of subjective class status is the following: "Sometimes people divide themselves into higher and lower classes. To which social class would you describe yourself as belonging?" Response categories include: upper class (*gao ceng*), upper middle class (*zhonggao ceng*), middle class (*zhong ceng*), lower middle class (*zhongxia ceng*), and lower class (*xia ceng*).

Political Values

A battery of eight questions from the World Values Survey is the basis of two measures of political values. First, three questions on the importance of economic rights plus three questions on the importance of political rights are the basis of a measure we term *the extent to which political rights should trump economic rights*. A higher value, reflecting a greater degree of relative importance attached to political rights, implies more liberal political values. Conversely, a lower value, reflecting a greater degree of relative importance attached to economic rights, implies more conservative political values.

Second, two additional questions from the World Values Survey are the basis of a measure we term *the extent to which democratic aspirations are fulfilled*. This measure is calculated simply as the extent to which the "current level of democracy" falls short of the "importance of democracy." A lower value, reflecting a lower degree of fulfillment and a greater degree of discontent with the political status quo, implies more liberal political values. Conversely, a higher value, reflecting a higher degree of fulfillment and greater satisfaction with the political status quo, implies more conservative political values.

In addition to the forgoing two measures of political values, we also analyze responses to an additional question in our 2009 CLE Survey: the extent to which "lawyers are inclined toward political reform." A higher extent implies more liberal political values, and a lower extent implies more conservative political values. More details both on these key dependent variables and on key independent variables are available from the authors upon request.

Economic Status and Class Identity

Chinese lawyers overwhelmingly define themselves as middle class. In the China World Values Survey, 43 percent of respondents identify themselves as middle class; if upper middle class is also counted, then 48 percent of respondents consider themselves middle class. Only 0.6 percent identify themselves as upper class. This distribution is very similar to that of the United States, where 47 percent of all respondents in the 2000–04 General Social Survey identify themselves as middle class and only 4 percent as upper class.[11] Compared to the general Chinese population, Chinese lawyers situate themselves more squarely in the middle class: 55 percent say they belong to the middle class; if the middle also includes upper middle, then 70 percent say they belong to this class. Meanwhile, similar to the World Values Survey, only 0.9 percent of lawyers say they belong to the upper class.

As one would expect, income is considerably higher in the legal profession than in the general population. With respect to perceived income decile, 58 percent of people in the China World Values Survey sample situate themselves below the 5th decile. By contrast, only 34 percent of the lawyers in the 2009 CLE Survey situate themselves below the 5th decile. According to the World Bank, the Chinese middle class is defined as people with personal annual income in the range of 20,000–90,000 yuan.[12] An alternative definition of middle class—created by the Economic Research Institute of the Chinese National Development and Reform Commission—includes individuals with an annual income in the range of 34,000–100,000 yuan.[13] By either definition, 84 percent of Chinese lawyers in our sample are in or above the middle class. Indeed, the median income of lawyers who self-identify as middle-class is 88,000 yuan. If upper middle class is included, the median increases to 100,000 yuan.

Many Chinese lawyers are also doing well by international standards. Of the lawyers in our sample, 9 percent report annual incomes above 500,000 yuan, or $73,000.[14] Indeed, twenty-five lawyers in the sample report incomes of at least 1 million yuan (or $146,000), and five respondents report incomes of at least 10 million yuan (or about $1.5 million). At the same time, as is the case with the general population, variation in education helps explain variation in income among lawyers. Median income among lawyers in our sample with junior college degrees or less, with B.A. degrees, with M.A. degrees, and with Ph.D. degrees is 50,000, 88,000, 138,000, and 231,000 yuan, respectively. According to official government data, 74 percent of full-time lawyers in 2005 possessed a university degree.[15] In our sample, almost every lawyer who reports educational data holds a B.A. degree or higher.

In sum, by all measures—income, education, and subjective class identification—lawyers are disproportionately represented in the middle class. Moreover, their overall income advantage appears to have remained stable between 2000 and 2009.[16]

Political Values

Lawyers' political values and aspirations are extreme both in international comparison and compared to other members of the legal system. The following is a very small selection of comments volunteered by our survey respondents:

—"The thirst for rights and democracy is far greater among Chinese lawyers than among any other segment of society!" (lawyer, respondent #91164, Henan)

—"Protect every citizen's freedom and equal rights. Democratic constitutions are the standard (*zhunsheng*) guiding our actions." (lawyer, respondent #30954, Jiangsu)

—"I greatly hope China will elevate political reform on its agenda. I greatly hope China can swiftly become a genuinely democratic and rule-of-law society." (lawyer, respondent #36071, Chongqing)

—"Democracy and rule of law! This is what we pursue!" (lawyer, respondent #63481, Fujian)

—"The rule of law is premised on democracy; rights are premised on the rule of law; rights defense (*weiquan*) is premised on rights; and lawyers are premised on rights defense." (lawyer, respondent #27619, Henan)

These comments also reflect Chinese lawyers' conflation of different dimensions of political rights. Even if lawyers in historical and comparative perspective have often pushed for a moderate state (that is, executive power "counterbalanced by forces outside the state") but not for democracy, Chinese lawyers in our survey tend to conflate these two sets of political rights.[17] The Cronbach's alpha value (a common measure of internal consistency among multiple measures) for the three items we include in our measure of political rights is .65, meaning that they can be meaningfully combined into a single scale. Indeed, Cronbach's alpha exceeds .60 in thirty-four of the forty-seven countries (with nonmissing data) in the 2005–07 wave of the World Values Survey, meaning that Chinese lawyers are no different from most people in the world in their conflation of these two dimensions of political rights.

International Variation

Table 14-1 shows that compared to people elsewhere in the world, China's general population tends to prioritize political rights over economic rights to a far smaller extent. With respect to our measure, *the extent to which political rights should trump economic rights,* China ranks toward the bottom. This finding supports the argument that Chinese people tend to privilege socioeconomic security over individual political rights.[18] At the same time, China ranks toward the top of the rankings with respect to our measure, *the extent to which democratic aspirations are fulfilled.* In other words, relative to most people elsewhere in the world, Chinese people tend to be content with the current level of democracy in their country. Although Internet users in China are no different from the general population in terms of the relative importance they attach to economic and political rights, they are less likely to be content with China's current level of democracy.

Differences between Internet users and the general population in China are, at best, modest. However, differences between lawyers and the general population in China are dramatic. If Chinese lawyers are treated like a country and compared to the populations of other countries, they rank in the top ten with respect to the relative importance they attach to political rights and near the very bottom with respect to the extent to which their aspirations for democracy are realized. In our survey, Chinese lawyers privilege political rights over economic rights to a similar degree as people in the World Values Survey samples from Sweden, Norway, Australia, the United States, and Argentina. Likewise,

TABLE 14-1. China and Chinese Lawyers in the Global Distribution of Political Values[a]

Subjective class	Extent to which political rights should trump economic rights			Extent to which democratic aspirations are realized		
	Rank of 49	Mean (95 % confidence intervals)	N	Rank of 47	Mean (95% confidence intervals)	N
Full China World Values sample						
Lower	42	0.27 (0.16, 0.39)	782	17	77.5 (75.6, 79.5)	637
Middle	43	0.28 (0.16, 0.40)	763	18	78.4 (76.6, 80.1)	671
Internet users						
Lower	37	0.39 (−0.05, 0.82)	69	31	68.3 (61.3, 75.2)	62
Middle	46	0.20 (−0.10, 0.50)	135	25	74.4 (70.5, 78.3)	133
Chinese lawyers						
Lower	4	1.74 (1.38, 2.10)	233	46	46.1 (42.5, 49.8)	241
Middle	10	1.63 (1.40, 1.85)	561	46	52.2 (50.0, 54.5)	563

Source: 2007 China World Values Survey; 2009 China Legal Environment Survey.

a. This table presents rankings (in descending order) of all countries in the 2005–07 wave of the World Values Survey plus two additional groups: Internet users in the China World Values Survey sample and lawyers in the 2009 CLE Survey. Thus Chinese Internet users are double-counted; they appear in both the full sample group and the Internet users group. The number of country samples is forty-five or forty-seven, depending on whether questions were omitted from country-specific questionnaires. Thus the total number of groups ranked is forty-seven or forty-nine. Details on measures used in the above rankings are available from the authors upon request. Rankings are disaggregated by subjective class identification: *lower class* is defined as respondents who identify their class status as lower class or lower-middle class, *middle class* is defined as respondents who identify their class status as middle class or upper-middle class. 95 percent confidence intervals: upper and lower bounds containing mean scores of 95 percent of samples drawn randomly from the same populations.

Chinese lawyers' contentment with their county's current level of democracy is surpassed by every World Values Survey sample except Ethiopia and Georgia and is not far below Ukraine, Bulgaria, and Morocco. We can also see in table 14-1 that, for the most part, subjective class identification has little effect on our measures of political values and political aspirations. The differences between self-identified members of the lower class and the middle class are trivial.

Variation within the Chinese Legal System

According to our measure, *the extent to which democratic aspirations are fulfilled,* lawyers are more discontented with the political status quo than any other occupational group in the legal system. According to our measure, *the extent to which political rights should trump economic rights,* lawyers' political values are more liberal than those of every other occupational group except law school faculty.[19] Two additional findings are noteworthy. First, the political values of legal actors as a whole are far more radical than those of the general population as a whole and than those of Internet users, as well. Second, although their overall class status is indistinguishable from that of the general Chinese population, spectators in our sample working outside the legal system attach markedly more importance to political rights and harbor markedly higher levels of political discontent. The reason is simple: many ordinary people who register as users on the websites from which we collected e-mail addresses do so in search of legal help with a long-standing, unresolved grievance, which often involves a government agency or other public organization. Many of these spectators provided details about their grievances and disappointments.

Vulnerabilities in Legal Practice

Our efforts to explain why Chinese lawyers' values are so liberal relative to those of both China's general population and other populaces focus on this group's sources of vulnerability. Our survey data suggest three primary sources of vulnerability in the Chinese bar: clients who fail to pay their legal fees, law firms that provide scant support to—while exacting heavy fees from—the lawyers they employ, and state actors who obstruct or otherwise undermine the work of lawyers.

Economic Vulnerability vis-à-vis Clients

Chinese lawyers experience difficulty collecting their fees from clients.[20] Among all lawyers in the sample, mean and median client arrears are 77,000 and 13,000 yuan, respectively. Lawyers reporting total client arrears of at least 100,000 yuan account for 15 percent of the total lawyer sample.[21] Lawyers in our survey were asked to rate the importance of seven factors they take into consideration when deciding whether or not to represent a client. The most important factor of all is "the probability that the client will refuse to pay your fee," which even edged out "the legal merit of the case" and "the chances of winning the case." In response to the statement "Lawyers have trouble collecting their fees from clients," lawyers in the sample are more than 50 percent more likely to choose one of the two most "prevalent" categories (33 percent chose category 4 or 5) than to choose one of the two most "rare" categories (20 percent chose category 0 or 1).

Economic Vulnerability vis-à-vis Law Firms

Lawyers' vulnerability vis-à-vis troublesome clients was compounded by the organization of law firms. Although almost all lawyers belong to law firms, they tend to work independently of their firms. "Most Chinese lawyers 'eat what they kill'; despite mandatory firm membership, they operate like solo practitioners, solely responsible for finding and representing clients from beginning to end."[22] Almost half (46 percent) of the lawyers in our sample indicate that they operate entirely independently of their firms (by selecting, "In reality I work independently of my law firm").

Lawyers' independence from their firms is reflected in their remuneration methods. More than half of the lawyers in Michelson's earlier 2000 lawyer survey report getting paid exclusively by commission—calculated as a percentage of the business they generate.[23] In a 2007 survey of lawyers in three major cities and five provinces, between 24 percent and 40 percent of lawyers in the cities (Beijing, Shanghai, and Guangzhou) report getting paid exclusively on a commission basis, while the spread is between 54 percent and 93 percent for the provincial samples.[24] In our 2009 CLE Survey, 54 percent of lawyers report getting paid "mainly by commission."[25] Another 9 percent of lawyers in our sample report making an annual lump-sum payment to their firms. Among the lawyers who report working entirely independently of their firms (lawyers who do not supervise or work with a team of junior lawyers and who receive no help or support from their firms with respect to finding and managing clients), the annual amount of money lawyers pay to their law firms in the form of client billings or lump-sum payments averages 131,000 yuan.

Not only do they receive little in the way of professional help or support in exchange for the "rents" they pay to their firms, but lawyers also receive little in the way of perks and benefits from their firms. Of twelve items that lawyers were asked to assess in terms of satisfaction, "the social security benefits supplied by my firm" registers far and away the highest levels of dissatisfaction. Lawyers are more than twice as likely to say they are "very dissatisfied" (32 percent) with their firms' perks and benefits than they are with the item generating the second-highest levels of dissatisfaction ("my chances for advancement," with which 15 percent of lawyers said they were "very dissatisfied"). In light of the high costs and negligible benefits of law firm membership, we should not be surprised that 71 percent of lawyers in our sample who report working entirely independently of their firms also report hoping or planning "in the future to take advantage of the provision in the revised Law on Lawyers to establish an individually owned firm."

In his earlier research, Michelson found that lawyers in general and commission-based lawyers in particular characterize themselves as "'fighting the battle alone' (*dan da du dou*), which fits into the larger rhetorical trope of fighting and hunting, of the combat character of lawyering."[26] In 2009 a lawyer in our survey echoes this theme: "Currently the vast majority of Chinese law firms are fake partnerships. Lawyers are all soldiers in war. Law firms only collect fees and do not shoulder any labor remuneration. They especially fail to provide any form of social insurance."[27] On the whole, law firms take much from their lawyers and give back very little. This source of economic vulnerability exacerbates the widespread problem of clients who renege on their lawyer fee agreements.

Institutional Vulnerability vis-à-vis State Actors

Lawyers' responses to seven statements describing their status in the criminal justice system, their relations with judges, levels of support and cooperation they receive in the course of their work, and their overall effectiveness in the legal system poignantly reveal additional sources of vulnerability. These are the same seven questions that Ethan Michelson combines into an aggregate measure of lawyers' "vexation with their institutional environment."[28] Only 9 percent of lawyers in our 2009 survey fail to assess at least one of these seven statements negatively; another 10 percent assess all seven statements negatively. More than half (58 percent) of the lawyers in our sample report negatively on at least four of the seven statements.[29]

Our questionnaire also includes a question about concrete, first-hand experiences with government interference and obstructionism. Lawyers were asked to identify organizations that, "over the past year . . . obstructed your work or failed to provide reasonable and lawful cooperation in other ways." Lawyers were asked to select all applicable organizations from a list: public security (police), procuracy (state prosecution), court, bureau of justice or lawyers association, and "other government agency." Only 23 percent of lawyers in the sample report no such direct experience with any of the listed state actors. Meanwhile, 54 percent report an experience of interference or obstructionism with at least two—and 20 percent with at least four—different types of state actor over the previous year. Overall, lawyers in the sample report this type of experience with an average of two different types of state actor.

Lawyers' high degree of vulnerability—both economic and institutional—helps explain why so many regret their choice of career. More than one in four lawyers in the sample (27 percent) say they would not become a lawyer if they "had it all to do over again," and almost one in five lawyers in the sample (18 percent) says he or she does not "hope to be working in the same job in five years."

Bivariate Associations between Vulnerabilities and Political Values

Chinese lawyers' aspirations for political rights, including democracy, reflect their craving for basic professional rights to carry out their work free of arbitrary state interference and obstructionism and with greater support from their law firms. They reflect more than anything else their desire for enhanced professional status, protection, and security.

Most of our measures of economic vulnerability (vis-à-vis clients and law firms) are strongly associated with the two measures of political values we analyze above, that is, *the extent to which political rights should trump economic rights* and *the extent to which democratic aspirations are fulfilled*. Lawyers who work independently of their firms, lawyers who are dissatisfied with their firms' social security benefits, and lawyers who regret their career decision or who plan to stop practicing law attach significantly greater importance to political rights and are more discontented with the political status quo than other lawyers. Lawyers who are owed at least 100,000 yuan in client arrears attach significantly more relative importance to political rights but are not significantly more discontented with the current level of democracy. The relationship between subjective class identification and political values is mixed: it is only weakly associated with the relative importance attached to political rights but strongly (and significantly) associated with the fulfillment of democratic aspirations.

Lawyers' institutional vulnerability (vis-à-vis state actors) also promotes liberal political values. Litigation, for example, exposes lawyers to the advantages as well as the potential interference and obstructionism of state actors. Bivariate associations between litigation work (measured as the proportion of total legal effort devoted to litigation) and these two measures of political values are both statistically significant. Consistent with this pattern, we also find that both measures of political values are positively and statistically significantly associated with lawyers' "vexation with their institutional environment" and direct experience with government obstructionism. CCP members and Communist Youth League (CYL) members are significantly less politically liberal than both members of the official state-sponsored democratic parties (*minzhu dangpai*) and lawyers with no political affiliation. However, we find no support for our expectation that lawyers with prior work experience in government agencies, including as former judges, prosecutors, and other state actors, would be less politically liberal than lawyers without this special background. We also find no evidence that the political values of self-identified rights defense (*weiquan*) lawyers differ from those of lawyers who do not identify as such. Our survey data thus fail to support popular accounts of rights defense lawyers as politically radical and instead support Fu Hualing and Richard Cullen's account of rights defense lawyers as generally nonthreatening politically.[30] Indeed, given that almost half of all the lawyers in our sample assume the rights defense moniker, it appears to be largely devoid of political significance.

Our third measure of political values yields similar findings. Overall, 32 percent of the lawyers in our sample selected "very prevalent" (response category 5) when assessing the following statement: "Lawyers are inclined toward political reform." An additional 19 percent chose response category 4, meaning over half of our sample believes that lawyers are inclined toward political reform. Although lawyers tend to attach importance to political reform, they do so mainly because they also tend to be highly vulnerable. With respect to economic vulnerabilities, lawyers who work independently of their law firms and lawyers who complain about their social security benefits report stronger overall support for political reform than their counterparts who receive more support from their law firms. Not surprisingly, frustration expressed in terms of regretting the decision to practice law is positively associated with support for political reform. Client arrears, however, are not associated with support for political reform. At the same time, neither subjective income nor subjective class status is associated with support for political reform.

As with our previous two measures of political values, institutional vulnerabilities are also closely associated with this measure of political values. Support for political reform increases commensurately with negative general assessments of and negative direct experiences with state actors.

Multivariate Associations between Vulnerabilities and Political Values

We performed multivariate regression analysis to test whether the bivariate associations reported above are robust to controls. Owing to space limitations, however, we do not present detailed results in this chapter.[31]

These multivariate regression models support our finding that, with the exception of law school faculty, Chinese lawyers' political values are more liberal than those of any other group of actors in the legal system. They also suggest that occupation explains some but not all of the effects of party affiliation. CCP and CYL members are, on the whole, more politically conservative than lawyers without these affiliations. Respondents who report attending a Communist Party school (*dang xiao*) are likewise more politically conservative than those who do not report this educational experience. The regression models also show that, with only a few exceptions, the effects of lawyers' economic and institutional vulnerability on their political values generally persist independent of controls.

Our finding that the political values of self-identified rights defense lawyers are no different from those of other lawyers also persists in multivariate analysis. Lawyers' "vexation" with their institutional environment is a statistically significant predictor of all measures of political values. Direct experiences with state interference or obstructionism are statistically significant determinants of all measures of political values except the relative importance attached to political rights.

The effects of lawyers' subjective economic status on their political values and aspirations are mixed and contradictory. In multivariate models, lawyers' subjective income is significantly positively associated with the relative importance attached to political rights, suggesting it is an engine of liberal political values. However, it is not significantly associated with the other two measures of political values. Furthermore, its strong and positive bivariate association with the extent to which democratic aspirations are realized—suggesting it is an engine of conservative political values—is explained by our measures of vulnerability. Results are similarly murky when we replace subjective income with subjective class identification.

Whereas the simple bivariate relationships described in the previous section reveal the effects of various dimensions of vulnerability one at a time, multivariate regression models allow us to simulate the effects

FIGURE 14-1. Predicted Probabilities of Support for Political Reform, with 95 Percent Confidence Intervals[a]

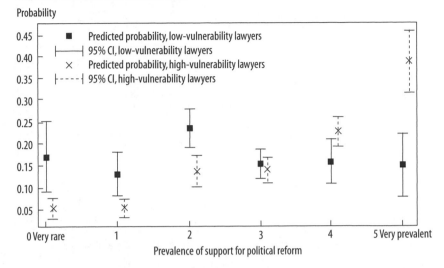

Source: 2009 CLE Survey.

a. *Low-vulnerability lawyers* are defined as those who do not operate independently of their firms, who devote 20 percent of their legal effort to litigation, with no negative evaluations of their institutional environment, and who report no state obstructionism in the past year. *High-vulnerability lawyers* are defined as those who do operate independently of their firms, who devote 80 percent of their effort to litigation, with at least one negative evaluation of their institutional environment, and who report three sources of state obstructionism in the past year. All remaining variables are set to sample means. Predicted probabilities for each group of lawyers sum to 100 percent. For details on postestimation techniques, see J. Scott Long and Jeremy Freese, *Regression Models for Categorical Dependent Variables Using Stata,* 2nd ed. (College Station, Texas: Stata Press, 2006). The multivariate regression model used to calculate the predicted probabilities in this figure is available from the authors upon request.

of simultaneously erasing multiple sources of vulnerability. If we plug low values of our vulnerability measures into our regression models, we can predict the political values of low-vulnerability lawyers. By the same token, if we plug in high values we can predict the political values of high-vulnerability lawyers. We define low-vulnerability lawyers as those who do not operate independently of their firms, devote 20 percent of their practice to litigation, have no negative evaluations of their institutional environment, and report no state obstructionism in the past year. We define high-vulnerability lawyers, by contrast, as those who operate independently of their firms, devoted 80 percent of their effort to litigation, have at least one negative evaluation of their institutional environment, and report three sources of state obstructionism in the past year. Figure 14-1 depicts the predicted distributions of these two

FIGURE 14-2. Predicted Values of Remaining Measures of Political Values, with 95 Percent Confidence Intervals[a]

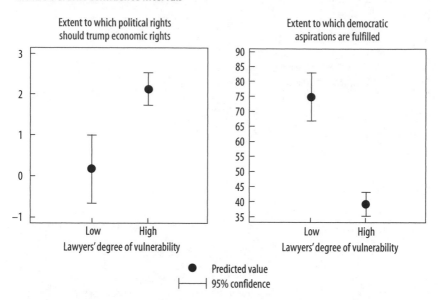

Source: 2009 CLE Survey.

a. See note a, figure 14-1, for definitions of *low-vulnerability* and *high-vulnerability lawyers*. The multivariate regression models used to calculate the predicted probabilities in this figure are available from the authors upon request.

groups' responses to the statement, "Lawyers are inclined toward political reform." High-vulnerability lawyers are 2.5 times more likely than low-vulnerability lawyers to choose "very prevalent" (39 percent and 15 percent, respectively), whereas low-vulnerability lawyers are more than three times more likely than high-vulnerability lawyers to choose "very rare" (17 percent and 5 percent, respectively). Confidence intervals show that these differences are statistically significant.

The effect of erasing lawyers' vulnerability is even more apparent in simulations of the remaining two measures of political values. Figure 14-2 depicts the predicted values of our measures of the relative importance attached to political rights and the extent to which democratic aspirations are realized. Recall from table 14-1 that according to the 2007 China World Values Survey, the general population of China averages between 0.27 and 0.28 on the first measure and 78 on the second measure. In figure 14-2 we can see that low-vulnerability lawyers are similarly politically conservative, clocking in at 0.16 on the first measure and 75 on the second measure. In other words, the political values of low-vulnerability lawyers are indistinguishable from those of the general population of China. By contrast, the predicted values of high-vulnerability lawyers are dramatically—and statistically significantly—more politically liberal.

Conclusions

The findings we report in this chapter suggest that, by any standard, Chinese lawyers' political values are highly liberal. The extent to which they embrace political rights (relative to economic rights) and the extent of their aspirations for more democracy in China are extreme relative to three reference standards: the general population of China, the general populations of forty-six additional countries included in the 2005–07 wave of the World Values Survey, and other members of China's legal system.

The story of political values in this chapter is not about "big classes"—aggregations of occupations whose inhabitants share similar socioeconomic outcomes.[32] We find that the effects of subjective class and subjective income on political values are small and mixed not only among lawyers but also among the general population. Data from the 2007 China World Values Survey fail to confirm findings reported elsewhere of a Chinese middle-class affinity for democracy.[33] In the Chinese population as a whole, people who identify as members of the middle class are no more liberal in their political values than people who identify as members of the lower class, at least according to the measures we analyze in this chapter. One implication of our findings is that existing and future research on Chinese middle-class attitudes that treats the middle class monolithically rather than disaggregating it into specific occupations could be seriously flawed.

This chapter's emphasis on the occupation-specific reasons for Chinese lawyers' liberal political values was inspired by and supports the microclass approach, in which big classes are disaggregated into their specific constituent occupations. Our findings are consistent with other microclass research insofar as they suggest that political values map onto specific occupations more reliably than onto aggregates of occupations.[34] Chinese lawyers' liberal political values are not reducible to their socioeconomic status. The generally great importance they attach to political rights, the generally small degree to which their democratic hopes are fulfilled, and their general perception that the bar as a whole is inclined toward political reform are, more than anything else, functions of the occupational hazards of their work. Chinese lawyers, as a whole, embrace liberal political values in large measure because their occupational vulnerability is so acute and widespread. Thus our findings further contribute to microclass research by identifying work experiences, work conditions, and work environments as occupation-specific causes of political values.

Notwithstanding their radically liberal character, Chinese lawyers' political values may be harmless to the political status quo. First, our data suggest that Chinese lawyers' demands fall far short of systemwide political change. Most lawyers simply want more and better-protected rights vis-à-vis their clients, law firms, and state actors. Chinese lawyers support political freedoms only to the extent that their professional livelihood is compromised by their marginal status and their weakly protected rights in the legal system. High-vulnerability lawyers—the majority—crave basic rights and protections to keep capricious state actors off their backs. Put another way, the importance they attach to political rights is conditioned by their demand for institutionalized constraints on the power of state actors who obstruct their work and compromise their livelihood, their demand for institutionalized protections in dealings with clients, and their demand for institutionalized support from their law firms. Redressing their sources vulnerability could thus serve to blunt their political demands and aspirations. By implication, Chinese lawyers' political values are unstable and could easily swing in the opposite direction if the sources of their discontent are remedied. It follows, then, that lawyers could potentially follow a trajectory similar to that of politically conservative business entrepreneurs and other politically conservative middle-class citizens who align their interests with the state and the CCP.

Second, if vulnerability breeds political radicalism within the Chinese bar, and if vulnerability causes lawyers to abandon legal practice, then politically liberal lawyers are at elevated risk of exiting the bar and taking their political values with them. Politically conservative lawyers, on the other hand, are more likely to survive, helping to color the political values of the bar as a whole. Ethan Michelson estimates an annual attrition rate of 5 percent in the Beijing bar between 1995 and 2004, meaning that every year in this time period one in twenty lawyers exited the bar. Over the nine years between 1996 and 2004, 35 percent—or more than one in three lawyers—dropped out.[35] As one lawyer in our 2009 survey comments, "I think it is essential to study young lawyers' survival difficulties, which is an important reason why the legal profession is losing so much talent" (respondent #47169, Chongqing).

Third, in historical and comparative perspective, lawyers' political mobilization efforts are generally more successful in response to the plight of ordinary people than in response to their own professional difficulties. They tend to be successful when mobilizing in support of universal political rights but not in support of their narrow professional interests. At the same time, a sine qua non of lawyers' successful mobilization in support of political liberalism is an alliance with judges and other members of the legal system.[36] Insofar as Chinese lawyers are relegated to "a marginal status of outside interloper" in the judicial system, and insofar as their political values are shaped by their narrow professional interests, Chinese lawyers are not likely to become the vanguard of political change.[37]

In sum, although Chinese lawyers' counterparts elsewhere in time and place often support political freedoms, such a natural affinity does not appear to extend to the contemporary Chinese bar.[38] If Chinese lawyers were more ideologically committed to political reform and political freedoms, our data would exhibit less variation between low-vulnerability and high-vulnerability lawyers. If Chinese lawyers' embrace of liberal political values were more deeply entrenched, even low-vulnerability lawyers' political values would be more liberal than those of the general Chinese population.

To be sure, however, we also recognize that countervailing forces may be at work. Lawyers' grievances—the primary engine of their liberal political values—may very well persist into the foreseeable future for at least two reasons. First, although we argue that political values are shaped by grievances, we also acknowledge the possibility that this relationship is endogenous. Lawyers with a prior inclination toward political reform may, by virtue of their more radical political values, deliberately choose cases that expose them to vulnerability and risk. Preexisting political values may help shape vulnerability insofar as lawyers most inclined toward political reform are also the most politically assertive and confrontational and therefore at greatest risk of administrative interference and obstructionism.

Second, from the CCP's standpoint, co-opting lawyers is more politically risky than co-opting entrepreneurs and other members of the middle class. The beginning of some measure of judicial autonomy from state interference and control is a necessary condition for assuaging the complaints of Chinese lawyers. Official measures to redress the sources of lawyers' vulnerability would, by necessity, include the enforcement of legal mechanisms designed to constrain the privileges—as well as the arbitrary and discretionary behavior—of state actors. Blunting lawyers' political aspirations by redressing their institutional vulnerability could paradoxically blunt the authority of the CCP and compromise its political monopoly. Thus compared to the political risks of alienating China's tens of millions of private business owners and employees, the political risks of alienating China's approximately 150,000 lawyers appear relatively trivial. Insofar as the political costs to the CCP of redressing lawyers' vulnerabilities outweigh the political benefits of ignoring them, we might expect lawyers' vulnerabilities and the liberal political values they spawn to persist for the foreseeable future.

Notes

1. For the conservative argument, see Minxin Pei, *China's Trapped Transition: The Limits of Developmental Autocracy* (Harvard University Press, 2006); Jonathan Unger, "China's Conservative Middle Class," *Far Eastern Economic Review* 169, no. 3 (2006): 27–31; Dali Yang, "China's Long March to Freedom," *Journal of Democracy* 18, no. 3 (2007): 58–64. For the liberal argument, see Jie Chen and Chunlong Lu, "Does China's Middle Class Think and Act Democratically? Attitudinal and Behavioral Orientations toward Urban Self-Government," *Journal of Chinese Political Science* 11, no. 2 (2006): 1–20; Merle Goldman, *From Comrade to Citizen: The Struggle for Political Rights in China* (Harvard University Press, 2005); Henry S. Rowen, "When Will the Chinese People Be Free?" *Journal of Democracy* 18, no. 3 (2007): 38–52; Min Tang, Dwayne Woods, and Zhao Jujun, "The Attitudes of the Chinese Middle Class Towards Democracy," *Journal of Chinese Political Science* 14 (2009): 81–95.

2. Li Lulu and Wang Yu, "Dangdai Zhongguo Zhongjian Jieceng de Shehui Cunzai: Jieceng Renshi Yu Zhengzhi Yishi" [The social presence of the middle class in contemporary China: class awareness and political consciousness], *Shehui Kexue Zhanxian* [Social science front] 10 (2008): 202–15.

3. Chen and Lu, "Does China's Middle Class Think and Act Democratically?"; Tang, Woods, and Zhao, "The Attitudes of the Chinese Middle Class Towards Democracy." For a review of the relevant Chinese-language literature, see Guo Yingjie, "Farewell to Class, except the Middle Class: The Politics of Class Analysis in Contemporary China," *Asia-Pacific Journal* 26, no. 2 (2009) (www.japanfocus.org/-Yinjie-Guo/3181).

4. An Chen, "Capitalist Development, Entrepreneurial Class, and Democratization in China," *Political Science Quarterly* 117, no. 3 (2002): 401–22; Bruce J. Dickson, *Wealth into Power: The Communist Party's Embrace of China's Private Sector* (Cambridge University Press, 2008); Kellee Tsai, *Capitalism without Democracy: The Private Sector in Contemporary China* (Cornell University Press, 2007); Tang Wenfang, *Public Opinion and Political Change in China* (Stanford University Press, 2005); Benjamin L. Read, "Democratizing the Neighborhood? New Private Housing and Homeowner Self-Organization in

Urban China," *China Journal* 49 (2003): 31–59; Li He, "Returned Students and Political Change in China," *Asian Perspective* 30, no. 2 (2006): 5–29; Guobin Yang, *The Power of the Internet in China: Citizen Activism Online* (Columbia University Press, 2009).

5. Kim A. Weeden and David B. Grusky, "The Case for a New Class Map," *American Journal of Sociology* 111, no. 1 (2005): 141–212; David B. Grusky and Kim A. Weeden, "Are There Social Classes? A Framework for Testing Sociology's Favorite Concept," in *Social Class: How Does It Work?* edited by Annette Laureau and Dalton Conley (New York: Russell Sage, 2008), pp. 65–90.

6. *Zhongguo Tongji Nianjian 2007* [China statistical yearbook 2007] (Beijing: Zhongguo Tongji Chubanshe, 2008), table 22-6 (www.stats.gov.cn/tjsj/ndsj/2008/html/W2206c.htm).

7. For example, Fu Hualing and Richard Cullen, "*Weiquan* (Rights Protection) Lawyering in an Authoritarian State: Building a Culture of Public-Interest Lawyering," *China Journal* 59 (2008): 111–27; Human Rights Watch, "*Walking on Thin Ice*": *Control, Intimidation and Harassment of Lawyers in China*, 2008 (www.hrw.org/en/reports/2008/04/28/walking-thin-ice-0); Mark O'Neill, "Legal Crusaders on the March: The Mainland Public Defenders Who Want to Reform the System," *South China Morning Post*, September 8, 2009.

8. Terence C. Halliday and Liu Sida, "Birth of a Liberal Moment? Looking through a One-Way Mirror at Lawyers' Defense of Criminal Defendants in China," in *Fighting for Political Freedom: Comparative Studies of the Legal Complex and Political Liberalism*, edited by Terence C. Halliday, Lucien Karpik, and Malcolm M. Feeley (Oxford: Hart Publishing, 2007), pp. 65–107.

9. *Zhongguo Lüshi Nianjian 2005* [China lawyer yearbook 2005] (Beijing: Renmin Fayuan Chubanshe, 2006), pp. 336–37.

10. World Values Survey, Official Data File c.20090621, 2009, World Values Survey Association (www.worldvaluessurvey.org), Aggregate File Producer (Madrid: ASEP/JDS, 2005).

11. Michael Hout, "How Class Works: Objective and Subjective Aspects of Class since the 1970s," in *Social Class: How Does It Work?* edited by Annette Laureau and Dalton Conley (New York: Russell Sage, 2008), p. 29.

12. The World Bank defines the middle class as people with annual incomes between $4,000 and $17,000 in 2005 purchase power parity, or international, dollars. "Beyond Wisteria Lane," *The Economist* 390, no. 8618 (February 14, 2009), pp. 7–13. The 2006 conversion rate was 3.462 yuan per PPP$1. International Monetary Fund, *World Economic Outlook Database, 2009*. Assuming an annual income growth rate of 11.9 percent, the World Bank's 2005 income range corresponds roughly to 20,000–90,000 yuan in 2009. See *Zhongguo Tongji Nianjian 2007*, table 9-2 (www.stats.gov.cn/tjsj/ndsj/2008/html/J0902c.htm).

13. Guo, "Farewell to Class, except the Middle Class."

14. During the period of the survey, the exchange rate averaged 6.841 yuan per $1 (www.oanda.com/convert/fxhistory).

15. *Zhongguo Lüshi Nianjian 2005*, p. 337; 2005 is the most recent year for which lawyer data disaggregated by province are available.

16. Income growth among lawyers seems to parallel income growth in the general population. If the average annual rate of income growth of 11.9 percent in China's general urban population between 2000 and 2007 corresponds to lawyers' income growth, then we should expect that Beijing lawyers' average income of 100,000 yuan in 2000 should have compounded to 275,000 yuan by 2009. Indeed, according to the 2009 CLE Survey, average income among lawyers in Beijing was 261,000 yuan. *Zhongguo Tongji Nianjian*

2007, table 9-2 (www.stats.gov.cn/tjsj/ndsj/2008/html/J0902c.htm); Ethan Michelson, "Unhooking from the State: Chinese Lawyers in Transition," Ph.D. dissertation, University of Chicago, 2003, p. 336.

17. Terence C. Halliday, "The Fight for Basic Legal Freedoms: Mobilization by the Legal Complex," in *Global Perspectives on the Rule of Law*, edited by James J. Heckman, Robert L. Nelson, Lee Cabatingan (New York: Routledge, 2010), p. 234; Lucien Karpik, "Political Lawyers," in *Fighting for Political Freedom: Comparative Studies of the Legal Complex and Political Liberalism*, edited by Terence C. Halliday, Lucien Karpik, and Malcolm M. Feeley (Oxford: Hart Publishing, 2007), pp. 463–94; Michelson, "Unhooking from the State"; Halliday and Liu, "Birth of a Liberal Moment?"

18. Ching Kwan Lee, *Against the Law: Labor Protests in China's Rustbelt and Sunbelt* (University of California Press, 2007); Elizabeth J. Perry, "Chinese Conceptions of 'Rights': From Mencius to Mao—and Now," *Perspectives on Politics* 6, no. 1 (2008): 37–50.

19. Other occupational groups include employees of foreign law firms, basic-level legal workers, employees of legal aid organizations, employees of government agencies, law teaching or research faculty, house counsel in state-owned enterprises, house counsel in foreign or private enterprises, legal consultants, police, law students, patent agents or other intellectual property workers, and employees of mass media organizations.

20. Ethan Michelson, "The Practice of Law as an Obstacle to Justice: Chinese Lawyers at Work," *Law and Society Review* 40, no. 1 (2006): 1–38.

21. Unlike income, which refers to the previous year (twelve months), client arrears refer to the respondent's entire career as a lawyer: "In the course of your career as a lawyer, roughly how much are you owed by clients who refused to pay your fee?" The mean value of client arrears is so much higher than the median because the distribution is so skewed. While almost half (46 percent) of the lawyers who supplied information reported arrears of less than 10,000 yuan, 9 percent reported arrears of at least 200,000 yuan, and 2 percent reported arrears of at least 1 million yuan.

22. Michelson, "The Practice of Law as an Obstacle to Justice," p. 11. Before the 2007 revised Law on Lawyers, individual law firms were banned; only a small number existed on a trial basis. Official statistics on law firm ownership in the time since the general prohibition on solo practice was lifted in 2007 are not yet available. The owners of individually owned law firms are not always solo practitioners. In our 2009 CLE Survey, only two lawyers indicated working alone in individually owned firms, while fifty-nine lawyers indicated that they were employed by individually owned firms.

23. Michelson, "Unhooking from the State," p. 43.

24. We are grateful to Professor Ji Weidong for generously sharing his 2007 survey data collected with the financial support of the Center for Legal Dynamics of Advanced Market Societies, Graduate School of Law, Kobe University, Japan.

25. In 2009 the modal commission rate (percent of billings kept as income) was 70 percent. Of all lawyers who reported commission-based income, 30 percent indicated this level, 15 percent reported 60 percent, and 14 percent reported 80 percent.

26. Michelson, "The Practice of Law as an Obstacle to Justice," p. 11.

27. Respondent #206901, Liaoning.

28. Ethan Michelson, "Lawyers, Political Embeddedness, and Institutional Continuity in China's Transition from Socialism," *American Journal of Sociology* 113, no. 2 (2007), p. 386.

29. The extent of lawyers' vulnerability vis-à-vis state actors appears to have remained fairly stable, and has perhaps even intensified, since 2000. In Michelson's 2000 survey, 8 percent of lawyers failed to assess at least one of these seven statements negatively; another 5 percent assessed all seven statements negatively; and 49 percent supplied negative

assessments of at least four of the seven statements. See Michelson, "Lawyers, Political Embeddedness, and Institutional Continuity in China's Transition from Socialism."

30. Ariana Eunjung Cha, "China Suspends Lawyers' Licenses: Representatives of Dissidents Are Targeted," *Washington Post*, June 28, 2009, p. 8; Peter Ford, "China Cracks Down on Human Rights Lawyers," *Christian Science Monitor*, February 25, 2009, p. 1; Louisa Lim, "Rights Lawyers in China Face Growing Threats," National Public Radio, May 3, 2009); O'Neill, "Legal Crusaders on the March"; Fu and Cullen, "*Weiquan* (Rights Protection) Lawyering in an Authoritarian State."

31. Detailed results are available from the authors upon request. None of our analyses considers regional variation because we found no obvious patterns with respect to local city-level characteristics (population, economic indicators, social indicators, and so on).

32. Weeden and Grusky, "The Case for a New Class Map."

33. Chen and Lu, "Does China's Middle Class Think and Act Democratically?"; Goldman, *From Comrade to Citizen*; Rowen, "When Will the Chinese People be Free?"; Tang, Woods, and Zhao, "The Attitudes of the Chinese Middle Class Towards Democracy."

34. Weeden and Grusky, "The Case for a New Class Map."

35. Ethan Michelson, "Gender Inequality in the Chinese Legal Profession," *Research in the Sociology of Work* 19 (2009): 337–76.

36. Halliday, "The Fight for Basic Legal Freedoms"; Terence C. Halliday and Lucien Karpik, "Politics Matter: A Comparative Theory of Lawyers in the Making of Political Liberalism," in *Lawyers and the Rise of Western Political Liberalism: Europe and North America from the Eighteenth to Twentieth Centuries*, edited by Terence C. Halliday and Lucien Karpik (Oxford: Clarendon Press, 1997), pp. 15–64; Terence C. Halliday and Lucien Karpik, "Political Lawyering," in *International Encyclopedia of the Social and Behavioral Sciences*, edited by Neil J. Smelser and Paul B. Bates (Amsterdam: Elsevier, 2001), pp. 11673–78; Terence C. Halliday, Lucien Karpik, and Malcolm M. Feeley, "The Legal Complex and Struggles for Political Liberalism," in *Fighting for Political Freedom: Comparative Studies of the Legal Complex and Political Liberalism*, edited by Terence C. Halliday, Lucien Karpik, and Malcolm M. Feeley (Oxford: Hart Publishing, 2007), pp. 1–40.

37. Quotation from Michelson, "Lawyers, Political Embeddedness, and Institutional Continuity in China's Transition from Socialism," p. 358.

38. On the relationship between lawyers and political liberalism, see Halliday, "The Fight for Basic Legal Freedoms"; Halliday and Karpik, "Politics Matter"; Halliday and Karpik, "Political Lawyering"; Halliday, Karpik, and Feeley, "The Legal Complex and Struggles for Political Liberalism."

CHAPTER FIFTEEN

Attitudes toward Democracy and the Political Behavior of China's Middle Class

JIE CHEN

According to the most recent nationwide, representative sample survey conducted by the Chinese Academy of Social Sciences, in 2000 the middle class accounted for 12 percent of the total population in China. The vice minister of foreign trade and economic cooperation, chief trade representative of the People's Republic of China (PRC), even predicted that by 2010 the size of the middle class would reach 30 percent of the population.[1] There is little doubt that the size and sociopolitical influence of the Chinese middle class will continue to grow as China continues to modernize. Facing such phenomenal emergence and expansion of the middle classes in China, political scientists and policy leaders constantly ponder two important and related questions: Do the middle classes in China support political democratization? And how do the middle class's attitudes toward democracy influence its political behavior? These questions have a lot to do with predicting the role of the middle class in political change in China.

Among scholars of the middle class and democratization, however, there seems to be no consensus on the attitudinal and behavioral orientations of China's emerging middle class toward democracy. Furthermore, almost none of the early studies on these issues are based on probability samples of middle-class individuals, samples that could provide more robust and conclusive findings regarding the middle class's orientations toward democracy. To help fill this gap, this chapter attempts to shed light on both the level of the middle class's democratic support and its behavioral consequences, based on data collected from a probability sample survey conducted in three Chinese cities in late 2006 and early 2007.

Theories of Middle-Class Support for Democracy

There is a large body of general literature on the orientation of the middle class in non-Chinese settings toward democracy and democratization. Within this literature there seem to be two distinct approaches. One tends to argue that the political orientations of the middle class result mainly from its interests and its size and strength relative to other social classes.[2] This approach suggests that once the middle class becomes the majority of the population and acquires significant economic power (and hence confidence), it will support democratization or an existing democratic system.[3] Scholars of this approach also argue that unlike individuals in the upper class (or bourgeoisie), who have abundant economic resources and close clientelist ties with political elites, those in the middle class have limited economic resources and lack connections with powerful patrons in the government.[4] Out of self-interest, therefore, the middle class supports a democratic system in which its individual rights and private (though modest) properties may best be protected from potential encroachment by the government and the upper class.[5] In addition, some of these scholars contend that those in the middle class tend to favor democracy because, compared to members of the lower class, they have the education and the leisure time to understand and participate in public affairs effectively.[6]

This approach is supported by evidence drawn mainly from studies of Western societies. These studies find that middle-class individuals do support democratic principles and do take action in support of the rise or the maintenance of a democratic system and against a nondemocratic system.[7] Yet this approach seems incapable of explaining why the middle classes in some nondemocratic developing countries are not enthusiastic about democracy and democratization even when their size and sheer economic power have become preponderant.[8]

The other approach explores the political orientations of the middle class mainly in developing countries, following Alexander Gershenkron's tradition emphasizing the vital role of the state in late-developing countries.[9] Most of these studies suggest that the state often plays a more active role in creating and shaping the middle class in the late-developing world than it did in early-industrialized countries. As Dale

Johnson points out, "In less developed societies the state tends to grow to the limits of resources that can be taxed or otherwise appropriated by government. . . . In part, this overdevelopment compensates for the presence of weak classes of local capitalists, or even their virtual non-existence: States assume entrepreneurial functions, giving birth to technocratic, managerial, and technical groupings."[10] These three groupings in fact compose the middle class. Therefore, the new middle classes in these countries are "illiberal" or "undemocratic" and generally support the authoritarian rule of the state because these middle-class individuals are dependent upon state power for their own survival and prosperity during development.[11]

This approach is supported by empirical evidence (though not representative sample studies) from late-developing countries. It has been found, for example, that middle classes in the late-developing countries of the Asia-Pacific tend to have a vested interest in the continuity and stability of authoritarian rule since they have been the main beneficiaries of state-led economic growth over the past several decades.[12] In Singapore the majority of the middle class accepts the undemocratic government as long as it continues to satisfy people's material needs.[13] In Malaysia the burgeoning middle class, especially ethnic Malays, has either actively supported an increasingly authoritarian state or remained politically apathetic.[14] In Indonesia the new middle class stood firmly on the side of the status quo.[15] In Thailand the new middle class is ambivalent toward democracy, which is also the case for the middle classes of other Southeast Asian countries.[16] Even in Taiwan and South Korea, both of which have become democratic, the new middle classes did little to stimulate democracy, their class interests being aligned with those of state elites.[17] In short, these studies support the theoretical approach that emphasizes the critical role of the states in shaping the middle class's attitudes toward democracy and democratization in late-developing countries. Thus this approach seems more suitable for analyzing the orientation of the new middle class in late-developing countries, such as China.

Research Methods: Survey Design and Middle-Class Identification

The data used in this study come from a public opinion survey conducted in three Chinese cities—Beijing, Chengdu, and Xi'an—between

December 2006 and January 2007. As the principal investigator of this research project, I collaborated with a research team from the Chinese Academy of Social Sciences (CASS) in designing the questionnaire and sample and in conducting the survey. The three cities were selected to represent three distinct levels of economic development in urban China: Beijing, Chengdu, and Xi'an represent, respectively, the most developed, the middle, and the least developed urban areas in China. The survey is based on a probability sample of urban residents of the three cities, aged eighteen years and older.[18] This probability sample was derived from a multistage sampling strategy. Three urban districts (*qu*) were randomly chosen at the first sampling stage in each city.[19] At the second sampling stage, twelve streets (*jiedao*) were randomly selected from the three districts in each city, with four streets being selected from each district.[20] From each of the twelve streets in each city, four residential communities were randomly chosen at the third stage of sampling, yielding forty-eight communities in each city. Then 1,200 households were randomly chosen from the forty-eight communities by using the technique of probability proportionate to size.[21] This process yielded 3,600 households in three cities. At the final stage, one individual was chosen randomly from each of the 3,600 households as the interviewee. The adjusted response rate of this survey was 88 percent (3,166).

This study uses occupations to identify the middle class in China. This is mainly because, in contemporary China, occupations are much easier to identify and more constant across regions than personal income, and they tend to represent "groupings that are distinct and separate from one another."[22] Moreover, compared to this occupation-based measurement, an income-based measurement of the middle class suffers from a serious drawback: it is very hard to achieve any consensus on the criterion of income when defining *middle class*, since actual personal income is hard to measure and varies dramatically by region in a fast-changing society like China.[23] Moreover, the occupation-based measure seems suitable for cross-nation comparison, since the modern occupations used in this measure are derived mainly from general trends of modernization and industrialization at the global level and hence share commonalities across countries.[24]

Consequently, I operationalized the middle class in urban China by combining three major occupational groups typically used in both Chinese and non-Chinese settings: managerial personnel, professionals, and

TABLE 15-1. Occupational Composition of the Chinese Middle Class

Occupation
Managers
The managers of state-owned, collectively owned, and privately owned enterprises; the managers of foreign and joint-venture enterprises (managers of privately owned enterprises are not their owners)
Professionals
Research, educational, and medical specialists (scientists, professors, teachers, doctors); engineers, technicians, and their assistants; economic and legal professionals (accountants, lawyers), culture and art and sports professionals; creative intellectuals (writers, musicians, consultants); other self-employed professionals
White-collar office workers
Staff members of government and party agencies; office workers and staff members of public organizations and enterprises

white-collar office workers.[25] Table 15-1 illustrates the components of each of these major occupational groups in Chinese society. Our survey results show that about 23 percent (739) of our respondents belonged to the middle class as defined by the three occupational groups.[26] Among these middle-class respondents, roughly 60 percent (441) were employed in the state apparatus.

Findings: Middle-Class Attitudes

As has been the case in other late-developing countries, China's new middle class has a dependent relationship with the state. Yet the state in China is even more effective than other late-developing countries in controlling the society and creating or shaping the new social classes, including the middle class. This is because this state still has two unique, powerful ruling pillars: the dominance of the single, Leninist party and the prerogative of the government to intervene in any socioeconomic sphere.[27] Due to the dominant role of the state in influencing the career and life opportunities of the newly rising middle class, this social class has become very dependent upon the party-state. As David Goodman points out, the Chinese middle class in general is "far from being alienated from the party-state or seeking their own political voice, and appears to be operating in close proximity and through close cooperation" with the party-state.[28] Thus the relations between the middle class and the communist state are in general positive and collaborative.

Furthermore, both the state and the middle class share fundamental interests: promotion of economic growth, protection of private property, maintenance of social stability, and restriction of mass political participation (particularly by the lower classes, who are still the majority of the population).[29] Finally, the middle class is by and large directly dependent on the state for employment and career advancement. According to some recent studies at least half of the new middle class in China is still employed in the public sector, such as government and party agencies, state-owned enterprises, and public organizations.[30] Access to these positions is subject to party membership and political loyalty to the party-state.[31]

In general, therefore, the middle class in China is not likely to be enthusiastic about democratization and democracy, because they could fundamentally and directly threaten the very survival of the party-state upon which it relies for its prosperity. Yet China's new middle class may be supportive of those individual rights that are less politically sensitive but mainly socioeconomic (such as private property and social mobility), since these rights are closely related to its own material interests as well as tolerated by the party-state. As An Chen argues, China's middle class may "expect a system of checks and balances that could effectively constrain party power" to infringe on their own economic and social interests.[32]

Furthermore, I suspect that in general the middle class might be even less enthusiastic than other classes about democracy, since the middle class has apparently benefited more from state-led reforms and has had a closer and more cooperative relationship with the state.[33] To explore this possibility, I compare the middle class's and the nonmiddle classes' democratic support.

Drawing on studies in both Chinese and non-Chinese settings, I operationalize support for democracy as positive attitudes toward a set of democratic norms and institutions.[34] The democratic supporter, according to James Gibson's synthesis of writings on democratic support, is "the one who believes in individual liberty and who is politically tolerant, who holds a certain amount of distrust of political authority but at the same time is trustful of fellow citizens, who is obedient but nonetheless willing to assert rights against the state, who views the state as constrained by legality, and who supports basic democratic institutions and processes."[35] In this study I measure this kind of support among our respondents by tapping into their attitudes toward three democratic norms—rights consciousness, valuation of political liberty, and popular

TABLE 15-2. Rights Consciousness, by Class, China

Percent

| Right | Believe that right ought to always be respected | |
	Middle class[a]	Other classes[b]
Right to work	94.0	93.6
Right to education and training	94.6	94.5
Freedom of information	93.1	94.2
Right to privacy of personal correspondence, telephone conversations, and so on	93.2	94.2
Right to travel abroad	91.1	90.2
Right to reside anywhere in the country	81.9	82.9
Religious liberty and Freedom of conscience	85.9	85.8

a. $N = 739$.
b. $N = 2,330$.

participation—and one fundamental democratic institution, the popular and competitive election of political leaders. While these norms and the institution do not exhaust all possible democratic principles, I believe they do represent the core of democracy and hence serve as a good test of democratic support among our respondents.

Rights Consciousness

Rights consciousness is the degree to which citizens are willing to assert individual rights for themselves. According to the scholars James Gibson, Raymond Duch, and Kent Tedin, "to the extent that citizens are vigilant about their rights, democracy tends to flourish."[36] Moreover, in China belief in individual rights is an especially important and sensible indicator of democratic values, since China's traditional culture is said to work against this democratic norm. Chinese traditional culture is thought to value collective (or group) interests and government authority over individual rights.[37]

To detect the strength of rights consciousness within the middle class relative to other classes, I asked our respondents to indicate whether a series of rights ought always to be protected or whether protection depends on the circumstances. The responses of the Chinese middle class are shown alongside those of other classes in table 15-2.

Like nonmiddle-class respondents, over 90 percent of middle-class respondents believe that individual rights—such as the right to work, to education, to free information, to privacy of personal correspondence, and to travel abroad—should always be protected. Moreover, over 80 percent of our respondents thought that individual rights such as the right to reside anywhere in the country and the right to worship freely ought to be protected. These findings suggest that, like the nonmiddle classes, the Chinese middle class is very eager to protect individual rights.

Valuation of Political Liberty

There are at least two distinct propositions on the valuation of political freedom by citizens in transitional societies, such as the former Soviet Union and the PRC. On the one hand, a group of scholars who studied such valuation in the former Soviet Union assume that "democracies require citizenries committed to liberty even when there is a prospect for disorder."[38] When designing instruments to measure the level of mass support for democracy in the former Soviet Union, therefore, they hypothesize that respondents who support democracy as a set of political institutions and principles should choose liberty over order. Moreover, Gibson suggests that even within a political culture that has a "penchant for order" (such as the Soviet political culture), democratic supporters should be more likely to choose liberty over order.[39] In short, this theoretical approach seems to suggest that the preference for political liberty over order is almost unconditionally positively related to support for democratic institutions and principles.

On the other hand, emphasizing the uniqueness of Chinese political culture, some analysts suggest that the Chinese conceptualize and prioritize certain democratic principles quite differently from their counterparts in some other societies, especially the West.[40] Specifically, in terms of the relationship between social order and democracy, as Andrew Nathan points out, Chinese political culture tends to assume that "democracy should be conducive to social harmony [or order]."[41] Moreover, Chinese political culture emphasizes social order and collective interests over individual rights and liberty. As Lucian Pye puts it, most Chinese "accept completely the need for order."[42] Certain findings from earlier survey studies of urban China also support this proposition.[43] In addition to this cultural explanation, material interests could also prompt the Chinese middle class to favor social order over democratization or democracy. This is because these interests—including

TABLE 15-3. Valuation of Political Freedom (versus Order), by Class, China

Percent

	Disagree with statement	
Statement	Middle class[a]	Other classes[b]
In general demonstrations should not be allowed because they frequently become disorderly and disruptive.	22.9	35.6[c]
The harmony of the community will be disrupted if people form their organizations outside the government.	23.5	37.4[c]

a. $N = 739$.
b. $N = 2,330$.
c. Difference significant at the .05 level.

professional mobility, employment stability, and a moderate level of private property—could be harmed by social disorder in a society where the majority of the population remains relatively poor. As a China scholar points out, it would make sense for the Chinese middle class to resist democracy if democracy might bring about chaos and cause social upheavals that could harm its self-interests.[44]

To explore these two propositions, I fashioned questions that postulate a conflict between political freedom and social order. Table 15-3 reports the responses of the Chinese middle class versus other members of society in three cities. Overall, the numbers in this table show that support for political freedom among the Chinese middle class is not strong in either absolute or relative terms. Only about 23 percent of middle-class respondents support the idea that a public demonstration as an expression of political freedom should be allowed even though it could turn disorderly and disruptive, whereas about 36 percent of nonmiddle-class respondents are in favor of the idea. Similarly, only 24 percent of middle-class respondents think that citizens should be able to form their own organizations outside the government even if the harmony of the community were disrupted, while a higher percentage (37 percent) of nonmiddle-class people share such a thought. These findings suggest that even though the Chinese middle class has become vigilant about its own rights, it still favors social order over political freedom. These findings apparently support one of the two propositions mentioned above: that is, when political freedom is pitted against social order, the Chinese middle class decisively chooses the latter.

TABLE 15-4. Support for Participatory Norms, by Class, China

Percent

	Disagree with statement	
Statement	Middle class[a]	Other classes[b]
Government leaders are like the head of a family; we should all follow their decisions and don't need to participate in government decisionmaking.	24.9	33.7[c]
Measures to promote political reform should be initiated by the party and government, not by ordinary people (laobaixing) like me.	28.1	40.1[c]

a. N = 739.
b. N = 2,330.
c. Difference significant at the .05 level.

Support for Participatory Norm

Another important democratic value is support for popular participation.[45] As many democracy scholars point out, democracy is a system wherein the people of a society control the government. In a democratic society, political power originates from the people living in this society and is delegated by the people to the government.[46] Thus those who support democracy must be willing to participate in politics in order to exercise such popular power. In China support for the participatory norm is an extremely critical indicator of democratic values, because there is said to be no native tradition of popular influence on the government. It is suggested that the political culture of China is rooted in Confucianism, which emphasizes deference to authority and grants a sage with the "mandate of heaven" to rule the country.[47] In our survey I include two items to measure support for this participatory norm. While one relates to citizens' participation in government decisionmaking in general, the other is about their role in initiating major political change. The frequency distribution of the two items is reported in table 15-4.

The results clearly indicate that support for the participatory norm is quite weak among our middle-class respondents in both absolute and relative terms. Only one-fourth of middle-class respondents (25 percent) are in favor of participating in the government's decisionmaking process, and less than one-third (28 percent) believe that ordinary people should have a role in initiating political reform. On the other hand, nonmiddle-class respondents scored higher than middle-class respondents on both questions. These findings suggest that the Chinese middle class is not supportive of this participatory norm, which is considered one of the most important democratic principles.

Support for Competitive Elections

Most scholars of democracy consider competitive, multicandidacy elections among independent political organizations to be imperative for a functioning democratic system.[48] They believe that only through such an institutionalized process can a government be established that is based on popular sovereignty and that serves the common good. As Joseph Schumpeter points out, democracy is an "institutional arrangement for arriving at political decisions in which individuals acquire the power to decide by means of a competitive struggle for the people's vote."[49] Therefore, a belief in competitive elections is an essential component of democratic values and one that democratic supporters must acquire in the transition from a nondemocratic regime to a democratic regime.[50]

The support for competitive elections is of particular interest in Chinese society. This is because a fully competitive election (a multicandidate and multiparty election) of government leaders has never happened in mainland China, at least since 1949. Furthermore, as some China analysts point out, "it is even more relevant to tap into the level of support for competitive elections in China, since Chinese political culture has been deemed inherently non-democratic."[51]

To measure levels of support for competitive elections, I employ two items in the three-city survey. One refers to the multicandidate election of government leaders at various levels (*geji*) in general, while the other relates to competition among political parties in elections. The results are reported in table 15-5.

About the same percentage (70 percent) of both middle-class and nonmiddle-class respondents supports multicandidate elections for government leaders. But respondents from the middle class had a lower level (25 percent) of support for multiparty competition than nonmiddle-class respondents (39 percent). These findings suggest that most middle-class respondents support the competitive, multicandidate election of leaders under the condition that these elections are not "among several parties." Because the Chinese Communist Party (CCP) has always dominated and controlled elections at almost all levels and the several so-called democratic parties have served in consultative roles, at best, rejection of

TABLE 15-5. Support for Competitive Election, by Class, China

Percent

	Agreement or disagreement with statement	
Statement	Middle class[a]	Other classes[b]
Government officials at various levels should be selected by multicandidate elections.	69.9 agree	71.2 agree
Competition among several parties in election of government leaders should not be allowed.	24.9 disagree	38.7 disagree[c]

a. $N = 739$.
b. $N = 2,330$.
c. Difference significant at the .05 level.

multiparty competition seems to imply consent to the current system of one-party dominance.

Thus far I implicitly argue that these four sets of attitudes toward democratic values and institutions are part of a more general belief system. I expect that the scales in these sets are themselves intercorrelated. To explore this expectation, I formed an additive index for each of the four sets and then ran a confirmatory factor analysis among them within the group of middle-class respondents.[52] The results from the factor analysis show that only a single dominant factor emerged from among these four sets, accounting for 56 percent of the original variance (figure 15-1).[53] Three of the four sets load strongly on this factor, and the remaining set has a moderate loading. The set of questions about support for participatory norms has the highest loading (.740). The sets for valuation of political freedom (.715) and support for competitive election (.649) also contribute substantially to the factor of democratic support. The set of questions on rights consciousness has a moderate loading (.427). A possible explanation for such a moderate loading could be that the results of this set of questions lacked variance: as reported earlier, almost 90 percent of the middle-class respondents in our sample believe that the individual rights listed in the questionnaire ought to be always respected and protected.

Based on these findings from the factor analysis, I conclude that there is a reasonable amount of coherence among the attitudes of the Chinese middle class toward these democratic values and institutions. In other

FIGURE 15-1. Middle-Class Support for Democratic Values and Institutions

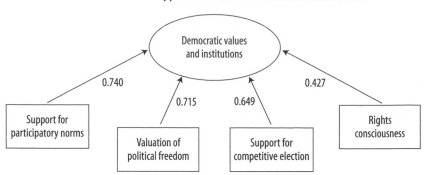

words, those who support one democratic value tend also to support other democratic values. Given such coherence, the factor score from this factor analysis is used as the collective indicator of democratic support in the analysis that follows.

Findings: Middle-Class Behavior

Thus far we have focused on the attitudes of China's middle class toward democracy and democratization. Do these attitudes significantly influence the middle class's political behavior or political participation in today's China? If so, how? The answers to these questions have direct implications for the prospects of democratic change in China as well as the likely trajectory of the current regime.

Major Forms and Intensity of Political Participation

Since the outset of post-Mao economic and political reforms in the late 1970s more and more ordinary citizens, including those in the middle class, have reportedly participated in public affairs and politics in both urban and rural areas of China, even though China's political system has never been democratic, especially by Western standards.[54] To understand the impact of the middle class's attitudes toward democracy on its political participation, I first assess the major forms of the middle class's political participation and their extent.

The questionnaire posed seven questions concerning the respondents' political participation (table 15-6). To identify major clusters or

T A B L E   1 5 - 6 . Factor Analysis of Participation Items, Middle Class, China[a]

Item	Election participation	Contacting and petitioning
Petitioning government individually	.746	
Petitioning government collectively	.716	
Contacting party or government officials	.685	
Contacting representatives of local people's congress	.620	.348
Voting in CRC election		.813
Participating in CRC nomination		.653
Voting in local people's congress election		.581

a. Figures are factor loadings of .25 or larger from the varimax rotated matrix for all factors with eigenvalues greater than 1.0.

categories of political participation, I ran an exploratory factor analysis of all seven items, using the sample of middle-class respondents.[55] As the table shows, two major factors emerged from the factor analysis, each of which deals with a category of political participation: election participation and contacting or petitioning. Election participation includes voting in elections of community residents' committees (CRCs) and local people's congresses and participating in the nomination of candidates for CRCs. The category of contacting/petitioning consists of contacting party or government officials, contacting representatives of local people's congresses, and petitioning the government at various levels collectively and individually. These two factors together explain over half (57.3 percent) of the variance among the seven items. While the contacting/petitioning category explains 31.2 percent of the variance, the election participation category explains 16.2 percent of the variance. The factor scores for these two categories are used as the indexes of the two categories of political participation in the analysis that follows.

There are two major reasons to choose these two categories of political participation for this study. One is that although the two do not exhaust all of the political acts conducted by the Chinese middle class, they are the most common.[56] Thus they are most likely to represent the fundamental trends of the middle class's political participation. The other reason is that these acts are "legitimate in China, at least in theory" (though certainly not risk free), so questions about these acts were "unlikely to make respondents give interviewers false answers."[57] Consequently, the responses to the questions in these two categories are expected to be truthful.

TABLE 15-7. Frequency of Political Participation, Middle Class, China

Item	Number	Percent[a]
Election participation		
Voting in local people's congress election	410	60.47
Voting in CRC election	115	16.96
Participating in CRC nomination	31	4.57
Contacting and petitioning		
Contacting party or government officials	25	3.69
Contacting representatives of local People's Congress	20	2.95
Petitioning government collectively	15	2.21
Petitioning government individually	7	1.03

a. Percentages represent positive (yes) responses. $N = 736$.

Table 15-7 shows the frequency of each of the seven political acts in the two categories of political participation. In the election category, voting in the elections for local people's congresses was most commonly engaged in by middle-class respondents. Over 60 percent of these respondents voted in the most recent elections of local people's congresses. By contrast, voting in CRC elections was lower (17 percent), and participating in CRC nominations was the lowest (5 percent).

In the contacting/petitioning category, the act of contacting party or government officials and representatives of local people's congresses was undertaken more frequently by the middle-class respondents in our sample than were the remaining two participatory forms (petitioning the government collectively and petitioning the government individually). Specifically, within the past year, 3–4 percent of respondents contacted party or government officials or representatives of people's congresses, while only 1–2 percent petitioned the government individually or collectively.

Impact of Democratic Support on Political Participation

In this study I assume that middle-class attitudes toward democracy and democratization may variably influence the two categories of middle-class political participation. Such a difference in the impact of democratic support between the two behavioral categories mainly results from the distinct natures of the two categories.

In terms of the impact of attitudinal support for democracy on electoral behavior in China, there are at least two distinct views. One argues that people's attitudes toward democracy and democratization have a positive effect on participation in government-sanctioned elections, such as the election of local people's congresses.[58] In other words, this view holds that those who support democratic values and institutions tend to engage in such elections in post-Mao China. It also suggests that the semidemocratic (versus totalitarian or nondemocratic) electoral system in China provides citizens with limited yet genuine opportunities to express their opinions and exert influence.

The other view contends that attitudinal support for democracy has either a negative impact or no impact on formal and conventional forms of participation, such as voting in local people's congress elections.[59] According to this view, all of these formal and conventional channels of participation are firmly controlled by the party, and such tight control in turn alienates democratic believers. Consequently, those who support democratic values and institutions tend to see the formal and conventional channel as a formality, which "serves only the function of legitimizing the non-democratic, one-Party rule."[60] As such, democratic supporters either ignore these channels or boycott them in protest of one-party rule.

From the contending views described above, one can derive two competing hypotheses concerning the impacts of democratic support on the middle class's participation through formal electoral channels, such as the election of local people's congresses and CRCs. The first is that those members of the middle class who support democratic principles and institutions are less likely to participate in those elections, because these democratic supporters consider the elections nondemocratic. The other hypothesis states that democratic supporters tend to participate in these elections because elections provide opportunities for political change. In the analysis that follows, I test these two competing hypotheses against my survey's sample of the middle-class respondents.

Similarly, there are also two contending views about the role of democratic support in shaping contacting/petitioning activities in nondemocratic settings. One view is that democratic supporters are not likely to contact government officials or petition governments because they regard officials and governments as the products of a nondemocratic political system.[61] The other view suggests that those who support democratic values and principles may engage in contacting/petitioning activities in a nondemocratic system, as they consider officials to be viable channels for making incremental changes and expressing their opinions.[62] Based on these two views, two competing hypotheses can be developed: members of the middle class who support democratic values and institutions are either likely to contact officials and petition governments at various levels or they are not likely to.

To test these two sets of competing hypotheses, I ran two multiple regression models (OLS) using the sample of middle-class respondents from this survey.[63] One model is for election participation; the other is for contacting/petitioning activities (table 15-8). In each of these models, I also include three categories of sociodemographic attributes as control variables in order to ascertain whether the middle class's attitudes toward democracy independently influence its political behavior. These three categories are affiliation with the state apparatus, key sociodemographic attributes, and local socioeconomic conditions.

Overall, the two regression models indicate that attitudinal orientations toward democratic values and institutions—the independent variable in both models—significantly and negatively affect the middle class's participation in elections (model 1), but significantly and positively influence the middle class's involvement in contacting and petitioning activities (model 2). The impact of democratic support on both kinds of political behavior is independent of the control variables. In other words, those in the middle class who strongly support democratic values and institutions are not likely to participate in elections for local people's congresses and CRCs but are at the same time likely to contact government officials and government institutions individually or collectively.

These findings appear to support two of the four hypotheses mentioned above. The first is that those who support democratic values and institutions tend to see the formal and conventional channels—such as local elections for people's congresses and CRCs—as a formality. Democratic supporters thus either ignore these channels or boycott them in protest of one-party rule. The other hypothesis substantiated by the findings is that those who support democracy (it should be stated, as a caveat, that the number of these democratic supporters in the survey is small) may engage in contacting/petitioning activities in a nondemocratic system, as they consider governments and individual officials at various levels—instead of the formal political procedures, such as local elections—to be meaningful channels through which to make incremental changes and express their opinions.

TABLE 15-8. Multiple Regression (OLS) of Political Participation by Democratic Support, Middle Class, China[a]

Estimated coefficient

Variable	Electoral category (model 1)[b]	Contacting/petitioning category (model 2)[c]
Democratic support[d]	−.080*	0.110**
	(.041)	(0.043)
Employment in the state apparatus[e]	.077*	−0.080*
	(.048)	(0.043)
Sex[f]	−.006	−0.027
	(.076)	(0.079)
Age	.018**	0.061*
	(.004)	(0.005)
Education[g]	−.038	0.064
	(.047)	(0.050)
Household gross income[h]	−.115	--0.170**
	(.074)	(0.077)
Party membership[i]	.231**	0.093
	(.094)	(0.107)
Location[j]		
Beijing	.432**	0.156
	(.102)	(0.107)
Chengdu	.603**	0.174
	(.111)	(0.116)
Summary statistic		
Constant	.295	1.102
	(.768)	(0.803)
R^2	.261	.256
Adjusted R^2	.248	.238
N	678	678

*$p < .05$, ** $p < .01$

a. Standard errors are in parentheses.

b. The value of electoral participation is the factor score of three items: participation in RC election, participation in RC nomination, and participation in local people's congress election.

c. The value of contacting or petitioning is the factor score of six items: individual *shangfang*, collective *shangfang*, contacting party or government officials, contacting representatives of local people's congress, contacting mass media, and working with others to solve community issues.

d. The value of support for democratic values and institutions is the factor score of the four dimensions: support for participatory norm, valuation of political liberty (versus order), support for competitive election, and rights consciousness.

e. The state apparatus includes government and party agencies, state-owned enterprises, and public organizations. Employment in the state apparatus = 1; employment outside of the state apparatus = 0.

f. Male = 0; female = 1.

g. Middle school and below = 1, high school = 2, postsecondary professional training = 3, four-year university education = 4, graduate school = 5.

h. Household income = natural log (gross household income).

i. Nonparty member = 0, party member = 1.

j. Xi'an is set as a reference group.

Among the sociodemographic attributes (control variables), employment in the state apparatus has a positive impact on election participation but exerts a negative impact on involvement in contacting/petitioning activities. These results suggest that those employed in the state apparatus are likely to participate in government-sanctioned elections, such as those for local people's congresses and for CRCs, and are unlikely to contact officials (outside of their own government agencies or state-owned enterprises) and petition governments.

The variables sex and education do not meaningfully influence either of the two categories of political action. However, age, income, and party membership variably affect both or one of the two categories. Specifically, the older the respondents are the more likely they are to participate in activities in both categories. Income does not significantly affect behavior in elections, but it does significantly, and negatively, influence involvement in contacting/petitioning activities. Those who have higher incomes are much less likely to contact officials and to petition governments at various levels. Moreover, party membership has a significant, and positive, impact on participation in elections, but it does not have a significant impact on contacting/petitioning activities.

Finally, the results are mixed when it comes to the impact of local socioeconomic conditions on political behavior. As indicated in table 15-8, those who live in more developed areas (Beijing and Chengdu) are more likely to vote in local elections than those who live in a less developed area (Xi'an). But location of residence is not significantly associated with the middle class's contacting/petitioning activities.

Discussion and Conclusion

What are the attitudes of China's new middle class toward democracy? How do these attitudes affect the middle class's political behavior? The findings presented throughout this chapter attempt to shed light on these two questions. In terms of the middle class's attitudes toward democratic values and institutions, I find that while most members of this new middle class are in favor of the individual rights that are typically hailed and protected in a democratic system, they shun certain political liberties—such as the freedom to demonstrate and to form organizations—and are not interested in certain democratic institutions, such as the fully competitive, multiparty election of leaders, nor are they enthusiastic about participating in government affairs and politics.

It should be noted that this study's empirical findings concerning the level of democratic support among the middle class may not be generalized directly to China in its entirety, as they are derived from a survey of three major cities. Nonetheless, these findings can help us to establish some needed statistical baselines about the level of democratic support within China's middle class, against which findings from other areas of the country can be compared. These baseline statistics will prove especially relevant for subsequent studies of political attitudes of the middle class in urban areas at the three levels of economic development under observation.

As for the impact of the middle class's attitudes toward democracy on its political behavior, I find that while those who strongly support democratic values and institutions tend to stay away from the voting booth in elections for local people's congresses and CRCs, they do tend to engage in activities such as contacting individual officials and petitioning governments at various levels. In other words, although most members of the middle class in China do not seem to support democracy, as mentioned above, those who support democracy tend to ignore local elections in favor of engaging directly in contacting/petitioning activities.

What are the political implications of these findings? First of all, the findings suggest that China's middle class is not likely to serve as an agent of democratization. This is not only because most members of the class do not seem to support most of the basic democratic norms and institutions investigated in this study but also because the middle class as a whole seems to be even less democratically oriented than other classes. Nonetheless, the middle class's current attitudes toward democracy and democratization may change as its relationship with (or dependence on) the state alters. It is because China's middle class relies heavily on the authoritarian state for its survival and prosperity that this class is currently "undemocratic." Following the same reasoning, however, the middle class may become enthusiastic about democracy and democratization if this class's dependence on the state is significantly weakened. It can be said, therefore, that a further expansion of the private sector—which may not only increase the size of the middle class but, more important, may pull more members of that class from the orbit of the state—would increase the middle class's support for democracy.

Second, but more critically, the findings imply that the formal political institutions in China—such as the election of local people's congresses and CRCs—do not seem to provide the middle class's democratic supporters with desirable channels to express their political preferences. On the other hand, these democratic supporters, while representing a minority of the middle class, find the informal political channels—such as contacting officials and petitioning governments individually or collectively—to be more meaningful ways to register their views and demands. Consequently, one may conclude that while the formal channels of political participation tend to solicit support for the current political system but to discourage the demand for democratic change from the middle class in contemporary China, the informal channels tend to facilitate a democratic tendency among the middle class. An increase in participation in the informal channels by the middle class, therefore, may presage a larger role for the middle class as the agent of democratic change in China in the near future.

Notes

1. Lu Xueyi, ed., *Dangdai zhongguo shehui jieceng yanjiu baogao* [Research report on contemporary China's social classes] (Beijing: Shehuikexue wenxian chubanshe, 2002); see also Zhou Xiaohong, *Zhongguo zhongchan jieceng diaocha* [Survey of the Chinese middle class] (Beijing: Shehuikexue wenxian chubaneshe, 2005), p. 1.

2. Seymour M. Lipset, "Some Social Requisites of Democracy: Economic Development and Political Legitimacy," *American Political Science Review* 53 (1959): 69–105; Seymour M. Lipset, *Political Man: The Social Bases of Politics* (Johns Hopkins University Press, 1981); Gregory M. Luebbert, *Liberalism, Fascism, or Social Democracy: Social Classes and the Political Origins of Regimes in Interwar Europe* (Oxford University Press, 1991); Norman H. Nie, G. Bingham Powell, and Kenneth Prewitt, "Social Structure and Political Participation: Developmental Relationships, Part I and II," *American Political Science Review* 63 (1969): 361–78, 808–32; Dietrich Rueschemeyer, Evelyne Huber Stephens, and John D. Stephens, *Capitalist Development and Democracy* (University of Chicago Press, 1992).

3. Lipset, "Some Social Requisites of Democracy"; Seymour M. Lipset, "Stratification: Social Class," in *International Encyclopedia of the Social Science*, vol. 15 (New York: Collier Macmillan, 1968), pp. 296–316; Luebbert, *Liberalism, Fascism, or Social Democracy*.

4. Rueschemeyer, Stephens, and Stephens, *Capitalist Development and Democracy*.

5. Ronald M. Glassman, *The Middle Class and Democracy in Socio-Historical Perspective* (Leiden, the Netherlands: E. J. Brill, 1995); Ronald M. Glassman, *The New Middle Class and Democracy in Global Perspective* (New York: St. Martin's Press, 1997).

6. C. Wright Mills, *White Collar: The American Middle Classes* (Oxford University Press, 1953); Robert E. Lane, *Political Life: Why People Get Involved in Politics* (Glencoe, Ill.: Free Press, 1959).

7. Heinz Eulau, "Identification with Class and Political Perspective," *Journal of Politics* 18 (1956): 232–53; Heinz Eulau, "Identification with Class and Political Role Behavior," *Public Opinion Quarterly* 20 (1958): 515–29; Lipset, "Some Social Requisites of Democracy"; Lipset, *Political Man*; Nie, Powell, and Prewitt, "Social Structure and Political Participation"; Lester W. Milbrath, *Political Participation: How and Why Do People Get Involved in Politics?* 2nd ed. (Chicago: Rand McNally College Publishing Company,

1977); Glassman, *The Middle Class and Democracy in Socio-Historical Perspective*; Glassman, *The New Middle Class and Democracy in Global Perspective*; Katherine Cramer Walsh, M. Kent Jennings, and Laura Stoke, "The Effects of Social Class Identification on Participatory Orientations towards Government," *British Journal of Political Science* 34 (2004): 469–95.

8. Peng Er Lam, "Singapore: Rich State, Illiberal Regime," in *Driven by Growth: Political Change in the Asia-Pacific Region*, edited by James W. Morley (New York: M. E. Sharpe, 1999), pp. 255–74; Garry Rodan, "The Growth of Singapore's Middle Class and Its Political Significance," in *Singapore Changes Guard: Social, Political, and Economic Directions in the 1990s*, edited by Garry Rodan (Melbourne: Longman Cheshire, 1993), pp. 52–71.

9. Alexander Gershenkron, *Economic Backwardness in Historical Perspective: A Book of Essays* (Harvard University Press, 1962).

10. Dale L. Johnson, "Class and Social Development: Toward a Comparative and Historical Social Science," in *Middle Classes in Dependent Countries*, edited by Dale L. Johnson (Beverly Hills: Sage, 1985), p. 15.

11. Daniel A. Bell, "After the Tsunami: Will Economic Crisis Bring Democracy to Asia?" *New Republic* 218, no. 10 (1998): 22–25; David Brown and David Martin Jones, "Growth and Democracy in Southeast Asia," *Comparative Politics* 30 (1995): 355–75; Neil A. Englehart, "Democracy and the Thai Middle Class," *Asian Survey* 43 (2003): 253–79; Johnson, "Class and Social Development"; David Martin Jones, "Democratization, Civil Society, and Illiberal Middle Class Culture in Pacific Asia," *Comparative Politics* 30 (1998): 147–69.

12. Bell, "After the Tsunami."

13. Lam, "Singapore"; Rodan, "The Growth of Singapore's Middle Class."

14. Bell, "After the Tsunami"; Jones, "Democratization, Civil Society, and Illiberal Middle Class Culture"; Takashi Torii, "The Mechanism for State-Led Creation of Malaysia's Middle Class," *Developing Economies* 41 (2003): 221–42.

15. Bell, "After the Tsunami"; Jones, "Democratization, Civil Society, and Illiberal Middle Class Culture."

16. Englehart, "Democracy and the Thai Middle Class."

17. Brown and Jones, "Growth and Democracy in Southeast Asia"; Jones, "Democratization, Civil Society, and Illiberal Middle Class Culture."

18. In a probability sample each member of a certain population should have an equal chance of selection set by the sampling procedure. For more detailed definition of probability sample, see Floyd D. Fowler, *Survey Research Methods* (Beverly Hills: Sage, 1988).

19. In Beijing the three districts are Dongcheng, Haidian, and Chaoyang. In Chengdu the three districts are Qingyang, Chenghua, and Wuhou. In Xi'an the three districts are Lianhu, Xincheng, and Beilin.

20. According to our agreement with the officials of the streets selected in the sample, the names of these streets must remain confidential.

21. At this stage, we obtained the household registration list of each community from the street office in which the community is located.

22. Martin Oppenheimer, *White Collar Politics* (New York: Monthly Review Press, 1985), p. 7.

23. There tends to be a huge gap between reported (or nominal) incomes and actual incomes in many occupational groups in China; the latter is often kept secret for various purposes, such as tax evasion (which is highly prevalent in China). For more detailed information about the gap between actual and nominal incomes in contemporary China, see Jie Chen, *Popular Political Support* (Stanford University Press, 2004), pp. 89–92. In addition, there are large differences in personal income among regions. For example, the average

monthly income of residents in developed East China is 2.5 times higher than the average of those in underdeveloped West China. See Li Chunling, "Zhongguo dangdai zhongchan jieceng de goucheng ji bili" [The composition and size of China's contemporary middle class], *Zhongguo renkou kexue* [Chinese population science] 6 (2003): 25–32.

24. Alan Marsh and Max Kaase, "Background of Political Action," in *Political Action: Mass Participation in Five Western Democracies*, edited by Samuel H. Barnes and others (Beverley Hills: Sage, 1979), pp. 97–136.

25. For the use of this occupation-based measure in identifying the middle class in the Western settings, see Robert Erikson and John H. Goldthorpe, *The Constant Flux: A Study of Class Mobility in Industrial Societies* (Oxford University Press, 1992); Glassman, *The Middle Class and Democracy in Socio-Historical Perspective*; Erik Olin Wright, *Class Counts: Comparative Studies in Class Analysis* (Cambridge University Press,1997). In the Pacific Asian settings, see Tamio Hattori, Tsuruyo Funatsu, and Takashi Torii, "Introduction: The Emergence of the Asian Middle Classes and Their Characteristics," *Developing Economies* 41 (2003): 129–39; Hsin-Huang Hsiao and Alvin Y. So, "The Making of the East Asian Middle Classes: The Five Propositions," in *East Asian Middle Classes in Comparative Perspective*, edited by Hsin-Huang Michael Hsiao (Taipei: Institute of Ethnology, Academia Sinica, 1999), pp. 3–49. In the Chinese settings, see Lu, ed. *Dangdai zhongguo shehui jieceng yanjiu baogao*; Lu Xueyi, ed., *Dangdai zhongguo shehui liudong* [Social mobility in contemporary China] (Beijing: Shehuikexue wenxian chubanshe, 2004); Zhang Wei, *Chongtu yu bianshu: Zhongguo shehui zhongjian jieceng zhengzhi fenxi* [Conflict and uncertainty: political analysis of the middle stratum in Chinese society] (Beijing: Shehuikexue wenxian chubanshe, 2005).

26. Our figure is higher than Lu Xueyi and his associates' result (15 percent) (see Lu, *Dangdai zhongguo shehui liudong*, p. 5). There are two important reasons for such a difference. One is that our result is based on three major cities (Beijing, Cheng'du, and Xi'an), which tend to have more middle-class individuals than rural areas. Yet Lu and his associates' result is based on the national survey that includes both rural and urban areas. The other reason is the time difference between Lu and his associates' and our surveys: their survey was conducted in 2001, while ours was conducted in 2006 and 2007. The size of the middle class might have increased between 2001 and 2006.

27. Andrew G. Walder, ed. *The Waning of the Communist State: Economic Origins of Political Decline in China and Hungary* (University of California Press, 1995).

28. David G. Goodman, "The New Middle Class," in *The Paradox of China's Post-Mao Reforms*, edited by Merle Goldman and Roderick MacFarquhar (Harvard University Press, 1999), pp. 260–61.

29. An Chen, "Capitalist Development, Entrepreneurial Class, and Democratization in China," *Political Science Quarterly* 117, no. 3 (2002): 401–22; Goodman, "The New Middle Class"; Gongqin Xiao, "The Rise of the Technocrats," *Journal of Democracy* 14 (2003): 59–65.

30. Zheng Hangsheng and Li Lulu, *Dangdai zhongguo chengshi shehui jiegou* [Social structure of the cities in contemporary China] (Beijing: Zhongguo renmin daxue chubanshe, 2004).

31. Zhang, *Chongtu yu bianshu*; Zheng and Li, *Dangdai zhongguo chengshi shehui jiegou*.

32. Chen, "Capitalist Development, Entrepreneurial Class, and Democratization in China," p. 416.

33. I pooled the rest of our sample together (excluding the private entrepreneurs of mid- and large-size firms and ranking government officials who account for only about 3 percent of the sample) to form a nonmiddle-class category. This category accounted for 73 percent of our sample, which included blue-collar industrial workers (skilled and

nonskilled) in state-owned, collectively owned, and privately owned enterprises; blue-collar employees in all types of service sector; the self-employed (*getihu*) with very little capital; the unemployed, underemployed, and retirees; and college students. The nonmiddle-class category is compared with middle-class respondents in terms of their democratic support. I conducted a series of one-tailed *t* tests to compare level of support of the middle class and that of private entrepreneurs. The results indicate that there is virtually no difference in the levels of democratic support between these two groups.

34. Gabriel Almond and Sidney Verba, *The Civic Culture: Political Attitudes and Democracy in Five Nations* (Princeton University Press, 1963); Robert A. Dahl, *Polyarchy: Participation and Opposition* (Yale University Press, 1971); Samuel P. Huntington, *The Third Wave: Democratization in the Late Twentieth Century* (University of Oklahoma Press, 1991); James L. Gibson, "The Resilience of Mass Support for Democratic Institutions and Processes in Nascent Russian and Ukrainian Democracies," in *Political Culture and Civil Society in Russia and the New States of Eurasia*, edited by Vladimir Tismaneanu (Armonk, N.Y.: M. E. Sharpe, 1995), pp. 53–111; Jie Chen and Yang Zhong, "Valuation of Individual Liberty versus Social Order among Democratic Supporters: A Cross-Validation," *Political Research Quarterly* 53 (2000): 427–39.

35. Gibson, "The Resilience of Mass Support for Democratic Institutions," pp. 55–56.

36. James L. Gibson, Raymond M. Duch, and Kent L. Tedin, "Democratic Values and the Transformation of the Soviet Union," *Journal of Politics* 54 (1992): 343.

37. Lucian W. Pye, *The Spirit of Chinese Politics* (Harvard University Press, 1992).

38. Gibson, Duch, and Tedin, "Democratic Values and the Transformation of the Soviet Union," p. 341.

39. Gibson, "The Resilience of Mass Support for Democratic Institutions," p. 80; Gibson, Duch, and Tedin, "Democratic Values and the Transformation of the Soviet Union"; James L. Gibson and Raymond M. Duch, "Emerging Democratic Values in Soviet Political Culture," in *Public Opinion and Regime Change*, edited by Arther H. Miller, William M. Reisinger, and Vicki L. Hesli (Boulder, Colo.: Westview Press, 1993), pp. 69–94.

40. Andrew J. Nathan, *China's Crisis: Dilemma of Reform and Prospects for Democracy* (Columbia University Press, 1990); Andrew J. Nathan, *China's Transition* (Columbia University Press, 1997); Robert Scalapino, "Current Trends and Future Prospects," *Journal of Democracy* 9 (1998): 35–40.

41. Nathan, *China's Transition*, p. 204.

42. Pye, *The Spirit of Chinese Politics*, p. 123.

43. Chen and Zhong, "Valuation of Individual Liberty versus Social Order among Democratic Supporters."

44. Xiao, "The Rise of the Technocrats," p. 62.

45. Almond and Verba, *The Civic Culture*.

46. Dahl, *Polyarchy*; John Locke, *Two Treatises of Government* (Cambridge University Press, 1967); Roy C. Macridis, *Contemporary Political Ideologies: Movements and Regimes* (New York: Harper Collins, 1992), chap. 2.

47. Pye, *The Spirit of Chinese Politics*.

48. Joseph A. Schumpeter, *Capitalism, Socialism, and Democracy* (New York: Harper, 1947); Dahl, *Polyarchy*; Huntington, *The Third Wave*.

49. Schumpeter, *Capitalism, Socialism, and Democracy*, p. 269.

50. Gibson, Duch, and Tedin, "Democratic Values and the Transformation of the Soviet Union."

51. Jie Chen and Yang Zhong, "Defining the Political System of Post-Deng China: Emerging Public Support for a Democratic Political System," *Problems of Post-Communism* 45 (1998), p. 32.

52. An additive index was formed for each of the four sets.

53. The eigenvalue of the first extracted factor is 2.66. The eigenvalue of the second factor is 0.95. $N = 739$.

54. Wenfang Tang and William L. Parish, *Chinese Urban Life under Reform: The Changing Social Contract* (Cambridge University Press, 2000); Jie Chen and Yang Zhong, "Why Do People Vote in Semicompetitive Election in China?" *Journal of Politics* 64 (2002): 178–97; Yang Zhong and Jie Chen, "To Vote or Not to Vote: An Analysis of Peasants' Participation in Chinese Village Elections," *Comparative Political Studies* 35 (2002): 686–712; Chen, *Popular Political Support.*

55. The exploratory factor analysis here is the statistical technique used to identify the underlying structure of the collection of all seven participation items.

56. Melanie Manion, "The Electoral Connection in the Chinese Countryside," *American Political Science Review* 90 (1996): 736–48; Tianjian Shi, *Political Participation in Beijing* (Harvard University Press, 1997); M. Kent Jennings, "Political Participation in the Chinese Countryside," *American Political Science Review* 91 (1997): 361–72; Tang and Parish, *Chinese Urban Life under Reform*; Chen, *Popular Political Support.*

57. Shi, *Political Participation in Beijing*, p. 27.

58. Tianjian Shi, "Voting and Nonvoting in China: Voting Behavior in Plebiscitary and Limited-Choice Elections," *Journal of Politics* 61 (1999): 1115–39; Tianjian Shi, "Village Committee Elections in China: Institutionalist Tactics for Democracy," *World Politics* 51 (1999): 385–412.

59. Jie Chen, "Subjective Motivation for Mass Political Participation in Urban China," *Social Science Quarterly* 81 (2000): 645–62; Chen and Zhong, "Valuation of Individual Liberty versus Social Order among Democratic Supporters"; Zhong and Chen, "To Vote or Not to Vote."

60. Zhong and Chen, "To Vote or Not to Vote," p. 185.

61. Chen, "Subjective Motivation for Mass Political Participation in Urban China."

62. Donna Bahry and Brian D. Silver, "Soviet Citizen Participation on the Eve of Democratization," *American Political Science Review* 48 (1990): 836.

63. Since the purpose of this part of the chapter is to study the impacts of the middle class's democratic values on its own political behavior, I run this regression model within the middle-class category.

Bibliography

English

Anagnost, Ann. "From 'Class' to 'Social Strata': Grasping the Social Totality in Reform-Era China." *Third World Quarterly* 29, no. 3 (2008): 497–519.

Barlow, James, and others. *Property, Bureaucracy, and Culture: Middle-Class Formation in Contemporary Britain*. London: Routledge, 1995.

Bergére, Marie-Claire. "'The Other China': Shanghai from 1919 to 1949." In *Shanghai: Revolution and Development in an Asian Metropolis*, edited by Christopher Howe, pp. 1–34. Cambridge University Press, 1981.

———. *The Golden Age of the Chinese Bourgeoisie, 1911–1937*. Translated by Janet Lloyd. Cambridge University Press, 1989.

Bhalla, Surji. *The Middle Class Kingdoms of India and China*. Washington: Peterson Institute for International Economics, 2010.

Bian Yanjie. "Chinese Social Stratification and Social Mobility." *Annual Review of Sociology* 28 (2002): 91–116.

Bian Yanjie and John Logan. "Market Transition and the Persistence of Power: The Changing Stratification System in Urban China." *American Sociological Review* 61 (1996): 738–58.

Bian Yanjie and Lu Hanlong. "Economic Reform and Socioeconomic Inequality: Status Perceptions in Shanghai." In *In Search of a Chinese Road Towards Modernization*, edited by Hu Jixuan and others, pp. 109–42. Lampetyer, Cerdigion, U.K.: Edwin Mellen Press, 1996.

Bian Yanjie and Zhang Lei. "Sociology in China." *Contexts* 7, no. 3 (2008): 20–25.

Bian Yanjie and others. "Occupation, Class, and Networks in Urban China." *Social Forces* 83, no. 4 (2005): 1443–68.

Birdsall, Nancy, Carol Graham, and Stefano Pettinato. "Stuck in the Tunnel: Is Globalization Muddling the Middle Class?" Working Paper 14. Center on Social and Economic Dynamics. Brookings, 2000.

Bourdieu, Pierre. *Distinction: A Social Critique of the Judgment of Taste.* Harvard University Press, 1984.

Bray, David. *Social Space and Governance in Urban China: The Danwei System from Origins to Reform.* Stanford University Press, 2005.

Buckley, Christopher. "How a Revolution Becomes a Dinner Party: Stratification, Mobility, and the New Rich in Urban China." In *Culture and Privilege in Capitalist Asia,* edited by M. Pinches, pp. 208–29. London: Routledge, 1999.

Butler, Tim, and Mike Savage, eds. *Social Change and the Middle Classes.* London: UCL Press, 1995.

Cai Yongshun. "China's Moderate Middle Class: The Case of Homeowners' Resistance." *Asian Survey* 45, no. 5 (2005): 777–99.

Chamberlain, Heath B. "On the Search for Civil Society in China." *Modern China* 19, no. 2 (1993): 199–215.

Chao, Lindam, and Ramon H. Myers. "China's Consumer Revolution: The 1990s and Beyond." *Journal of Contemporary China* 7, no. 18 (1998): 351–68.

Chen, An. "Capitalist Development, Entrepreneurial Class, and Democratization in China." *Political Science Quarterly* 117, no. 3 (2002): 401–22.

Chen Jie and Bruce J. Dickson. *Allies of the State: China's Private Entrepreneurs and Democratic Change.* Harvard University Press, 2010.

Chen Jie and Lu Chunlong. "Does China's Middle Class Think and Act Democratically? Attitudinal and Behavioral Orientations toward Urban Self-Government." *Journal of Chinese Political Science* 11, no. 2 (2006): 1–20.

Chen Jie and and Yang Zhong. "Valuation of Individual Liberty versus Social Order among Democratic Supporters: A Cross-Validation." *Political Research Quarterly* 53 (2000): 427–39.

Clammer, John. "Globalization, Class, Consumption, and Civil Society in Southeast Asian Cities." *Urban Studies* 40, no. 2 (2003): 403–19.

Cleveland, John W. "Does the New Middle Class Lead Today's Social Movements?" *Critical Sociology* 29, no. 2 (2003): 163–88.

Cui Zhiyuan. "A Petite Bourgeoisie Manifesto." In *The Chinese Model of Modern Development,* edited by Tian Yucao. New York: Routledge, 2005.

Davis, Deborah, ed. *Consumer Revolution in Urban China.* University of California Press, 2000.

———. "Urban Consumer Culture." *China Quarterly* 183 (September 2005): 677–94.

———. "Urban Chinese Homeowners as Citizen-Consumers." In *The Ambivalent Consumer,* edited by Sheldon Garon and Patricia Maclachlan, pp. 281–99. Cornell University Press, 2006.

Davis, Deborah, and Feng Wang, eds.. *Creating Wealth and Poverty in Post Socialist China*. Stanford University Press, 2008.

Dickson, Bruce J. *Red Capitalists in China: The Party, Private Entrepreneurs, and Prospects for Political Change*. Cambridge University Press, 2003.

———. *Wealth into Power: The Communist Party's Embrace of China's Private Sector*. Cambridge University Press, 2008.

Durkheim, Emile. *The Division of Labor in Society*. New York: Free Press, 1964.

Englehart, Neil A. "Democracy and the Thai Middle Class." *Asian Survey* 43 (2003): 253–79.

Farrell, Diana, Ulrich A. Gersch, and Elizabeth Stephenson. "The Value of China's Emerging Middle Class." *McKinsey Quarterly*, special issue, "Serving the New Chinese Consumer." 2006.

Fernandez, Leela, and Patrick Heller. "Hegemonic Aspiration: New Middle-Class Politics and India's Democracy in Comparative Perspective." *Critical Asian Studies* 38, no. 4 (2006): 495–522.

Finnemore, Martha. *National Interest in International Society*. Cornell University Press, 1996.

Finnemore, Martha, and Kathryn Sikkink. "International Norm Dynamics and Political Change." *International Organization* 52, no. 4 (1998): 887–917.

Fu Hualing and Richard Cullen. "*Weiquan* (Rights Protection) Lawyering in an Authoritarian State: Building a Culture of Public-Interest Lawyering." *China Journal* 59 (2008): 111–27.

Gallagher, Mary E. "'Reform and Openness': Why China's Economic Reforms Have Delayed Democracy." *World Politics* 54, no. 3 (2002): 338–72.

Giddens, Anthony. *The Class Structure of Advanced Societies*. New York: Harper Collins, 1975.

———. *The Consequences of Modernity*. Stanford University Press, 1990.

Gilbert, Dennis. *The American Class Structure in an Age of Growing Inequality*. Belmont, Calif.: Wadsworth, 2002.

Gilley, Bruce, and Larry Diamond, eds. *Political Change in China with Comparisons with Taiwan*. Boulder, Colo.: Lynne Rienner, 2008.

Glassman, Ronald M. *The Middle Class and Democracy in Socio-Historical Perspective*. Leiden, the Netherlands: E. J. Brill, 1995.

———. *The New Middle Class and Democracy in Global Perspective*. New York: Macmillan, 1997.

Goldthrope, John H. *Social Mobility and Class Structure in Modern Britain*. Oxford, U.K.: Clarendon Press, 1987.

Goodman, David S. G. "The New Middle Class." In *The Paradox of China's Post-Mao Reform*, edited by Merle Goldman and Roderick MacFarquhar. Harvard University Press, 1999.

———, ed. *The New Rich in China: Future Rulers, Present Lives*. New York: Routledge, 2008.

Gries, Peter Hays, and Stanley Rosen, eds. *Chinese Politics: State, Society, and the Market*. New York: Routledge, 2010.

Guo Yingjie. "Farewell to Class, except the Middle Class: The Politics of Class Analysis in Contemporary China." *Asia-Pacific Journal* 26, no. 2 (2009).

Halliday, Terence C., and Liu Sida. "Birth of a Liberal Moment? Looking through a One-Way Mirror at Lawyers' Defense of Criminal Defendants in China." In *Fighting for Political Freedom: Comparative Studies of the Legal Complex and Political Liberalism*, edited by Terence C. Halliday, Lucien Karpik, and Malcolm M. Feeley, pp. 65–107. Oxford, U.K.: Hart Publishing, 2007.

Hattori, Tamio, Tsuruyo Funatsu, and Takashi Torii. "Introduction: The Emergence of the Asian Middle Classes and Their Characteristics." *Developing Economies* 41 (2003).

Hong Zhaohui. "Mapping the Evolution and Transformation of the New Private Entrepreneurs in China." *Journal of Chinese Political Science* 9, no. 1 (2004): 23–42.

Hsiao, Hsin-Huang Michael, ed. *Discovery of the Middle Classes in East Asia*. Taipei: Academia Sinica, 1993.

———. *East Asian Middle Classes in Comparative Perspective*. Taipei: Academia Sinica, 1999.

———, ed. *Exploration of the Middle Classes in Southeast Asia*. Taipei: Academia Sinica, 2001.

———, ed. *The Changing Faces of the Middle Classes in Asia-Pacific*. Taipei: Academia Sinica, 2006.

Hsiao, Hsin-Huang Michael, and Hagen Koo, "The Middle Classes and Democratization." In *Consolidating the Third Wave Democracies*, edited by Larry Diamond and others. Johns Hopkins University Press, 1997.

Jones, David Martin. "Democratization, Civil Society, and Illiberal Middle Class Culture in Pacific Asia." *Comparative Politics* 30 (1998): 147–69.

Howell, Jude, ed. *Governance in China*. Lanham, Md.: Rowman and Littlefield, 2004.

Huang Yasheng. *Capitalism with Chinese Characteristics: Entrepreneurship and the State*. Cambridge University Press, 2008.

Huntington, Samuel. *Political Order in Changing Socie*ties. Yale University Press, 1968.

———. *The Third Wave: Democratization in the Late Twentieth Century*. University of Oklahoma Press, 1993.

Iriye, Akira. *Cultural Internationalism and World Order*. Johns Hopkins University Press, 1997.

Jaffrelot, Christophe, and Peter van der Veer, eds. *Patterns of Middle-Class Consumption in India and China*. Los Angeles: Sage, 2008.

Johnston, Alastair Iain. "Chinese Middle-Class Attitudes toward International Affairs: Nascent Liberalization?" *China Quarterly* 179 (September 2004): 603–28.

Katzenstein, Peter. *The Culture of National Security: Norms and Identity in World Politics.* Columbia University Press, 1996.

Kennedy, Scott. *The Business of Lobbying in China.* Harvard University Press, 2005.

Kerbo, Harold R. *Social Stratification and Inequality: Class Conflict in Historical and Comparative Perspective.* New York: McGraw-Hill, 1991.

Kharas, Homi, Laurence Chandy, and Geoffrey Gertz, eds. *The Four-Speed World.* Brookings, 2010.

Koo, Hagen. "The Social and Political Character of the Korean Middle Class." In *Discovery of the Middle Classes in East Asia,* edited by Hsin-Huang Michael Hsiao. Taipei: Academia Sinica, 1993.

Lee, Ching Kwan. *Against the Law: Labor Protests in China's Rustbelt and Sunbelt.* University of California Press, 2007.

Li Cheng. "'Credentialism' versus 'Entrepreneurism': The Interplay and Tensions between Technocrats and Entrepreneurs in the Reform Era." In *Chinese Business Networks: State, Economy, and Culture,* edited by Chan Kwok Bun, pp. 86–111. New York: Prentice Hall, 1999.

———. "Diversification of Chinese Entrepreneurs and Cultural Pluralism in the Reform Era." In *Chinese Political Culture, 1989–2000,* edited by Shiping Hua, pp. 219–45. Armonk, N.Y.: M. E. Sharpe, 2001.

———, ed. *Bridging Minds across the Pacific: U.S.-China Educational Exchanges, 1978–2003.* Lanham, Md.: Lexington Books, 2005.

———. "Introduction: Making Democracy Safe for China." In *Democracy Is a Good Thing: Essays on Politics, Society and Culture in Contemporary China,* edited by in Yu Keping, pp. xvii–xxxi. Brookings, 2009.

———. *Rediscovering China: Dynamics and Dilemmas of Reform.* Lanham, Md.: Rowman and Littlefield, 1997.

———. "Rediscovering Urban Subcultures: Contrast between Shanghai and Beijing." *China Journal* 36 (July 1996): 139–53.

Li Cheng and Jordan Lee. "Obama's China Trip: Forging Middle Class Ties." *China Brief* 9, no. 20 (October 2009): 4–6.

Li He. "Middle Class: Friends or Foes to Chinese Leadership?" *Journal of Chinese Political Science* 8, nos. 1, 2 (2003): 87–100.

———. "Returned Students and Political Change in China." *Asian Perspective* 30, no. 2 (2006).

Li Jian and Niu Xiaoha. "The New Middle Class(es) in Peking: A Case Study." *China Perspectives* 45 (2003): 4–20.

Li Jun. "Fostering Citizenship in China's Move from Elite to Mass Higher Education: An Analysis of Students' Political Socialization and Civic Participation." *International Journal of Educational Development* 29 (2009): 382–98.

Lin Jing. *Social Transformation and Private Education in China.* New York: Praeger, 1999.

————. "Educational Stratification and the New Middle Class in China." In *Education and Social Change in China: Inequality in a Market Economy*, edited by Gerard Postiglione, pp. 179–98. Armonk, N.Y.: M. E. Sharp, 2006.

Lipset, Seymour Martin. *Political Man: The Social Bases of Politics*. Garden City, N.J.: Anchor Books, 1963.

————. "Some Social Requisites of Democracy: Economic Development and Political Legitimacy." *American Political Science Review* 53, no. 1 (1959): 69–105.

Logan, John, and Bian Yanjie. "Inequalities in Access of Community Resource in Chinese Cities." *Social Force* 72 (1993): 555–76.

Luebbert, Gregory M. *Liberalism, Fascism, or Social Democracy: Social Classes and the Political Origins of Regimes in Interwar Europe*. Oxford University Press, 1991.

Maurer-Fazio, Margaret. "Earnings and Education in China's Transition to a Market Economy." *China Economic Review* 1 (1999).

Michelson, Ethan. "Unhooking from the State: Chinese Lawyers in Transition." Ph.D. dissertation, University of Chicago, 2003.

————. "The Practice of Law as an Obstacle to Justice: Chinese Lawyers at Work." *Law and Society Review* 40, no. 1 (2006): 1–38.

————."Lawyers, Political Embeddedness, and Institutional Continuity in China's Transition from Socialism." *American Journal of Sociology* 113, no. 2 (2007).

Mills, C. Wright. *White Collar: The American Middle Classes*. Oxford University Press, 1951.

Moore, Barrington, Jr. *The Social Origins of Dictatorship and Democracy: Lord and Peasant in the Making of the Modern World*. Boston: Beacon Press, 1966.

Nan Lin and Xie Wen. "Occupational Prestige in Urban China." *American Journal of Sociology* 93, no. 4 (1988): 793–832.

Nee, Victor. "A Theory of Market Transition: From Redistribution to Market in State Socialism."*American Sociological Review* 54 (1989): 663–81.

————. "The Emergence of a Market Society: Changing Mechanisms of Stratification in China." *American Journal of Sociology* 101 (1996): 908–48.

Nie, Norman H., G. Bingham Powell, and Kenneth Prewitt. "Social Structure and Political Participation: Developmental Relationships." *American Political Science Review* 63 (1969): 361–378, 808–32.

Ninkovich, Frank A., and Bu Liping, eds. *The Cultural Turn: Essays in the History of U.S. Foreign Relations*. Chicago: Imprint Publications, 2001.

Norris, Pippa, ed. *Critical Citizens: Global Support for Democratic Government*. Oxford University Press, 1999.

Nye, Joseph S. *Soft Power: The Means to Success in World Politics*. New York: Public Affairs, 2004.

Ong, Aihwa. *Flexible Citizenship: The Cultural Logics of Transnationality*. Duke University Press, 1999.

Oppenheimer, Martin. "The Political Missions of the Middle Strata." In *Class and Social Development: A New Theory of the Middle Class*, edited by Dale Johnson, pp. 109–32. London: Sage, 1982.

Parish, William L. "Destratification in China." In *Class and Social Stratification in Post-Revolution China*, edited by J. Watson. Cambridge University Press, 1984.

Parker, Richard. *The Myth of the Middle Class*. New York: Harpers, 1972.

Parkin, Frank. *Marxism and Class Theory: A Bourgeois Critique*. Columbia University Press, 1979.

Parsons, Talcott. *The Social System*. New York: Free Press, 1951.

Pearson, Margaret M. *China's New Business Elite: The Political Consequences of Economic Reform*. University of California Press, 1997.

Peerenboom, Randall. *China Modernizes: Threat to the West or Model for the Rest?* Oxford University Press, 2007.

Perry, Elizabeth J. "Chinese Conceptions of 'Rights': From Mencius to Mao—and Now." *Perspectives on Politics* 6, no. 1 (2008): 37–50.

———. "A New Rights Consciousness?" *Journal of Democracy* 20, no. 3 (2009): 17–20.

Pilbeam, Pamela M. *The Middle Classes in Europe, 1789–1914: France, German, Italy, and Russia*. London: Macmillan, 1990.

Polanyi, Karl. *The Great Transformation: The Political and Economic Origins of Our Time*. Boston: Beacon Press, 1944.

Pow, Choon-Piew. *Gated Communities in China: Class Privilege and the Moral Politics of a Good Life*. London: Routledge, 2009.

Read, Benjamin L. "Democratizing the Neighborhood? New Private Housing and Homeowner Self-Organization in Urban China." *China Journal* 49 (2003): 31–59.

———. "Assessing Variation in Civil Society Organizations." *Comparative Political Studies* 41, no. 9 (2008): 1240–65.

Rodan, Garry. "The Growth of Singapore's Middle Class and Its Political Significance." In *Singapore Changes Guard: Social, Political, and Economic Directions in the 1990s*, edited by Garry Rodan, pp. 52–71. Melbourne: Longman Cheshire, 1993.

Rona-Tas, Akos. "The First Shall Be Last? Entrepreneurship and Communist Cadre in the Transition from Socialism." *American Journal of Sociology* 100 (1994): 40–69.

Saich, Tony. "Citizens' Perceptions of Governance in Rural and Urban China." *Journal of Chinese Political Science* 12, no. 1 (2007): 1–28.

Sautman, Barry. "Sirens of the Strongman: Neo-Authoritarianism in Recent Chinese Political Theory." *China Quarterly*, no. 129 (March 1992): 72–102.

Schultz, Theodore W. "Capital Formation by Education." *Journal of Political Economy* 68 (1960).

Schumpeter, Joseph A. *Capitalism, Socialism, and Democracy*. New York: Harper, 1947.

Shi Tianjian. "China: Democratic Values Supporting an Authoritarian System." In *How East Asians View Democracy*, edited by Yun-han Chu and others. Columbia University Press, 2008.

Smail, John. *The Origins of Middle-Class Culture: Halifax, Yorkshire, 1660–1780*. Cornell University Press, 1994.

Solinger, Dorothy J. "Urban Entrepreneurs and the State: The Merger of State and Society." In *State and Society in China: The Consequences of Reform*, edited by A. L. Rosenbaum, pp. 121–41. Boulder, Colo.: Westview Press, 1992.

Steinfeld, Edward. *Playing Our Game: Why China's Rise Doesn't Threaten the West*. Oxford University Press, 2010.

Szelényi, Ivan. "Social Inequalities in State Socialist Redistributive Economies." *International Journal of Comparative Sociology* 19 (1978): 63–68.

Szelényi, Ivan, and Eric Kostello. "The Market Transition Debate: Toward a Synthesis?" *American Journal of Sociology* 101 (1996): 1082–96.

Tang Min, Dwayne Woods, and Zhao Jujun. "The Attitudes of the Chinese Middle Class Toward Democracy." *Journal of Chinese Political Science* 14 (2009): 81–95.

Tang Wenfang. *Public Opinion and Political Change in China*. Stanford University Press, 2005.

Tang Wenfang and William L. Parish. *Chinese Urban Life under Reform: The Changing Social Contract*. Cambridge University Press, 2000.

Thompson, William, and Joseph Hickey. *Society in Focus: An Introduction to Sociology*. 5th ed. Boston: Pearson, Allyn, and Bacon, 2005.

Tomba, Luigi. "Creating an Urban Middle Class: Social Engineering in Beijing." *China Journal* 51 (2004): 1–26.

Torii, Takashi. "The Mechanism for State-Led Creation of Malaysia's Middle Class." *Developing Economies* 41 (2003): 221–42.

Tsai, Kellee S. *Capitalism without Democracy: The Private Sector in Contemporary China*. Cornell University Press, 2007.

Varma, Pavan K. *The Great Indian Middle Class*. New Delhi: Viking, 1998.

Vidich, Arthur J. *The New Middle Class: Life-Style, Status Claims, and Political Orientation*. London: Macmillan, 1995.

Vogel, Ezra F. *Japan's New Middle Class; The Salary Man and His Family in a Tokyo Suburb*. University of California Press, 1963.

Walder, Andrew G. "Sociological Dimensions of China's Economic Transition: Organization, Stratification, and Social Mobility." Stanford: Shorenstein Asia/Pacific Research Center, 2003.

Wang Jing. "Bourgeois Bohemian in China? Neo-Tribes and the Urban Imaginery." *China Quarterly* 185 (2005): 532–48.

Wang Jun and Stephen Siu Yu Lau. "Gentrification and Shanghai's New Middle

Class: Another Reflection on the Cultural Consumption Thesis." *Cities* 26, no. 2 (2009): 57–66.

Wang Xin. "Seeking Channels for Engagement: Media Use and Political Communication by China's Rising Middle Class." *China: An International Journal* 7, no. 1 (2009): 31–56.

Wang Yaping. "Housing Reform and Its Impacts on the Urban Poor in China." *Housing Studies* 15, no. 6 (2000): 845–64.

Wang Yaping and Alan Murie. "Commercial Housing Development in Urban China." *Urban Studies* 36, no. 9 (1999): 1475–94.

———. *Housing Policy and Practices in China*. New York: St. Martin's Press, 1999.

Wang Zhengxu. "Public Support for Democracy in China." *Journal of Contemporary China* 16, no. 53 (November 2007): 561–63.

Weber, Max. "Class, Status, and Party." In *Class, Status, and Power: Social Stratification in Comparative Perspective*, edited by Beinhard Bendix and Seymour Lipset. New York: Free Press, 1966.

———. *Economy and Society: An Outline of Interpretive Sociology*, 2 vols. University of California Press, 1978.

Wendt, Alexander. *Social Theory of International Politics*. Cambridge University Press, 1999.

Whyte, Martin K. "Urban China: A Civil Society in the Making?" In *State and Society in China: The Consequences of Reform*, edited by Arthur Lewis Rosenbaum, pp. 77–101. Boulder, Colo.: Westview Press, 1992.

Wilson, Dominic, and Raluca Dragusanu. "The Expanding Middle: The Exploding World Middle Class and Falling Global Inequality." Global Economics Paper 170. New York: Goldman Sachs, 2008.

World Bank. *Governance, Investment Climate, and Harmonious Society: Competitiveness Enhancements for 120 Cities in China*. Washington: 2006.

———. *From Poor Areas to Poor People: China's Evolving Poverty Reduction Agenda*. Washington: 2009.

———. *World Development Indicators 2009*. Washington: 2009.

Wright, Erik Olin. *Classes*. London: Verso, 1985.

———. *Class Counts: Comparative Studies in Class Analysis*. Cambridge University Press, 1997.

Yang Guobin. *The Power of the Internet in China: Citizen Activism Online*. Columbia University Press, 2009.

Yu Keping. *Democracy Is a Good Thing: Essays on Politics, Society, and Culture in Contemporary China*. Brookings, 2009.

Zunz, Olivier, ed. *Social Contracts under Stress: The Middle Classes of America, Europe, and Japan at the Turn of the Century*. New York: Russell Sage, 2004.

Zweig, David. *Internationalizing China: Domestic Interests and Global Linkages*. Cornell University Press, 2002.

Chinese

Ao Daiya. *Siying qiyezhu jieceng de zhengzhi canyu* [Political participation of private entrepreneurs]. Zhongshan University Press, 2005.

Bao Yaming. *Youdangzhe de quanli xiaofei shehui yu dushi wenhua yanjiu* [The right of a flaneur: consumer society and urban cultural studies]. Renmin University Press, 2004.

Bao Zonghao and Hu Yishen. *Wenhua: guoji dadushi de linghun* [Culture: the spirit of metropolis]. Shanghai: Shanghai shehui kexueyuan chubanshe, 2004.

Bian Yanjie, Wu Xiaogang, and Li Lulu. *Shehui fenceng yu liudong: guowai xuezhe dui Zhongguo yanjiu de xinjinzhan* [Social stratification and mobility: overseas scholar's advanced research on China]. Beijing: Zhongguo renmin daxue chubanshe, 2008.

Cao Shichao. *Diyi jingzhengli: Chengjiu shijie yiliu de wenhua zhanlue* [The first competitive power: strategy for achieving a world-class culture]. Shanghai: Shanghai wenhua chubanshe, 2003.

Chen Guanzhong, Liao Weitang, and Yan Jun. *Boximiya Zhongguo* [Bohemian China]. Guilin: Guangxi shifan daxue chubanshe, 2004.

Chen Shuhong. *Zhongguo zhongjian jieceng jiaoyu yu chengjiu dongji* [China's middle-income stratum: education and motivation]. Beijing: Zhongguo dabaike quanshu chubanshe, 2007.

Chen Xinnian. *Zhongdeng shouruzhe lun* [Middle-income stratum]. Beijing: Zhongguo jihua chubanshe, 2005.

Chen Yiping. *Fenhua yu zuhe: Zhongguo zhongchanjieceng yanjiu* [Separation and coherence: a study of China's middle class]. Guangzhou: Guangdong renmin chubanshe, 2005.

Dongfang zaobao. *Shanghai zhongchan quanjing baogao* [Shanghai middle-class landscape]. Shanghai: Shanghai shehui kuxue chubanshe, 2004.

Fan Lizhu, ed. *Quanqiuhua xia de shehuibianqian yu fei zhengfuzuzhi (NGO)* [Social transformation and NGOs in the age of globalization]. Shanghai: Shanghai renmin chubanshe, 2003.

Fang Ning, Wang Bingquan, and Ma Lijun. *Chengzhang de Zhongguo: Dangdai zhongguo qingnian de guojia minzu yishi yanjiu* [Growing China: a study of Chinese youths' consciousness of state and nation]. Beijing: Renmin chubanshe, 2002.

Fu Chonglan, Chen Guangting, and Dong Liming, eds. *Zhongguo chengshi fazhan wenti baogao* [Report on China's urban development]. Beijing: Zhongguo shehuikexue chubanshe, 2003.

Gan Yang and Li Meng. *Zhongguo daxue gaige zhi dao* [The road of reform for China's universities]. Shanghai: Shanghai renmin chubanshe, 2003.

Guo Dingping. *Shanghai zhili yu minzhu* [Governance and democracy in Shanghai]. Chongqing: Chongqing chubanshe, 2005.

Hu Lianhe and Hu Angang. "Zhongchan jieceng: Wendingqi haishi xiangfan huo qita" [Middle stratum: a stabilizer, a disrupter, or something else]. *Zhengzhixue yanjiu* [Political science studies] 2 (May 2008).

Jiang Shan. *Zhongchan luxiantu* [A road map to become middle class]. Wuhan: Changjiang chubanshe, 2004.

Li Chunling. "Zhongguo dangdai zhongchan jieceng de goucheng ji bili" [The composition and size of China's contemporary middle class]. *Zhongguo renkou kexue* [Chinese population science] 6 (2003): 25–32.

———. *Duanlie yu suipian: Dangdai Zhongguo shehuijieceng fenhua shizheng fenxi* [Cleavage and fragment: an empirical analysis of social stratification in contemporary China]. Beijing: Shehuikexue wenxian chubanshe, 2005.

———. "Zhongguo zhongchan jieji yanjiu de dongli yu quxiang" [The motives and trends of studying China's middle class]. In *Hexie shehui yu shehui jianshe* [Harmonous society and social development], edited by Fang Xiangxin. Beijing: Shehuikexue wenxian chubanshe, 2008.

———, ed. *Bijiao shiyexia de zhongchan jieji xingcheng: guocheng, yingxiang yiji shehui jingji houguo* [Formation of the middle class in comparative perspective: process, influence, and socioeconomic consequences]. Beijing: Social Sciences Academic Press, 2009.

Li Chunling and Lu Peng. *Shehui fenceng lilun* [Theories of social stratification]. Beijing: Zhongguo shehuikexue chubanshe, 2008.

Li Chunling and Wang Boqing. "Zhongguo daxuesheng jiuye yu gongzi shuiping diaocha baogao" [Survey on employment and wage levels of college graduates]. In *2009 nian Zhongguo shehui xingshi fenxi yu yuce* [China in 2009: analysis and forecasts], edited by Ru Xin, Lu Xueyi, and Li Peilin. Beijing: Social Sciences Academic Press, 2009.

Li Lulu. *Zhuanxing shehuizhong de siying qiyezhu* [Private entrepreneurs in transitional society]. People's University Press, 1998.

———. *Zhongguo de danwei zuzhi: Quanli, ziyuan yu jiaohuan* [China's danwei: power, resources, and exchanges]. Hangzhou: Zhejiang Renmin Chubanshe, 2000.

———. "Zhongjian jieceng de shehui gongneng: xin de wenti quxiang he duowei fenxi kuangjia" [The social function of the middle class: the new question-oriented approach and multidimensional analysis framework]. *Journal of Renmin University* 4 (April 2008).

Li Lulu and Li Sheng. "Shutu yilei: Dandai Zhongguo chengzhen zhongchan jieji de leixing fengxi" [Different approaches and different types: a typological analysis of the middle class in Chinese cities and towns]. *Shehuixue yanjiu* [Sociology studies] 22, no. 6 (2007): 15–37.

Li Lulu and Wang Yu. "Dangdai Zhongguo zhongjian jieceng de shehui cunzai: Jieceng renzhi yu zhengzhi yishi" [The social existence of the middle stratum in contemporary China: strata recognition and political consciousness]. *Shehuikexue zhanxian* [Social sciences frontline], no. 10 (2008): 202–15.

Li Peilin. *Ling yizhi kanbujian de shou: Shehui jiegou zhuanxing* [Another invisible hand: the transformation of social structure]. Beijing: Shehuikexue wenxian chubanshe, 2005.

Li Peilin, Li Qiang, and Sun Liping. *Zhongguo shehui fenxing* [Social stratification in China today]. Beijing: Shehuikexue wenxian chubanshe, 2004.

Li Peilin and Zhang Yi. "Zhongguo zhongchan jieji de guimo, rentong, he shehui taidu" [The scale, recognition, and attitudes of China's middle class]. In *Daguoce tongxiang Zhongguo zhilu de Zhongguo minzhu: Zengliang shi minzhu* [The strategy of a great power: incremental democracy and a Chinese-style democracy], edited by Tang Jin, pp. 188–99. Beijing: Renmin chubanshe, 2009.

Li Peilin and others. *Shehui chongtu yu jieji yishi:dangdai Zhongguo shehui maodun wenti yanjiu* [Social conflicts and class consciousness in present-day China]. Beijing: Shehuikexue wenxian chubanshe, 2005.

———. *Zhongguo shehuihexie wending baogao* [Social harmony and stability in China today]. Beijing: Social Sciences Academic Press, 2008.

Li Qiang. *Zhuanxing shiqi Zhongguo shehui fenxi* [Chinese social stratification in the transition period]. Shenyang: Liaoning jiaoyu chubanshe, 2004.

———. "Guanyu zhongchan jieji de lilun yu xianzhuang" [Theories and status assessment of the middle class]. *Shehui* [Society], no. 1 (2005).

Li Youmei. *Zhongguo shehui shenghuo de bianqian* [The transformation of Chinese social life]. Beijing: Zhongguo dabaike quanshu chubanshe, 2008.

Li Youmei, Liu Yuzhao, and Zhang Huxiang. *Shanghai shehuijiegou bianqian shiwu nian* [Social structural changes in Shanghai during the past fifteen years]. Shanghai: Shanghai daxue chubanshe, 2008.

Liu Xin. *Shichang zhuanxing yu shehui fenceng* [Market transition and social stratification]. Shanghai: Shanghai Renmin Chubanshe, 2005.

Lu Hanlong. *Shehui jianshe yu shehui zhili* [Social constructions and social governance]. Beijing: Shehuikexue wenxian chubanshe, 2005.

———. *Zhuanbian zhong de Shanghai shimin* [Shanghai citizens in transition]. Shanghai: Shanghai Shehuikexueyuan chubanshe, 2008.

Lu Xueyi. *Dangdai Zhongguo shehuijieceng yanjiu baogao: Zhongguo shehuijieceng congshu* [Research report on social strata in contemporary China]. Beijing: Shehuikexue wenxian chubanshe, 2002.

———. *Dangdai Zhongguo shehui liudong* [Social mobility in contemporary China]. Beijing: Shehuikexue wenxian chubanshe, 2004.

———. *Dangdai Zhongguo shehui jiegou* [Social structure of contemporary China]. Beijing: Shehuikexue wenxian chubanshe, 2010.

Lu Xueyi and others. "Woguo siyou qiye de jingying zhuangkuang yu siyou qiyezhu de qunti tezheng" [Operational conditions of private enterprises in China and group characteristics of private entrepreneurs]. *Zhongguo shehuikexue* [Social sciences in China], no. 4 (1994).

Ni Pengfei and others, eds. *Zhonguo chengshi jingzhengli baogao* [Annual report on urban competitiveness], no. 3. Beijing: Shehuikexue wenxian chubanshe, 2005.

Pan Wei and Ma Ya. *Jujiao dangdai Zhongguo jiazhiguan* [Focusing on contemporary Chinese values]. Beijing: Shenghuo dushu xinzhi sanlian shudian, 2008.

Ru Xin and others. *Erlinglingba nian Zhongguo shehui xingshi fenxi yu yuce* [Society of China: analysis and forecast for 2008]. Beijing: Social Sciences Academic Press, 2008.

———. *Erlinglingjiu nian Zhongguo shehui xingshi fenxi yu yuce* [Society of China: analysis and forecast for 2009]. Beijing: Social Sciences Academic Press, 2009.

Shen Hui. *Dangdai Zhongguo zhongjian jieceng rentong yanjiu* [China's middle-income stratum: a study of identity]. Beijing: Zhongguo dabaike quanshu chubanshe, 2008.

Song Guokai. "Zhongguo zhongchan jieceng jin shinianlai jiakuai jueqi de zhuyao yuanyin" [The main factors in the rapid rise of the Chinese middle-income stratum in the past decade]. *Chinese Sociology*, January 29, 2010.

Sun Liping. *Duanlie: 20 shiji 90 niandai yilai de Zhongguo shehui* [Cleavage: Chinese society since the 1990s]. Beijing: Shehuikexue wenxian chubanshe, 2003.

———. *Zhuanxing yu duanlie* [Transition and cleavage]. Tsinghua University Press, 2004.

Wang Jianping. *Zhongguo chengshi zhongjian jieceng xiaofei xingwei* [China's middle-income stratum: consumption behavior]. Beijing: Zhongguo dabaike quanshu chubanshe, 2007.

Wang Ning. *Cong Kuxingzhe Dao Xiaofeizhe Shehui* [From the ascetic society to the consumer society]. Beijing: Social Sciences Academic Press, 2009.

Wei Cheng. *Suowei zhongchan: yingguo jinrong shibao zhongwenwang dui Zhongguo zhongchan jieji de diaocha* [China's emerging middle class: a survey by the *Financial Times*'s Chinese website]. Guangzhou: Nanfang ribao chubanshe, 2007.

Wei Liqun. *Zhongguo jingji tizhi gaige sanshi nian huigu yu zhanwang* [The retrospect and prospect of China's thirty-year economic structure reform]. Beijing: Renmin chubanshe, 2009.

Xia Jun and Yin Shan. *Juzhu gaibian Zhongguo* [How housing has transformed China]. Beijing: Qinghua daxue chubanshe, 2006.

Xu Rong. *Zhongguo zhongjian jieceng wenhua pinwei yu diwei konghuang* [China's middle-income stratum: cultural tastes and social anxiety]. Beijing: Zhongguo dabaike quanshu chubanshe, 2007.

Xu Zhiyuan. *Xinglai, 110 nian de Zhongguo biange* [Awakening: China's 110-year reform]. Hubei: Hubei renmin chubanshe, 2009.

Yan Zhimin. *Zhongguo xianjieduan jieji jieceng yanjiu* [A study of class and social strata in present-day China]. Beijing: Zhonggong zhongyang dangxiao chubanshe, 2002.

Yang Dongping, ed. *Zhongguo huanjing fazhan baogao 2010* [Report on China's environmental development 2010]. Beijing: Shehuikexue wenxian chubanshe, 2010.

Yuan Yue and Zhang Hui. "2008 nian Zhongguo jumin shenghuo zhiliang diaocha baogao" [Survey of the living standards of Chinese citizens]. In *2009 nian Zhongguo shehui xingshi fenxi yu yuce* [Society of China: analysis and forecasts for 2009], edited by Ru Xin and others. Beijing: Social Sciences Academic Press, 2008.

Zhang Wanli. "Zhongguo shehui jieji jieceng yanjiu ershi nian" [Research on classes and social status during the last twenty years in China]. *Shehuixue yanjiu* [Sociological research], no. 1 (January 2000): 24–39.

Zhang Wei. *Chongtu yu bianshu: Zhongguo shehui zhongjian jieceng zhengzhi fenxi* [Conflict and uncertainty: political analysis of the middle-income stratum in Chinese society]. Beijing: Shehuikexue wenxian chubanshe, 2005.

Zhang Yi. "Dangdai Zhongguo zhongchan jieceng de zhengzhi taidu" [Political attitudes of the middle stratum in contemporary China]. *Zhongguo shehuikexue* [Chinese social sciences], no. 2 (2008).

Zheng Hangsheng and Li Lulu. *Dangdai zhongguo chengshi shehui jiegou* [The social structure of cities in contemporary China]. Beijing: Zhongguo renmin daxue chubanshe, 2004.

Zhou Xiaohong. *Quanqiu zhongchan jieji baogao* [Report on the world's middle classes]. Beijing: Social Sciences Academic Press, 2005.

Zhou Xiaohong. *Zhongguo zhongchan jieji diaocha* [A survey of the Chinese middle class]. Beijing: Shehuikexue wenxian chubanshe, 2005.

Zhou Yaohong. *Zhongguo shehui zhongjie zuzhi* [Intermediary organizations in Chinese society]. Shanghai: Shanghai jiaotong daxue chubanshe, 2008.

Zhou Yunqing. *Zhongguo chengzhen jumin zhufang juzhu zhiliang* [The residential quality of Chinese urban households]. Beijing: Shehuikexue wenxian chubanshe, 2008.

Zhu Guanglei. *Dangdai Zhongguo ge jieceng fenxi* [Analysis of social strata in contemporary China]. Tianjin: Tianjin Renmin Chubanshe, 2007.

Contributors

Jɪᴇ Cʜᴇɴ is Louis I. Jaffe Professor of Political Science and serves as chair of the Department of Political Science and Geography at Old Dominion University. He also holds the titles of Changjiang Scholar and Zhiyuan Chair Professorship, bestowed respectively by the Ministry of Education and the PRC and Shanghai Jiaotong University. He served as a Fulbright Scholar conducting survey research in China in 2002. He has authored and coauthored four books on Chinese politics. His most recent books include *Popular Political Support in Urban China* (2004) and *Allies of the State: China's Private Entrepreneurs and Democratic Change* (coauthored with Bruce Dickson, 2010). He has also authored and coauthored many refereed articles on contemporary Chinese politics, which have appeared in such scholarly journals as *Journal of Politics, Comparative Political Studies, Public Opinion Quarterly, Social Science Quarterly, Political Research Quarterly, China Quarterly, Asian Survey, Modern China,* and *Journal of Contemporary China.* He received a research grant from the National Science Foundation to conduct research projects on the political roles of the middle class and private entrepreneurs in China.

Dᴇʙᴏʀᴀʜ Dᴀᴠɪꜱ is a professor of sociology at Yale University. Her primary teaching interests are inequality and stratification, contemporary Chinese society, and methods of fieldwork. In addition to teaching at Yale, she runs a summer fieldwork seminar in which Yale students work collaboratively with students from Hong Kong and China. She is associate editor of the *Journal of Asian Studies,* and in 2004 she helped launch the *Yale China Health Journal.* Past publications have analyzed the politics of the Cultural Revolution, Chinese family life, social welfare policy, consumer culture, property rights, social stratification, and occupational mobility. In 2009 *Creating Wealth and Poverty in Post-Socialist China,* which she coedited with Wang Feng, was published. She is completing a monograph, *A Home of Their Own,* that is a study of the social consequences of the privatization of real estate in urban China.

BRUCE J. DICKSON is professor of political science and international affairs at the George Washington University. His research and teaching focus on comparative politics, the political dynamics of authoritarian regimes, and the prospects for political change in China. His research has been funded by the National Science Foundation, the Smith Richardson Foundation, and the United States Institute of Peace. His most recent books are *Wealth into Power: The Communist Party's Embrace of China's Private Sector* (2008) and *Allies of the State: China's Private Entrepreneurs and Democratic Change* (coauthored with Jie Chen, 2010). His articles have appeared in *China Quarterly, Comparative Political Studies, Comparative Politics, Journal of Democracy, Political Science Quarterly,* and other journals.

GEOFFREY GERTZ is a research analyst at the Wolfensohn Center for Development at the Brookings Institution. His research interests include international political economy, long-run trends in the global economy, and international development. Previously he was a junior fellow in the Carnegie Endowment's Trade, Equity, and Development Program.

HAN SANG-JIN is professor emeritus of sociology at Seoul National University and the director of the Han Sang-Jin Institute for Social Theory in Seoul. Since 2010 he has taught at Beijing University and Tsinghua University as a distinguished visiting professor. Specialized in critical social theory and democratic transformations, he is currently doing research on the second modern transformation, intercultural dialogue on human rights, middle-class politics, and third-way development. He has lectured at Columbia University, at the École des hautes études en sciences sociales, and at the University of Buenos Aires. He has served as chairman of the Presidential Commission on Policy Planning of the Republic of Korea and as president of the Academy of Korean Studies, among others. He is the author or editor of the following volumes: *Divided Nation and Transitional Justice* (2010), *Asian Tradition and Global Democracy* (2011), *Human Rights in North Korea* (coeditor, 2007), *Global Forum on Civilization and Peace* (coeditor, 2007), and *Habermas and the Korean Debate* (1998).

HSIN-HUANG MICHAEL HSIAO is the director of the Institute of Sociology–Academia Sinica and a research fellow at both the Institute of Sociology and the Center for Asia-Pacific Area Studies. He is also professor of sociology at National Taiwan University as well as chair professor at National Central University. He served as a national policy adviser to the president of Taiwan between 1996 and 2006. His areas of specialization include civil society and new democracies, middle classes in Asia, sustainable development, and NGO/NPO studies. His most recent books include *Recharging Social Movements in Taiwan* (coeditor, 2010), *Cross-Border Marriages with Asian Characteristics* (coeditor, 2009), *Rise of China: Beijing's Strategies and Implications for the Asia-Pacific* (coeditor, 2009), *Non-Profit Sector: Organization and Practice* (coauthor, 2009), *Deepening Local Sustainable Development in Taiwan* (coauthor, 2008), *Asia-Pacific Peace Watch* (coeditor, 2008), *Social Movements and Democratization in East Asia* (in Japanese, coeditor, 2007), and *Civil Society and Democratization in East Asia* (in Japanese, coeditor, 2007).

HOMI KHARAS is a senior fellow at the Brookings Institution. He is also a member of the working group for the Commission on Growth and Development, chaired by Michael Spence; a nonresident fellow at the OECD Development Center; and a member of the National Economic Advisory Council to the prime minister of Malaysia. His research interests are now focused on global trends, Asian growth and development, and international aid for the poorest countries. Previously, he served as the chief economist for the World Bank's East Asia and Pacific region. He is the author or editor of the following volumes: *Delivering Aid Differently (2010), An East Asian Renaissance (2007), East Asian Visions (2007),* and *East Asia Integrates (2004).*

CHENG LI is senior fellow and director of research at the Brookings Institution's John L. Thornton China Center. He also currently serves as a director of the National Committee on U.S.-China Relations, as a member of the Academic Advisory Team of the Congressional U.S.-China Working Group, as an adviser to the World Bank, and as a vice chairman of the Committee of 100. He is the author or editor of *Rediscovering China: Dynamics and Dilemmas of Reform* (1997), *China's Leaders: The New Generation* (2001), *Bridging Minds across the Pacific: The Sino-U.S. Educational Exchange 1978–2003* (2005), and *China's Changing Political Landscape: Prospects for Democracy* (2008). He is also the principal editor of the Thornton Center Chinese Thinkers series, published by the Brookings Institution Press. He has frequently appeared on CNN, C-SPAN, BBC, and PBS. He is a columnist for the Stanford University journal, *China Leadership Monitor*.

LI CHUNLING is a professor of sociology at the Institute of Sociology, Chinese Academy of Social Sciences. Her academic interests include social stratification and mobility, gender studies, and the sociology of education. Her main publications include *Formation of Middle Class in Comparative Perspective: Process, Influence, and Socioeconomic Consequences* (2009), *Theories of Social Stratification* (2008), *Cleavage or Fragment: A Quantitative Analysis on the Social Stratification of the Contemporary China* (2005), *Social Mobility in Chinese Cities* (1997), *Social Mobility in the Contemporary China* (coauthor, 2004), *A Research Report on Social Classes of the Contemporary China* (coauthor, 2002), *China Social Stratification* (coauthor, 2004), and *The Development, Participation, and Social Status of Professional Females* (coauthor, 1996).

JING LIN is professor of international education policy at the University of Maryland, College Park. She has done extensive research on Chinese education, culture, and society. In particular, she has systematically studied social changes in China and educational reforms undergone in that country since 1978. She is the author of five books on Chinese education: *The Red Guard's Path to Violence* (1991), *Education in Post-Mao China* (1993), *The Opening of the Chinese Mind* (1994), *Social Transformation and Private Education in China* (1999), and *Portraits of 21st Century Chinese Universities: In the Move to Mass Higher Education* (coauthor, 2010). Her research also concentrates on peace education, environmental education, and spirituality education. She has published *Love, Peace, and Wisdom in Education: Vision for Education in the 21st Century* (2006), *Educators as Peace Makers: Transforming Education for Global Peace* (2008), and *Spirituality, Religion, and Peace Education* (2010).

SIDA LIU is assistant professor of sociology and law at the University of Wisconsin–Madison. He has written widely on various aspects of China's law reforms and legal profession, including lower court justice, popular legal advice, the criminal justice system, and the corporate law market. He has published articles in *Law & Society Review*, *Law & Social Inquiry*, *Annual Review of Law and Social Science*, and *China Quarterly* as well as extensively in leading law and social science journals in China, including *Social Sciences in China*, *Peking University Law Review*, and *Sociological Studies*. His first book, *The Lost Polis: Transformation of the Legal Profession in Contemporary China* (in Chinese), was published in 2008. He is finishing a book manuscript in Chinese, *The Logic of Fragmentation: An Ecological Analysis of the Chinese Legal Services Market*, which explains why China's legal reform since the late 1970s has produced a fragmented market for legal services. He is also working on a large research project on the politics of Chinese criminal defense lawyers, funded by the National Science Foundation and the American Bar Foundation.

LU HANLONG is a professor at the Institute of Sociology at the Shanghai Academy of Social Sciences and is also the chair of sociology at East China Normal University. He has been vice president of the Society of Sociology China since 2005, an elected representative of the Shanghai Municipal People's Congress since 1993, and one of the appointed counselor members of Shanghai's municipal government since 2006. He has had extensive international academy experience and has been a visiting scholar at SUNY-Albany, Duke University, University of Minnesota, Yale University, Cornell University, and the UK's Institute of Development Studies. His expertise includes social development studies, social indictors, and the quality of life; his publications have focused on income inequality and social stratification, urban and community studies, consumer culture, and NGOs. He is the editor of a collection called *Market Transition in China* (SASS) and the annual blue book, *Shanghai Social Development Report*.

JOYCE YANYUN MAN is director of Peking University–Lincoln Institute Center for Urban Development and Land Policy (PKU–Lincoln Center) and senior fellow and director of the China Program at Lincoln Institute of Land Policy. She is also professor of economics, College of Urban and Environmental Sciences, Peking University. Her teaching and research interests focus on urban and regional economics, public finance, housing economics, land policy, and sustainable development. She has contributed articles to such journals as *Journal of Urban Economics, Public Finance Review, National Tax Journal, Public Budgeting and Finance,* and *Urban Studies.* She is coeditor of *Tax Increment Finance and Economic Development: Uses, Structures, and Impact* (with Craig Johnson, 2001) and has written the following forthcoming books: *China's Local Public Finance in Transition* (coedited with Yu-hung Hong) and *China's Housing Reforms and Outcomes.* She has been based at Peking University in Beijing since 2007.

ETHAN MICHELSON is associate professor of sociology and East Asian languages and cultures and associate professor of sociology and law at Indiana University–Bloomington. His research on Chinese lawyers and social conflict in rural China has been published in a variety of disciplinary and area studies journals, including *American Sociological Review, American Journal of Sociology, China Quarterly, Law & Society Review, Social Problems,* and *Journal of Conflict Resolution.* His research has been funded by the Ford Foundation, the National Science Foundation, the Social Science Research Council, the U.S. Department of Education (Fulbright-Hays), the American Bar Foundation, and the Hopkins-Nanjing Center.

QIN CHEN is a doctoral student in sociology at the School of Social and Behavioral Sciences at Nanjing University and a lecturer at the College of International Languages and Cultures at Hohai University. Her research focuses on the Chinese people's cultural identity in the era of globalization and on the way people from different cultures think and act in different ways. She is a recipient of Hohai University's Distinguished Teaching Award. Her published works include "Conformity and Deviation: A Psychoanalysis of the 'Flashmob,'" "Humanities, Sciences, and the 'Split Personality' of Universities," "Debate on *Dragon*: A Case Study of Cross-Cultural Communication," and "The *How* and *Why* of China's Internationalization." She is also co-translator of Iris Murdoch's *The Sea, the Sea* and Thomas Gilouich and others' *Social Psychology.*

XIAOYAN SUN is a doctoral student at the School of English and International Studies, Beijing Foreign Studies University. She received a bachelor's degree in international studies and a law and master's degree in international relations from the Beijing Foreign Studies University. Her research focus is on peace studies. She is currently doing research on United Nations peace building from a gender perspective under her adviser Li Yingtao. During 2009–10 she spent five months at the School of Education, University of Maryland, as a visiting doctoral student under the supervision of Jing Lin.

LUIGI TOMBA is a senior fellow with the Department of Political and Social Change, Australian National University. A native of Italy, he has lived and worked in China for many years and has written extensively on a number of issues related to contemporary Chinese politics and social change. He joined the Australian National University in 2001 and has since been researching urban politics, labor reform, the impact of housing commodification, and the formation of a Chinese middle class and its meaning for urban governance. Since 2005 he has been coeditor, with Andrew Kipnis, of *China Journal*.

JIANYING WANG earned a doctorate in sociology from Yale University. Her primary research interests include social inequality, gender and work, life-course analysis, and China studies. In her doctoral dissertation, "Self-Employment in Urban China: The Interplay of Gender, Capitalism, and Labor Market," she analyzes the changing pathways and returns to self-employment in postreform urban China as institutional transformation reshaped opportunity structures in the urban labor market. She is currently working on two manuscripts based on her dissertation, one focusing on the rise of managerial self-employment since the late 1990s and the other focusing on the experience of women in self-employment.

ZHOU XIAOHONG is professor of sociology and dean of the School of Social and Behavioral Sciences, Nanjing University. He completed undergraduate and graduate work at Nanjing Medicine College and Nankai University in 1987 and in 1997 received his doctorate from the Department of History at Nanjing University. He was a visiting scholar at Harvard University's Fairbank Center for Eastern Asian Research in 1999–2000. His major area of research is sociological theory, social psychology, and modern China studies. He has published more than eighty academic papers and is chief editor of the *Journal of China Studies* (Beijing).

Index

Academy of Chinese Reform and Development (Beijing), 75
Advertising, 95, 140
Africa, 36
All-China Federation of Industry and Commerce, 121, 299
Anagnost, Ann, 17, 211
Argentina, 317
Aristotle, 72
ASEAN. *See* Association of Southeast Asian Nations
Asia: emerging economies in, 37; financial crisis, 94; global consumption and, 33, 38; global middle class and, 33, 37; global output and, 36; growth and expansion in, 40, 48; middle class in, 245, 251–59, 336. *See also individual countries*
Asian Tigers, 40, 87
Association of Southeast Asian Nations (ASEAN), 37
Australia, 317
Authoritarian regimes, 76, 283, 306
Automobile industry, 9, 41, 94
Aziz, Jahangit, 47

Banerjee, Abhijit, 34, 180, 183–84
Beijing (China): community-level action and participation in, 205; five-class structure in, 119; gentrification in,

207; housing subsidization in, 200, 201; middle class in, 16, 17, 203; migrant workers in, 199; representative of most-developed Chinese cities, 337; residential developments in, 197; white- and blue-collar workers in, 219
Beijing Medical University, 222–23
Beijing Middle Class Survey of 2007, 136, 149, 155n2
Beijing Olympic Games (2008), 124, 233
Bell, Daniel, 87
Bernstein, Eduard, 87
Bhalla, Surjit, 34
Bian Yanjie, 66, 115, 220
Birdsall, Nancy, 34, 180, 182
Black-collar stratum (*heiling jieceng*), 77–79
Black society (*heishehui*), 77
BNP Paribas Peregrine (French investment bank), 9, 10
Brazil, 37, 44, 45, 74
BRIC economies (Brazil, Russia, India, China), 37
Bulgaria, 318
Burtless, Gary, 13
Business sector (China), 78, 246, 249

Cashell, Brian, 180
CASS. *See* Chinese Academy of Social Sciences

collar workers, 123–26; *xiaokang* (middle class), 119; *zhongchan cheng* (middle properties stratum), 267, 268, 271, 273, 279, 286n19. *See also* Employment issues (China); Middle class (China)

Class issues (China)—capitalist/private entrepreneur class: development of, 121, 145, 146–47; economic status of, 121; educational issues of, 148; family background of, 150; gender gap in, 149; income issues of, 151; occupation and employment of, 146–47, 150; size of, 145; as a subset of the middle class, 143, 149, 154, 156n12. *See also* Private sector and entrepreneurs (China)

Class issues (China)—marginal middle class: definition of, 15; democratic consciousness of, 259, 281–82; educational issues of, 148; income issues of, 151; members of, 143; occupation and employment of, 146, 150–51, 249, 257, 281; public and private sector employment of, 146, 147; size of, 145; socioeconomic status of, 145, 156n15; social stability and, 258; as a subset of the middle class, 143, 145, 149, 154, 249, 257, 281

Class issues (China)—"old" and "new" middle classes: democratic consciousness of, 259, 260, 281–82; educational issues of, 148; family background of, 150; gender issues of, 149; income issues of, 151; occupation and employment of, 146–47, 150, 154–55, 157, 249, 257, 281; as a subset of the middle class, 143, 144, 145, 249, 281, 284n5; working class and, 282

Class issues (China)—working class: Chinese Communist Party and, 114; family background of, 150; income issues of, 162, 170, 172; middle class and, 154; "new" middle class and, 282; occupation and employment of, 114, 117, 249; satisfaction of, 173–74; size of, 114–15, 145–46, 161; social stability and, 258

Class Stratification in Present China (report), 247

CLE. *See* China Legal Environment (CLE) Survey

Climate change, 41

CNNIC. *See* China Internet Network Information Center

Colleges. *See* Educational issues

Community building (*shequ jianshe*), 208

Communism. *See* Chinese Communist Party

Communist Youth League, 237, 323

Community residents' committees (CRCs), 208, 209, 347, 349, 350, 352, 353

Consumer issues (China), 124, 125

Consumption. *See* Spending and consumption

Cosmopolitan magazine, 124, 130n45

CRCs. *See* Community residents' committees

Criminal underground (*heishehui*), 77

Cui Zhiyuan, 114

Cullen, Richard, 323

Cultural issues (China): belief in individual rights, 340; Chinese revolution, 115; *datong* and *xiaokang*, 111–12, 127; democracy social harmony/order, 341–42; influence on government, 343; middle-class identity, 269–70

Cultural Revolution. *See* Great Proletarian Cultural Revolution

Datong (ideal society). *See* Socioeconomic issues

Davis, Deborah, 15, 23, 66, 157–76

Definitions, characteristics, and criteria (middle class): absolute and relative approaches to, 34–35; definitional criteria, 13–14, 22, 32; conventional view, 264, 269; identity and, 266–69; income and, 107, 135, 159, 189–90, 218, 331n12; occupational and educational credentials, 218; precision of, 71; sociocultural and economic characteristics of, 104, 107, 120, 135, 159–62, 179–80; Western experience in the formation of the middle class, 105–07